Mythologies o

Work maps of the Ancient World

Mythologies
of the
Ancient World

EDITED AND WITH AN INTRODUCTION BY

Samuel Noah Kramer

WITH CONTRIBUTIONS BY

Rudolf Anthes

Derk Bodde

W. Norman Brown

M. J. Dresden

Cyrus H. Gordon

Hans G. Güterbock

Michael H. Jameson

Samuel Noah Kramer

Miguel León-Portilla

E. Dale Saunders

Anchor Books
Doubleday & Company, Inc.
Garden City, New York

COVER DESIGN BY ANTONIO FRASCONI
TYPOGRAPHY BY SUSAN SIEN

*The illustration on page 16 is reproduced by kind permission
of the Institut Français d'Archéologie Orientale, Cairo.*

ACKNOWLEDGMENTS

Excerpts from *And Now All This* by W. C. Sellar and R. J.
Yeatman, published in the United States by E. P. Dutton &
Co., Inc., are reprinted by permission of Methuen & Co. Ltd.

Excerpts from *Agamemnon* from *Complete Greek Tragedies,*
translated by Richmond Lattimore, and from *The Iliad,* translated by Richmond Lattimore, copyright 1951 by The University of Chicago, are included by permission of The
University of Chicago Press.

Excerpts from Hesiod: *The Works and Days; Theogony; The
Shield of Herakles,* translated by Richmond Lattimore and
published in 1959 by The University of Michigan Press, are
reprinted by permission of The University of Michigan Press.

Excerpts from *Essays and Addresses* by Gilbert Murray, published in the United States by Houghton Mifflin Company
under the title *Tradition and Progress,* are reprinted by permission of George Allen & Unwin Ltd.

Mythologies of the Ancient World, an Anchor Original, is
also available in a hardbound edition from Quadrangle
Books, Inc., 119 West Lake Street, Chicago, Illinois.

Table of Contents

Introduction

The mythologies of the ancient world consist largely of tales of gods and heroes: their birth and death, loves and hates, spites and intrigues, victories and defeats, acts of creation and destruction. Not a few of the ancient myths are concerned with the creation and organization of the universe, the fashioning of man, and the establishment of civilization. In spite of certain basic similarities of theme, the ancient mythologies differ widely in the choice and treatment of the individual plots and motifs, in accordance with the history and culture, the character and temper of the people which produced them.

Modern students of mythology disagree radically in their views of the nature, scope, and significance of the ancient myths. There are those who look upon them as trivial, superstitious fairy tales of little intellectual and spiritual import—the infantile products of undisciplined imagination and capricious fantasy. Diametrically opposed to them are scholars who believe that the myths of the ancients represent one of the most profound achievements of the human spirit, the inspired creation of gifted and unspoiled mythopoeic minds, uncontaminated by the current scientific approach and analytic mentality, and therefore open and prone to profound cosmic insights which are veiled to modern thinking man with his inhibiting definitions and impassive, soulless logic.

There are whole schools of modern mythologists who argue that ancient myth is closely bound to rite and ritual;

that myth was, as it were, nothing other than the "rite spoken"; and that myth and ritual were practically two sides of the same cultic coin. On the other hand, there are historians of religion who claim that the ancient myths were primarily etiological in character—fictitious tales evolved for the purpose of explaining the nature of the universe, the destiny of man, and the origin of the customs, beliefs, and practices current in their days, as well as the names of holy places and outstanding individuals.

There are psychologists who see in the ancient myths depositories of primordial archetype motifs which reveal and illuminate man's collective subconscious. On the other hand, there are linguists and philologists who are convinced that myth is a "disease of language," the product of man's vain, futile, and misguided attempts to express the inexpressible and to verbalize that which is ineffable.

But no matter what view one takes of the origin, character, and significance of the ancient mythologies, it would seem not unreasonable to expect that it be based on the actual texts of the myths as contained in the written documents of the ancients, and not on the versions surmised and improvised, transformed and recast by some modern enthusiast with an ax to grind and a point to make. Unfortunately, the reading of the original documents on which the ancient myths are inscribed is no simple matter; it is an intricate, thorny, and often frustrating task demanding many years of highly specialized linguistic and philological training. Practically all serious students of the ancient mythologies have to depend on the translations and interpretations prepared by specialists over the years. But in not a few cases the available translations are seriously outdated and misleading. And in the case of the ancient peoples, especially those who had their home in the Near East, new documents are being discovered constantly, either through excavations or as a result of renewed and concentrated study of material excavated in the distant past.

All this struck me with particular force and meaning on reading a recently published book on the mythologies of the ancient Near East entitled *Myth and Ritual in the Ancient Near East: An Archaeological and Documentary Study.* Its author, E. O. James, is a distinguished, anthropologically orientated historian of religion who in the course of a lifetime of productive research has written numerous works on the history of religion and on its origin, nature, and function. But though he makes a brave attempt in his book to be thorough, objective, and discriminating in his examination of the written documents, he often relies on misleading translations which he cannot control, and tends to take at face value secondary interpretations of the textual material, and even some of the more synthetic inferences and surmises, theories and hypotheses which pervade this rather rarefied and elusive area of humanistic studies. It seemed high time to take a fresh look at the generally accepted, but not always trustworthy data and at the clichés and shibboleths not infrequently utilized in interpreting them.

The opportunity came at the time of the annual 1959 meetings of the American Anthropological Association and the American Folklore Society, when I found it possible and practical to arrange for a symposium on ten ancient mythologies, those of Egypt, Sumer and Akkad, Anatolia, Canaan, Greece, India, Iran, China, Japan, and Mexico. Each of these mythologies was covered by a specialist in the field, one who had devoted much of his scholarly career to the translation and interpretation of the relevant texts. The participating scholars were free to choose the material they deemed best for their particular contribution, and were not circumscribed by the imposition of a single, rigid, and overriding definition of mythology—the time is hardly ripe for ultimate consistency and absolute homogeneity in the field of mythological research. Each of the contributors made a determined effort to cover within the limited space afforded by a composite book of this nature, what seemed to him the essentials relevant to his area, utilizing for this purpose the most up-to-date translations which he himself controlled, verified, and if necessary corrected and revised.

A concrete illustration of one of the major goals of the collection of essays presented in this volume, which is to help correct and rectify at least some of the more obvious of the current misconceptions and misstatements relating to the myths of the ancients, is provided by the hitherto largely unknown Sumerian myth concerned with the death of the god Dumuzi, or to use the modified form of his name known from Biblical and post-Biblical sources, Tammuz (see page 110 for a detailed sketch of its contents). For when taken together with the myth "Inanna's Descent to the Nether World" (see pages 107–9) with which it is intimately related, its contents demonstrate beyond reasonable doubt that Dumuzi dies and "stays dead"; indeed he must not under any circumstances leave the Nether World and return to the upper regions, since in that case Inanna would have no substitute and would therefore be forced to return to the Nether World. It is for this reason, too, that we find only laments for Dumuzi's death; there are no songs of rejoicing to celebrate his resurrection. But for more than half a century now, students of mythology (see, for example, Stephen Langdon's *Tammuz and Ishtar* and the chapter bearing the same title in his *Semitic Mythology*) have taken Dumuzi to be the original prototype of the dying god who rises annually from the dead, the very archetype of the deity who dies every summer and is revived every spring. In an effort to get at the reasons for this erroneous but well-nigh universal view of the Dumuzi myth, I combed the relevant cuneiform literature patiently and carefully, but could find no supporting evidence whatever from the texts; it is based on nothing but inference and surmise, guess and conjecture.

To judge from the available texts, including the new material just mentioned, the origin and development of the myth revolving about the death of Dumuzi may be tentatively and partially reconstructed as follows. Dumuzi, whose life and deeds made a deep impression upon his own and future generations, was a prominent ruler of the important Sumerian city-state of Erech early in the third millennium B.C. The tutelary deity of Erech was Inanna, a goddess who

throughout Sumerian history was deemed to be the deity
primarily responsible for sexual love, fertility, and procreation, and the names of Dumuzi and Inanna no doubt became
closely intertwined in the early myth and ritual of Erech.
Sometime about the middle of the third millennium, however, when the Sumerians were becoming more and more
nationally minded, and the theologians were in the process
of systematizing and classifying the Sumerian pantheon
accordingly, there arose the seemingly quite plausible and
not unattractive idea that the king of Sumer, no matter who
he was, or from what city he originated, must become the
husband of the life-giving goddess of love, that is, Inanna of
Erech, if he were to insure effectively the fecundity and prosperity of the land and its people. After the initial idea had
become accepted dogma it was actually carried out in ritual
practice by the consummation of a marriage ceremony which
was probably repeated every New Year, between the king
and a specially selected hierodule from Inanna's temple in
Erech. To lend importance and prestige, however, to both
the credo and the rite, it was advisable to carry them back to
earlier times, and the honor of being the first mortal ruler to
have become the husband of Inanna, Erech's most revered
deity, not unnaturally fell to Dumuzi, the Erech ruler who
over the centuries had become a memorable figure in Sumerian legend and lore. But Dumuzi, as was known to all, had
died like any other mortal, while the husband of a goddess
might have been expected to become immortal. To explain
this puzzling enigma, one or another of the more imaginative
of the Sumerian theologians and poets originated and developed the myth of the death of Dumuzi according to which
the latter was deprived of the gift of eternal life because of
his unseemly and ungrateful behavior toward his wife Inanna,
to whom he owed his "godship" in the first place.

The new myth "The Death of Dumuzi" is a promising
example of what Sumerian mythology still holds in store for
us. For the Sumerian literary documents are only now in the
process of restoration and translation, although many of the
tablets on which they are inscribed were excavated more than

fifty years ago. This is not true for the mythological source
material of the other Near Eastern peoples. In the case of the
Egyptians, Akkadians, Hittites, and Canaanites, practically
all the extant mythological texts have been published and
translated in one way or another. The essays devoted to these
mythologies have therefore concentrated primarily on rein-
terpretation and clarification in the light of deeper insight
into the original texts and their meaning.

One of the more noteworthy chapters in the book is that on
the mythology of the ancient Greeks, a subject which has
been discussed so often and written about so voluminously
that it would seem to have little new to offer. The compactly
written, informative, and comprehensive essay ranges over
the invaluable and imperishable Greek literary material from
pre-Homeric times to the days of Alexander, and explores
their social, cultural, religious, and psychological implications, as well as the possible Greek-Oriental interrelations.

Another outstanding chapter in the book is that devoted to
the mythology of ancient India from Vedic days on. The
original literary documents in which the tales concerning the
gods and demigods, the heroes and sages of ancient India
are often involved, abstruse, esoteric, and equivocal. But the
essay searches out, analyzes, and sketches the essential facts
with the sure hand and clear phrasing generated by a lifetime
of devoted study and research.

In the case of ancient Iran and China, the essays are of
rather unusual significance not only for their effective handling of the elusive and complex subject matter, but for an
instructive analysis of the scholarly methodology essential to
a trustworthy reconstruction of the pertinent myths. The essay
on ancient Japan provides a straightforward description of
the rather sprightly and sensitive tales of its people, together
with a valuable sketch of the relevant sources. Finally, there
is the illuminating essay on the mythology of ancient Mexico,
tapping sources written in the Nahuatl language but in the
Latin alphabet. It sketches the myth of the Nahuatl peoples
of Central Mexico, of which the Aztecs are but the last and
best-known branch. Although the Nahuatl peoples are sep-

arated by thousands of miles from those of the ancient Eurasian world, their mythologies reveal a number of significant parallels and thus pose the ever-intriguing problem of possible cultural dissemination from the new world to the old in pre-Columbian times. All in all, the present volume should turn out to be a significant contribution not alone to mythology but humanistic research in general.

SAMUEL NOAH KRAMER

Mythology in Ancient Egypt

BY RUDOLF ANTHES

1. THE HEAVENLY COW

The picture of the heavenly cow, here represented on page 16, was cut in the stone walls of several royal tombs between 1350 and 1100 B.C. The mythological tale accompanying it may be summarized as follows.

When the sun god Re, the king of mankind and the gods, had grown very old, he learned that upstream and in the desert man was plotting against him. Therefore, he summoned his council of gods which included the males, Shu, Geb, and Nunu, and the females, Tefnut, Nut, and the Eye of Re. This was done secretly, lest man should know about it. On the advice of the gods, Re sent his Eye, in the form of the goddess Hathor, to kill mankind. When she came back rejoicing, after having accomplished part of her task, Re repented and decided to spare the rest of mankind. He ordered red beer to be poured out onto the fields during the night, and then when the bloodthirsty Eye came back in the morning, she found the red beer pleasant for her heart. She became intoxicated and failed to recognize men. Thus, adds the narrator, originated the custom of preparing intoxicating drinks on the Feast of Hathor.

But Re was still weary of remaining with mankind on earth. Nunu, the ancient one, whose name means "the primeval ocean," advised him to mount the back of the cow Nut. When dawn came and men began to shoot at each other with arrows the cow Nut arose with Re on her back and became the sky. Then Re expressed his "satisfaction" and his wish to "plant green herbs" in the sky—the narrator punning on those words says that by means of these utterances the "Field of Satisfaction" and the "Field of Rushes" came into existence. These old names originated in the idea of a heavenly lake although later on, in the present context, they indicated the ideal of the peasants, a land for cultivation in the beyond. The cow standing up on high, however, felt giddy and trembled. "Then the Majesty of Re said, 'If I only had a *heh*-number [meaning: a million of deities?] to support her,' and by saying this he brought into existence the (eight) *heh*-deities" who held the legs of the heavenly cow. Finally, Re ordered the god Shu to place himself beneath the cow to support her belly and to guard the eight *heh*-deities.

The tale ends with the prescription that it is to be recited over the picture of a cow, apparently by a father as he holds his newly born child over his head so as to protect it against any evil (*The Shrines*, pp. 27–31; the first section also *ANET*, pp. 10–11).

The first portion of the tale represents a combination of older mythological concepts: The sun god Re in his character as the king of mankind and the gods is identical with the primeval god Atum and thus, by his very nature, is a very old man. The transgression of mankind against Atum is attested at about 2100 B.C. As to the rather cryptic concept of the Eye of the highest god, I should like to restrict myself here to saying that it is equal to the aggressive Uraeus viper, to the goddess Hathor, and to other deities as well. The Eye of Atum is attested as a messenger of Atum at about 2000 B.C. (*C.T.* II 5b). The gentle goddess Hathor, who is usually incorporated in a cow, is introduced here as the bloodthirsty Eye. Apparently the whole story is designed to explain the custom of drinking to excess on the Feast of Hathor. The skeptical historian, however, is inclined to think that these excesses might, instead, be traced back to the character of Hathor the protector of love.

The second part of the tale is linked with the first through the mutual motif of Re's weariness with mankind. Taken by itself, it interprets the picture of the heavenly cow with the slight deviation that, in the picture, Re is not seated on the back of the cow but is rather traveling in his two boats. It is a cosmogonic tale in that it explains how the sky came into being. Furthermore, the existence of the heavenly fields and of the eight deities who are depicted holding the legs of the cow is explained by puns. Punning is a popular feature in Egyptian mythology. New mythological concepts were often created in this unimaginative and clumsy manner, for instance, in hymns and rituals.

The picture is not an illustration of the complete tale of the heavenly cow, nor does the tale conform with the picture in every detail. Let us, therefore, discuss the picture in its own right. We shall see that it is composed of several heterogeneous elements just as was the preceding story of the blood-thirsty goddess.

The details of the picture are, I think, clear enough. We see a standing cow. Her belly is decorated with a line of stars. Two boats travel along her belly, with a man in one of them wearing the sun disk as a headdress. The belly of the cow is carried on the raised hands of a man, and each of her legs is supported by two men. It may be added that the hieroglyphs between the horns and in front of the breast of the cow read "*heh*" which means either "the millions" or "the *heh*-deities," and the hieroglyphs in front of the forehead of the cow read "beauty," which may or may not designate the cow.

In addition to the stars which indicate that this picture represents the sky, four different and contradictory concepts of the sky are represented, each of them well known to us elsewhere in allusions transmitted in hymns and other religious texts. First, the cow has been a concept of the sky since prehistoric times. Since a cow, according to the earliest texts, was also in the primeval ocean, the idea that she arose out of the ocean to be the sky may or may not have existed before the present tale was composed. Second, the two boats of the sun indicate the concept of the sky as the body of water through which the sun sails in the morning boat and in the evening boat. This heavenly body of water corresponds to the ocean below just as the heavenly cow corresponds to the cow below. It was certainly not the heavenly replica of the Nile, since the Egyptians were well aware that the Nile flowed from the south to the north, in contrast to the path of the sun from the east to the west. Third, the man who carries the belly of the cow is the god Shu, who, as we shall see later, raised up his daughter Nut, the sky, from her brother and husband Geb, the earth, so that only her finger tips and toes touched the ground. The idea that Nut carried the boats of the gods with her when she was raised, and that they became the stars, is attested early (*Pyr.* 785). To understand the popular idea that the gods, the stars, and the sun god traveled in their boats, we must realize that in the valley of the Nile the boat is both a natural and convenient medium of transportation. The fourth concept of the sky which is indicated in the picture is relatively rationalistic: the sky is a roof which is carried by four supports, each guarded by a deity. The four legs of the cow stand here for the four pillars of the sky. The eight *heh*-deities may be traced back to the guards of the pillars which represented the four chief points of the compass. Four, the number of the cardinal points, has always been looked on as a holy number by the Egyptians.

What then may we learn from this picture?

Four different Egyptian concepts of the sky are attested here: a cow, an ocean, the woman Nut, and a roof. All of these concepts were accepted as correct by those who were responsible for the ornamentation of the royal tombs in the centuries around 1300 B.C. It is true that in this very period the Egyptians were highly sophisticated. The slightly sarcastic approach to their mythological tales, which is displayed in contemporaneous secular works of literature, is reminiscent of the very human portrayal of the Greek gods in Homer. This, then, might suggest an understanding of the composite picture of the heavenly cow as an artist's fanciful joke in spite of the solemnity of the royal tombs. However, such an interpretation does not hold good. A simpler picture, in which the sky is depicted as the wings of a vulture supported by two of the heavenly pillars, originated about 2900 B.C. It proves that the combination of various concepts of the sky was accepted as valid in the very beginning of Egyptian history. Similar evidence is found in the Pyramid Texts which originated in the course of the third millennium B.C. and were inscribed in stone in the centuries around 2300 B.C. In these texts a cow, an ocean, a vulture, and the woman Nut appear among other concepts of heaven alternatively combined in sentences as the following: "The star travels through the ocean beneath the body of Nut" (*Pyr.* 802) and "He [i.e., the deceased king] is the son of the great wild-cow. She conceives him and gives birth to him and they place him inside of her wing" (*Pyr.* 1370). In this context the multitude of concepts of heaven is taken most seriously. It is neither a poetic fiction nor an artistic joke.

Nobody in Egypt was supposed to believe in one single concept of the sky, since all the concepts were accepted to be valid by the same theologians. Furthermore, since the Egyptians had as much common sense as we have ourselves, we may conclude with certainty that no one, except perhaps a very unsophisticated mind, took the composite picture of the heavenly cow at its face value. This conclusion is supported by the fact that there exist, in the same royal tombs about 1300 B.C., other pictures of the sky, e.g., in the form of the human figure of Nut and with the sun disk in place of the sun boats. Whoever might have sought for a replica of the actual shape of the sky in these pictures would have become completely confused. Consequently, they were meant to be symbolic of the sky. The picture under discussion is an artistic combination of symbols, each of which stands for the sky or heaven. We have seen that the composite pictures of heaven in the royal tombs about 1300 B.C. have their counterparts in a drawing of about 2900 B.C. and in the Pyramid Texts. There is no question that at the very beginning of their history, about 3000 B.C., the Egyptians were aware that the concept of the sky could not be understood directly by means of reason and sensual experience. They were conscious of the fact that they were employing symbols to make it understandable in human terms. As no symbol can possibly encompass the whole essence of what it stands for, an increase in the number of symbols might well have appeared enlightening rather than confusing. Besides, this variety contributed to a certain picturesqueness and liveliness of the representation of heaven in words and pictures.

2. THE CHARACTER OF EGYPTIAN MYTHOLOGY

A further discussion of Egyptian mythology will bring forth ample evidence that we may legitimately generalize on the example of the sky. A multitude of mythological concepts may exist for any single entity. Moreover, the liberality which is displayed here with respect to mythological concepts holds good for Egyptian religion as a whole. There existed no dogmas in which belief was compulsory, and thus heresy was inconceivable. Consequently, intolerance and religious zeal do not appear before periods which have already become decadent to some extent. To our knowledge, they occur only in the second millennium, about 1370 B.C., when King Akhenaton tried to unshackle Egyptian religion from mythology with hate and persecution, and later, in the centuries around the time of the birth of Christ, wherever magic and fetishism prevailed. On the other hand, individual skepticism and the rejection of transcendental concepts are attested as early as about 2000 B.C. These were not eliminated by Egyptian society. They appear in the secular literature and were inscribed on the walls of tombs which, at the same time, were covered with hymns and prayers in the standard terms of the Egyptian religion.

We have already found evidence of certain characteristics of Egyptian mythological thinking in the tale of the attempted destruction of mankind and in the composite picture of the heavenly cow. In order to make it possible for the reader to follow more readily the discussions, I will now present a series of relevant definitions developed out of my research into Egyptian myths.

An Egyptian "mythological concept" is a concept by which man tried to make comprehensible in human terms a figure, an event, a group of figures, or a sequence of events which appear to him to belong to the "divine world."

The expression "divine world" encompasses whatever cannot be explained directly by human reasoning and sensual perception even though it appears to exist. Naturally, many entities which can be grasped and explained directly in our present time, such as the sky and the sun, belonged to the divine world in the mind of the ancient Egyptians. In no event and in no time, however, can an entity of the divine world be grasped by the human mind except by means of a "symbol."

A "symbol" is the manifestation of a human attempt to make an element of the divine world conceivable in human terms, that is, in terms of logic and sensuous perception, although these do not necessarily conform with the laws of nature. The Egyptian sages of about 3000 B.C. were aware of this fact and did not mistake a symbol for an actual replica of what it represented. An Egyptian symbol in this sense may take the form of either an object or an action or words. While not every symbol is a mythological concept, every mythological concept is symbolical of an entity of the divine world. Obviously, the truth of a symbol cannot possibly be judged by reason. A mythological concept is true if it makes something of the divine world conceivable in human terms and as long as it is accepted by man's faith.

"Egyptian mythology" is the sum of all Egyptian mythological concepts.

The expression "myth" may be used to designate a defined composite sector of Egyptian mythology.

"Egyptian religion" in this context is the administered manifestation of the implicit consensus of the ancient Egyptians for a common use of mythological concepts.

"Egyptian theology" in this context is the dealing of the Egyptian sages with mythology in constructive and interpretative activities.

Egyptian mythological concepts may take shape in words (e.g., hymns, prayers, tales, and rituals), in actions (dramatic performances and other rites), in objects and pictures (e.g., images, non-figural emblems, plants, and heavenly bodies), or in living beings (e.g., the king and animals). Virtually every manifestation of these expressions causes, is, or recalls a spiritual experience. Most mythological concepts may be experienced in several of these forms of expression. For instance, the myth of Osiris and Horus was experienced in the funeral rites of the king and, at the same time, known by heart as a tale of the past, early in the third millennium B.C.

The former discussion of the tale and the picture of the heavenly cow has displayed some characteristics of Egyptian mythology. We have seen that diverse concepts were composed artistically into a tale or a drawing by which either a cosmic entity or a cosmogonic event or a religious custom was explained. The use of the tale for a magical purpose points to the fact that, on the one hand, a mythological tale might well be composed either for this very purpose or for mere entertainment; on the other hand, it appears that the context of the rites or hymns in which a mythological item is employed, may create a new version of a tale. Furthermore, we have seen that playing on words might well create a new detail of a mythological concept, e.g., the utterance of a deity in a certain situation. In conclusion, these as well as other features support the general impression evoked by the tales and the picture, that Egyptian mythology was reflective rather than imaginative and poetic.

Two more characteristics are significant. One is that a single entity of what we have called the divine world can be conceived in various incompatible concepts by the same theologians. This feature has been fully discussed above. The other striking feature, which we have not yet discussed, is that one deity can be easily identified with another. The discussion of the tales and the picture has shown that Re occurs as Atum in one context and as the sun disk in another. The Eye which in other contexts is identified with the venomous aggressive Uraeus viper appears as Hathor here. Consequently, Hathor appears as a cruel deity in contrast to her otherwise gentle nature as a cow. These incidental examples of the intricacy of mythological concepts point to a fundamental characteristic of Egyptian mythology: the tendency to both change and continuity.

The tendency to change naturally came about as the result of the non-dogmatic character of Egyptian mythology and the resulting attempt to find as many different mythological concepts of a single entity as possible. We have already encountered a number of combinations by means of which new concepts were created, e.g., the king Re who by means of his identification with the primeval Atum became the aged ruler, and the god Shu, who eventually supported the belly of the cow rather than the body of his daughter, Nut. The old idea of the heavenly cow protecting her son, the deceased king, with her "wings"—we have already seen that the concept of the protecting wings originated in the idea of the heavenly vulture—became most popular in Egyptian iconography. First the heavenly Nut and then any other motherly goddess in the shape of a woman was represented as protecting her child with her wings. Otherwise winged human-shaped deities are virtually unknown in Egyptian mythology. These and other similar concepts originated more or less incidentally, as did, for example, those which resulted from a play on words. More purposeful was the theological tendency to equate, for instance, a local deity with one of the great gods in order to give him greater local authority. In these cases the name of the minor god was put in front of that of the major one (as Hermann Junker first pointed out) to form a combined name such as Re-Atum or Amon-Re. Since, in Egypt, the name was looked upon as an essential element of the personality, the combination of their names accomplished the transfer of the mythological attributes of the higher deity to the minor one. Egyptian mythology was thus in a state of change throughout, virtually, the three millenniums of Egyptian history, as a result of the creation of new concepts. It is true that after about 2200 B.C. these changes continued mainly with new combinations of the older basic ideas. But it was those very combinations which gave Egyptian mythology a kaleidoscopic and intricate appearance, and resulted in new mythological tales. It may be added that some influence of Asiatic mythologies is also found, mainly in the second millennium B.C., but, to my knowledge, it never played an important role in the development of Egyptian myths.

The changing pattern and liberal mood prevalent in Egyptian religion were balanced by the characteristic tendency to conservatism. This shows itself in the fact that any mythological concept which had once proved valid was virtually never abandoned. The composite picture of the heavenly cow, which we have discussed, by no means represents the final or any other state of a development in which the earlier individual concepts of the cow, the woman Nut, the heavenly ocean, and the roof were absorbed. All four of these concepts were simultaneously retained in their own right. We shall see that the role of the highest god was attributed successively to Horus, Re, and Amon-Re, to whom the Serapis of the Ptolemaic period may be added here. Each of these gods who was superseded by his successor preserved his dominant role in whatever context permitted it. We may well assume that the conservative character of its mythology saved Egyptian religion from disintegration as early as in the fourteenth century B.C. and again after the middle of the last millennium B.C. However, the same perseverance which caused the permanence and continuity of Egyptian religion contributed no less to the increase of mythological concepts and the intricacy of Egyptian mythology since the earlier elements and combinations were preserved together with the new ones.

As I have stated previously, the basic concepts of Egyptian mythology were already established about 2200 B.C., and the succeeding changes represented an increase in variations and combinations rather than alterations of these concepts. In view of this it will be useful here to present first the mythology of the third millennium until about 2200 B.C. and only subsequently the elaboration on it as it appears from about 2300 B.C. on. The dates are suggested by our main sources for early Egyptian mythology. It was between 2300 and 2200 B.C. that the latest genuine versions of the Pyramid Texts were incised on walls in the interior of pyramids and that the earliest versions of the Coffin Texts were prepared. This change indicates an epochal turning point. It is true that these two main sources of early Egyptian mythology have very different characters. The Pyramid Texts consist mainly of rituals, incantations, and hymns referring to the funeral and transfiguration of the king of Egypt, while the Coffin Texts appear to be mainly literary elaborations on mythological concepts, which were designed for the deification and eternal life of those commoners who could afford to have them inscribed or written on their coffins. We shall see, however, that this difference in design is by no means accidental. The shift from the Pyramid Texts to the Coffin Texts coincides with the invalidation of the mythological concept of the divine king. It was this very concept in which Egyptian mythology was rooted.

3. EGYPT ABOUT 3000 B.C. AND HER MYTHOLOGICAL INHERITANCE

The foundation of ancient Egyptian civilization was laid before 3000 B.C. by the development of a uniform culture. This was the so-called Later Naqada Civilization or, Naqada II, which is attested by burials, implements, pottery, and figurative art. It extended from the Fayyum to the south through Middle and Upper Egypt into Nubia. Lower Egypt including the Delta had reached a state of civilization which cannot be defined with certainty although it appears to have been on a level not lower than in Upper Egypt. The beginning of Egyptian recorded history in the centuries around 3000 B.C. is marked by two decisive events: the invention of writing, that is, the employment of pictures as phonograms, and the political unification of Egypt as the "Kingdom of Upper and Lower Egypt." These events were simultaneous with other great achievements which made the period about 3000 B.C. one of the most remarkable epochs in history. The administration of the new kingdom whose extent exceeded any former community in Egypt was established. A permanent calendar of 365 days replaced the farmer's moon calendar for administrative purposes. Legal documents are attested as early as about 2800 B.C. The casebook of a surgeon and two medical treatises have been dated with more or less certainty to the centuries around 2500 B.C. The potter's wheel was invented about 3000 B.C. Progressive elements gathered in the capital, Heliopolis, at the site of present-day Cairo, and in the royal residence, Memphis, on the left bank of the Nile, opposite Heliopolis. This concentration promoted the shaping of Egyptian civilization. Masonry came into existence. The distinctly Egyptian characteristics first appeared in works of architecture and representative art as well as in objects of daily use. Further, as we shall see, Egyptian mythology was created as a result of the country's political unification.

This was not a period of primitive men. The idea that a qualitative change of the human mode of thinking took place in history, from a "magical," "prelogical," or "mythopoeic" mind in the past to a rational and scientific mind in our period, is not supported by the history of Egypt. Medicine in the third millennium B.C. apparently did without magic in contrast to the recourse to magic in recipes of the second millennium. The oracle of the god does not appear to have intruded into the rational administration of the law before about 1500 B.C. It is true that the rule of *noli me tangere* concerning the live incarnation of a god was as valid about 3000 B.C. as it was three millenniums later. The pyramids, however, were not built by magic means. It is true that the foundation of the pyramid was laid ceremonially and its consecration was celebrated with magical services. There was nothing magical, however, about their actual construction. Blocks of masonry were prepared with stone and copper tools, and only ramp and lever were used to lift them up to a height of four hundred and fifty feet. The decisive criterion of the employment of logic and reason by the earliest Egyptians is the fact that they achieved so much in spite of their lack of those physical and intellectual tools which are available for us after 5000 years of development. If we apply this standard we cannot but have the highest esteem for the power of their logical and creative minds. As mentioned earlier, the number of those entities in man's environment, which could not be grasped by logic and reason, was, naturally, inconceivably greater for the Egyptians than for us. However, it is not the quantity of knowledge which decides the quality of intellect. A necessary criterion for the intelligence of man seems to be the question of whether or not he is aware of the limits of his knowledge. He has to know his proper place in respect to reason as well as reverence. When all is said and done, Egyptian history suggests that at about 3000 B.C. in Egypt "magical mind" and "rational mind," i.e., religious and logical manners of thinking, were in a better balance than they were at about 1000 B.C. in Egypt, or in the present-day world, for that matter. The early Egyptians employed reason in the highest degree where it was called for and approached with due reverence what was beyond their understanding.

The preceding discussion of the mentality of the Egyptians about 3000 B.C. was necessary for an adequate evaluation of the origin of Egyptian mythology. With the same purpose in mind, the attempt must be made to answer the question as to which mythological concepts already existed at the end of the prehistoric period. In this discussion we must keep in mind that the prehistoric period encompasses many millenniums in which numerous significant developments and alterations took place. The variety of parallel prehistoric concepts might well have originated in local and temporal differences. Furthermore, the following sketch of what appears to have existed before writing was invented, is based almost entirely on the written documents of the succeeding historical period. The conclusions appear to me well founded although there are some uncertainties.

First, the idea of the primeval ocean appears to have been transmitted from earliest times. The primeval earth hill arose out of the water with flaming appearance and bore the first living being. This was either a serpent, which was looked at as the primary "body" of any autochthonic deity in historical times; or it was a beetle, which subsequently became the scarab beetle of the Egyptian religion. Probably the following concepts of the first living being also originated in prehistory: the frog, which eventually became a Christian symbol of resurrection; an egg, which is also looked on as a symbol of life outside of Egypt; and the lotus flower, which, according to later belief, gave birth to the sun, or endowed it with life. The conception of the primeval ocean on earth might have implied the idea that the sky also was an ocean. The concepts of the primeval earth hill and the first living being appear characteristic of Egypt, where the reoccurrence of a corresponding experience is repeated each year, as the inundation of the Nile decreases to make place for cultivation. As to the further primeval development, the Egyptians have always been vague. The sun was looked on in general terms as the creator of whatever existed on earth. Men were sometimes thought of as the descendants of the gods. The idea that "men" originated in the "tears" of Re represents a play on two Egyptian words which are similar in sound; it is not attested before 2000 b.c. The idea that men were shaped individually in clay by the god Khnum occurs later, and is not cosmogonic; that is, it does not include the notion that there was a *first* man who was created of clay.

Second, there exist the concepts of the sky. We have already encountered the heavenly ocean and the heavenly cow. We do not know when the idea that the cow arose out of the ocean originated. In any event, her counterpart below was known in the third millennium as Methyer, "the great cow in the water." The idea of the heavenly cow appears to have survived, in her name as "Gold," "the golden one," as that of the cow in the wilderness of the Delta, which was looked on as the tutelary deity of lovers from the third millennium. She was then identified with Hathor, "the (deified) house of Horus." The same Hathor later appears as a cow dwelling in the mountains of Upper Egypt, where she received the deceased at their burial. The opinion that the cow in prehistory was the Egyptian version of a very early concept of a mother goddess and source of fertility has been proffered by Elise Baumgartel as an interpretation of certain discoveries in prehistoric tombs. The exact interrelation of the various concepts of cows has not yet been clarified, however. The same holds true for the various concepts of bulls. From the beginning the heavenly cow appears connected with the "bull of heaven." Presumably, the idea was that when she gave birth each day to a calf, that is, the sun, that calf grew into a bull in order to engender the calf of tomorrow. The concept of the bull of heaven was, early in the historical period, applied to the king and other gods of heaven. It later appears in the designation of Min of Coptos, who will be discussed below, as Kamuthis, "the bull of his mother." Furthermore, the idea of the heavenly calf survived in the later popular belief that the king was nursed by a cow. In addition to the concept of the fertile bull, the idea that the king was the strong bull, the victor over his enemies, is attested as early as the very beginning of writing in Egypt. Apparently, the concept of heaven as a vulture is also prehistoric. Its influence on the iconography of mother goddesses has already been discussed. In the historic period the various Egyptian female deities appear either as a cow or as a vulture or as a snake, and also in hieroglyphic writing as an egg, notwithstanding any other appearance as either an animal or a woman. This holds true even of the major female deities, Isis, Hathor, and Nephthys, who certainly did not exist in prehistoric times.

In addition to the idea of heaven as either a cow or a vulture, its concept as a roof appears to be prehistoric. The picture of the heavenly roof carried by supports of a specific shape, the *zam*-supports, is well known in the iconography of the historic period. It appears to be already misunderstood in the Pyramid Texts, where the supports are conceived as the youthful Four, who are standing, sitting, or leaning on "their *zam*-supports" all together in one or the other of the four quarters of the heaven, and not each one in his own quarter. There they are identified as "the four sons of Horus," whose mummiform standing figures usually appear together as a single group and are depicted, for instance, upon the primeval lotus. The four youths with their *zam*-supports are replaced as the carriers of the sky by the eight *heh*-deities in the Coffin Texts.

Third, there existed other deities in the shapes of either animals, plants, or inanimate objects. We may call these "fetish" deities to distinguish them from the other groups. Their common characteristic is that their images were carried on standards. They appear as local deities in the historical period. It is possible that they all originated in local deities, but there appear among them cows and bulls who otherwise have a cosmic character, and the problematical emblem of Min of Coptos, which may have been a symbol of animal fertility. We must, therefore, leave open the question whether or not the "fetish" deities are grouped together here correctly as far as their origin is concerned. Perhaps it was not before the beginning of the historical period that they were conceived in human form, or in the case of the animal gods, with human bodies and the heads of animals. A few of them became significant mythological characters such as Thoth of Hermopolis, who was the prototype of wisdom and who appeared as a baboon as well as an ibis; and the jackal Anubis, who, dominating the necropolis in the desert, took care of the deceased and the tombs. Min, the goddess Neit, and the canine Upwawet were early connected with the kingship of Horus in one way or another, though without mythological implications. Those animal-shaped deities of this group which were most important for Egyptian mythology were the falcon Horus, the unidentified mammal Seth, which was later looked at as a donkey, and the ibis Thoth. The early historical evidence seems to suggest that the falcon and the Seth-animal were identified with those prehistoric rulers who worshiped them. Many problems about this group remain.

Fourth, there exist allusions to prehistoric deities which cannot be identified. The Egyptian words for earth, e.g., *geb,* were masculine, and those for the sky, e.g., *nut,* were feminine except when the sky was conceived as the ocean. This difference of gender seems to indicate some undefined prehistoric concepts of heaven and earth, which should have been mythological in character, and accords with the fact that the moisture which fertilizes the soil is brought forth by the Nile and not by rain in Egypt. Furthermore, the concept of vegetation in its name *osiris* presumably originated before the historic period, as well as the attribution of creative power to the sun disk, *re.* We shall discuss all this more thoroughly in the following chapters.

4. THE CONCEPT OF HORUS AND HIS LINEAGE

All the prehistoric concepts which we have mentioned survived in the Egyptian religion, which was the result of the unification of the Two Lands and the creation of the Kingdom of Upper and Lower Egypt, about 3000 B.C. The basic fact of Egyptian religion was the idea that the king was a god. The later ritual of daily service stresses the point that the priest in front of the god's image acted only as the substitute of the king. In festival rites the king represented the gods to his people with the same authority as he represented his people to the gods. Since he, the king, was the sole mediator and link between men and the gods, the concept of a hero who intrudes into the world of the gods is not known in Egyptian mythology. Only the king and the gods play a role in mythology. The non-mythological idea that the sages of the past might well have "joined heaven and entered among the lords of the necropolis" as did the kings, is very rarely attested and not before 1400 B.C. (Pap. Chester Beatty IV 6, 14).

The king of Egypt was looked on as the god Horus at the very beginning of the First Dynasty, and at the same time Horus was embodied in the image of a seated or standing falcon. This phenomenon suggests that in prehistory Horus, a local falcon deity at Hierakonpolis in Upper Egypt, was embodied in the local leader either before or after this leader vanquished his rivals and became the king of Egypt. The original character of Horus is a problem, however, and it is still more complicated by the fact that kings in the Second Dynasty, about 2800 B.C., were called "Horus and Seth," or "the two falcons," and not merely "Horus," and that in early sections of the Pyramid Texts, Horus and Seth appear as brothers and equal rulers of the two parts of Egypt, Lower and Upper. Notwithstanding the problematical character of the development, however, the fact remains that in the very beginning of history the god Horus was the falcon and the king of Egypt. Moreover, he was "the heavenly Horus," "the lord of heaven," "the king of the gods," "the unique one," and he was a heavenly body, either a star or the sun. This apparent universal and eternal character of Horus may well have come into existence as the result of the situation that Horus was the ruler of all Egypt and thus virtually of the inhabited world. Horus is attested as a true trinity of the heavenly king, the king on earth, and the falcon.

It may appear striking to find both the concepts of the universal, eternal god and the trinity of this god as early as 3000 B.C. Therefore, I should like to clarify the meaning of these expressions in the present context by summarizing the textual evidence. As for the trinity, the earliest evidence is the carving on the ivory comb of King Zet, "the Serpent," of about 2900 B.C. It represents the Horus falcon twice: the one stands in a boat above the sky, thus indicating a heavenly body; the other stands beneath the sky and is unmistakably identified as the king, Zet. The identification of "Horus of heaven" or "the heavenly Horus" as a star and the "king of the gods" on the one hand, and the identification of the earthly Horus as the king of Egypt on the other hand is frequently attested and has been generally accepted. As for the concept of the universal god, it is first attested in the Pyramid Texts about 2400 B.C. By that time Re had already replaced Horus, and the epithet, "the greatest god," is given Horus, Osiris, the king, and Re—the intricacy of these figures will be cleared in the due course of the present discussion. The significant epithets, "the lord of all" and "the unlimited one," are given the heavenly ruler who is in one case identified as Re. Finally, the eternal character of Horus is indicated mainly by the statement which is found in the Pyramid Texts saying that the king existed in the primeval beginning before heaven and earth came into being.

Thus the idea that the eternal and universal god exists is attested at the very beginning of Egyptian history. The opinion that this concept came into existence in consequence of the political unification of the country and did not exist previously, is supported by two facts: First, the heavenly appearance of the trinity, the heavenly Horus, is the sun in daytime and a star in the twilight. Obviously, this is a speculative concept designed for the sake of Horus, the god and king, and can only have come into being after the unification of Egypt. Second, the conclusion that the concept of Horus was not preceded by any other idea of the universal god is made plausible by the character of the concept of the lineage of Horus, which we shall discuss now.

The crucial problem in the conception of the universal and eternal god, Horus, was: how could it be explained that he was subjected to death in his appearance as the earthly king? This question is answered in the Pyramid Texts, which gradually developed during the third millennium and were cut in stone about 2400 and 2300 B.C. in seven pyramids. According to the Pyramid Texts which refer to the funeral and transfiguration of the king, the king Horus became Osiris, the Vegetation, after his death. In his character as both Horus and Osiris the king was then transfigured into his permanent aspect of the eternal king, united with the ruler of heaven, while another incarnation of Horus on earth succeeded him.

The great cosmogonic concept of Heliopolis is shown on page 37. It was early identified with the concept of the great court of Heliopolis which installed the new king by acclamation and therefore was also looked on as a primeval entity. Therefore, the members of the genealogy of which the cosmogonic concept consists are often called the Ennead, the "Nine Gods," who are the members of this court. This genealogy originated in about the First Dynasty, is attested in the Third Dynasty, about 2700 B.C., and in the Pyramid Texts, and was a standard concept of Egyptian religion in all succeeding periods. Summarized as a tale, it runs as follows: The primeval god, Atum, engendered the pair, Shu and Tefnut, by himself, in an unnatural though human manner. The children of Shu and Tefnut were Geb and Nut. Father Shu raised Nut up from Geb and so separated the sky from the earth. A quarrel about the kingship in Egypt arose among the sons of Geb and Nut: Seth killed the king Osiris and took his throne until Horus, the son of Osiris and Isis, grew up, fought his uncle, Seth, and was acclaimed by the court of Heliopolis as the true king of Egypt and heir to Osiris. This tale, therefore, relates the coming into existence of the world and the kingdom of Horus. There are, however, some inconsistencies, of which three are most striking. First, the idea that it was the father, Shu, and not a son who separated heaven from earth, does not fit well in a logical cosmogonic tale. Second, Seth is called the brother of Osiris and the brother of Horus. Third, the characteristics of Geb as the representative of the royal ancestry, and of Atum, as a king, are hardly compatible with the idea as expressed in the tale, that Osiris was the first king of Egypt. Furthermore, the whole composition gives the impression that there was a break in the middle of the tale. The first section is a cosmogonic tale with the cosmic entities conceived in human forms. The second section is a human story in which only Osiris was a genuine cosmic concept. Therefore, it has

THE COSMOGONIC CONCEPT OF HELIOPOLIS
OR
THE LINEAGE OF HORUS
(*indicates the females)

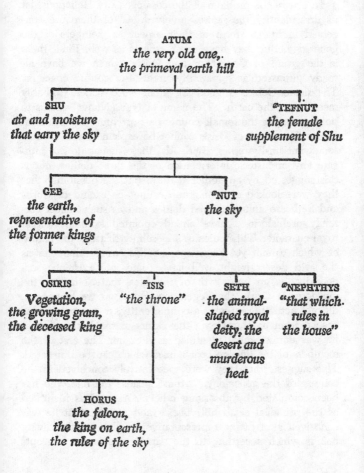

ATUM
the very old one,
the primeval earth hill

SHU
air and moisture
that carry the sky

*TEFNUT
the female
supplement of Shu

GEB
the earth,
representative of
the former kings

*NUT
the sky

OSIRIS
Vegetation,
the growing grain,
the deceased king

*ISIS
"the throne"

SETH
the animal-
shaped royal
deity, the
desert and
murderous
heat

*NEPHTHYS
"that which
rules in
the house"

HORUS
the falcon,
the king on earth,
the ruler of the sky

often been assumed that this was a tale composed of divergent elements just like the story about old king Re, which we discussed at the very beginning. But this fails to explain the inconsistencies just enumerated. Moreover, the context of the Pyramid Texts hardly bears out the opinion that the concept of the lineage of the gods was inconsistent in any respect.

To clarify the problem of the cosmogony of Heliopolis, let us first identify the figures involved. All of them are conceived in human form in their aspect as members of the genealogy. But they have other aspects as well. First, there is the group of Geb, Nut, and Osiris, whom we have already discussed as apparently prehistoric cosmic concepts. The name Geb is a good Egyptian word which probably meant just "the earth." The name of Nut (Nunut) seems to point to her as the female counterpart of Nunu, the primeval ocean. The name of Osiris cannot be explained and appears somewhat un-Egyptian. Evidently, these names do not indicate any prehistoric interrelation of the three deities, nor is this suggested by any other feature; but the possibility that they were looked at as a group cannot be excluded. Horus and Seth are animal-shaped deities and as such almost certainly prehistoric. I have already pointed to their mutual royal character. This indicates a close interrelation, the nature of which cannot yet be grasped. Seth's cosmic character as the arid desert might well have come into existence secondarily, as an outgrowth of the idea that Seth was the murderer of Osiris, the Vegetation. Horus, as we have seen, did not actually represent a cosmic entity; it was only in his special form as Harakhty, "the Horus of the horizon," that he was unmistakably identified as the sun. The rest of the members of the lineage bear names which can be translated. This suggests that they were speculatively conceived in the context of the genealogy. "Atum" means "the one who has been completed by absorbing others." Also, he is identified as the primeval earth hill. These facts suggest that he was conceived as a divine representative of all those first living beings which according to the various prehistoric concepts originated in the primeval earth hill. Presumably, they were fused in him according to a theological interpretation. This conclusion appears corroborated by textual evidence according to which, however, "the gods" rather than "the first living beings" are amalgamated in Atum. The word "Shu" can be translated either as "the empty one," "the dry one," or "the sunlight" (but not the sun himself). The word "Tefnut" is a general designation for "woman" as contrasted with "man." In the context of the cosmogony, Tefnut appears to indicate "the (first) woman" who was paired with Shu in contrast to their lonely father, Atum, the primeval One. Finally, Isis and Nephthys represent a very different group, outsiders in a cosmogonic tale. They appear as the sisters and wives of Osiris and Seth, and as mothers of Horus, but they are not once indicated as daughters of Geb and Nut in the Pyramid Texts. Correspondingly, their names point to the concept of kingship exclusively. They are translated "the throne" (Isis) and "she who [or, that which] rules in the house" (Nephthys). As the meaning of the "throne" is clear enough we may be allowed to guess that "she who rules in the house" designates an indoor counterpart of the open-air throne, perhaps another seat, or the bed of the king.

Thus a very heterogeneous group was united in the concept of the cosmogony of Heliopolis. This concept evidently originated in speculation, but for what purpose? Certainly not for entertainment. In fact, the tale has never been narrated in so many words either in the Pyramid Texts or in any later text in Egyptian language. The very numerous allusions to it which occurred in the proceedings of the royal funerary rites according to the Pyramid Texts prove that this myth was an integral part of the transfiguration of the deceased king as well as of the deification of the former crown prince when he ascended the throne.

We have concluded previously that a crucial question in the conception of the divine king was raised by the death of the god, Horus. A second crucial problem concerned the beginning of the existence of the same god: how did it come to pass that a human being, the crown prince, became the god, Horus, when he ascended the throne as his father's successor? We have certain evidence that the transfiguration of the deceased king in heaven mirrored the enthronement of the earthly king. A sequence of birth and rebirth seems indicated. When all is said and done, I think that the genuine purpose of the Heliopolitan cosmogony, the genealogy of the gods, was to prove the divine character of the king and not to interpret the coming into existence of world and kingship. This means that the lineage of the gods should be read not from above, starting with Atum; it can be correctly understood only if we start with the scion of the gods, the divine king, Horus. I may mention here that I first published the outlines of this interpretation of the genealogy of the gods for the Egyptologists in 1955, and to my knowledge, the reader would seek in vain for it in any earlier presentation of Egyptian mythology.

We know that, as a rule, kingship was carried over from father to son and that there existed in the earliest period a highest court which acclaimed the crown prince as the true divine king after the death of his father. The assumption that a ceremonial questioning of the crown prince preceded his acclamation is a mere guess, but formal questioning as a medium of identification is well attested in the mythical world according to the Pyramid Texts. The following series of questions and answers is completely fictitious, but it illustrates the manner in which the establishment of the lineage of Horus might perhaps have come to pass. Let us assume that after the death of the old king his son appeared before the court with the claim that he was the god, Horus.

Question on the part of the court: You are a human being. It is your father who is Horus.

Answer on the part of the crown prince: I am the god Horus because my father, the Horus, has died. He has become Osiris for his body is buried in the earth as a grain and his spirit rises to heaven as vegetation.

Q. How did it come to pass that Horus, the god, died?

A. The death of the god could not be effected but by murder. It was the only equal of Horus, his brother Seth,
who was powerful enough to kill him.

Q. You have said that your father who thus has become
Osiris is buried in the earth and at the same time lives in
heaven. What does that mean?

A. The king who was Horus and is now Osiris originated
in the primeval beginning, in eternity, and he has gone
back to where he originated, that is, to his parents.
Geb, the earth, is his father, and Nut, the sky, is his
mother.

Q. Eternity is oneness, but Geb and Nut are separated
from each other. How can they possibly be the parents
of Osiris?

A. One who was more powerful than they separated them:
their father, Shu, who raised Nut up from Geb.

Q. Are you claiming that Shu is your first ancestor?

A. The pair, Shu and Tefnut, are the children of the One
who existed by himself in the primeval beginning, Atum.
I am one with my father, Atum.

In this fictitious development of the lineage of the gods, the
inconsistencies concerning Shu and Seth have vanished. As
to what seemed to be an inconsistency concerning Geb, we
must realize that in this context Osiris is the individual deceased king and not the first king of Egypt. Thus his father,
Geb, is the representative of the royal ancestry.

It is the identification of the king with his first ancestor,
Atum, which is the purpose and result of this fictitious formal
questioning; the mythological genealogy was primarily a
concept of identification and not of chronology. The identification of king and Atum is supported by other concepts
which are also attested in the Pyramid Texts. First, we have
already mentioned that Atum appears as a king, evidently
as an adaptation of the concept of the king of Egypt. Second, the king is expressly called the bodily son of Atum,
conceived by the primeval ocean in the same manner as
Atum arose out of the ocean. Accordingly, Atum was looked

upon as a replica of the king of Egypt, and the king, like Atum, was looked upon as the primeval god who was born before heaven and earth, gods and men, and everything else came into existence; he is characterized as such in the Pyramid Texts.

In view of this close interrelationship between the conceptions of king and Atum, we may well ask why a genealogy of five generations was established to prove the divine and primeval character of the king. The answer lies in the fact that the lineage of Horus encompasses cultivated land and desert, heaven and earth and whatever is in between, as well as the ocean out of which Atum arose. This can be best understood as the systematic demonstration that all the world was identified with, or belonged to the realm of, Horus. If so, the fact that this demonstration was felt to be necessary would indicate that the idea of the existence of a universal god, a ruler of all, was only now realized, and did not exist earlier. Thus the lineage of Horus was established, to the best of my understanding, as a mythological concept to make it clear on the one hand, that the very death of the god king was presupposed to effect the final stage of his eternal existence and, on the other hand, that this god king was the ruler of the universe, the "universe," that is, that centered on Egypt, and consisted of heaven and earth, Egypt and "the desert." Since the hieroglyphic ideogram which pictured the desert was likewise used for any foreign country "the desert," in this context, meant whatever was outside of Egypt.

Naturally, once established, the lineage of Horus was looked at as a perfect cosmogony. It may be added that, later on, in historical retrospect, the male members of the lineage, augmented by Re and other relevant deities, were regarded as the early divine kings of Egypt who preceded the First Dynasty.

The character of the king as the supreme being should not be understood as an autocrat free to rule the country at his own pleasure. We should rather think that he was enveloped in ceremonies while the actual rulership lay in the hands of his subordinates. Accordingly, the highest positions in Egypt were held by members of the royal family in the period of Kheops, about 2650 B.C., and his successors, and doubtless in the preceding period. With the beginning of the Fifth Dynasty, however, about 2550 B.C., the same positions were held by men who were commoners by birth. This shift suggests that the position of the king had changed. Simultaneously, the concept of Horus as the highest god was replaced, or rather superseded, by the idea that the highest god was the sun, Re, and that the king was merely the son of Re. The most suggestive interpretation of this change is the assumption that it was due either to an evolution or to a revolution in the administration for the benefit of the royal power and against a clique of princes who earlier controlled the administration. In any event, the concept of Re as the highest god was clearly established at the very beginning of the Fifth Dynasty.

5. THE SUPREMACY OF THE SUN GOD, RE, AND ITS EFFECT ON MYTHOLOGY

Re, the sun disk, was looked upon as a god by the kings as early as in the Second Dynasty. The path which led to his elevation as the highest god, therefore, appeared already prepared. We know of very few mythological concepts which were connected with him innately. One was the idea that he fought the serpent of darkness, an idea which, as we shall see, was further developed later. Another was the notion that the primeval lotus flower gave life to him daily by means of its fragrance, just as once it gave life to him in the primeval beginning. The lotus was called Nefertem in this context. Its name has a similar meaning as that of Atum, namely, "the young lotus has been completed by absorbing others (meaning, the other first living beings)." Just as in the concept of

Horus the primeval Atum gave life to the highest god, Horus, as his ancestor, so the primeval Nefertem gave life to the highest god, Re, by means of his lotus-flower fragrance. Obviously, the figure of Nefertem originated as the product of theological speculation, probably as late as about 2550 B.C. It should be mentioned, by the way, that there existed another concept of the lotus flower and the sun which is clearly different from that of the lotus Nefertem. This was the idea that the young sun arose out of the opening lotus. We do not know when this concept originated, since it is not attested before 1500 B.C. The sun was identified as the young Horus in this context. The corresponding iconographic motif represents the child Horus seated on the lotus flower.

The lack of a genuine mythological background for Re was counterbalanced by his adaptation into the concept of Horus. As Re-Atum he was the heavenly ruler of primeval times, the king of the gods and men, the father of all. As Re-Harakhty he was identified with Horus in his aspect of "Horus of the horizon," the heavenly falcon which was embodied in the sun. Horus, the son of Osiris, had been, and continued to be, the prototype of the earthly king as a youth. Consequently, the earthly king became the son of Re. At the same time, confusingly enough, the youthful Nefertem who, as we have seen, gave life to Re, was identified with the king of Egypt as a primeval being and, later on, with the child "Horus, the son of Isis." Thus, the king being Nefertem gave life to Re and at the same time he was the son of Re; he was the lotus flower, Nefertem, and at the same time he was the young sun, Horus, who arose out of the lotus. This is a characteristic example of the intricacy of Egyptian mythology, but part of it becomes somewhat more understandable if we realize that "giving life" is not necessarily identical with "giving birth." On earth the son gives offerings to his deceased father to bestow him with life in the beyond, and likewise the king, being the son of Re, offers to his father the nourishment on which the god lives.

The old concept of Horus and his ancestry was carried on beside the new concept of Re, in accordance with that conservatism in Egyptian religious thinking, which contributed so much to its complexity. However, some simplification was also brought forth by the new concept which centered on Re. The complicated ideas that both the heavenly god and the earthly ruler were Horus, and that the divine king was both Horus and Osiris, were no longer effective elements, although they survived in certain contexts. The highest god Re, the earthly king, and the god Osiris emerged as distinct individual concepts, whose separate developments were clearly discernible after 2300 B.C. and will be discussed presently. At that time the centralized political unit which we call the "Old Kingdom" broke down and gave space to a feudalistic form of government throughout Egypt until about 2000 B.C., when the country, again united by kings, had a character very different from that of the Old Kingdom.

Re himself was apparently involved in the further development of mythology only when he represented either Atum or Harakhty or when he appeared in the fight of the sun against the serpent of darkness. Otherwise, the figure of Re started a development which eventually led to the disintegration of Egyptian mythology. For while the main seat of the worship of Re remained in Heliopolis, he penetrated into the cults of other gods, because of his connection with the concept of kingship. Thus in the Middle Kingdom (about 2000–1700 B.C.) the local deities connected with the royal house of the Twelfth Dynasty were assimilated to him. The crocodile Sobek (Sukhos) of the Fayyum near the royal residence became Sobek-Re, and Amun of Thebes in the South, where the royal family originated, became Amon-Re. Although the tendency to assimilate a local god to Re became widespread, only the Amon-Re combination proved to be of utmost importance. For about 1600 B.C. Thebes became the royal residence and, subsequently, the capital of the New Kingdom, the Egyptian Empire which encompassed Palestine, Syria, and the Sudan. Amon-Re was thus the true successor of Re as the god of the universe, both of heaven and the Empire. Nor was this due exclusively to political circumstances; the very character of Amon-Re led to a new theological concept. While Amun was sometimes represented as a ram and occasionally as a goose, he was not a local fetish god of oldest tradition. He appears first in the Pyramid Texts as a primeval deity and about 2100 B.C. as a deity at Thebes, in either case as a male and, at the same time, female—this duality being a feature which we shall discuss in the context of the Ogdoad as a characteristic of primeval deities. His name means "the hidden one," so he was identified with the air. In the mythology of Thebes he appears equated with his neighbor god, Min of Coptos, whose character as Kamuthis, "the bull of his mother," we have mentioned before. This character paved the way for his assimilation with Re, and the fact that he was deemed invisible contributed much to the later, final idea of the universal god.

This latest concept of the universal god, "Amon-Re, the king of the gods," was preceded by a number of variations. These were prompted mainly by political changes. King Akhenaton (about 1370 B.C.) overthrew the domination of Amon-Re and his priests at Thebes and rejected the spiritual leadership of Heliopolis. He took his residence in Amarna in Middle Egypt and made it the center of a religion of his own. He acknowledged only the sun god Re (Re-Harakhty) and taught that Re appeared only in the sun disk which was then called Aton. Consequently, he rejected all mythology. Akhenaton called himself merely the son of Re and Aton. His followers, however, were induced to look upon him as a god and identified him with both Re and Aton. Thus the old concept of the trinity revived in the idea of the oneness of Re, Aton, and the king. Developed along a strictly rationalistic basis in a period of mere lip service to the gods, this concept of Amarna revealed the dangers involved in the exaltation and deification of a living individual: autocracy and sub-missiveness. The idea of trinity appeared again in the period of religious and political restoration which set an end to the interlude of Amarna. Then the three gods of the traditional capitals of Egypt—Re-Harakhty of Heliopolis, Amon-Re of Thebes, and Ptah of Memphis, to whom we shall come back later—were regarded as a unit. Finally, about 1000 B.C., the so-called "Credo of a Highpriest of Thebes," reveals a spiritual concept of the highest order: Amon-Re is looked on as the one god whose form is hidden like the shape of the radiating sun in whom he manifests himself. He is the first who came into existence and the creator of all, the king of heaven, earth, and the beyond, the lord of life and light, beloved and feared. In this hymnal composition (*Mythological Papyri,* p. 13 ff.) the mythological ideas are employed as metaphors in a manner similar to those in which the conception of God is expressed in the prophetic literature and psalms of the Old Testament. Still, all of the other gods are acknowledged as well, since they are his own various forms of appearance. Strictly speaking, he is the god of the gods. In consequence of the historical situation, this highly spiritual concept of God was not permitted to affect Egyptian popular religion, in contrast to the effect of the similar concept in Israel. On the contrary, in Egypt it marks the final separation of priestly theology and popular religion.

I have summarized the way in which the concept of the universal god developed as it did, as a consequence of the elevation of the sun god Re in the middle of the third millennium. By the same token, the concept of the earthly king was free to develop in the opposite direction, toward its secularization. In fact, the "Instruction for King Mery-ka-Re," a literary work of about 2100 B.C., shows clearly that the king himself as well as the readers of this popular "Instruction" considered him a mere human being dependent on the will of god. This, however, is by no means the complete picture. The fact that early kingship and early mythology had been virtually the same caused Egyptian government and religion to remain inseparable in actuality until 525 B.C. and in theory for another millennium. In this official context the king remained always the god, Horus as well as the Son of Re, and he was approached accordingly in ceremonies; he was then also called Re. The aspect of the king as the son of Re actually prompted a new mythological elaboration of the old concept that the king was the son of Atum. A tale of the Middle Kingdom relates that the first kings of the Fifth

Dynasty who established the predominance of Re actually were the children of Re and the wife of a priest of Re. About 1500 B.C., Queen Hatshepsut stressed her right to rule as a king by recording the story of her divine birth in the mural reliefs of her temple in Deir-el-Bahari at Thebes (Breasted, *Ancient Records* II, pp. 75–86). According to this representation, which apparently was based on earlier tradition, Amon-Re visited with the queen Ahmose in the appearance of her husband to engender the new king and to fix the name of the child, Hatshepsut; then he ordered Khnum to fashion the child on the potter's wheel; Ahmose gave birth to her; Hathor, the cow goddess, presented her to her father, Amon-Re, who called her the king; and Hathor nursed her. On the one hand, it is evident that old concepts which we discussed before were combined with new aspects in this theological tale. On the other hand, very similar scenes are found in the mural pictures and inscriptions of the so-called Mammisis, meaning "the houses of birth," which occur as special separate buildings on the premises of the great temples from about 400 B.C. The Mammisi of a temple served for the performance of the ceremonies concerned with the birth of the child god, the son of the main god of the temple. In these ceremonies the mythological aspect of the divine birth of the king as depicted in Deir-el-Bahari merged with the myth of the birth of Horus by Isis in the solitude of the Delta wilderness. After all, both concepts were basically the same as they can be traced back, in different ways, to the question: how was it possible for the god to appear as a human being?

Just as the old question of the birth of the god was still valid in the concept that the king was the son of Re, so also was the problem of the meaning of his death. The famous novel of Sinuhe, about 1950 B.C., was the first to express the popular idea of the death of the king: "he was taken away, so he joined the sun disk (Aton), and the divine body was united with him who made him." The theological answer to the problem was not so simple. It is attested in the mural reliefs of the tombs of the kings between about 1500 and 1100 B.C., which have also provided us with the "Book of the

Heavenly Cow," with which we started this discussion. I should like to give an idea of the main mythological concept which is to be found there with the following quotation from Alexandre Piankoff's studies on this difficult topic: "The deceased king comes as Osiris in his tomb, where a cycle of transformation is going to begin: the dead god will be born again, Osiris will appear as a new Re, a new sun god. In the royal tombs this transformation of a dead god into a new sun, and of a king identified with him, is described in the great religious compositions, the 'Book of What Is in the Nether World,' the 'Book of the Gates,' and the 'Book of the Caverns'" (*The Shrines*, p. 23). These three books are illustrated descriptions of the journey of the sun during the night through twelve enclosures, each of which represents one hour of the night. The sun god changes his appearance from a scarab to a ram-headed man at the beginning of this journey, and from the ram-headed man into the scarab at its end.

Osiris was the third mythological character to emerge from the differentiation of the early concepts, which was prompted by the elevation of Re. Osiris, we have seen, was the deceased king who was then transfigured as the Lord of Heaven. Now, when Re was acknowledged as the Lord of Heaven, there was no room in heaven for the Osiris king. His struggle to emerge from his tomb and be accepted by Re as his peer, or replace Re in heaven, is clearly attested in the Pyramid Texts. Presumably this very desire caused the Pyramid Texts to be inscribed on the walls of the later pyramids in contradiction to the uninscribed earlier ones: the spells rendered permanent the magical means by which the desire of the deceased king could be enforced upon Re. Theologically speaking, this struggle of Osiris represents an effort to reaffirm the idea that the individual king who was Osiris would further be the divine ruler in the light of heaven rather than in the darkness of the pyramid tomb and the nether world. As a result, the concept of the deceased king became separated from that of Osiris as an individual deity. We have seen that the deceased king was transformed from his character as Osiris into the new sun, Re, according to the texts in the royal tombs of the period of the Empire. The god Osiris, however, was the ruler of the dead forever. His situation is elaborated on in the famous dialogue of Atum and Osiris (*ANET*, p. 9): When Osiris complained about his life alone in the darkness, he was comforted by the words of Atum that only the two of them, Atum and Osiris, would survive in eternity when the world would have vanished and returned to its primeval state as the ocean, Nunu. Then Atum and Osiris would take the shape of serpents, and there would be neither gods nor men to perceive them. Evidently, the old concepts of the primeval serpent and of the primeval existence of both the king and Atum are combined here. Besides, Atum tells Osiris that for the time being it is only for his benefit that he is separated from the light of the sun; for his enemy, Seth, is fighting the serpent of darkness (who is now called Apophis) in the boat of Re; Seth will never reach him to kill him again.

Another aspect of Osiris crystallized as a result of his vain struggle for life in the light. Osiris, being the deceased king, was the ruler of the necropolis which adjoined the pyramid of the individual king. By the same token he was the judge who punished tomb robbers and would have prevented the admission to his "roads" of those deceased who were accused of a crime and not acknowledged as righteous by their contemporaries. The concept that the righteousness of man depended on its acknowledgment by his fellow men, however, changed with the breakdown of the social order of the Old Kingdom about 2300 B.C. The individual consciousness of self-responsibility emerged from this debacle, and from then on it was no longer the acknowledgment of his contemporaries which proved the righteousness of a man. The individual now had to fit into a divine order which was no longer mirrored on earth, and he had to answer to God for the deeds of his life after death. Thus the god Osiris, who was now the king of the beyond in his own right and no longer the deceased king, became the judge in a trial in the beyond, to which every man was subjected.

6. MYTHOLOGY AND THE IDEA OF LIFE AFTER DEATH

Leaving for later consideration the discussion of the trial in the beyond, which, as we have seen, originated after 2300 B.C. and applied then to the kings and commoners alike, there seem to be hardly any mythological concepts which originated in the belief that human life continued after death. However, the impact of Egyptian mythology on this belief and vice versa was very great. Our knowledge of the Egyptian mythology would be most limited without the funerary texts. The close interrelation of mortuary and mythological ideas is due to the fact that human goal after death was deification. This idea too came into existence after 2300 B.C. To understand it we must briefly summarize the ideas concerning the hereafter in the preceding centuries.

The remarkable development of tombs and funeral rites in Egypt during the third millennium B.C. resulted from an extensive elaboration of two basic ideas: The first was the belief that the deceased carried on some spectral form of existence by which they might be either dangerous or beneficial to their survivors, and in which they themselves were exposed to various dangers. The second idea was what I think is the natural human urge to provide the deceased with what belonged to him, what he needed and loved on earth so that he might enjoy it and employ it as long as, and in whatever manner, he could. The elaboration of these basic ideas, neither of which implied the belief that the human spirit or soul was immortal, originated in the royal residence. The employment of masonry for the tombs, the depth of the burial chamber with its deposits, the establishment of permanent offerings and incantations, the wall pictures of daily life and funerary rites, the statue, or statues, of the deceased, and the other features, including mummification, probably served the sole purpose of pacifying them and providing them as long as possible with what they had been used to during their lifetime. Since these funeral practices, gifts, and offerings appeared to be fixed for eternity, there gradually developed the idea of everlasting life beyond death. Furthermore, the tomb was built in the vicinity of the pyramids. As the pyramid was the dwelling place of the body of the Great God, the divine and transfigured king, the wish was expressed in the tomb inscriptions that the deceased who was a true servant of his king in his lifetime might be accepted gracefully by the eternal god and permitted to "walk on his divine roads." This also implied everlasting life. The hope for eternal life thus originated with, and was restricted to, those who could afford the means to provide for it, and it depended on the continuance of the society in its accustomed structure. When the concept of the king as being Horus and Osiris was superseded by that of the two gods, Re and Osiris, the idea of the future life with the god became a little more vague, since the designation, the Great God, was then applied to either of these different divine characters. The catastrophical end of the whole concept, however, came when the order of the Old Kingdom broke down. Kingship lost its meaning, tombs were destroyed, there were no means to maintain the funerary cult. Despair and skepticism pervade the contemporaneous works of literature. They make it very clear that, according to popular belief, then as well as later on, orderly existence after death could not be expected if there was no orderly burial.

The belief that life after death depended on the burial continued to exist side by side with a new idea of everlasting life: the earlier concept of the deceased king in both his divine forms as Horus and Osiris was applied to the deceased commoner to grant him the eternal character of the gods. It is true that the clearest indications of the new idea appeared gradually about 2000 B.C. These were the designations which were added to a man's name after his death: the word "Osiris" was put before it, and the appellation of Horus when he was acclaimed as the right king, "the vindicated one," succeeded the name—"Osiris NN, the vindicated one" meant "the late NN" who would live on as both Osiris and Horus. However, the most important documentation of the new belief, the so-called Coffin Texts, appeared earlier, about the same time in which the latest Pyramid Texts were engraved.

The aim of the Coffin Texts is to give those who had them written on their coffins the power to enforce either a fairly comfortable form of existence in the beyond or, more presumptuously, deification for eternal life. Their contents is not exclusively mythological. Remarks are often added to the individual spells to inform the deceased for which magical purpose they should be recited; moreover, some spells are for the living rather than the deceased. Except for these latter, the remarks added to the spells exemplify the prevailing melancholy prospect in regard to the existence hereafter. They are recommended, for example, for maintaining the functioning of heart and all the other organs; getting air with which to breathe; not having to walk upside down or eat excrement; avoiding another death. Other spells were designed to transform oneself into any possible form: for instance, into the divine falcon, the goddess Hathor, a crocodile, a flame, or "into whatever god he wishes to." The beginning of the first spell in our modern arrangement of the spells is apt to give an idea of both the arbitrariness of the identifications which occur in it, and of the mixture of mythological and funeral concepts: "O Osiris NN, you are the *ru*-lion, you are Ruruty (a deity who was identified as a pair of lions meaning Shu and Tefnut), you are Horus who revenges his father, you are the four gods, those spirits who bring the water and make the Nile, who rejoice with the (bones of the) thighs of their fathers (apparently in the funeral procession according to an obsolete rite). O Osiris NN, raise yourself on your left side, put yourself on your right side (in the tomb to rise in renewed life)." Naturally, the identification of Osiris, the lion, Ruruty, Shu and Tefnut, Horus, and the personifications of the four chief points of the compass would leave room for any number of new combinations of mythological concepts. It is thus clear that the Coffin Texts represent a vast documentation of the Egyptian mythology of about 2000 B.C. Only gradually, however, shall we learn which concepts were old and which were the product of the speculation of those literary men who composed them in the form which has been transmitted to us.

Only two of the desired identifications will be discussed here, those with Re and Horus, as they play a more than casual role. They are closely related to the wished-for royal character of the deceased, which was also expressed in his identification with Osiris. They also continue the leading ideas concerning the king as expressed in the Pyramid Texts, though with new arguments. The deceased wished to be, or to join, Re in heaven, for in daytime Re gave the light which the deceased particularly wished to enjoy, while during the night he was safe in his tomb. Furthermore, Re was identical with the ancient one, Atum, and thus the concepts of the first living being, the divine king, and the genealogy of the gods with all its ramifications would apply to the deceased. Finally, Re was the victor over his enemy, the hostile serpent of darkness, which was then called Apophis, while Seth, the royal killer, fought it on behalf of old king Re in the bow of the sun boat.

The same desire for the defeat of one's enemies—those slanderers who might prevent the admission of the deceased into the more enjoyable features of existence after death—was also effective in the context of the popular identification of the deceased with the young and vigorous king, Horus, for Horus was vindicated in the face of the claims of his enemy, Seth, and was acknowledged as the true king and god by the court of the gods. Therefore, the deceased was supposed to undergo the same court procedure, in which the god Thoth would bring about his vindication. This identification had a strange bearing on the myth. We have already seen that the deceased was called "Osiris NN." This designation was used in the context of the lawsuit as well as elsewhere in the Coffin Texts. Consequently, the texts some times refer to Osiris instead of Horus as the adversary of, and victor over, Seth. Accordingly, the new name of Wennofer, "he who exists anew," was given to Osiris in the course of this development. He is called, "the king of Upper and Lower Egypt, Wennofer, the vindicated one," and "the king of Upper and Lower Egypt, Osiris Wennofer," in two texts of the very beginning of the second millennium. The idea of Wennofer, the victorious and rejuvenated Osiris, corresponded with those ideas which were expressed in the royal tombs in later centuries and "King Wennofer" became especially popular in the last millennium B.C. To begin with, it implied an identification of Osiris with Horus, which appears, incidentally, to fit with the old idea that the king was both Horus and Osiris. It is no wonder, then, that scholars have always thought that the idea of Osiris fighting Seth in the court was as genuine as that of the lawsuit between Horus and Seth. However, it should be stressed that the notion that Osiris himself overcame his enemy in one way or another is not attested before the Coffin Texts.

Another consequence of the identification of the deceased with both Osiris and Horus is even more striking. We have already discussed the concept of the trial in the beyond which was presided over by the Great God who eventually became Osiris. When this was inserted in the funerary texts, the defendant, i.e., the deceased, was as usual himself called "Osiris NN." Thus Osiris was judged by Osiris. When all is said and done, the court procedure in the beyond appears to have been a rather complicated idea. Let me summarize the evidence, therefore. In the Coffin Texts the lawsuit between Horus and Seth was identified as the lawsuit which, according to the old concept of the royal necropolis, the deceased individual as a defendant carried on with his enemies, the accusers and slanderers. Thus, on the one hand, the spells represented a magical means "to vindicate a man against his enemies in the necropolis" (*C.T.* I 19). On the other hand, it was Geb, the god who had once judged Horus and Seth, who presided over the court, and not the Great God. In a few texts, however, the Great God, Osiris, joined Geb in his position as the chief of the court. Consequently, the situation that "Osiris NN" was judged by the god Osiris occurs for the first time in these spells (*C.T.* I 32; 43). The idea that doing right and avoiding sin during one's lifetime was the best manner in which the accusations might be invalidated is expressed in the "Instruction for King Mery-ka-Re" which dates from the same period. We would seek for it in vain in the Coffin Texts for the simple reason that such an admonition to avoid sin during his lifetime would come too late for the deceased, for whom these texts were designed, and thus be useless.

The classical conception of the trial in the beyond originated in the intellectual temper of the "Instruction" and not of the Coffin Texts. It was not included in the collection of mortuary magical spells until the Coffin Texts were replaced by the so-called Book of the Dead about 1600 B.C. This is distinguished from the Coffin Texts mainly by the fact that it was written on papyrus rolls and not on the coffins. The trial in the beyond is dealt with in what we call the 125th chapter of the Book of the Dead. It consists of two elements, the Protestation of Guiltlessness, which does not concern us here, and a picture of the trial, which appears as the first item in the finest manuscripts of the Book of the Dead. After all, only the acquittal in the trial made the admittance to the world of the gods possible. An extensive description of this trial (*B.o.D.*, Chap. 30, according to Any) shows that the court consisted of the Great Ennead of the Gods and was presided over by Osiris although he himself did not take any action. The god of wisdom, the ibis-headed Thoth, was the public attorney. He made the jackal-headed Anubis weigh the heart of the deceased on the scale, where it was supposed to balance the weight of an ostrich feather, the symbol of Maat, "law and righteousness." In addition, Thoth made the *ba*-soul of the deceased testify about him. Finally, he transmitted his judgment, duly based on evidence and testimony, to the court. The court accepted Thoth's judgment and completed the verdict by ruling that the deceased was vindicated: "The *amemet*-beast, 'the devourer,' shall not have power over him. He shall be given the food yielded to Osiris and a permanent

(share of an) acre in the Field of Satisfaction." The mythological concept of the trial, therefore, appears to be a replica
of an earthly and well-conducted court procedure. Likewise,
the illustration factually presents as its main features the
king Osiris with his court, the deceased, Thoth writing,
Anubis weighing the heart, the *ba*-soul in the form of a
human-headed bird, and the Chimera-like monster, the Devourer, waiting for his prey, though in vain. Both the illustration and the Protestation of Guiltlessness are evidently used
to enforce the acquittal by magical means. Still, the trial
might have been a matter of concern to serious people then,
as it was five hundred years earlier. The notion that evil
deeds will be punished in the beyond is well attested in the
centuries around the birth of Christ.

7. VARIOUS MYTHOLOGICAL TEXTS

Almost every mythological character and situation which I
have mentioned thus far appears to have occurred more
than once and each time in a different context. This happens
neither by accident nor because I intended it that way.
After all, Egyptian mythology does not appear to differ
from other mythologies for, like them, it has a restricted
number of major mythological characters. However, it seems
to be characteristic of Egypt that the major myths can easily
be traced back to one main concept, the lineage of Horus.
The knowledge of its two elements, the cosmogony of the
first generations and the family story of the fourth and
fifth, is indispensable for the understanding of, I would say,
any mythological tale of logical continuity. In the following
discussion of some of them, therefore, only a few additional
facts must be introduced.

The concept of the Eye of the highest god was mentioned
in the story of the heavenly cow at the very beginning of

the present discussion. The Eye occurs either as the Eye of
Horus or the Eye of Re, though not exclusively: we encountered the Eye of Atum before. The characteristic of the Eye
appears to be that its removal from the highest god means
disturbance, while its return means pacification and the
restitution of order. It seems that the concept of the Eye
was closely connected with the idea of kingship and not
with cosmic ideas, although, later on, the moon might be
called the Eye of Horus and the sun and the moon together
the Eyes of either Re or Horus. The Eye is identified in
the Pyramid Texts with the Uraeus viper which spat venom
and fire against its enemies and was fastened at the forehead
of the king as the sign of kingship in both heaven and earth.
There also appears to exist a close relation between the Eye
and the primeval serpent. The Eye of Horus was fused with
the story of Osiris, Horus, and the wretched Seth through
the tale of a fight between Horus and Seth. They wounded
each other to mutual exhaustion as Seth tore out the eye
of Horus and Horus tore off the testicles of Seth. This Horus
was the king who, through his death, became Osiris, and
whose son, Horus, then was acknowledged as the king. This
young Horus fought Seth, took the Eye of Horus out of
Seth's head, affixed it to his own forehead, while at the same
time he restored it to his father, to whom it originally
belonged and who then was Osiris. Thus he made good
the wrong which had been done to his father and revived
him. Accordingly, then, the Eye of Horus was a symbol
first of the offerings with which Horus gave life to his
deceased father, and subsequently of all offerings for the
gods. The Eye of king Re appears as a messenger just as,
according to the Coffin Texts, Atum sent his Eye to find his
children, Shu and Tefnut. It is terrifying to the enemies of
Re, such as those who gathered to the south of Egypt, in the
desert, to plot rebellion against Re. A popular version of the
story of the Eye of Re was first discovered by Hermann
Junker in allusions and other references in the inscriptions
and reliefs of some temples dating from the centuries around
the birth of Christ, and confirmed not long afterward by a

contemporaneous lengthy novel. This story may be summarized as follows: Tefnut, who was the Eye of Re and the daughter of Re, was separated from her father for reasons unknown to us. She then dwelled in the desert of Nubia as a bloodthirsty lion. Re, longing for her, sent the baboon Thoth, who succeeded in persuading her to return to Egypt. There she appeared as Hathor and was received by all the Egyptians, especially in the temples of Hathor-Tefnut, with jubilation. Variants of this story depict Tefnut as a cat, the goddess Bastet, who changed into a lion only when she became angry. The discussion of Thoth with Tefnut, which occasioned such an outburst of anger, is the main topic of the late novel; it then gives way to the telling of various fables. A picture of the dispute between the cat and the baboon is preserved from about 1300 B.C. In fact, the basic elements of the tale have been found in the religious literature of all periods, including the Pyramid Texts.

The Eye of Re was also often identified with Maat. Apparently it is she who was called "the unequaled Eye, the mistress of the Ennead, the mistress of the universe" (*C.T. IV* 86). Maat is the personification of divine and political order, of law and individual righteousness. Maat was early represented as a female bearing the ostrich feather on her head. Simultaneously, in the middle of the third millennium, the highest judge bore the title "priest of Maat." While she was, therefore, regarded as a goddess, her character as the cosmic, political, and social order prevented her from being conceived of as a mythological character. However, she was associated with mythology in a twofold manner. The expression, "who lives on Maat," is attested in the Pyramid Texts for the four "guards in Upper Egypt" whom we have identified with the four points of the compass; this exemplifies the idea, which is also expressed elsewhere, that Maat was looked on as a primeval entity. Later on, it is mainly Re who "lives on Maat." In this expression it is the idea of actual food, namely the offerings which were delivered in accordance with the social order of Egypt, which was involved in Maat, in addition to that of the order itself. Secondly, Maat was associated with mythology by means of her appellation as "the daughter of Atum" and, more regularly, "the daughter of Re." In both the implications of "living on Maat" and "daughter of Atum," which are not exactly mythological, she occurs in a mythological tale (*C.T.* II 34–35): "Then Atum said to Nunu (the primeval ocean): 'I am swimming in the water, very tired, for men are lazy (in giving offerings). My son Geb (the earth) is he who can elevate my heart (please me). He shall make my heart alive when he has gathered together my limbs (being the limbs) of one who is very tired.' (Evidently, Atum wishes to die and to be buried.) Nunu said to Atum: 'Smell your daughter Maat after putting her at your nose (kiss her), so your heart will live. They will not leave you, namely, your daughter Maat and your son Shu whose name is Life. Thus you will feed on your daughter Maat, and it will be your son Shu who elevates you.'" The latter activity of Shu may be understood from the raising of Re by Shu as told in the story of the heavenly cow, which is an elaboration on the present dialogue in more than one respect. The idea that a child may give life to his father has been mentioned before, and the motif of the pleasure which the daughter gives her elderly father occurs also in the story of Horus and Seth. The word "to smell" is the usual Egyptian expression for "to kiss." Here the kissing involves the well-known idea that life is given by means of the breath which enters the nose. Finally, to return to the non-mythological aspect of Maat: She is related most closely to three figures, Re, the earthly king, and, according to the earliest as well as to later evidence, Ptah; all three are evidently called "Lord of Maat" more genuinely and regularly than any other deity.

Ptah was mentioned before as one of the trinity which consisted of Amon-Re, Re-Harakhty, and Ptah, about 1300 B.C. His highly important theological role originated in the fact that he was the god of the residence of the king at Memphis in the third millennium. Like Maat, he does not display any genuine mythological characteristics. He might well have

been invented in one way or another at the beginning of the
historical period in his character as a governmental theological concept. The genuine local deity of Memphis was
the Apis bull and, furthermore, there was Ta-tenen, "the
raised land," who may or may not have been a theologically
conceived variation of the primeval earth hill. Both the
apparent "newcomers" in Memphis, Ptah and Ta-tenen, are
involved in a document which represents the most interesting theological treatise which we possess in Egypt, the "Monu-
ment of the Theology of Memphis," or the "Theology of
Memphis" (*ANET*, pp. 4–6). It is a badly preserved inscription on a monolith erected about 700 B.C., which King
Shabaka ordered to be prepared as a copy of an old and
worm-eaten papyrus roll. The king's claim that the text was
copied from an old papyrus is supported by certain characteristics of the inscription. The dating of the text to about
2500 B.C. appears possible and has been generally accepted
for the time being.

This "Theology of Memphis" is composed in the narrative
form, with inserted dialogues and stage directions of a type
which we shall discuss later in the context of another document. Its content represents an elaboration on the concept of
the lineage of Horus. Its aim is to prove that Memphis has
been the seat of the king since mythical times and that Ptah
is the creator of all. These two points are dealt with one
after the other. The first portion is based on elements of the
family story of king Osiris. Possibly, the link between Heliopolis and Memphis is provided by Geb, the representative
of the royal ancestry who was the earth just as was Ta-tenen,
who is identified with Ptah. The second part is based on the
idea that Atum engendered Shu and Tefnut by masturbation,
which is here elevated to a spiritual level by means of the
interpolation of Ptah. This is an extremely difficult text, which
has been the subject of most careful studies by such distinguished scholars as Breasted, Erman, Sethe, and Junker,
but still many problems remain. I will now try to relate its
main features as follows.

The first part, which includes the references to a dramatic

performance, is a historical treatise. In the beginning, Horus and Seth quarreled. Then Geb, presiding over the Ennead, installed Seth as the king of Upper Egypt and Horus as the king of Lower Egypt. Seeing that Horus was the son of his oldest son, Osiris, however, Geb changed his mind and gave the whole country to Horus. Thus Horus became he who united the Two Lands in his name of Ta-tenen, and Memphis was the "Balance of Egypt," where Horus and Seth were reconciled. Then Osiris drowned and was taken ashore at Memphis by Horus, Isis, and Nephthys. He joined Ta-tenen through his interment. The royal palace was established by Geb and Thoth, and Isis accomplished the reconciliation of Horus and Seth. In order better to follow the logic of the tale, we must recall that Horus was always the son of Osiris and, at the same time, became Osiris himself after his death. We may well assume, therefore, that in the beginning of the tale "Horus" meant the father and in its second part the son. We have made the same distinction between Horus the father and Horus the son in the discussion of the Pyramid Texts' version of the fights concerning the Eye.

The second part of the "Theology of Memphis" is introduced by the statement that the major gods of the primeval beginning originated in Ptah. This is proved by means of eight identifications of Ptah, only four of which are preserved, however: Ptah is both the male and the female primeval ocean, the father and the mother of Atum; he is Nefertem, who is at the nose of Re to bestow breath upon him; and he is "the heart and tongue which belong to the Ennead." The latter expression is discussed in the rest of the text, which Hermann Junker has analyzed as a fusion of two treatises. One elaborates on the physiological and psychological idea that the sensual organs of the human body report their impressions to the heart which is the seat of the thoughts, and the tongue repeats the thoughts by means of the creative word. This part of the text concerned with the creative power of heart and tongue laid the foundation for the second treatise which is mythological in character and which seems to indicate that Atum was absorbed by Ptah, whose heart is Horus, whose mouth is Thoth, and whose teeth and lips are the Ennead. Out of his mouth, consisting of tongue, teeth, and lips, Shu and Tefnut were spat. By means of the creative word of Ptah the gods with their images and temples, life and death, every craft, and all the actions of the human body were then created.

It is impossible to state exactly which features of this text occur here for the first time. The idea of thought and word being definite and effective entities was perhaps characteristic of the concept of Ptah, but it is not unique and has its counterpart in the concept of Sia and Hu, who appear connected with Re. Genuinely Memphite elements are introduced with Memphis, Ta-tenen, and Ptah. It has become customary to understand this elaboration as polemic and directed against Heliopolis in an attempt to create a predominant role for Ptah and Memphis. This interpretation may be debated, however, if we bear in mind our discussion of the absence of dogmatism in Egyptian mythology and our interpretation of the genealogy as the lineage of Horus. We can readily imagine that this Memphite version of the genealogy was gladly acknowledged by the theologians of Heliopolis as a product of theology which served a local and governmental purpose, although they did not have any reason to take it over for themselves. The identification of Horus and Osiris with Ptah-Ta-tenen could not possibly do any harm to the former—there existed precedents in the identification of a number of provincial deities as "Horus," but such an identification by name was not possible of course in the residence of Horus, the king. Furthermore, where else could Ptah have fitted into the lineage if not at its end, that is, at the very beginning of the genealogy? Ptah's identification with the primeval ocean, Nunu, and its female counterpart, i.e., as father and mother of Atum, is expressly stated in the "Memphite Theology." It is quite compatible with the well-known Heliopolitan idea that Atum was born out of the ocean, which was omitted in the context of the lineage of Horus for the very good reason that Horus was conceived as equal with Atum and not with Nunu. Further, the character of Memphis as the residence of the king, once established, was of course undisputed. Finally, I cannot agree with the opinion that the "Memphite Theology" was a polemic treatise, since we have no other indications of a controversy between Memphis and Heliopolis in the centuries before and around 2500 B.C. or at any other time in the third millennium. While the problem of whether or not the "Memphite Theology" was deigned for polemics cannot be solved here, it appears relevant to our understanding of Egyptian mythology. The widely spread assumption that mythological concepts were employed as political chessmen by belligerent theologians in ancient Egypt is not in harmony with the character of Egyptian mythology and theology: such a move could not possibly have had any effect. Nor does it appear to be supported by the facts of Egyptian history. The influence of an established political fact upon mythological concepts, however, is something different and well attested. The "Memphite Theology" should be understood as the theological explanation and justification of the undisputed fact that Memphis was the residence of the kings. It was adapted to the concept current in Heliopolis, and was not designed for competition.

The sky has appeared more often than any other entity in our summary of prehistoric concepts. We have, furthermore, discussed its appearance as Nut and as the heavenly cow in the historic period. Another tale of Nut, similar to the tale of the cow, appears about 1300 B.C., in a royal tomb structure. It accompanies the picture of Nut with her body raised by Shu and her toes and finger tips touching the ground. The text deals with the stars: "They sail to the end of the sky (Nut) surrounding her body at night whilst they show themselves and are seen. They sail in her inside in the day-time whilst they do not show themselves and are not seen. They enter after this god (i.e., the sun, Re) and they come forth after him. So they sailed after him on what Shu raised . . . and they entered the mouth of Nut in the

MYTHOLOGY IN ANCIENT EGYPT 65

place of her head in the West. So she ate them. So Geb
quarreled with Nut because he was angry with her because
of the eating of her young ones. Her name was called
'Sow who eats her piglets,' because she ate them. So her
father Shu lifted her and raised her to his head and said:
'Guard Geb. Let him not quarrel with her because she
eats their children. She shall give birth to them and they
shall live, and they shall come forth in the place at her hinder
part in the East every day.'" (This translation is based on
that of Adriaan de Buck in H. Frankfort, *The Cenotaph*,
p. 82 ff.) In other versions of this story Nut appears as
either a woman or a hippopotamus. The same concept is
attested by figurines of either a sow or a hippopotamus, and
the same identifications of Nut appear in hymns. Some of the
texts including that which we have quoted were written down
in the context of astronomical treatises. The oldest elements of
the tale are familiar to the reader of this chapter as the
prehistoric concept of the heavenly cow which gives birth to
her calf, the sun, everyday and most probably devours the
bull in the evening to give birth again to the calf in the
morning, and as the concept of Nut, Geb, and Shu. Since
the idea that Nut devours her children is reminiscent of
the Greek myth of Kronos who devoured his children, a
tale which is related by Plutarch (*De Iside et Osiride*, Chap.
12) may be added. Kronos (Geb) loved Rhea (Nut), but
in consequence of a curse of Helios (Re) she was not permitted to bear children on any day of the year. Hermes
(Thoth), however, prepared five days which he added to
the 360 days of the year. Thus Nut mothered Osiris, Haroëris ("the eldest Horus"), Seth (Typhon), Isis, and Nephthys on these five intercalary days. In fact, the five days which
were added to the twelve months of thirty days each, every
year in the Egyptian calendar, had always been called with
the names of those five gods.

The myth of the Ogdoad, "the eight gods," of Hermopolis
deals with the primeval beginning. In discussing the prehistoric ideas about heaven I have mentioned the eight
heh-deities who since about 2000 B.C. replaced the four

guards of the supports of the sky. Heh appears already as a single deity in the Pyramid Texts. According to the Coffin Texts (IV 86) he was apparently fed on Maat, just as were those four guards according to the Pyramid Texts. Heh is depicted kneeling with his arms raised like Shu when he raises his arms to support Nut. The same kneeling figure represents the members of the Ogdoad, "the eight *heh*-deities," as an ideogram in the hieroglyphic writing of the Coffin Texts. In the illustration of the heavenly cow, on page 16, this shape of the *heh*-deities occurs in front of the breast and between the horns of the cow, while their pose holding the legs of the cow is exceptional. All this evidence suggests the conclusion that Heh, the supporter of the sky, was identical with Shu and became a unit of four in analogy to the four cardinal points. In any event, we shall see below how the four became eight. The Ogdoad is called "the eight *heh*-deities whom Shu conceived, bore, created, knotted, and engendered" (*C.T.* II 19c–e). They were also the direct offspring of Atum and Nunu (*C.T.* II 7d; 20a). They "elevate Nut beneath Re-Atum" (*C.T.* II 20a). The most comprehensive description of them runs, "Oh ye eight *heh*-deities in millions (*heh*) of millions, who bind the sky in their arms, who gather the sky and the earth together for Geb. Shu has given birth to you as Hehu, Nunu, Tenmu, and Keku. He assigned you to Geb and Nut when Shu was in *neheh*-infinity and Tefnut was in *zet*-infinity" (*C.T.* II 27–28). Their four names, according to other versions, were created by Atum in accordance with a word of Nunu (*C.T.* II 7e; 23–24) and occur in these texts again and again. Heh(u) is the appellative *heh*, probably in its meaning "a million," "an indefinite number"; Nunu is the primeval ocean; Tenmu is translated, "Those who go astray or, who rove"; Keku means "darkness" or "the dark one." The number eight of the *heh*-deities, which does not appear to correspond with the number four of their names, might be explained as follows: The primeval deities appear as dual entities in contrast to Atum, the One. Already in the Pyramid Texts, the pair, Shu and Tefnut, were paralleled to the couples Nunu and Nunut (Naunet), Amun and Amunet (Amaunet) (*Pyr.* 446/447). Correspondingly, the four names of the *heh*-deities actually indicate eight figures, four males and four females. We should also remember in this context that, according to the "Memphite Theology," Ptah was identified with eight primeval deities, though not the Ogdoad of the *heh*-deities. Moreover, there is a certain significance of the number eight in its relation to the seat of the worship of the Ogdoad, which was Hermopolis in Middle Egypt. This town, or at least one of its quarters, was called Shmun (the present-day Eshmunein), which simply means "eight." Evidently, in one way or another the name of the place and the number of the *heh*-deities were genuinely interrelated.

The Ogdoad was rarely mentioned in the millennium succeeding the Coffin Texts; in a variant form, however, it became rather significant at a much later period, after about 600 B.C. At that time the name of Tenmu was replaced by other names, mainly that of Amun. Amun, however, was the great god of Thebes, who by then had been Amon-Re, the King of the Gods, for a millennium. Consequently, the late concept of the Ogdoad is known mainly from inscriptions of the latest period in the temples of Thebes. The Ogdoad is then conceived of as the eight first living beings who appeared on the flaming isle of the Primeval Beginning, four couples in which the males were frogs and the females serpents. Their names, in the Greek pronunciation, are interpreted as follows: Nun and Naunet, the primeval unlimited ocean; Huh and Hauhet, representing the infinity of space; Kuk and Kauket, representing the darkness; and Amun and Amaunet, the invisible ones, the air. They were looked upon as the elements of the primeval chaos out of which the sun arose. That the whole concept originated in the North was acknowledged by a Theban version of the myth: The Ogdoad originated at Thebes and was then carried downstream by the waves of the Nile to Hermopolis, where they accomplished the act of creation on the flaming isle; subsequently, they reached Memphis to create the sun by means of their word—a reminder of the "Theology of Memphis"; and finally they brought Atum into existence at Heliopolis. While virtually all the elements of the myth of the Ogdoad may be traced back to the third millennium, it appears in a new form in the Theban theology of the last millennium B.C.

8. THE MYTH OF OSIRIS, ISIS, AND HORUS

Finally, the myth of Osiris must be discussed. The most significant of the Egyptian myths, it was not only popular with the Egyptians, but has even been known in Europe for over two thousand years. Naturally, the story of the good king who was murdered by his covetous brother, his faithful widow who protected their son from the outside world and who brought him up in solitude, and the boy who eventually avenged his father and regained his kingdom appealed to people since everybody was ready to identify himself and his experiences with one or another of its features. The survival of the tale in Europe is due to another reason. The Roman mysteries of Isis, upon which the eighteenth-century idea of Osiris as expressed in Mozart's *Magic Flute* is based, featured the tale of Isis and her deceased husband in a spiritual rather than bodily aspect. Osiris was accepted as a mythological symbol by those who sought that ceremonial guidance to a religious experience which a predominantly rationalistic conception of religion could not offer to its followers.

To the best of our knowledge, the myth of Osiris was never written down by the Egyptians in a single comprehensive tale. The Greek authors were the first whose versions of the story have been directly transmitted. The Egyptian documents allude to it frequently in all kinds of religious texts, and they relate episodes in the form of ritual and tales. I should first like to deal with that form of the tale which is alluded to in our earliest source, the Pyramid Texts, and then discuss some of the major Egyptian elaborations on the myth. Finally, a hymn to Osiris from the time of the Empire may give an impression of how the Egyptian theologians of that period looked upon the myth.

We have already seen that the myth of Osiris originated in the genealogy of Horus. This might have been established in a ceremony such as the one which I have invented to illustrate the proceedings of the elevation to the throne in the earliest period. The elements of the myth, therefore, originated in two actions: the death of the king with his transformation into Osiris, and the installation of his son upon the throne, which meant the son's deification on earth as Horus. Evidently, no historical reminiscence of any figure of the past was involved, and folklore, too, played little if any role in it. Moreover, a significant observation of Siegfried Schott should be mentioned here: The fact that our first knowledge of the myth of Osiris originates in the funerary rituals of the king should not lead us to conclude that this ritual was some sort of performance of the myth of Osiris. The proceedings of the funeral were prompted by the factual necessity of a ceremonial interment in the pyramid as befitted the king, and they inspired the incidental mythological allusions. However, these allusions fit into the pattern of a tale. While any change in the proceedings of the funerary rites was apt to add new details to the story, its basic facts appear well established in the Pyramid Texts. We have evidence that the myth of Osiris was then already understood to have happened in the past, notwithstanding the fact that it was experienced anew in every performance of the rites. In our understanding, the myth was about six hundred years old when the Pyramid Texts were first written down in stone, and the ritual underwent considerable changes during this period. The funeral rites were certainly rooted in the prehistoric period. Thus many elements of the ceremonies contributed to the final appearance of the tale.

According to the Pyramid Texts, the tale of Osiris runs about as follows: The king, Osiris, was killed by his brother, Seth, in Nedyt (or Gehesty). Isis and Nephthys, the sisters of

Osiris, sought for the body, found it in Nedyt, and lamented over it. Isis restored Osiris to life temporarily so that he might get her with child. She then gave birth to Horus, suckled him, and brought him up in Khemmis, a place in the Delta. As a child, Horus overpowered a snake. He reached manhood through a ceremony which centered on the fastening of the belt, which Isis performed, and went out to "see" his father (*Pyr.* 1214–15). Apparently he found him. Then a court over which Geb presided was held at Heliopolis. Seth denied the murder of Osiris; presumably, too, the question arose whether or not Horus was the true heir to Osiris; in any event, Isis testified on behalf of her son by taking him to her breasts. Horus was made the king by the acclaim of the court. I have mentioned before that an additional story which centered on the Eye was fused with the main one: Seth stole the eye of Horus who subsequently became Osiris, when they fought at Heliopolis, and the younger Horus, the son of Osiris, regained it in a fight with Seth and took it to his murdered father, Osiris, to revive him. According to the first story, the kingdom which was lost by murder was reassigned to the right heir by the court. According to the second story, the sign of kingship, the Eye, was first taken away from its owner and then restored to him by means of fights. The fusion of these two tales was accomplished by introducing the son into the combat; furthermore, the second fight was vaguely associated with the court procedure, and Horus restored the Eye to his father at Gehesty, the very place where Osiris was slain, according to the first story. Apparently, for reasons which are unknown to us, it was necessary to connect the idea of the Eye which was lost and then regained with the concept that the king was Horus and Osiris. In view of this interrelation we may venture the opinion that the idea of fights was not genuinely connected with the loss and recovery of the Eye; it was the criminality of Seth, originating in the concept of the slaying of Osiris, which might well have first suggested that the fate of the Eye was due to struggles with that evil character. In addition to the elements of the combined story as presented here, two other features are alluded to in the Pyramid Texts, which are not yet fused into the main story. First, the drowning of Osiris, which refers to his cosmic character as the vegetation which arises out of the inundation of the Nile; this, as we have seen, plays a role in the version of the tale of Osiris which is related in the "Memphite Theology." Second, references to the dismemberment of the body of the deceased king who was Osiris seem to be reminiscent of a very ancient burial custom, which was no longer practiced early in the third millennium; the dismemberment of Osiris by Seth is a significant element of the tale of Osiris chiefly in the versions which are transmitted from the Greek period.

A papyrus roll written about 1970 B.C. deals with a series of ceremonies which were performed in connection with the accession of King Sesostris I to the throne. The ceremony probably represents a much older tradition. I should like to present the contents on the basis of Sethe's first edition as well as Drioton's most recent interpretation, which is, however, preliminary in character. The papyrus presents, in a very sketchy manner, a text in forty-six parts and thirty-one illustrations. They feature individual scenes apparently in a logical sequence, which represent what we may call the action, as a pantomime. The actors are the king, his children, some officials, and men and women. Objects and activities include the slaughtering of a bull, the preparation and offering of bread, boats, branches of trees, the insignia of the king, the figure of the deceased king, et al. The pantomime appears to be accompanied by the acting out of mythological scenes with the actors speaking. The following translation of the main part of the eighteenth scene, which is illustrated with the "mena"-fight of two men without weapons, may exemplify the evidence: "(The) action (is): (the performance of a) mena-fight.——This (corresponds to): Horus fights with Seth. ——Geb (addresses) Horus and Seth. Speech (of Geb): 'Forget (it).'——Horus, Seth, fight.——Mena-fight." Evidently, both text and picture are only notes which serve for the harmonizing of two different performances. The pantomime follows in logical sequence although it cannot be reconstructed as a whole. Each scene contains a verbal or figurative allusion which directs the selection of the corresponding scene of the mythological performance. The mythological scenes, consequently, do not follow in logical order. They do not represent either a continuous drama or a tale. Again, however, just as in the Pyramid Texts, we may try to use the mythological notes as elements for reconstructing the underlying narrative. This appears as the myth of Osiris: the slaying of Osiris, the fight for the Eye, and the proclamation of Horus as the king. It seems to run in summary as follows:

Seth and his followers killed Osiris. Horus and his sons sought for Osiris on the earth and in heaven with the help of fish and birds. Horus found his father and lamented over him. He addressed Geb in order to seek justice and promised his deceased father to avenge him. The children of Horus brought the body of Osiris. Then they bound Seth and put him under the body of Osiris to serve as a bier. Then Seth with his followers and Horus with his children fought and Geb first encouraged their fight. The eye of Horus was torn out and the testicles of Seth were torn off. Thoth gave the eye of Horus to both Horus and Seth. The eye of Horus escaped. It was caught by the children of Horus who brought it back to Horus. Eventually it was restored to Horus and healed by Thoth. The details of the fight and the Eye are not too well understood at present, and it should be mentioned that both the intervention of Thoth and the escape of the Eye of Horus are alluded to in the Pyramid Texts as well as here. The end of the tale appears clearer: Geb ordered Thoth to assemble all the gods. These in turn did homage to their lord, Horus. Apparently Geb proclaimed an amnesty by which the followers of Seth as well as the children of Horus regained the heads which they lost during the fight.

Abydos in Upper Egypt, where the kings of the first two dynasties were buried, was the main seat of the worship of Osiris. Its great festival featured the finding, burying, and bringing back to life of Osiris in a ceremonial performance. This festival is attested mainly about 1850 B.C. in the autobiographical inscriptions of those men who were commissioned by the king to participate in it. It appears to be an exception that, in the eighteenth century B.C., a king, Nefer-hotep, personally attended the performance and seems to have even participated in it in the role of Horus (Breasted, *Ancient Records* I, pp. 332–38). It is an open question whether this feast was repeated annually or only upon special occasions. The following reconstruction of the ceremony is based mainly on the inscriptions of the chancellor of Sesostris III, Ikherno-fret (*ANET*, pp. 329–30): The standards of those gods who guarded Osiris in his holy chapel were brought from the temple in the "Procession of Upwawet." Upwawet (trans-lated "he who finds or prepares the ways") was the canine deity of Asiut. He acted here as Horus when he went out to fight for his father. The enemies of Osiris were overthrown and those who rebelled against the Neshmet-boat of Osiris were driven away. Then, presumably on the second day of the feast, there took place the "Great Procession," in which Osiris, the deceased god, was brought from the temple and placed in the Neshmet-boat, which floated on a lake. Accord-ing to the Neferhotep inscription, it was here that Horus "joined" his father, that is, found him and made a great offering for him. The funeral procession was drawn up on the lake and on the land and proceeded to the tomb of Osiris in Peker, the ancient royal necropolis. The death of Osiris was avenged in a fight which took place on the island of Nedyt. A triumphant procession brought Osiris back to Abydos in a boat which was then called "the great one." At Abydos he was conducted into his holy chapel. The stress which is laid upon the fights in the narrations of this festival leads us to think that they actually were performed and, consequently, that the processions were accompanied with the lamentation and the jubilation of the onlooking population, just as on the corresponding occasions in the late period. The character of this ceremony differs basically from that previously dis-cussed. There we saw royal ceremonies which were inter-preted by mythological references; here, however, the subject of the performance was the very myth of Osiris and Horus who, as divine beings, were only reminiscent of their former identity with the king. No direct connection appears to exist between these different types of performances. The following attempt to find affinities for the Abydian ceremony may, however, throw some light on the character of the myth itself.

From about 1500 B.C. we know of a funeral rite which brought about the identification of the deceased with what we call a grain-Osiris, i.e., moist earth and grain molded in a clay form. The growing of the grain indicated the Osirian rebirth. The rite is attested in the funerals of both kings and commoners. It took place in the last month of the inundation season when the water started to recede. This was the same month in which, fifteen hundred years later, the festival of the resurrection of Osiris was celebrated in all the forty-two nomes of Egypt. These ceremonies centered around the finding of Osiris as did the Abydian celebrations, but Osiris now was represented by a grain-Osiris, and the jubilant cry, "We have found him, we rejoice," sounded loud throughout the country when the water of the Nile was mixed with the earth and the grain in the clay form. After Osiris was "found," the new grain-Osiris was taken in procession to the temple. There it was deposited in the upper chamber of that room of the temple which represented the tomb of Osiris, where it replaced its predecessor from the preceding year. The latter was prepared for burial and exposed in front of the tomb either upon branches of sycamore, which was the tree in which Hathor, and subsequently Nut, had been embodied since ancient times, or else it was placed inside a wooden cow representing the ancient heavenly cow which was Nut and subsequently Hathor. These ceremonies of the latest period appear closely related to the funerary rites of the grain-Osiris, and not with the Abydian ceremonies of Osiris. As the god of vegetation who had deceased and was revived, Osiris appears only incidentally identified with the mythological character.

There exists, however, a certain affinity between the late ceremonies of Osiris and those which were performed in Abydos. Diodorus Siculus (*Bibliotheca Historica* I 87, 2–3) tells us that, according to some of his authorities, Anubis the dog was "a 'guard of the body' among those who were around

Osiris and Isis; others, however, think that the dogs guided Isis during her search for Osiris." These two statements are confirmed by Egyptian sources. Anubis is the leader of those who guard the body of the deceased Osiris, according to the Coffin Texts, and together with the children of Horus he slays the enemies of Osiris according to a ritual of the late period. All this activity of Anubis is duplicated by the canine Upwawet, who is represented by the figure of a wolf standing upon a standard in Abydos where, according to pictures and the report of Ikhernofret, he was the first of the guardians in the chapel of Osiris and went forth in the "procession of Upwawet" to seek Osiris and to slay his enemies. Since the canines Upwawet and Anubis are interrelated and are sometimes substituted for each other, the fact that they acted alike in the service of Osiris can hardly be accidental. Another close parallel between the late mysteries of Osiris and the Abydian ceremonies is their virtual restriction to the finding, the burial, and the revival of the god. To be sure, it has been often assumed that the death of Osiris was represented in the ceremonies of Abydos but that it was not mentioned in the inscriptions because it was something secret and unspeakable. But this is hardly likely. The ceremony expressly starts with the departure of Horus in the guise of Upwawet to "fight for [or, to avenge]" Osiris, an expression which always indicates the activity of the son Horus for his deceased father. The departure of Upwawet mirrors that of Horus from Khemmis. Now, it is striking that the ceremonial reiteration of the extensive myth of Horus was restricted to the mere finding and resurrection of the god, just as it was in the late mysteries. Thus, the Abydian and the late ceremonies have something significant in common although the latter, which concern the god of vegetation, cannot possibly be traced back directly to the representation of the myth of the god who once was the deceased king. It is true that this agreement was possibly accidental. Abydos was the site of what was regarded as the tomb of Osiris and therefore the question of how his death occurred might have appeared less significant. Nor did the grain-Osiris ceremony pose the question of how the god died.

However, the possibility that a historical reason for the conformity existed should be taken into consideration. It might be that the ceremony by which a deceased person was identified with vegetation goes back to earlier, and possibly prehistoric, times. Deposits of heaps of grain in tombs of commoners of the Early Dynastic period have been tentatively interpreted by Alexander Scharff as the prototype of the grain-Osiris. This interpretation of the grain deposits has been disputed for good reasons and must not be accepted as certain. Still, it is not altogether impossible, in spite of the lack of positive evidence, that the Osirian ceremonies at Abydos were influenced by agricultural rites as was the rite of the grain-Osiris. This brings up the further question of whether the identification of the deceased king with Osiris in the context of the lineage already had some prototype in popular belief. I am submitting to the reader this problem which cannot be solved with the available evidence, as an example of the difficulties confronting the student of Egyptian mythology.

There exist a number of additional features of the myth of Osiris and his family which throw light on the popularity which it enjoyed. I may mention the political implications which were given the fights between Horus and Seth. The hostile character of Seth, who ruled the desert outside of Egypt, and his affinity to the Asiatic storm god, eventually led to his identification as Apophis, although, according to the Coffin Texts, it was he who fought Apophis. The Hyksos who invaded Egypt about 1700 B.C. worshiped him more than any other Egyptian god. Later on, in retrospect, the Hyksos as well as the destructive Assyrians and the Persians who made Egypt a Persian satrapy, were identified with Seth. A myth recorded on the walls of the Ptolemaic temple of Horus at Edfu in Upper Egypt featured Horus as the victorious king who, on behalf of his father, Re, overcame Seth and his followers in Egypt and expelled them to Asia; this version of the myth was doubtless influenced by the experience of foreign invasions into Egypt. The character of Horus as a warrior developed mainly in the figure of Haroëris, "the great, or the elder Horus," who was regarded as the son of Re, in contrast to Harsiese, "Horus, the son of Isis," and Harpokrates, "Horus the child." The differentiation between Horus, the son of Re, and Horus, the son of Isis, is reminiscent of the fact that, in the ancient period, as we have seen, the king, Horus, was thought of as the bodily son of Atum and, at the same time, as the son of Osiris and Isis. However, Horus, the king, and Haroëris were clearly distinguished from each other as early as in the Pyramid Texts, as were several other forms of Horus, including Harakhty or Re-Harakhty.

Isis was looked on as an especially powerful magician, since it was she who revived her husband and protected her child against all the dangers of the wilderness. She still occurred as such in magical spells of the Christian period in Egypt. A longish tale which was recommended for use as a magical spell to "kill the poison—really successful a million times" is preserved from about 1300 B.C. and describes how she tricked Re into betraying his "name" to her, because, except for this name, "there was nothing that she did not know in heaven and earth." She created a serpent which bit Re as he took his evening walk. There was no remedy against the poison except for the magic of Isis, but Isis claimed that her magic was powerless in this case if she did not know Re's name. He tried to sell her many of his numerous names for this purpose, but the poison still burned "more powerful than flame and fire." Eventually, Re divulged his secret name to her, and Isis healed him with her spell, which, by the way, did not reveal the name (*ANET*, pp. 12–14). "He whose name is not known" occurs elsewhere in Egyptian religious literature as early as the Pyramid Texts. The tale of Isis indicates that this epithet was used for the highest god because he could not be submitted to magic, and not for any other reason.

In narrative fiction the separation of the world of the gods and the king on the one hand, and of non-royal individuals on the other, was, as a rule, observed. In the "Story of the Two Brothers" (*ANET*, pp. 23–25), the gods fashioned a woman for Bata, but then Bata was a divine being and not a mere mortal. This tale was written down about 1300 B.C., as were the other tales which we shall discuss. It is what we may call a semi-mythological tale. The names given to the two brothers, Bata and Anubis, are the names of deities and are so indicated in the writing, which makes it clear that the divine character inherent in them applies also to the two brothers themselves. The jackal-headed god Anubis and the very minor deity Bata are known from other sources but, in contrast to the two brothers of the tale, are in no way related, to the best of our knowledge. Neither the characters of the two brothers, nor the experiences which are related in the tale display any similarity to what we know about the gods whose names they bear. However, the tale contains several incidents which are clearly reminiscent of the story of Osiris. An essential part of the tale, the experiences of Bata and his wife in Byblos and in the palace of Pharaoh, is almost exactly like Plutarch's story of what happened to Isis when she sought for Osiris in these same places (*De Iside et Osiride,* Chap. 15). In contrast to this similarity of setting, however, the behavior of Bata's wife is just the opposite of that of the faithful Isis. Another story of the same kind, that of the two hostile brothers, Right and Wrong, is obviously reminiscent of the tale of Osiris: Wrong blinds Right, and the latter's son fights Wrong in court to avenge his father. Neither in this tale is the boy's mother reminiscent of Isis.

Besides these works of literature which are merely influenced by mythological motifs, there are others which are mythological in the strict sense of the word. We have already encountered some of them. The story of the sorceress Isis and the hidden name of Re is a good example; while it was recommended for use as a magical spell, it was doubtless composed for entertainment. The most sophisticated and most extensive example of this type of fiction is the story of the contest of Horus and Seth for the rule of Egypt (*ANET,* pp. 14–18). It adds considerably to our knowledge of mythological details since it relates at length episodes which are otherwise known only from allusions. Moreover, it throws some light upon the question of how mythological tales came into existence. All the characters of this tale are divine beings, as is to be expected in an Egyptian mythological text, but they are all very human, including the sorceress Isis.

The theme of the tale centers about the lawsuit between the clumsy, boorish fellow, Seth, who is introduced as the brother of Isis, and the clever child, Horus, who is assisted by his resourceful mother, Isis. The lawsuit deals, of course, with the inheritance of Osiris, the kingship in Egypt, which is claimed by Horus and Isis on the basis of the law, and by Seth on the basis of his strength and power. The court is the Ennead, the ancient court of Heliopolis, and is presided over by Shu, who is also called Onuris, "the bringer of her [i.e., the Eye] who was far away." Thoth, the recorder, is expressly described as the keeper of the Eye on behalf of Atum during the interregnum—the Eye, as we have seen above, being the royal Uraeus viper and crown, identical with Maat meaning law and order. Atum, who is also called Re, Re-Harakhty, "Re-Harakhty and Atum," the Lord of All, et al., is "the Great one, the Oldest one, who is in Heliopolis," and his consent is necessary for the validity of the decision of the court. The episodes occur because Atum favors the powerful Seth, while the court clearly decides in favor of the lawful heir, Horus. The tale opens with this decision of the court, and with the same decision the quarrel is finally brought to a happy end, with Horus crowned the king of Egypt. A characteristic feature of the end is the appearance of Seth here as in the "Memphite Theology" as a good loser. Once the decision is final, he agrees to it willingly and is then assigned to Re-Harakhty to be with him like a son, the frightful warrior in the sun boat. Between its beginning and end, the tale is replete with incidents which either delay or expedite the proceedings and decisions of the court. Atum hopes to find support for Seth in the goddess Neit, "the mother of the god," to whom Thoth writes a letter on behalf of the Ennead. In her answer Neit threatens to cause the sky to collapse if Horus is not made the king of Egypt. She recommends that the Lord of All compensate Seth by doubling his property and giving him Anat and Astarte, his (the Heliopolitan's) daughters. At another time, Re-Harakhty is placed in a situation where he cannot deny the right of Horus. Angry, as always, he blames the court for delaying the procedure and orders them to give the crown to Horus, but when they start to do so Seth throws a tantrum and the Heliopolitan gladly yields to his protest. Eventually, Thoth, the god of wisdom, recommends that the court ask the opinion of Osiris, the old king who is in the realm of the dead and is thus prevented from performing his former office. Naturally, the answer of Osiris favors the claim of his son, Horus, and prompts the final decision.

The tale is a parody on delayed court procedures and red tape, and is spiced with gibes at the leading figures. Baba, definitely a minor deity but apparently a member of the court, insults Re-Harakhty by claiming, "Your chapel is empty,"— though, in fact, Re was always worshiped in the open and not inside a temple. This impudent remark, which offends even the other gods, enrages Re. He lies down on his back in his tent, and, like Achilles, sulks. Then his daughter, Hathor, enters and displays her naked beauty to his eyes. This gesture makes him laugh. Later on, however, Re-Harakhty shows his own impudence toward Osiris. For when Osiris boasts in his letter that he created barley and emmer which are indispensable for all life, Re answers him, "If you had never existed, if you had never been born—still, barley and emmer would exist." Osiris, however, keeps his temper, even though he appears sensitive about his banishment to the realm of the dead. He earnestly reminds Re of his spectral "messengers who do not fear either god or goddess," and intimates that mankind and the gods eventually rest in his kingdom beneath in accordance with the word which Ptah once spoke when he created heaven.

In addition to all this, a major part of the tale consists of interludes which are prompted either by the crafty Isis or the plodding, muscle-bound Seth. Seth boasts of his strength. Isis insults him. Seth refuses to attend the court as long as Isis is admitted. The court adjourns to an island, and the ferryman Anty is forbidden to ferry any woman over to it. Isis deceives him and induces Seth to concede unwittingly that his claim is unjustified. At the suggestion of Seth, both he and Horus engage in a contest for which they turn into hippopotami. After an initial failure, Isis succeeds in spearing the Seth-hippopotamus, but then, driven by sisterly love, she frees him and is promptly beheaded by her son, Horus—this detail, however, does not diminish in any degree her activity throughout the balance of the story. Horus hides, but Seth finds him and rips his eyes out, and Hathor heals them with milk of a gazelle. Then Seth tries to overcome Horus by sexually attacking him, for this would make Horus despicable to all the gods. Horus, however, thinking quickly, nullifies this attack without Seth's knowledge, while Isis ingeniously turns Seth's scheming back on himself: in the presence of all the gods, a golden disk, unmistakably engendered by Horus, arises out of the head of Seth. Seth then suggests another test, a fight in boats on the Nile, and again Isis helps Horus to victory. He sails downstream to Neit of Sais to urge her to bring about the final decision, which, however, as we have seen, is actually prompted by Osiris's favorable opinion.

All of these ludicrous episodes have a mythological background, or, putting it more cautiously, most of their details also occur more or less explicitly elsewhere in mythological texts. This makes us wonder how far such details are genuinely mythological, and how far they originated in the fanciful imagination of the storytellers. We may remember that it was the activity of literary men rather than theologians which appears to have played a significant role in the composition of the Coffin Texts. Two of the episodes enumerated above may be stressed here because of their etiological origin: the ferryman Anty is punished by the removal of the "forepart of his feet," the god Anty is "he with claws," a falcon. The story could then refer to an anthropomorphic image of the god in which the toes were replaced by claws, in accordance with a suggestion first proffered by Joachim Spiegel. An etiological tendency is also evident in the beheading of Isis. She then appears to the gods as a headless statue of flint or obsidian. This might well have referred to a local image of hers. However, her decapitation also occurs contemporaneously elsewhere, and Plutarch (*De Iside et Osiride*, Chap. 19) relates that Horus beheaded his mother because she freed Seth. According to Plutarch, her head was replaced by that of a cow, and this is thought to explain the appearance of Isis as the cow-headed Hathor.

The origin, aim, and composition of this tale might well be explained in a serious light, and the fact remains that it is a purely mythological tale with respect to all its elements and its final appearance. In spite of the gravity of the topic, however, neither the exalted station of the gods nor the calamities which befell them were taken seriously by those who enjoyed the story. The tale is unmistakably the humorous product of, presumably, generations of storytellers. They and their audience identified themselves with the characters of this tale, and the fact that these were actually the gods of Egypt might not have been a matter of great concern. Perhaps listening to a story like this one was like remembering the youthful pranks of a man of undisputed dignity, which could not do any harm to his authority. Whether we regard this tale as a joke or as blasphemy, one fact is certain: a thousand years and more after this tale of the gods was written down, the common people of Egypt clung to these same gods with a worship which was both fanatic and fetishistic, and the teachers and sages interpreted Egyptian mythology reverently in a manner which brought it world-wide recognition. The humorous story of the contest of Horus and Seth did no harm to the myth of Osiris and Isis.

The great hymn to Osiris which was engraved on the tombstone of a certain Amenmose about 1550 B.C. may conclude this discussion. In the first section of the hymn Osiris is invoked in his characters of the god who is worshiped in all temples; the personification of Egypt, to whom Nunu yields the water of the Nile and for whom the beneficent north wind blows; the ruler of the starry sky; and the king of the deceased and the living. Throughout the hymn Osiris appears as the glorious ruler, terrifying only to his enemies. No allusion is made to the sinister aspect of his kingdom beyond, nor is the death of the god mentioned in the myth which is presented in the second and concluding part of the hymn. The glory of the kingdom of Osiris, the deeds of Isis, and the happiness of the kingdom of Horus are extolled. This is a paraphrase of the myth and at the same time the glorification of the kingship in Egypt, with both Osiris and Horus representing the kingship whose continuity is guaranteed by Isis, "the throne"; the author might well have been aware of the ancient meaning of these mythological figures. This part of the hymn, translated here with only a few minor omissions and introduced with the first line of the hymn, follows:

*Praise to you, O Osiris, Lord of Eternity, King of the
          Gods. . . .*
*Great One, First of his brothers, Eldest of the Primeval
          Deities,*
*who established Maat (the law) throughout the two banks
          of the river,*
who put the son upon the seat of the father,
whom his father, Geb, favors and his mother, Nut, loves,
great of strength when he overthrows the rebel,
mighty of arm when he kills his enemy. . . .
who inherited Geb's kingship of the Two Lands.
*He (Geb) saw his virtue, he bequeathed to him the leader-
          ship of the countries,*

                    that coming events might be happy,
     He fashioned this country (Egypt) with his hand,
its water, its wind, its herbs, all its herds,
and whatever flies in the air and alights on earth,
its worms, and its small game of the desert
     *being rightly given to the son of Nut, and the Two Lands
          were pleased with this.*
Who appeared on the throne of his father like Re
          *when he shines forth in the horizon and gives light
               in the face of the darkness.*
*He brightened the sunlight with his plumes and inundated
          the Two Lands like the sun disk at dawn.*
His crown, it pierced the heaven and mingled with the stars,
the leader of every god, clear of command,

whom the Great Ennead favors and the Little Ennead loves.

His sister protected him, she who repelled the enemies

*and who caused the deeds of the mischief-maker to retreat
     by the power of her mouth,*

*she who is excellent of tongue, whose words do not fail, who
     is clear of command,*

*Isis, the mighty, who took action for her brother, who sought
     him without tiring,*

*who roved through Egypt as the (wailing) kite without rest
     until she found him,*

*who provided shade with her feathers and created wind
     with her wings,*

who made jubilation and brought her brother to rest,

*who strengthened the weakness of him who was tired of
     heart,*

who received his seed, who bore an heir,

*who suckled the infant in solitude—the place where he was
     was unknown—*

*who introduced him, when his arm was strong, into the
     hall of Geb,*

while the Ennead rejoiced:

> *"Welcome, O Son of Osiris, Horus, firm of heart,
>   vindicated,*
>
> *Son of Isis, Heir of Osiris,*
>
> *for whom the proper court, the Ennead and the All-Lord
>   himself, has assembled.*
>
> *The Lords of Maat are united in it,*
>
> *those who shun wrongdoing, and sit in the hall of Geb
>   in order to give the office to its lord and the kingship
>   to whom it should be rendered."*

*They found that the acclamation given to Horus was, "He
     is right."*

The office of his father was given to him.

He came forth wearing the fillet and with the mace of Geb.

*He took the rule of the two banks of the river, the white
     crown firm on his head.*

The earth was reckoned to him to be his property.

Heaven and earth were under his supervision.

Mankind, common folk, gentle folk, and humanity were en-
    trusted to him,
Egypt, the northern regions, and the circuit of the sun were
        under his counsels and also the north wind, the
        river, the flood, the trees of life, and all green
        plants. . . .
Everyone rejoices, hearts are pleased, hearts are filled with joy.
Everyone is happy, everyone worships his beauty.
How sweet is his love in our presence.
His grace traverses hearts and his love is great in every body,
        when they have rightly offered to the son of Isis.
His enemy has fallen because of his crime, and evil is done to
        the mischief-maker.
He who has done evil, his deed has returned to him.
The son of Isis has avenged his father so that he is satis-
        fied and his name has become excellent. . . .
Let your heart be glad, Wennofer.
The son of Isis, he has assumed the crown,
the office of his father has been assigned to him in the hall
        of Geb.
(When) Re spoke and Thoth wrote, the court was pleased.
Your father, Geb, has given command for your benefit,
and it has been done according to that which he said.

9. CONCLUSION WITH AN ADDITIONAL NOTE ON THE MYTH OF THE EYE

In the course of this summary of the ancient Egyptian mythology the reader will have become aware that, in Egypt, we
have the unique opportunity of determining the time and
the circumstances in which the most substantial sector of her
mythology, the myths centering on Horus, originated. The
time was the beginning and the middle of the third millennium B.C., starting with the earliest documentation of history,

and the circumstances were prompted by the establishment of the kingship in Egypt. The myth of Horus encompassed the concepts of the lineage of Horus which then became the Heliopolitan cosmogony; of Horus and Seth; of Osiris and Isis; and of the Eye of Horus; it became the prototype of the concept of Re, the sun who was the king of heaven. This myth was rooted in the first known conception of the highest god, the ruler of All, who appeared in the trinity of the Horus falcon, the Horus king of Egypt, and the heavenly Horus. It came into existence through speculations that were conducted in a clearly logical manner, based upon the faith in the universal and eternal character of the king of Egypt, and enriched by cosmogonic ideas that had been transmitted from prehistoric times; and it was made effective by the amalgamation with the rites that were performed in the service for the divine king and, particularly, for his ascension to the throne and his interment. Subsequently, although very early, the myth of Horus with all its affiliations was regarded as a tale, or a group of tales, of bygone ages, while, simultaneously, it was experienced as a present reality in the performance of the ceremonies. This origin of mythology in Egypt bears specific Egyptian characteristics and must not be generalized upon with respect to the origin of mythology in other civilizations. However, it is worth while to keep in mind that, in Egypt, mythology arose out of the creation of a new form of society whose structure was expressed in theological terms. It is true that a few mythological concepts of the sky and the sun, the earth and vegetation had been carried over from the prehistoric period into the myth of Horus and, later, that of Re. Other ideas of the cosmos, however, originated as replicas of ideas of the kingship on earth. One of these more recent cosmic concepts was that of the heavenly king Horus who was incorporated in the sun and a star. There exist a few more, and we shall see that the concept that a heavenly body was the eye of a god belongs to them.

It was one of the goals of our presentation of Egyptian mythology to convey the understanding that, on the one hand, much of it can be explained if we realize that a continuous change of mythological conceptions took place: only those documents which date in the third millennium B.C., before the great social breakdown of Egypt, should be used in the attempt to understand the mythology that prevailed in the period of the foundation and the first culmination of Egyptian kingship. On the other hand, however, since it is exactly this research on the earliest period that is still going on, much remains unexplained for the time being. While those results of it that have been obtained so far are presented in this study, I wish to stress that this picture of Egyptian mythology is certainly not complete. The transitory situation of our research can be well exemplified with the most recent research on the myth of the Eye.

My presentation of the origin of the myth of the Eye on p. 58 and of its unification with the myth of Horus, Seth, and Osiris on p. 68 ff., differs from the opinion that has been generally accepted until now. According to this former opinion, the concept of both the Eye of Horus and the Eye of Re originated in the idea of the sun and the moon being the eyes of the heavenly god. While I realized that this opinion could not be maintained according to my understanding of the heavenly Horus, I was not ready to do better than to enumerate those facts that were attested about the Eye; I felt compelled to refer to the concept of the Eye as being rather cryptic in the first chapter of this study. Since this situation was quite unsatisfactory I started research on the original meaning of the Eye as attested in the third millennium as soon as I finished the manuscript of the present paper. The results of this research will be published in two papers, "Beilaeufige Bemerkungen zum Mythos von Osiris und Horus" and "Das Sonnenauge in den Pyramidentexten," in the *Zeitschrift fuer Aegyptische Sprache und Altertumskunde.* I am happy to have the opportunity of adding the results here to this paper. The factual elements of the myth as presented above will be much more easily understood after they are presented in their correct context here; besides, the new results may shed some new light on other topics that we have discussed.

The idea of the Eye came into existence as that of the Eye of Horus. This was a third eye in addition to the natural pair of eyes of either the falcon or the king. The Eye was basically identical with the Uraeus viper, the likeness of which was attached to either one of the crowns or a fillet at the forehead of the king. Both the Uraeus and Eye appear to have originated in the idea that the divine *zet*-serpent, the embodiment of the gods and, simultaneously, a form of the primeval serpent, was also an attribute of the divine king: the *zet*-serpent was the Uraeus at the forehead of the king in reality while, in the myth of Horus and Osiris, it was the third eye of Horus. Because of this basic identity of the Eye of Horus and the Uraeus, the former can be best understood in terms of the Uraeus viper. As long as the king lived, the Uraeus was, as the Pyramid Texts express it, magically "guarded" by the king. When the king died, however, the venomous viper would escape unless it was taken in custody. Left loose, it was frightening and hostile; going abroad, it would leave disturbance and chaos behind in Egypt and, consequently, Maat, that is, law and order, would leave the country. Maat would not be restored until the Uraeus again came to rest at the forehead of the king, this time the successor of the deceased one. This basic concept of the Uraeus viper appears as the concept of the Eye of Horus in the myth of Horus who became Osiris when Seth killed him. Then Seth, the representative of rebellion and disturbance, took the Eye from Horus, who simultaneously became Osiris, and law and order were not restored until the new Horus on earth, the son of Osiris, recaptured it. Thoth also plays a role as the custodian of the Eye of Horus in the context of the fights between Horus and Seth. We now can understand that both the existence of Seth as the foe of Horus-Osiris and the loosening of the Eye from the king's magic protection were mythological facts which were featured in ceremonies only in the period between the death of the old king and the nomination by acclaim of the new king. Therefore, these simultaneous concepts necessarily were amalgamated. Furthermore, we now can understand that, as I have pointed out in the discussion of the tale of Seth and Horus, Seth appears as a good loser, for as soon as the new king was installed, Seth was no longer the enemy of Horus; he then appears rather as his complement in his genuine character of the peer of Horus. When Horus, being rightly the king, regained the Eye, he became its guardian and it dwelled at his forehead until he himself became Osiris; the Eye was then loosened and gained by Seth, and came to rest again at the forehead of the new earthly Horus king. However, Horus did not regain the Eye only for himself. As soon as he got it—that is, when the new king was nominated before the burial of his father—he took it to his father, Osiris, who had been robbed of it when he was Horus, and by giving the Eye, the symbol of kingship, to Osiris, Horus prompted his father's reinstallation as a king but this time not as the king on earth: Osiris instead became one with both his predecessors and those who would be the earthly kings in the future. He was transfigured into the eternal form of Horus, the king of heaven, embodied in a heavenly body, either the sun or, mainly, according to the Pyramid Texts, in the morning star. Here again a typical example of the intricacy of Egyptian mythology should be mentioned. The transfigured deceased king became the heavenly Horus, the morning star; the morning star, therefore, was the divine body, the *zet*-serpent, of the transfigured king; since the *zet*-serpent, which was a single entity although it represented the divine form of every god, was identical with the Eye of Horus, the transfigured form of the Eye of Horus was also the morning star; thus both Horus and the Eye of Horus in their eternal aspects were the morning star.

Like Horus, his mythological counterpart, Atum, also had his royal Eye, and when Re became the king of heaven, the Uraeus of Re and the Eye of Re also came into existence. Only the Eye of Re is identified as a heavenly body in a few sentences of the Pyramid Texts. We used to understand them as though the Eye of Re was identified as the sun, but a careful interpretation of them has unmistakably shown that the Eye of Re was the morning star. Therefore, the morning star, according to the Pyramid Texts, was simultaneously Osiris after his transfiguration, the heavenly Horus, the eternal aspect of the Eye of Horus, and the Eye of Re. Outside of the Pyramid Texts that centered on the transfiguration of the deceased king, however, the morning star played no role in mythology. Therefore, it appears quite plausible that the idea that both the Eye of Horus and the Eye of Re appeared as a celestial body, gave room to the further idea, which is attested in later texts, that the two main celestial bodies, the sun and the moon, were the two eyes of either Re or Horus. Then sometimes the moon was called the Eye of Horus, for just as the Eye of Horus was robbed and then restored, so the moon vanished and reappeared every month. The Eye of Re, however, apparently was never the sun; it became the mythological figure, identified as Maat, the daughter of Re, who, like the Eye of Atum, was sent out as a messenger by her father whenever disturbance and rebellion arose; and peace was not restored before she came back to where she belonged —that is, to Egypt and the heavenly king.

BIBLIOGRAPHY

1. TEXTS

ANET, *Ancient Near Eastern Texts*, edited by James B. Pritchard. 2nd edition. Princeton 1955 (The Egyptian Texts are translated by John A. Wilson).

James H. Breasted. *Ancient Records of Egypt*, Vols. I–IV. New York 1906.

E. A. Wallis Budge. *The Book of the Dead*. An English Translation with Introduction, Notes, etc. London 1898.

————. The Book of the Dead: The Papyrus of Ani. London 1895 (with translation).

Adolf Erman. *The Literature of the Ancient Egyptians*, translated by Ailward M. Blackman. London 1927 (the "Hymn to Osiris" on pp. 140–45).

Henri Frankfort. *The Cenotaph of Seti I at Abydos*. 39th Memoir of the Egypt Exploration Society. London 1933.

Samuel A. B. Mercer. *The Pyramid Texts in Translation and Commentary*, Vols. I–IV. New York 1952.

Mythological Papyri Texts. Translated with Introduction by Alexandre Piankoff. Edited with a chapter on the Symbolism of the Papyri by N. Rambova (Bollingen Series XL, Vol. 3). New York 1957.

Kurt Sethe. *Dramatische Texte zu altaegyptischen Mysterienspielen* (Untersuchungen zur Geschichte und Altertumskunde Aegyptens, Band 10). Leipzig 1928 (the text concerning the coronation of Sesostris I on p. 81 ff.).

The Shrines of Tut-ankh-Amon. Texts translated with Introductions by Alexandre Piankoff. Edited by N. Rambova (Bollingen Series XL, Vol. 2). New York 1955.

The abbreviations *Pyr.*, *C.T.*, and *B.o.D.* refer to the hieroglyphic text editions of the Pyramid Texts, Coffin Texts, and Book of the Dead respectively. For translation see above the books of Budge and Mercer.

2. BOOKS OF REFERENCE, DISCUSSIONS, ETC.

Rudolf Anthes. "Egyptian Theology in the Third Millennium B.C.," *Journal of Near Eastern Studies,* Vol. 18 (1959), pp. 170–212.

Hans Bonnet. *Reallexikon der aegyptischen Religionsgeschichte.* Berlin 1952.

Etienne Drioton. "Le papyrus dramatique du Ramesséum," *Annuaire du Collège de France,* 59e année (1959). Résumé des cours de 1958–59, pp. 373–83.

Etienne Drioton et Jacques Vandier. *L'Égypte.* Contains an extensive bibliography of mythology and religion with introductions, on pp. 107–28. Paris 1952.

Henri Frankfort. *Kingship and the Gods.* Chicago 1948.

Henri Frankfort et al. *The Intellectual Adventure of Ancient Man.* Chicago 1946. (Reprinted with the title, *Before Philosophy,* as a Pelican Book, 1951.)

Hugo Gressmann. *Tod und Auferstehung des Osiris nach Festbraeuchen und Umzuegen* (Der Alte Orient, Band 23, Heft 3). Leipzig 1923.

Hermann Kees. *Der Goetterglaube im alten Aegypten.* 2. Auflage. Berlin 1956.

Alexandre Piankoff. "The Theology in Ancient Egypt," *Antiquity and Survival,* no. 6 (1956), pp. 488–500.

Siegfried Schott. "Mythen in den Pyramidentexten," in Samuel A. B. Mercer, *The Pyramid Texts,* Vol. IV, pp. 106–23.

Mythology of Sumer and Akkad

BY SAMUEL NOAH KRAMER

The extant myths of the Sumerians and Akkadians revolve primarily about the creation and organization of the universe, the birth of the gods, their loves and hates, their spites and intrigues, their blessings and curses, their creative and destructive acts. Only rarely do the Sumero-Akkadian myths revolve about the struggle for power between the gods, and even then the struggle is not usually depicted as a bitter, vindictive, and gory conflict. Intellectually speaking, the Sumero-Akkadian myths reveal a rather mature and sophisticated approach to the gods and their divine activities; behind them can be recognized considerable theological and cosmological reflection.

SUMER

As yet no Sumerian myths have been recovered dealing directly and explicitly with the creation of the universe; what little is known about the Sumerian cosmogonic ideas has been inferred and deduced from laconic statements scattered throughout the literary documents. But we do have a number of myths concerned with the organization of the universe and its cultural processes, the creation of man, and the establishment of civilization. The deities involved in these myths are relatively few in number: the air-god Enlil, the water-god Enki, the mother goddess Ninhursag (also known as Nintu and Ninmah), the god of the south wind Ninurta, the moon-god Nanna-Sin, the Bedu-god Martu, and above all the goddess Inanna, particularly in relationship to her unlucky spouse Dumuzi.

Enlil was the most important deity of the Sumerian pantheon, "the father of the gods," "the king of heaven and earth," "the king of all the lands." According to the myth "Enlil and the Creation of the Pickax," he was the god who separated heaven from earth, brought up "the seed of the land" from the earth, brought forth "whatever was needful," fashioned the pickax for agricultural and building purposes, and presented it to the "blackheads" (the Sumerians, or perhaps mankind as a whole). According to the myth "Summer and Winter," Enlil was the god who brought forth all trees and grains, produced abundance and prosperity in "the land," and appointed "Winter" as the "farmer of the gods," in charge of the life-producing waters and of all that grows. The gods—even the most important among them—are all eager for his blessing. One myth relates how the water-god Enki, after building his "sea house" in Eridu, journeyed to Enlil's temple in Nippur in order to obtain his approval and benediction. When the moon-god Nanna-Sin, the tutelary deity of Ur, wants to make sure of the well-being and prosperity of his domain he journeys to Nippur on a boat loaded with gifts and thus obtains Enlil's generous blessing.

But although Enlil is the chief of the Sumerian pantheon, his powers are by no means unlimited and absolute. One of the more "human" and tender of the Sumerian myths concerns Enlil's banishment to the Nether World and tells the following story:

When man had not yet been created and the city of Nippur was inhabited by gods alone, "its young man" was the Enlil; "its young maid" was the goddess Ninlil; and "its old woman" was Ninlil's mother Nunbarshegunu. One day the latter, having evidently set her mind and heart on Ninlil's marriage to Enlil, instructs her daughter thus:

"In the pure stream, woman, bathe in the pure stream,
Ninlil, walk along the bank of the stream Nunbirdu,
The bright-eyed, the lord, the bright-eyed,
The 'great mountain,' father Enlil, the bright-eyed, will see
    you,
The shepherd . . . who decrees the fates, the bright-eyed,
    will see you,
Will forthwith embrace (?) you, kiss you."

Ninlil joyfully follows her mother's instructions:

In the pure stream, the woman bathes, in the pure stream,
Ninlil walks along the bank of the stream Nunbirdu,
The bright-eyed, the lord, the bright-eyed,
The "great mountain," father Enlil, the bright-eyed, saw her,
The shepherd . . . who decrees the fates, the bright-eyed,
    saw her.
The lord speaks to her of intercourse (?), she is unwilling,
Enlil speaks to her of intercourse (?), she is unwilling;
"My vagina is too little, it knows not to copulate,
My lips are too small, they know not to kiss . . ."

Whereupon Enlil calls his vizier, Nusku, and tells him of his desire for the lovely Ninlil. Nusku brings up a boat and Enlil rapes Ninlil while sailing on the stream, and impregnates her with the moon-god Sin. The gods are dismayed by this immoral deed, and though Enlil is their king, they seize him and banish him from the city to the Nether World. The relevant passage, one of the few to shed some indirect light on the organization of the pantheon and its method of operation, reads:

Enlil walks about in the Kiur (Ninlil's private shrine),
As Enlil walks about in the Kiur,
The great gods, the fifty of them,
The fate-decreeing gods, the seven of them,

Seize Enlil in the Kiur (saying):
"Enlil, immoral one, get you out of the city,
Nunamnir (an epithet of Enlil), immoral one, get you out
*   of the city."*

And so Enlil, in accordance with the fate decreed by the
gods, departs in the direction of the Sumerian Hades. Ninlil,
however, now pregnant with child, refuses to remain behind,
and follows Enlil on his forced journey to the Nether World.
This disturbs Enlil, for it would mean that his son Sin,
originally destined to be in charge of the largest luminous
body, the moon, would have to dwell in the dark gloomy
Nether World instead of in the sky. To circumvent this, he
seems to devise this rather complicated scheme. On the way
to Hades from Nippur he meets up with three individuals,
minor deities no doubt: the gatekeeper in charge of the
Nippur gates; the "man of the Nether World river"; and the
ferryman, the Sumerian "Charon" who ferries the dead
across to Hades. Enlil takes the form of each of these in
turn—the first known example of divine metamorphosis—
and impregnates Ninlil with three Nether World deities as
substitutes for their older brother Sin, who is thus free to
ascend to heaven.

One of the more detailed and revealing of the Sumerian
myths concerns the organization of the universe by Enki,
the Sumerian water-god who was also the god of wisdom.
The myth begins with a hymn of praise addressed to Enki
which exalts Enki as the god who watches over the universe
and is responsible for the fertility of field and farm, of flock
and herd. There follows a paean of self-glorification put into
the mouth of Enki, and concerned primarily with his relationship to the leading deities of the pantheon, An, Enlil, and
Nintu, and to the lesser gods known collectively as the
Anunnaki. Following a brief five-line passage which tells
of the Anunnaki doing homage to Enki, Enki "for a second
time" utters a paean of self-glorification. He begins by exalt-
ing the power of his word and command in providing the
earth with prosperity and abundance; continues with a de-

scription of the splendor of his shrine, the Abzu; and con-
cludes with an account of his joyous journey over the
marshland, in his *makurru*-boat, "the ibex of the Abzu," after
which the lands Magan, Dilmun, and Meluhha sent their
heavily laden boats to Nippur with rich gifts for Enlil.
Then the Anunnaki once again pay homage to Enki, particularly as the god who "rides" and directs the *me*'s, the
divine laws which govern the universe.

The poet now introduces a description of the various rites
and rituals performed by some of the more important priests
and spiritual leaders of Sumer in Enki's Abzu-shrine. After
which we find Enki in his boat once again all set to "decree
the fates." Beginning, as might have been expected, with
Sumer itself, he first exalts it as a chosen, hallowed land
with "lofty" and "untouchable" *me*'s, where the gods have
taken up their abode, then blesses its flocks and herds, its
temples and shrines. From Sumer he proceeds to Ur, which
he extols in lofty, metaphorical language and blesses with
prosperity and pre-eminence. From Ur he goes to Meluhha
and blesses it most generously with trees and reeds, oxen and
birds, gold, tin, and bronze. Following which, he proceeds
to provide Dilmun, Elam, Marhashi, and Martu with some
of their needs.

Enki now turns from the fate and destiny of the various
lands which made up the Sumerian inhabited world, and performs a whole series of acts vital to the earth's fertility and
productiveness. Directing himself first to its physical features,
he begins by filling the Tigris with fresh, sparkling, life-
giving water—in the concrete metaphorical imagery of our
poet, Enki is a rampant bull who mates with the river
imagined as a wild cow. Then, to make sure that the Tigris
and Euphrates function properly, he appoints the god En-
bilulu, the "canal inspector," to take charge of them. Enki
next "called" the marshland and the canebrake, supplied
them with fish and reeds, and appointed a deity "who loves
fish"—the name is illegible—to take charge of them. He
then turns to the sea, erects there his holy shrine, and places
the goddess Nanshe, "the Lady of Sirara," in charge. Finally

Enki "called" the life-giving rain, made it come down on earth, and put the storm-god Ishkur in charge.

Enki applies himself to the earth's cultural needs. He attends to the plow, yoke, and furrow and appoints Enlil's farmer, Enkimdu, in charge of them. He next "calls" the cultivated field, brings forth its varied grains and vegetables, and makes the grain-goddess Ashnan responsible for them. He looks after the pickax and brick mold, and puts the brick-god Kulla in charge of them. He lays foundations, aligns the bricks, builds "the house," and puts Mushdamma, "the great builder of Enlil," in charge.

Leaving farm, field, and house, Enki directs his attention to the high plain, covers it with green vegetation, multiplies its cattle, and makes Sumugan, "the king of the mountains," responsible for them. He next erects stalls and sheepfolds, supplies them with the best fat and milk, and appoints the shepherd-god Dumuzi to take charge of them. He fixes the "borders"—presumably of cities and states—sets up boundary stones, and appoints the sun-god Utu "in charge of the entire universe." Finally Enki attends to "that which is woman's task," specially the weaving of cloth, and puts Uttu, the goddess of clothing, in charge.

The myth now takes a rather unexpected turn, as the poet brings on the scene the ambitious and aggressive Inanna, who feels that she has been slighted and left without any special powers and prerogatives. Bitterly she complains that Enlil's sister Aruru, alias Nintu, and her (Inanna's) sister goddesses Ninisinna, Ninmug, Nidaba, and Nanshe have all received their respective powers and insignia, but that she, Inanna, has been singled out for neglectful and inconsiderate treatment. Enki seems to be put on the defensive by Inanna's complaint, and he tries to pacify her by pointing out that she actually does have quite a number of special insignia and prerogatives—"the crook, staff, and ward of shepherdship"; oracular responses in regard to war and battle; the weaving and fashioning of garments; the power to destroy "the indestructible" and to make perish the "imperishable"—as well as by giving her a special blessing. Following Enki's reply to Inanna the poem closes with a four-line hymnal passage to Enki.

Another Enki myth tells an intricate and as yet somewhat obscure tale which involves the paradise-land Dilmun, perhaps to be identified with ancient India. Very briefly sketched, the plot of this Sumerian "paradise" myth, which treats of gods, not humans, runs thus:

Dilmun is a land that is "pure," "clean," and "bright," a "land of the living," which knows neither sickness nor death. What is lacking, however, is the fresh water so essential to animal and plant life. The great Sumerian water-god Enki, therefore, orders Utu, the sun-god, to fill it with fresh water brought up from the earth. Dilmun is thus turned into a divine garden, green with fruit-laden fields and meadows.

In this paradise of the gods eight plants are made to sprout by Ninhursag, the great mother goddess of the Sumerians, perhaps more originally Mother Earth. She succeeds in bringing these plants into being only after an intricate process involving three generations of goddesses, all conceived by the water-god and born—so our poem repeatedly underlines —without the slightest pain or travail. But probably because Enki wanted to taste them, his messenger, the two-faced god Isimud, plucks these precious plants one by one and gives them to his master Enki, who proceeds to eat them each in turn, whereupon the angered Ninhursag pronounces upon him the curse of death. Evidently to make sure that she does not change her mind and relent, she disappears from among the gods.

Enki's health begins to fail, eight of his organs become sick. As Enki sinks fast, the great gods sit in the dust. Enlil, the air-god, the king of the Sumerian gods, seems unable to cope with the situation when up speaks the fox. If properly rewarded, he says to Enlil, he, the fox, will bring Ninhursag back. As good as his word, the fox succeeds in some way— the relevant passage is unfortunately destroyed—in having the mother goddess return to the gods and heal the dying water-god. She seats him by her vulva and after inquiring which eight organs of his body ache him, she brings into existence eight corresponding healing deities, and Enki is brought back to life and health.

Although our myth deals with a divine rather than a human paradise, it has numerous parallels with the Biblical paradise story. First, there is some reason to believe that the very idea of a paradise, a garden of the gods, is of Sumerian origin. The Sumerian paradise is located, according to our poem, in Dilmun. It is in this same Dilmun where later, the Babylonians, the Semitic people who conquered the Sumerians, located their "land of the living," the home of their immortals. And there is good indication that the Biblical paradise, too, which is described as a garden planted *eastward* in Eden, from whose waters flow the four world rivers including the Tigris and Euphrates, may have been originally identical with Dilmun, the Sumerian paradise-land.

Again the passage in our poem describing the watering of Dilmun by the sun-god with fresh water brought up from the earth is reminiscent of the Biblical, "But there went up a mist (?) from the earth, and watered the whole face of the ground" (Genesis 2:6). The birth of the goddesses without pain or travail illuminates the background of the curse against Eve that it shall be her lot to conceive and bear children in sorrow. And obviously enough, Enki's eating of the eight plants and the curse uttered against him for this misdeed recall the eating of the fruit of the tree of knowledge by Adam and Eve, and the curses pronounced against each of them for this sinful action.

But perhaps the most interesting result of our comparative analysis of the Sumerian poem is the explanation which it provides for one of the most puzzling motifs in the Biblical paradise story, the famous passage describing the fashioning of Eve, "the mother of all living," from the rib of Adam. For why a rib? Why did the Hebrew storyteller find it more fitting to choose a rib rather than any of the other parts of the body for the fashioning of the woman whose name, Eve, according to the Biblical notion, means approximately "she who makes live." The reason becomes quite clear if we assume a Sumerian literary background, such as that represented by our Dilmun poem, underlying the Biblical paradise tale. For in our Sumerian poem one of Enki's sick members is the rib. Now the Sumerian word for "rib" is *ti* (pronounced "tee"). The goddess created for the healing of Enki's rib therefore was called in Sumerian Nin-ti, "the lady of the rib." But the very same Sumerian word *ti* also means "to make live." The name Nin-ti may thus mean "the lady who makes live," as well as "the lady of the rib." In Sumerian literature, therefore, "the lady of the rib" came to be identified with "the lady who makes live" through what may be termed a play of words. It was this, one of the most ancient of literary puns, which was carried over and perpetuated in the Biblical paradise story, although here, of course, it loses its validity, since the Hebrew word for "rib" and that for "who makes live" have nothing in common.

There is also an Enki-Ninhursag myth concerned with the creation of man from "clay that is over the abyss." The story begins with a description of the difficulties of the gods in procuring their bread, especially, as might have been expected, after the female deities had come into being. The gods complain, but Enki, the water-god, who, as the Sumerian god of wisdom, might have been expected to come to their aid, is lying asleep in the deep and fails to hear them. Thereupon his mother, the primeval sea, "the mother who gave birth to all the gods," brings the tears of the gods before Enki, saying:

"O my son, rise from your bed, from your . . . work what is wise,
Fashion servants of the gods, may they produce their doubles (?)."

Enki gives the matter thought, leads forth the host of "good and princely fashioners," and says to his mother, Nammu, the primeval sea:

"O my mother, the creature whose name you uttered, it exists,
Bind upon it the image (?) of the gods;

Mix the heart of the clay that is over the abyss,
The good and princely fashioners will thicken the clay,
You, do you bring the limbs into existence;
Ninmah (the earth-mother goddess) will work above you,
The goddesses (of birth) . . . will stand by you at your
    fashioning;
O my mother, decree its (the newborn's) fate,
Ninmah will bind upon it the mold (?) of the gods,
It is man. . . ."

The poem now turns from the creation of man as a whole
to the creation of certain imperfect human types in an obvious attempt to explain the existence of these abnormal beings.
It tells of a feast arranged by Enki for the gods, no doubt to
commemorate man's creation. At this feast Enki and Ninmah
drink much wine and become somewhat exuberant. Ninmah
then takes some of the clay which is over the abyss and
fashions six different varieties of abnormal individuals, while
Enki decrees their fate and gives them bread to eat.

After Ninmah had created these six types of man, Enki
decides to do some creating of his own. The manner in which
he goes about it is not clear, but whatever it is that he does,
the resulting creature is a failure; it is weak and feeble in
body and spirit. Enki is now anxious that Ninmah help this
forlorn creature; he therefore addresses her as follows:

"Of him whom your hand has fashioned, I have decreed the
    fate,
    Have given him bread to eat;
Do you decree the fate of him whom my hand has fashioned,
    Do you give him bread to eat."

Ninmah tries to be good to the creature but to no avail.
She talks to him but he fails to answer. She gives him bread
to eat, but he does not reach out for it. He can neither sit nor
stand, nor bend the knees. Following a long but as yet unin-
telligible conversation between Enki and Ninmah, the latter
utters a curse against Enki because of the sick, lifeless crea-

ture which he produced, a curse which Enki seems to accept as his due.

Of Ninurta, the god of the stormy South Wind, there is a myth with a dragon-slaying motif. Following a brief hymnal passage to the god, the plot begins with an address to Ninurta by the Sharur, his personified weapon. For some unstated reason the Sharur had set his mind against Asag, the demon of sickness and disease, whose abode is in the Kur, or Nether World. In a speech which is full of phrases extolling the heroic qualities and deeds of Ninurta, he urges him to attack and destroy the monster. Ninurta sets out to do as bidden. At first, however, he seems to have met more than his match, and he "flees like a bird." Once again the Sharur addresses him with reassuring and encouraging words. Ninurta now attacks the Asag fiercely with all the weapons at his command, and the demon is destroyed.

With the destruction of the Asag, however, a serious calamity overtook Sumer. The primeval waters of the Kur rose to the surface, and as a result of their violence no fresh waters could reach the fields and gardens. The gods of Sumer who "carried its pickax and basket," that is, who had charge of irrigating Sumer and preparing it for cultivation, were desperate. The Tigris did not rise, it had no "good" water in its channel.

> *Famine was severe, nothing was produced,*
> *At the small rivers, there was no "washing of the hands,"*
>   *The waters rose not high.*
> *The fields are not watered,*
>   *There was no digging of (irrigation) ditches.*
> *In all the lands there was no vegetation,*
>   *Only weeds grew.*
> *Thereupon the Lord put his lofty mind to it,*
> *Ninurta, the son of Enlil brought great things into being.*

He set up a pile of stones over the Kur and heaped it up like a great wall in front of Sumer. These stones held back "the mighty waters," and as a result the waters of the Kur could rise no longer to the surface of the earth. As for

waters which had already flooded the land, Ninurta gathered
them and led them into the Tigris, which is now in a position
to water the fields with its overflow. Or, as the poet puts it:

> *What had been scattered, he gathered,*
> *What of the Kur had been scattered,*
> *He guided and hurled into the Tigris,*
> *The high waters it pours over the fields.*
> *Behold, now, everything on earth,*
> *Rejoiced afar at Ninurta, the king of the land.*
> *The fields produced abundant grain,*
> *The vineyard and orchard bore their fruit,*
> *The harvest was heaped up in granaries and hills,*
> *The Lord made mourning to disappear from the land,*
> *He made happy the spirit of the gods.*

Hearing of her son's great and heroic deeds, his mother
Ninmah was taken with love for him; she became so restless
that she was unable to sleep in her bedchamber. She therefore addresses Ninurta from afar with a prayer for permission
to visit him and gaze upon him. Ninurta looks at her with the
"eye of life," saying:

> *"Oh lady, because you would come to the Kur,*
> *Oh Ninmah, because for my sake you would enter the inimi-*
>   *cal land,*
> *Because you have no fear of the terror of the battle surround-*
>   *ing me,*
> *Therefore, of the hill which I, the hero, have heaped up,*
> *Let its name be Hursag (Mountain) and you be its queen."*

Ninurta then blesses the Hursag that it may produce all
kinds of herbs; wine and honey; various kinds of trees; gold,
silver, and bronze; cattle, sheep, and all "four-legged creatures." Following this blessing he turns to the stones, cursing
those which had been his enemies in his battle with the
Asag-demon, and blessing those which had been his friends.

Not a few of the Sumerian myths revolve about the ambitious, aggressive, and demanding goddess of love, Inanna—
the Akkadian Ishtar—and her husband, the shepherd-god

Dumuzi—the Biblical Tammuz. The wooing of the goddess by Dumuzi is told in two versions. In the one he contends for her favor with the farmer-god Enkimdu, and is successful only after a good deal of quarrelsome argument leading to threats of violence. In the other, Dumuzi seems to find ready and immediate acceptance as Inanna's lover and husband. But little did he dream that his marriage to Inanna would end in his perdition and that he would be literally dragged down to Hell. This is told in one of the best-preserved Sumerian myths, "Inanna's Descent to the Nether World," which has been published and revised three times in the course of the past twenty-five years, and is about to be revised a fourth time with the help of several hitherto unknown tablets and fragments; it tells the following tale:

Inanna, "queen of heaven," the ambitious goddess of love and war whom the shepherd Dumuzi had wooed and won for wife, decides to descend to the Nether World in order to make herself its mistress, and thus perhaps to raise the dead. She therefore collects the appropriate divine laws and, having adorned herself with her queenly robes and jewels, she is ready to enter the "land of no return."

The queen of the Nether World is her older sister and bitter enemy, Ereshkigal, Sumerian goddess of death and gloom. Fearing, not without reason, lest her sister put her to death in the domain she rules, Inanna instructs her vizier, Ninshubur, who is always at her beck and call, that if after three days she has failed to return he is to set up a lament for her by the ruins, in the assembly hall of the gods. He is then to go to Nippur, the city of Enlil, the leading god of the Sumerian pantheon, and plead with him to save her and not let her be put to death in the Nether World. If Enlil refuses, Ninshubur is to go to Ur, the city of the moon-god Nanna, and repeat his plea. If Nanna, too, refuses, he is to go to Eridu, the city of Enki, the god of wisdom, who "knows the food of life," who "knows the water of life," and he will surely come to her rescue.

Inanna then descends to the Nether World and approaches Ereshkigal's temple of lapis lazuli. At the gate she is met by the chief gatekeeper, who demands to know who she is and why she has come. Inanna concocts a false excuse for her visit, and the gatekeeper, on instructions from his mistress, leads her through the seven gates of the Nether World. As she passes through one gate after another her garments and jewels are removed piece by piece in spite of her protests. Finally, after entering the last gate, she is brought stark naked and on bended knees before Ereshkigal and the Anunnaki, the seven dreaded judges of the Nether World. They fasten upon her their eyes of death, and she is turned into a corpse, which is then hung from a stake.

Three days and three nights pass. On the fourth day Ninshubur, seeing that his mistress has not returned, proceeds to make the rounds of the gods in accordance with her instructions. As Inanna had surmised, both Enlil and Nanna refuse all help. Enki, however, devises a plan to restore her to life. He fashions the *kurgarru* and the *kalaturru*, two sexless creatures, and entrusts to them the "food of life" and the "water of life," with instructions to proceed to the Nether World where Ereshkigal, "the birth-giving mother," lies sick "because of her children" and, naked and uncovered, keeps moaning, "Woe my inside" and "Woe my outside." They, the *kurgarru* and *kalaturru*, are to repeat sympathetically her cry and add: "From my 'inside' to your 'inside,' from my 'outside' to your 'outside.'" They will then be offered water of the rivers and grain of the fields as gifts but, Enki warns, they must not accept them. Instead they are to say, "Give us the corpse hanging from a nail" and proceed to sprinkle "the food of life" and "the water of life" which he had entrusted to them, and thus revive the dead Inanna. The *kurgarru* and *kalaturru* do exactly as Enki bid them and Inanna revives.

Though Inanna is once again alive, her troubles are far from over, for it was an unbroken rule of the "land of no return" that no one who had entered its gates might return to the world above unless he produced a substitute to take his place in the Nether World. Inanna is no exception to the rule. She is indeed permitted to reascend to the earth, but is accompanied by a number of heartless demons with instructions to bring her back to the lower regions if she fails to provide another deity to take her place. Surrounded by these ghoulish constables, Inanna first proceeds to visit the two Sumerian cities Umma and Bad-tibira. The protecting gods of these cities, Shara and Latarak, terrified at the sight of the unearthly arrivals, clothe themselves in sackcloth and grovel in the dust before Inanna. Inanna seems to be gratified by their humility, and when the demons threaten to carry them off to the Nether World she restrains the demons and thus saves the lives of the two gods.

Inanna and the demons, continuing their journey, arrive at Kullab, a district in the Sumerian city-state of Erech. The king of this city is the shepherd-god Dumuzi, who, instead of bewailing the fact that his wife had descended to the Nether World when she had suffered torture and death, "put on a noble robe, sat high on a throne," that is, he was actually celebrating and rejoicing. Enraged, Inanna looks down upon him with "the eye of death" and hands him over to the eager and unmerciful demons to be carried off to the Nether World. Dumuzi turns pale and weeps. He lifts his hands to the sky and pleads with the sun-god Utu, who is Inanna's brother and therefore his own brother-in-law. Dumuzi begs Utu to help him escape the clutches of the demons by changing his hand into the hand of a snake, and his foot into the foot of a snake.

But there, right in the middle of Dumuzi's prayer, the available tablets break off, and the reader was left hanging in the mid-air. Now, however, we have the melancholy end. Dumuzi, in spite of the three-time intervention of Utu, is carried off to die in the Nether World as a substitute for his angered and embittered wife, Inanna. This we learn from a hitherto largely unknown poem which is not actually a part of the "Inanna's Descent to the Nether World" but is intimately related to it and which, moreover, speaks of Dumuzi's changing into a gazelle rather than a snake. This new composition has been found inscribed on twenty-eight tablets and fragments dating from about 1750 B.C., and the full text has only recently been pieced together and translated, at least tentatively, although some of the pieces were published decades ago. In fact the first of the pieces belonging to the myth was published as early as 1915 by a young Sumerologist, Hugo Radau, but it contained only the last lines of the poem and its contents therefore remained obscure. In 1930 the French scholar, Henri de Genouillac, published two additional pieces which contained the initial fifty-five lines of the poem. But since the entire middle portion was unknown there was no way of knowing that the Radau and the de Genouillac pieces belonged to the same poem. By 1953 six additional pieces, published and unpublished, became available, and Thorkild Jacobsen, of the Oriental Institute, one of the world's leading Sumerologists, was the first to give an idea of its plot and to translate several passages in the *Journal of Cuneiform Studies*, vol. XII, pp. 165–66, and in Leo Oppenheim's *The Interpretation of Dreams in the Ancient Near East*, p. 246. Since then, I have identified nineteen additional tablets and fragments, ten of which are in the Museum of the Ancient Orient in Istanbul; these have been copied by Mmes. Muazzez Cig and Hatice Kizileyay, the curators of the tablet collection in Istanbul, and myself. As a result of all these new documents it was possible, at long last, to restore the text of the poem almost in full and to prepare the tentative translation on which the following sketch of its contents is based.

The myth begins with an introductory passage in which the author sets the melancholy tone of the tale he is to tell. Dumuzi the shepherd of Erech has a foreboding premonition that his death is imminent, and so goes forth to the plain with tearful eyes and bitter lament:

His heart was filled with tears,
*   He went forth to the plain,*
The shepherd—his heart was filled with tears,
*   He went forth to the plain,*
Dumuzi—his heart was filled with tears,
*   He went forth to the plain,*
He fastened his flute (?) about his neck,
*   Gave utterance to a lament:*

"Set up a lament, set up a lament,
*   O plain, set up a lament!*
O plain, set up a lament, set up a wail (?)!
Among the crabs of the river, set up a lament!
Among the frogs of the river, set up a lament!
*   Let my mother utter words (of lament),*
Let my mother Sirtur utter words (of lament),
Let my mother who has (?) not five breads (?)
*   utter words (of lament),*
Let my mother who has (?) not ten breads(?)
*   utter words (of lament),*
On the day I die she will have none to care (?) for her,
On the plain, like my mother, let my eyes shed tears (?),
On the plain, like my little sister, let my eyes shed tears."

Dumuzi, the poem continues, then lies down to sleep and has an ominous and foreboding dream:

Among the buds (?) he lay down, among the buds (?) he
*   lay down,*
*   The shepherd—among the buds (?) he lay down,*
As the shepherd lay down among the buds (?), he dreamt a
*   dream,*
He arose—it was a dream, he trembled (?)—it was a vision,
He rubbed his eyes with his hands, he was dazed.

The bewildered Dumuzi now has his sister Geshtinanna, the divine poetess, singer, and dream interpreter, brought before him and tells her his portentous vision:

"My dream, oh my sister, my dream,
*   This is the heart of my dream:*
Rushes rise up all about me, rushes sprout all about me,
One reed standing all alone, bows its head for me,
Of the reeds standing in pairs, one is removed for me,
In the wooded grove, tall (?) trees rise fearsomely all about
*   me,*
Over my holy hearth, water is poured,
Of my holy churn—its stand (?) is removed,

The holy cup hanging from a peg, from the peg has fallen,
My shepherd's crook has vanished,
An owl holds a . . . . . . ,
A falcon holds a lamb in its claws,
My young goats drag their lapis beards in the dust,
My sheep of the fold paw the ground, with their bent limbs,
The churn lies (shattered), no milk is poured,
The cup lies (shattered), Dumuzi lives no more,
    The sheepfold is given over to the wind."

Geshtinanna, too, is deeply disturbed by her brother's dream:

"Oh my brother, your dream is not favorable, which you
    tell me!
Oh Dumuzi, your dream is not favorable which you tell me!
Rushes rise up all about you, rushes sprout all about you.
(This means) outlaws will rise up to attack you.
One reed standing all alone, bows its head for you,
(This means) your mother who bore you will lower her head
    for you.
Of the reeds standing in pairs, one is removed,
(This means) I and you—one of us will be removed. . . ."

Geshtinanna thus proceeds to interpret, item by item, her brother's somber and foreboding dream, ending with a warning that the demons of the Nether World, the *galla*'s, are closing in on him and that he must hide immediately.

Dumuzi agrees, and implores his sister not to tell the *galla*'s of his hiding place, thus:

> *"My friend, I will hide among the plants,*
>   *Tell no one my (hiding) place,*
> *I will hide among the small plants,*
>   *Tell no one my (hiding) place.*
> *I will hide among the large plants,*
>   *Tell no one my (hiding) place.*
> *I will hide among ditches of Arallu,*
>   *Tell no one my (hiding) place."*

To which Geshtinanna replies:

"If I tell your (hiding) place, may your dogs devour me,
The black dogs, your dogs of 'shepherdship,'
The wild dogs, your dogs of 'lordship,'
*   May your dogs devour me."*

And so the *galla's*, the inhuman creatures who

> *Eat no food, know not water,*
> *Eat not sprinkled flour,*
> *Drink not libated water,*
> *Accept no gifts that mollify,*
> *Sate not with pleasure the wife's bosom,*
> *Kiss not the children, the sweet . . . .*

come searching for the hidden Dumuzi but cannot find him. They seize his sister Geshtinanna and try to bribe her to tell them of Dumuzi's whereabouts, but she remains true to her given word.

Dumuzi, however, returns to the city, probably because he fears that the demons will kill his sister. There the *galla's* catch hold of him, belabor him with blows, punches, and lashes, bind fast his hands and arms, and are all set to carry him off to the Nether World. Whereupon Dumuzi turns to the sun-god Utu, the brother of his wife, Inanna, the tutelary goddess of his city Erech, with the prayer to turn him into a gazelle, so that he can escape the *galla's* and carry off his "soul" to a place (as yet unidentified) known by the name of Shubirila, or as Dumuzi himself puts it:

"Utu, you are my wife's brother,
*   I am your sister's husband,*
I am he who carries food for Eanna [Inanna's temple],
In Erech I performed the marriages
I kissed the holy lips (?)
Caressed (?) the holy lap, the lap of Inanna—
Turn my hands into the hands of a gazelle,
Turn my feet into the feet of a gazelle,
Let me escape my galla-demons,
Let me carry off my soul to Shubirila. . . ."

The sun-god harkened to Dumuzi's prayer. In the words of the poet:

> *Utu took his tears as a gift,*
> *Like a man of mercy, he showed him mercy,*
> *He turned his hands into the hands of a gazelle,*
> *He turned his feet into the feet of a gazelle,*
> *He escaped his* gala-*demons,*
> *Carried off his soul to Shubirila. . . ."*

But to no avail. The pursuing demons catch up with him once again, and beat and torture him as before. A second time, therefore, Dumuzi turns to the sun-god Utu with the prayer to turn him into a gazelle; only this time he will carry off his soul to the house of a goddess known as "Belili, the wise old lady." Utu does so, and Dumuzi arrives at the house of Belili pleading:

> *"Wise old lady, I am not a man, I am the husband of a god-*
>   *dess,*
> *Of the libated water, let me drink a little (?)*
> *Of the flour which has been sprinkled, let me eat a little (?)."*

He had barely had time to partake of food and drink, when the *galla's* appear and beat and torment Dumuzi a third time. Again Utu turns him to a gazelle, and he escapes to the sheepfold of his sister Geshtinanna. But all in vain, five of the *galla's* enter the sheepfold, strike Dumuzi on the cheek with nail and sticks, and Dumuzi dies. Or, to quote the melancholy lines which end the poem:

> *The first* galla *enters the sheepfold,*
> *He strikes Dumuzi on the cheek with a piercing (?) nail (?),*
> *The second one enters the sheepfold,*
> *He strikes Dumuzi on the cheek with the shepherd's crook,*
> *The third one enters the sheepfold,*
> *Of the holy churn, the stand (?) is removed,*
> *The fourth one enters the sheepfold,*
> *The cup hanging from a peg, from the peg falls,*
> *The fifth one enters the sheepfold,*

The holy churn lies (shattered), no milk is poured,
The cup lies (shattered), Dumuzi lives no more,
    The sheepfold is given to the wind.

Thus Dumuzi comes to a tragic end, a victim of Inanna's love and hate. Not all the Inanna myths, however, relate to Dumuzi. There is one, for example, which relates how the goddess obtained through trickery the divine laws the *me*'s which govern mankind and his institutions. This myth is of considerable anthropological interest. Because its author found it desirable in connection with the story to give a full list of the *me*'s, he divided civilization as he conceived it into over one hundred culture traits and complexes relating to man's political and religious and social institutions, to the arts and crafts, to music and musical instruments, and to a varied assortment of intellectual, emotional, and social patterns of behavior. Briefly sketched, the plot of this revealing myth runs as follows:

Inanna, Queen of Heaven, the tutelary goddess of Erech, is anxious to increase the welfare and prosperity of her city, to make it the center of Sumerian civilization and thus to exalt her name and fame. She, therefore, decides to go to Eridu, the ancient and hoary seat of Sumerian culture where Enki, the Lord of Wisdom, "who knows the very heart of the gods," dwells in his watery abyss, the Abzu. For Enki has under his charge all the divine decrees that are fundamental to civilization. And if she can obtain them, by fair means or foul, and bring them to her city Erech, its glory and her own will indeed be unsurpassed. As she approaches the Abzu of Eridu, Enki, no doubt taken in by her charm, calls his messenger Isimud, whom he addresses as follows:

"Come, my messenger Isimud, give ear to my instructions,
A word I shall say to you, take my word.
The maid, all alone, has directed her step to the Abzu,
Inanna, all alone, has directed her step to the Abzu,
Have the maid enter the Abzu of Eridu,
Give her to eat barley cake with butter,
Pour for her cold water that freshens the heart,

Give her to drink beer in the 'face of the lion'
At the holy table, the Table of Heaven,
Speak to Inanna words of greeting."

Isimud did exactly as bidden by his master, and Inanna
and Enki sit down to feast and banquet. After their hearts
had become happy with drink, Enki exclaims:

"By the name of power, by the name of my power,
To holy Inanna, my daughter, I shall present the divine
*   decrees."*

He thereupon presents, several at a time, the over one
hundred divine decrees which, according to our author, control the culture pattern of civilization as he knew it. Inanna is
only too happy to accept the gifts offered her by the drunken
Enki. She takes them and loads them on her Boat of Heaven,
and makes off for Erech with her precious cargo. But after
the effects of the banquet had worn off, Enki noticed that the
me's were gone from their usual place. He turns to Isimud
and the latter informs him that he, Enki himself, had presented them to his daughter Inanna. The upset Enki greatly
rues his munificence and decides to prevent the Boat of
Heaven from reaching Erech at all cost. He therefore dispatches his messenger Isimud together with a group of sea
monsters to follow Inanna and her boat to the first of the
seven stepping stations that are situated between the Abzu
of Eridu and Erech. Here the sea monsters are to seize the
Boat of Heaven from Inanna; Inanna herself, however, must
be permitted to continue her journey to Erech afoot.

Isimud does as bidden. He overtakes Inanna and the Boat
of Heaven and informs her of Enki's change of heart, and
that while she is free to go on to Erech, he will have to take
the boat and its precious cargo from her and bring it back to
Erech. Whereupon Inanna berates Enki roundly for breaking
his word and oath, turns to her vizier, the god Ninshubur, for
help, and the latter rescues her and the boat from Isimud
and the sea monsters. Enki is persistent; again and again he
sends Isimud accompanied by various sea monsters to seize

the Boat of Heaven. But on each occasion Ninshubur comes to the rescue of his mistress. Finally Inanna and her boat arrive safe and sound at Erech, where amidst jubilation and feasting on the part of the delighted inhabitants she unloads the precious divine *me*'s, one at a time.

There is one Inanna myth in which a mortal plays an important role; its plot runs as follows:

Once upon a time there lived a gardener by the name of Shukallituda, whose diligent efforts at gardening had met with nothing but failure. Although he had carefully watered his furrows and garden patches, the plants had withered away; the raging winds smote his face with the "dust of the mountains"; all that he had carefully tended turned desolate. He thereupon lifted his eyes east and west to the starry heavens, studied the omens, observed and learned the divine decrees. As a result of this newly acquired wisdom he planted the (as yet unidentified) *sarbatu*-tree in the garden, a tree whose broad shade lasts from sunrise to sunset. As a consequence of this ancient horticultural experiment Shukallituda's garden blossomed forth with all kinds of green.

One day, continues our myth, the goddess Inanna, after traversing heaven and earth, lay down to rest her tired body not far from Shukallituda's garden. The latter, who had spied her from the edge of his garden, takes advantage of Inanna's extreme weariness and cohabits with her. When morning came and the sun rose, Inanna looked about her in consternation and determined to ferret out at all costs the mortal who had so shamefully abused her. She therefore sends three plagues against Sumer. Firstly, she fills all the wells of the land with blood, so that all the palm groves and vineyards are saturated with blood. Secondly, she sends against the land destructive winds and storms. The nature of the third plague is uncertain, since the relevant lines are too fragmentary. But in spite of all three plagues she is unable to locate her defiler. For after each plague Shukallituda goes to his father's house and informs him of his danger. The father advises his son to direct his step to his brothers, the "black-headed people," that is, the people of Sumer, and to stay close to the urban centers. Shukallituda follows this advice, and as a result Inanna is unable to find him.

After her third failure Inanna realizes bitterly that she is unable to avenge the outrage committed against her. She therefore decides to go to the city Eridu, to the house of Enki, the Sumerian god of wisdom, and ask his advice and help. But here unfortunately the tablet breaks off, and the end of the story remains unknown.

Except for references to mankind as a whole, mortals play little role in the Sumerian myths. In addition to the Inanna-Shukallituda myth just described, there is only one other myth involving a mortal. This is the long-known flood-story so important for comparative Biblical studies. Unfortunately only one tablet inscribed with this myth has been excavated to date, and this tablet is only one-third preserved. The beginning of the myth is broken away, and the first intelligible lines concern the creation of man, vegetation, and animals; the heavenly origin of kingship; the founding and naming of five antediluvian cities, which are presented to five tutelary deities. We then learn that a number of deities are bitter and unhappy because of a divine decision to bring the flood and destroy mankind. Ziusudra, the Sumerian counterpart of the Biblical Noah, is next introduced in the story as a pious god-fearing king who is constantly on the lookout for divine dreams and revelations. He stations himself by a wall, where he hears the voice of a deity, probably Enki, informing him of the decision taken by the assembly of the gods to send a deluge and "destroy the seed of mankind."

The myth must have continued with detailed instructions to Ziusudra to build a giant boat and thus save himself from destruction. But all this is missing because of a rather large break in the tablet. When the text resumes we find that the flood in all its violence had already come upon the earth where it raged for seven days and nights. Following which, the sun-god Utu comes forth lighting and warming up the earth, and Ziusudra prostrates himself before him and offers him sacrifices of oxen and sheep. The last extant lines of the myth describe the deification of Ziusudra: after he had prostrated himself before An and Enlil, he was given "life like a god" and translated to Dilmun, the divine paradise-land, "the place where the sun rises."

Finally, there is a Sumerian myth which, although concerned with gods only, provides an interesting bit of anthropological information about the Semitic Bedu-people known as Martu. The action of the story takes place in the city of Ninab, "the city of cities, the land of princeship," a still unidentified locality in Mesopotamia. Its tutelary deity seems to have been Martu, god of the nomadic Semites who lived to the west and southwest of Sumer. The relative time when the events took place is described in cryptic, antithetical, and obscure phrases, thus:

> Ninab existed, Aktab existed not,
> The holy crown existed, the holy tiara existed not,
> The holy herbs existed, holy nitrum existed not. . . .

The god Martu, the story begins, decides to marry. He asks his mother to take him a wife, but she advises him to go and find a wife for himself in accordance with his own desire. One day, the story continues, a great feast is prepared in Ninab, and to it comes Numushda, the tutelary deity of Kazallu, a city-state located to the northeast of Sumer, together with his wife and daughter. During this feast Martu performs some heroic deed which brings joy to the heart of Numushda. As a reward, the latter offers Martu silver and lapis lazuli. But Martu refuses; it is the hand of Numushda's daughter which he claims as a reward. Numushda gladly consents; so, too, does his daughter, although her girl friends try to dissuade her from marrying Martu since:

> He lives in tents, buffeted by wind and rain,
> Eats uncooked meat,
> Has no house while he lives,
> Is not brought to burial when he dies.

AKKAD

The myths of the Akkadians (that is, of the Babylonians and Assyrians) derive largely from Sumerian prototypes. At least two of them—"Ishtar's Descent to the Nether World" and the "Flood"-story as told in the Epic of Gilgamesh—are well-nigh identical with known Sumerian originals. But even those for which no Sumerian counterparts have as yet been recovered contain mythological themes and motifs which reflect Sumerian sources, not to mention the fact that most of the deities involved are part of the Sumerian pantheon. This is not to say that the Akkadian poets imitated slavishly their Sumerian prototypes; they introduced many innovations and changes in both theme and plot. But by and large, the Akkadian men of letters could not escape the deep and all-pervading influence of their Sumerian heritage.

The best-known of the Akkadian myths is the "creation" poem usually called *Enuma-Elish,* from its initial two words which mean "when above." Actually the poem was composed not so much to tell the story of creation, but to glorify the Babylonian god Marduk and the city of Babylon. But in the course of doing so it introduces and relates Marduk's acts of creation, and is thus a prime source for the Akkadian cosmogonic ideas. Thus the poem tells us that at the very beginning, when as yet "the heavens had not been named on high" and "the earth had not been called by name below," there existed only the primordial oceans, Tiamat and Apsu (the Sumerian Abzu). Then, at some unspecified time, several generations of gods were born, one of whom was Ea, the Sumerian Enki, the god of wisdom. These gods, however, distressed Apsu and Tiamat with their unceasing bustle and clamor, and Apsu decided to do away with them, although his wife Tiamat urged him to have compassion on them. Fortunately for the gods, however, Ea succeeded in killing Apsu with the help of a magic incantation. Ea then established his own abode upon the dead Apsu, and there his wife gave birth to Marduk, a heroic and imposing figure of a god who soon had occasion to show his bravery by saving the gods from Tiamat, bent on avenging the death of her husband Apsu, with the help of some renegade gods and a host of vicious monsters. Following this victory, Marduk created heaven and earth from Tiamat's huge corpse by splitting it in two. He then created special "stations" for the gods, set up the stellar constellations, constructed gates through which the sun might enter and depart, and caused the moon to shine forth. Then, to free the gods from menial labor, Marduk, with the help of his father Ea, created mankind from the blood of Kingu, the rebel god who had been leader of Tiamat's inimical host. Following which, the appreciative gods built the Esagila, Marduk's temple at Babylon, prepared a joyous banquet, and recited Marduk's fifty names which attributed to him the powers of practically all the major gods of the Akkadian pantheon.

In addition to the *Enuma-Elish* version, there are a number of other and much briefer creation accounts which differ in numerous details from each other and from that of *Enuma-Elish*. Thus there is one account used as an introduction to an incantation for the purification of a Babylonian temple, which relates that at first nothing existed, neither reed nor tree, neither house nor temple, neither city nor living creatures, and that "all lands were sea." Then the gods were created and Babylon was built. After which Marduk fashioned a reed frame over the face of the waters and created mankind with the help of the mother goddess Aruru (the Sumerian Ninmah, alias Nintu, alias Ninhursag). Following man, Marduk created the beasts of the plain, the rivers Tigris and Euphrates, grass, rushes, and reeds, the green herbs of the fields, lands, marshes, and canebrakes, the cow and her young, the ewe and her lamb, the sheep of the fold. And thus it was that dry land came into being, and cities such as Nippur and Erech together with their temples and houses were built of bricks fashioned in brick molds.

According to another brief creation account, one that was intended for recitation in connection with a ritual for the restoration of a temple, it was the god Anu (the Sumerian heaven-god An) who created the heavens, while Ea (the Sumerian Enki) created the dry land and everything on it. He "pinched off clay" from over his sea dwelling, the Apsu, and created the brick-god Kulla. He created the reed marshes, and forests, the mountains and the seas, together with the gods in charge of such crafts as carpentry, metal work, engraving, and stonecutting. In order that the temples, once built, might be provided with regular offerings, he created the deities in charge of grain, cattle, and wine, as well as a divine cook, cupbearer, and high priest. Finally, in order to maintain the temples and perform the labor which the gods would otherwise have to do themselves, they created men and kings.

There is a fragmentary creation myth used as an introduction to a childbirth incantation, of which only the passage dealing with the creation of man is preserved. According to this version, the gods turn to Mami, alias Aruru, the mother goddess, also known by her Sumerian names Nintu, Ninhursag, and Ninmah, with a request to create man "to bear the yoke" of the gods. Mami asks Enki for counsel, and he advises that Mami fashion man as a partly divine creature by mixing clay with the blood and flesh of a deity slain by the gods.

There is one "creation" poem devoted primarily to the creation of man alone. This version begins with the statement that after "heaven had been separated from earth" and the earth had been fashioned, after the "fate" of the universe had been decreed, and the Tigris and Euphrates together with their dykes and canals had been "established" and given their proper direction, then all the gods seated themselves in their exalted sanctuary and Enlil, the king of the gods, asks:

"Now that the 'fate' of the universe has been decreed,
Dyke and canal have been given proper direction,
The banks of the Tigris and Euphrates have been established,

What else shall we do?
What else shall we create?
O Anunnaki, great gods,
What else shall we do?
What else shall we create?"

The Anunnaki thereupon urge upon Enlil that the gods should create man out of the blood of two *Lamga* (crafts-man) gods whom they will slay for this purpose. Man's portion, the gods continue, will be to carry out the service of the gods for all time, by tilling and irrigating the fields and building temples and sanctuaries for them. Accordingly there were created two mortals having the names Ullegarra and Zallegarra (two Sumerian words whose meaning is still uncertain), and these were blessed by the gods with generous increase and rich abundance, so that they might celebrate the festivals of the gods "day and night."

How the Akkadian poets felt free to modify the current cosmogonic ideas in accordance with the need of the moment is well illustrated by a creation version used as an incantation against toothache which, according to the Akkadian medical practitioners, was due to a blood-sucking worm lodged in the gums. As the author, who was a poet, priest, and physician combined, puts it:

> *After Anu had created heaven,*
> *Heaven had created earth,*
> *Earth had created rivers,*
> *Rivers had created canals,*
> *Canals had created marsh,*
> *Marsh had created worm—*
> *The worm came weeping before Shamash,*
> *His tears flowing before Ea:*
> *"What will you give me to eat?*
> *What will you give me to drink?"*
>
> *"I will give you the ripe fig,*
>   *The apricot."*

"What to me are the ripe fig,
*   The apricot?*
Lift me up and let me dwell
Among the teeth and the gums,
I will suck the blood of the tooth,
And will gnaw away of the gum its roots."

The text closes with instructions to the dentist-incantator to "insert the needle and seize its (the worm's) foot"—that is, presumably, to pull the sick nerve—and to perform an accompanying ritual involving the mixing of "second-grade beer" and oil.

Among the non-cosmogonic myths there is one which tells of the slaying of the huge sea-born monster Labbu, who brought havoc and destruction to the people and their cities. Another myth revolves about the slaying of the monstrous Zu-bird, who in its inordinate lust for power stole the "Tablets of Fate" right from under Enlil's nose, as it were, and thus usurped the sovereignty over the gods. The plot motif of the two stories is similar; several deities ordered to go and do battle with the monsters decline the honor in cowardly terror, in spite of the promised reward; then one courageous deity—probably Marduk or Ninurta—agrees, slays the monster, and is rewarded accordingly.

One myth concerns the Nether World and relates how the god Nergal, originally a sky-god, became king of Hades where until then the goddess Ereshkigal had reigned supreme. The story begins with an invitation by the gods to Ereshkigal, queen of the Nether World, to send a representative to a banquet which they had prepared, since she herself cannot leave her dominion. Ereshkigal accepts and sends Namtar, that is, Fate, the demon of death. Namtar arrives in heaven and is welcomed with due honor by the gods except for Nergal, who insults him by remaining seated when all the gods rise to greet him. To avenge this insult Ereshkigal demands that Nergal be extradited to the Nether World, where she will put him to death. On the plea of Nergal, however, the god Ea comes to his rescue by giving him fourteen

demons to accompany him to the Nether World and stand by
him against Ereshkigal. Upon arrival in Hades, Nergal posted
the fourteen demons at its fourteen gates while he himself,
after being admitted by the gatekeeper of the Nether World,
rushed into Ereshkigal's palace, dragged her from the
throne by her hair, and was all set to cut off her head. But
she tearfully pleaded with him not to kill her, and to become
her husband instead, and take dominion over Hades. Whereupon Nergal kissed her, wiped away her tears, and agreed
to become lord and king of the Nether World with Ereshkigal
as his lady and queen.

There are three mythological compositions in which mortals play the major role. In one of these the protagonist is a
sage of Eridu by the name of Adapa, who might have secured
eternal life for himself and all mankind had he not followed
the unwise advice of Ea, the god who is usually depicted as
man's best friend. The myth begins with a description of
Adapa as "the wise son of Eridu," "the most wise," "a leader
among men," the "skillful and exceedingly wise," "the blame-
less and clean of hands," who daily provided Eridu, the city
of Ea, with food and drink. One day, as Adapa set sail in the
Persian Gulf in order to catch fish to provision Ea's sanctuary,
the South Wind blew up a gale and submerged him and his
boat. Enraged, Adapa uttered a curse against the South Wind
and thus broke his wings. When the South Wind had failed
to blow upon the land for seven consecutive days, the heaven-
god Anu inquired what was the trouble, and his vizier,
Ilabrat, told him what had happened. Anu, beside himself
with anger, rose from his throne, cried out, "Let them fetch
him (Adapa) hither."

Here Ea comes into the story and unwittingly, it seems,
deprives Adapa and mankind of the gift they desire most,
that of immortality. For he counsels Adapa thus: On his
journey to heaven and Anu's palace he is to wear his hair
long and unkempt and dress in mourning. This will arouse
the curiosity of the two heavenly gatekeepers, Tammuz and
Gishzida, two deities who had once lived on earth. Upon
their questioning him as to why he is in mourning, Adapa is

to answer them ingratiatingly that he is mourning "two gods who had disappeared from the land." When they further ask him, "Who are the two gods who have disappeared from the land?" he is to say, "They are Tammuz and Gishzida." Delighted by this flattering response, they will intercede for Adapa before the irate Anu.

So far so good. Ea then, however, adds a bit of advice which, intentional or not, turns out to be tragic for Adapa and mankind. This, in Ea's own words, runs as follows: "As you stand before Anu they will offer you the food of death— do not eat it. They will offer you the water of death, do not drink it." But when Adapa arrives in heaven, garbed in mourning, and Tammuz and Gishzida, upon learning the purported reason for his mourning, intercede with Anu in his behalf, the latter offers, not the food and water of *death*, but the food and water of *life*. Unfortunately, true to Ea's counsel, Adapa rejects both and misses the golden opportunity to secure immortality for himself and mankind. Anu sends him back to earth where man continues to be the victim of sickness and disease, although these can be allayed to some extent by Ninkarrak, the goddess of healing and medicine.

Another mortal who plays a major role in an Akkadian myth is Etana, reputed to be a mighty ruler of the dynasty of Kish, the first after mankind had recovered from the legendary flood. He, too, ascended to heaven, but not as in the case of Adapa to answer to the gods for a misdeed he had committed; his burning desire was to obtain "the plant of birth." For though he was a pious, god-fearing king who practiced the divine cult faithfully and assiduously, he was cursed with childlessness and had no one to carry on his name. According to the myth, he is borne to heaven by an eagle whom he had rescued from a pit where it had been cast by a serpent whose friendship it had betrayed and whose nests it had devoured. The Etana myth was popular among the seal cutters, to judge from a number of seals depicting a mortal climbing toward heaven on the wings of an eagle.

The third Akkadian myth in which a mortal plays a significant role revolves about a sage named Atrahasis and his repeated efforts to save mankind from destruction at the hands of the gods angered by man's chronic depravity and evil-doing. Unfortunately only a few fragmentary passages of the composition, originally 1245 lines in length, are preserved. From these we gather that the gods, disturbed and oppressed by "the clamor of mankind," sent famine, plagues, pestilence, and disease against it, so that people were reduced to cannibalism and self-destruction. But again and again Atrahasis pleads with the god Ea to intercede, and in one way or another mankind is saved, only to multiply once again and become noisy, rebellious, and clamorous. One of the decimating inflictions sent against man by the gods, according to this myth, is the flood, and in this case man is saved when Atrahasis, on the advice of Ea, builds himself a huge boat and boards it with his wife, family, and craftsmen, his grain, goods, and possessions, as well as the beasts of the field, "as many as eat herbs." All this sounds like just another version of the well-known and not too different Sumerian, Akkadian, and Biblical flood-stories in which the hero's name, however, is not Atrahasis, but Ziusudra, Utanapishtim, and Noah.

Finally, there is a myth concerned with the trials and tribulations of mankind, and particularly the Akkadians, though it ends on a note of hope and salvation; in this case, however, it is not a mortal, but a god who acts as the savior of mankind. This myth, which is not readily accessible to the layman, will be treated here in considerable detail since it is noteworthy in several respects: its diction is highly poetic; some of its ideas and expressions seem to have Biblical echoes; it ends with an unusual epilogue which illuminates to some extent the literary practices and conventions of the ancient myth writers.

The two major protagonists of the myth are Irra, the god of pestilence, and his vizier and constant companion, Ishum, the god of fire. Following a description of Irra as "the fearful slaughterer" who "lays waste the plain" and who takes joyous delight in devastating the land, the story begins with Irra lying lazily about, uncertain of what cruel and destructive deed to perform next. Whereupon Sibbi, his strange and unnatural seven-bodied weapon, whose "breath is death" and who inspires all with dread and terror, speaks up to the dilatory Irra in bitter anger:

> "Rise up and march forth, Irra,
> Like a pale old man you linger in the city,
> Like a whimpering child you linger in the house,
> Like one who rides not the plain we eat woman's food,
> Like one who knows not battle we dread the combat.
>
> Arise, hero, ride the plain,
> Lay low man and beast,
> Gods will hear and be dismayed,
> Kings will hear and be affrighted,
> Demons will hear and be terrified,
> The mighty will hear and quake,
> The towering mountains will hear and tremble,
> The billowy seas will hear and be convulsed.
>
> Irra, hear, I have said my word,
> Taut is the good bow, pointed the sharp arrow,
> Drawn is the sword for slaughter."

Whereupon mighty Irra calls to his vizier and guide, his "torch," Ishum, and says:

> "Open the path, I would take to the road,
> Sibbi, the hero unrivaled, will march at my side,
> While you, my guide, will walk behind."

Ishum heard these words with anguished heart. He took pity on man and says to Irra:

> "Lord! Against god and king you have planned evil,
> To destroy all the land, you have planned evil,
> Will you not turn back?"

Irra opened his mouth and speaks,
Addresses Ishum, his guide:
> "Silence, Ishum, and hear my words,
> Let me answer you concerning man and his fate,
> Guide of the gods, Ishum the wise, hear my words:

In the heavens I am a wild ox,
        On earth I am a lion,
                In the land I am a king,
Among the gods I am mighty,
        Among the Igigi (heaven-gods) I am valorous,
                Among the Anunnaki (here, the Nether World
                        gods) I am powerful,
Because man feared not my utterance,
        And heeded not the word of Marduk,
                But acted according to his own heart,
I will arouse Marduk, the princely,
        Will summon him forth from his dwelling place,
                Will destroy man."

And so Irra proceeds to Babylon, the city of Marduk, the king of the gods. He enters Marduk's temple, the Esagila, and urges Marduk to leave his dwelling place and go forth toward a place which he describes as "the house where the fire will purify your garments," perhaps the mountain to the east where the gods live. Or in the words of the poet:

Mighty Irra toward Babylon, the city of the king of the gods,
        set his face,
Entered Esagila, the palace of heaven and earth, and stood
        before him,
Opened his mouth and to the king of the gods speaks:
        "Lord, the nimbus, the symbol of your lordship,
        Full of brightness like a heavenly star—
                Darkened is its light,
        The crown of your lordship is cast down;
        March you forth from your dwelling place,
        Toward the house where fire will purify your garments,
                Set your face."

But Marduk is troubled lest if he leave Babylon and the Esagila, complete chaos will follow on earth; evil winds, demons, and the gods of the Nether World will destroy the lands, devour its inhabitants, and kill all living creatures, with none to turn them back. Irra reassures him that he will take full charge while Marduk is away, and see to it that the earth and its inhabitants are unharmed either by the heaven-gods or the Nether World demons. But as soon as Marduk leaves Babylon, Irra calls Ishum and says:

"Open the path, I will take to the road,
The day is come, the hour is passed,
I will speak, and the sun will drop its rays,
I will cover with darkness the face of day;
Who was born on a day of rain
    Will be buried on a day of thirst,
Who went forth on a well-watered path
    Will return by a road of dust.

I shall speak unto the king of the gods:
    'Come not forth from the house you entered,
    Faithfully will I carry out your commands,
    When the blackheaded people (the Akkadians) cry out
        to you,
    Receive not their prayers.'
I will put an end to all habitations
    And turn them into mounds,
I will devastate all the cities
    And make them into ruins,
I will destroy the mountains
    And wipe out their flocks,
I will convulse the seas
    And destroy their bounty,
I will uproot canebrake and forest
    And crush the mighty,
I will lay man low
    And wipe out all living creatures."

Ishum is filled with pity for man thus doomed to destruction. He therefore pleads with Irra to renounce his evil plans. But to no avail. He first destroyed Babylon and its inhabitants, as well as its walls and outskirts. Babylon a ruin, he turned to Erech, "the city of hierodules, courtesans, and sacred prostitutes to whom Ishtar (the goddess of love) was husband and master"; the city "of eunuchs and sodomites, the merrymakers of Eanna (Ishtar's temple), whose maleness Ishtar had turned to femaleness, in order to terrify man." Erech a ruin, Irra still found no peace and rest, saying in his heart:

> "Slaughter I shall multiply, and vengeance,
> I shall kill the son,
>> And his father will bury him,
> I shall kill the father,
>> And there will be none to bury him.
> Who has made himself a house, saying:
>> 'This is my resting chamber,
>> This I have made to rest therein,
>> The day the fates carry me off, I shall lie in its midst'—
> Him I shall put to death
>> I shall destroy his resting chamber,
> After it had become a ruin
>> I shall give it to another."

But Ishum, deeply disturbed by Irra's indiscriminate slaughter and destruction, pleads with him and tries to pacify him in these words:

> "Mighty Irra!
> The righteous you have put to death,
>> The unrighteous you have put to death,
> Him who has sinned you have put to death,
>> Him who has sinned not you have put to death,
> Him who burned offerings to the gods you have put to death,
>> The courtiers and the king's man you have put to death,
> The elder in the assembly you have put to death,
>> The young maiden you have put to death,
> And yet you refuse to rest, and say unto your heart
>> 'I shall crush the mighty
>>> And lay low the weak,
>> I shall kill the leader of the host
>>> And make the host turn back,

I shall destroy the tower chamber, the wall coping,
　　And wipe out the wealth of the city,
I shall rip out the mast—the ship will be lost,
I shall break the tying post—it will not touch shore,
I shall tear asunder the cable, rip off its flag,
I shall make dry the breast—the babe will not live,
I shall make dry the springs—the rivers will not bring
　　the waters of abundance,
I shall make fall the planet's light—leave the stars un-
　　tended,
I shall tear out the roots of the tree—its fruit will not
　　grow,
I shall rip out the foundation of the wall—its top will
　　totter,
To the dwelling of the king of the gods I shall betake
　　me—there is none to oppose me.' "

Ishum's address seems to pacify Irra to some extent, and
he proffers at last a note of hope, at least for the Akkadians,
if not for mankind as a whole:

Mighty Irra heard him,
　　And the word which Ishum spoke was soothing as oil,
　　And thus did mighty Irra speak:
　　　　"The Sealander—the Sealander,
　　　　　　The Subarean—the Subarean,
　　　　The Assyrian—the Assyrian,
　　　　　　The Elamite—the Elamite
　　　　The Kassite—the Kassite,
　　　　　　The Sutaean—the Sutaean,
　　　　The Gutaean—the Gutaean,
　　　　　　The Lullamaean—the Lullamaean,
　　　　Land—land, city—city,
　　　　House will attack house,
　　　　　　Brother will not spare brother,
　　　　　　They will kill one another,
　　　　Then will the Akkadian rise up,
　　　　　　And subdue them all."

And so Irra at last finds peace and rest, and he informs the gods that while it is true that he had formerly been angered by man's sins, and had planned his total destruction and annihilation, he had a change of heart as a result of Ishum's counsel and urging; he will now see to it that the Akkadians defeat and conquer their enemies and carry off their booty to Babylon; that the land will prosper in peace and war; and that once again Babylon will rule the world. Or, in Irra's own words to the happy Ishum:

"The people of the land, the few, will turn into many,
The short and the tall will seek out its roads,
The Akkadian, the weakling, will capture the Sultaean, the
            mighty,
One will carry off seven like sheep,
His cities you will turn into ruins, his mountains to mounds,
His heavy booty you will carry off to Babylon.
The gods of the land, the irate,
    Appeased, you will bring them to their dwellings,
Cattle and grain will prosper in the land,
The fields which had been made desolate,
    You shall make to bear produce,
All the governors, from the midst of their cities,
    Will bring their tribute to Babylon,
The Ekur temples which have been destroyed—
    Like the rising sun, their peaks will shine forth in light,
The Tigris and Euphrates with waters of abundance will
        overflow,
        And unto distant days Babylon will rule the cities
        all."

The poem closes with an epilogue which sheds some light on the psychological attitude of the author of the myth, as well as of the audience for whom it was intended. The first part reads:

That for the glory of Irra
    This song might be sung years without count—

How Irra had become angry,
*   And had set his face to devastate the land,*
*   To lay low man and beast,*
How Ishum his counselor had pacified him,
*   And a remnant was saved—*
To Kabti—Ilani—Marduk, his tablet keeper,
*   The son of Dabibi,*
Ishum showed it in a vision of the night,
When he arose at dawn, not a line did he miss,
*   Not a line did he add.*

To judge from this statement, which is hardly likely to have
corresponded to the facts, the ancient myth writer deemed
it important to proclaim to his intended audience that he did
not create the poem himself, but merely reproduced what
a god had "shown" him in a vision. Nor is it unlikely that
his claim was doubted by those who heard it—it may well
be that the author himself was convinced of its truth. In any
case our poet is very eager to have his song endure through
the ages, and to this end he closes his epilogue as follows:

Irra heard and welcomed it,
The song of Ishum was pleasing to him,
*   All the gods revered it with him.*
And thus did mighty Irra speak:
*   "Who honors this song—in his sanctuary abundance will*
*   overflow,*
*   Who causes it to be neglected will not smell incense,*
*   The king who exalts my name will rule the four quarters,*
*   The prince who utters the glory of my might will*
*   have no rival,*
The singer who chants it will not die in slaughter,
*   To prince and king his word will be pleasing,*
The scribe who learns it by heart will be saved from the
*   enemy's land,*
In the assembly of the learned, where my name is honored
*   unceasingly,*
*   I shall open wide the ears,*

To the house where this tablet is stored,
    Should Irra be irate and Sibbi rage,
The sword of slaughter will come not near,
    Peace and well-being will be its lot,
May this song exist for all time,
    May it endure unto eternity,
All the lands shall hear and revere my might,
All the inhabited earth will say and exalt my name."

BIBLIOGRAPHY

Alexander Heidel. *The Babylonian Genesis*, second edition. University of Chicago Press, 1951.

A careful but rather heavy-handed translation and interpretation of *Enuma-Elish* and related texts. The book also contains a long chapter on the Old Testament parallels found in the Akkadian "creation" texts, which is quite detailed and informative, but whose conclusions are rather superficial and tendentious.

Thorkild Jacobsen in *The Intellectual Adventure of Ancient Man* (Editor, Henri Frankfort). University of Chicago Press, 1946.

An original, imaginative, stimulating, but rather subjective presentation of Sumero-Akkadian mythological and religious concepts by one of the world's leading cuneiformists; a penetrating and invaluable contribution in spite of its exaggerated emphasis on supposedly "mythopoeic mind" attributed to the ancients.

Samuel Noah Kramer. *Sumerian Mythology*. Memoir No. XXI of the American Philosophical Society, Philadelphia, 1944.

———. "Sumerian Myths and Epic Tales" in *Ancient Near Eastern Texts Relating to the Old Testament* (Editor, James Pritchard). Princeton University Press, 1957.

———. *History Begins at Sumer*. Doubleday Anchor Book, 1959.

E. A. Speiser. "Akkadian Myths and Epics" in *Ancient Near Eastern Texts Relating to the Old Testament* (Editor, James Pritchard). Princeton University Press, 1957.

Excellent, up-to-date translations of the Akkadian material. Prepared with care and precision, they retain much of the poetic rhythm and flavor of the original text.

Hittite Mythology

BY HANS G. GÜTERBOCK

Speaking of Hittite mythology we have to keep in mind that the Hittite Empire, as it spread over all of Anatolia and parts of Syria and north Mesopotamia, included regions of different background, culturally as well as ethnically and linguistically. Soon after the Hittite language had been deciphered in 1915, it was noticed that among the cuneiform tablets of the Hittite capital there were texts in several other languages beside Hittite. Apart from Sumerian and Akkadian, the languages of higher learning, a number of local languages could be identified. As the number of texts and, with it, our knowledge of these languages increased, it became apparent that there existed mythical tales in all languages. For a better understanding of the myths of ancient Anatolia it will therefore be best to start with a brief survey of the various languages, so as to enable us to attribute the individual myths to the different components of Hittite civilization.

The oldest population of the central part of the Anatolian plateau whose language is known are the Hattians. Their language does not belong to any of the better-known linguistic groups but rather stands by itself, with a vague, though possible, relation to some of the idioms spoken in recent times in the Caucasus. The Hittites called this language

Copyright © 1961 by Hans G. Güterbock. This is an adaptation of a chapter in the author's forthcoming book *The Art and Literature of the Hittites* to be published by The University of Chicago Press.

hattili, that is, the language of the country of Hatti. While taking over the name of that country for their own kingdom, the Hittites reserved the term *hattili* for the language of the old inhabitants in contrast to their own Indo-European language, which they called *nesili* after the town of Nesa, the center of their own first settlement. Since moderns had already used the name "Hittite" for the official *nesili* language, they had to invent another term for *hattili*, namely, "Hattic." We thus say "Hattic" for the non-Indo-European *hattili* language, but Hittite or sometimes, for clarity's sake, "Nesian" for the Indo-European *nesili* language, which was the official language of the kingdom and, as such, most productive in literature.

There are two more Indo-European languages in Anatolia beside Hittite: Luwian and Palaic. Palaic was spoken in the north (according to the most likely localization proposed, in Paphlagonia, northwest of Hatti); like Hittite, it was superimposed on a Hattic substrate. Luwian, on the other hand, was spoken in the south: probably in the southwest and certainly in the Cilician plain. We have to assume that the Luwians, too, superseded a population that spoke another language, but this substrate still remains unknown and unnamed. The language written with the so-called Hittite hieroglyphs is nothing else but a Luwian dialect. But since no mythological material has so far been found in hieroglyphic inscriptions—which, for the most part, are of votive character—we may safely leave hieroglyphic Luwian out of our consideration.

There finally is the non-Indo-European Hurrian language of north Mesopotamia and north Syria. The Hurrian element came to play an important part in Hittite civilization, especially in the New Kingdom or Empire period (fourteenth and thirteenth centuries B.C.), during which probably the dynasty and certainly many scribes were of Hurrian background. Kizzuwatna, the region in southeastern Anatolia including the Cilician plain, was the one Hittite province in which Hurrian scribal schools must have flourished most prominently. Since, as we have seen, Luwian was also spoken in Cilicia, we find a certain amount of linguistic mixture in that region, as evidenced by Hurrian loanwords in Luwian and by Luwian loanwords in Hittite texts dealing with Hurrian myths.

Our task, then, will be to ascribe, as far as possible, the individual myths to these various ethno-linguistic groups: Hattic, Nesian (Hittite), Palaic, Luwian, and Hurrian. In so doing we immediately make an observation concerning the literary form in which mythological tales have been handed down: only the myths of foreign origin were written as real literary compositions—we may call them epics—whereas those of local Anatolian origin were committed to writing only in connection with rituals. By foreign origin in this context we mean mainly Hurrian; beside it, Babylonian, for which it can be shown that Hurrian served as intermediary, and Canaanite, for which we can only assume that the way of borrowing went from Syria via Cilicia to the Hittite capital. By local Anatolian we mean the material perserved in Hattic, Palaic, and Luwian, and those Hittite myths whose protagonists are local, chiefly Hattic, deities.

In Hattic we have, apart from brief and, as yet, hardly intelligible allusions to mythological concepts, only one little story: "The Moon Who Fell from Heaven."[1] Although this tale is contained in a bilingual text where the Hattic original is provided with a Hittite translation, the story itself is far from clear. We can only make out that the moon fell down from heaven and that various deities, among them the Storm-god, saw it and sent messengers after it. From the ritual that precedes and follows the tale we learn that it was told "when the Storm-god thunders" and that the Storm-god with his helpers, the clouds, thunders, and rains, received offerings; so the story seems to have been told *in maiorem gloriam* of the Storm-god, who must have played a major part in it.

Much more important is the myth of "The God Who Disappeared." The best-preserved versions of this myth are in Hittite, but the locale as well as the *dramatis personae* clearly point to a Hattic background. There are many versions of this myth. Not only do we find different deities in the role of the Vanished God, but even the versions dealing with one and the same god differ in detail. This textual instability is certainly the result of the non-literary character of the texts: all versions were written down in connection with a ritual. Contrary to what might be expected on the analogy of—real or alleged—myths of "dying gods" of other peoples,[2] this ritual has nothing to do with seasonal patterns but rather serves to reconcile the vanished deity with a certain individual, who may be a queen or a private person, and to secure well-being, probably also offspring, for that person and his or her household. Nor does the god die in these Hittite tales; he rather goes into hiding, as we shall see.

In the best-known version of this myth the god who disappears is Telipinu, and the story is therefore mostly referred to as the Telipinu Myth. The name of the god is Hattic. Telipinu is a son of the great Storm-god, and he himself bears many traits of a Storm-god.[3] There is also a version in which the vanished god is simply called Storm-god; since this version has never been translated in full, and since it contains an episode not included in the Telipinu version, it may be good to give a translation of it here.[4] (Brackets indicate restorations and parentheses, additions made for the sake of idiom or clarity; roman type indicates uncertainty of translation or restoration.)

The beginning of the story, which must have contained a description of the god's anger and probably a statement of its cause, is so fragmentary that it cannot be understood. In another version of the Storm-god myth[5] it is said that the god "was angry at (queen) Ashmunikal" and that in his rage "he put his right shoe on his left foot . . . and left." This is immediately followed by the description of the results of the Storm-god's leaving. At this point our main version of the Storm-god myth becomes available, in part restored from the Telipinu version.

Fog *seized the windows, smoke seized the house:*
In the fireplace the logs were "oppressed" (*smouldering*).

On the pedestal the gods were "oppressed,"
in the fold the sheep were "oppressed,"
in the corral the cows were "oppressed":
The ewe refused its lamb, the cow refused its calf.
. . . . (two and one-half fragmentary lines not paralleled by
        the Telipinu version)
    Barley and emmer-wheat no longer grow,
cattle, sheep and humans no longer become pregnant,
and even those who are pregnant do not give birth.
    The mountains dried up, the trees dried up
(so that) shoots did not come (forth).
The meadows dried up, the springs dried up.
    [*The great Sun*]-*god prepared a feast and invited the*
        thousand gods.
They ate but could not satisfy their hunger,
they drank but could not satisfy their thirst.
    [*The Father of the Storm-god sa*]*id* [*to the gods*]:
"*My son* [*is not there; he became enraged*]
[*and carried away*] *growth,*
he carried away everything good!"
    The great gods and the small gods set out to search for
        the Storm-god.
The Sun-god sent out the swift Eagle (saying):
"*Go, search the high mountains,*
search the deep valleys,
search the darkblue waves!"
    The Eagle went but did not find him.
The Eagle swiftly brought the Sun-god news:
"*The high mountains I searched,*
the deep valleys I searched,
the darkblue waves I searched,
but I did not find him, the Storm-god of Heaven!"
    The Storm-god's Father went to his (i.e., the Storm-
        god's) Grandfather and said to him:
"*Who sinned (so that) the seed perished and everything*
        dried up?"
The Grandfather said:
"*No one sinned, but you alone sinned!*"

The Storm-god's Father replied:
"In no way did I sin!"
But the Grandfather said:
"This matter I shall investigate,
and (if I find you guilty) I shall kill you!
Now go, search for the Storm-god!"
     The Storm-god's Father went to Hannahanna of the Gul-
     sas (the Mother-goddess),
Hannahanna of the Gulsas said to the Storm-god's Father:
"Why did you come?"
The Storm-god's Father said:
"The Storm-god became enraged,
(so) everything dried up and the seed perished.
Now my father says to me:
'It is your fault!
I shall investigate the matter and kill you!'
Now, how shall I proceed? What has happened?"
     Hannahanna replied:
"Fear not!
If it is your fault I shall put it straight,
and if it is not your fault I shall (also) put it straight.
Go, search for the Storm-god
(while) his Grandfather has not yet heard (about it)!"
     The Storm-god's Father said:
"Where shall I go and search?"
Hannahanna replied:
"I shall hand him over to you.
Go, bring (me) [the Bee]!
I myself shall instruct it,
and it will search for [the Storm-god]."
     The Storm-god's Father said t[o Hannahanna]:
"The great gods and the small gods searched for him
and did not find him;
shall now this Bee go and search for him?
Its wings are weak, and it is weak itself:
They will........!"
     Hannahanna replied:
"[.......] not [.......]"

In this version the continuation is lost. Since the individual versions differ in detail, it is better to refrain from a verbal restoration taken from other versions. It seems likely, however, that Hannahanna, in the speech that originally followed, dispelled the misgivings expressed by the Storm-god's Father about the Bee's fitness and, after the Bee had been brought into her presence, gave it instructions for the search. In a small fragment of which it is not clear whether it belongs to this particular version but which at least deals with the Storm-god,[6] parts of these instructions and of the ensuing search are preserved, and in this context "a grove at the town of Lihzina" is mentioned, that is, the god's hiding place where the Bee found him.

The corresponding section of the Telipinu version tells the story roughly as follows: Following Hannahanna's instructions, the Bee searches everywhere until it finds the god sleeping in a grove at Lihzina. (Note that this town, although mentioned as the hiding place of both Telipinu and the Storm-god in the two versions of our myth, is known from ritual texts as a cult center of the Storm-god only.) The Bee stings the god, thus awakening him. As a result his anger only increases; he now brings destruction over man and beast and the whole land. The gods, left in consternation, have recourse to magic.

In our Storm-god version the corresponding parts are lost. What is left of the second column of the tablet is very fragmentary and without parallel. It completely differs from the part of the Telipinu version just outlined, but we cannot tell yet whether we have here a different story or merely an addition.

The entreaty and ritual aimed at bringing the vanished god back follow the same patterns in all versions, though with variations in detail; we may safely leave them aside.[7] The ritual is followed by the narrative of the god's return:

The Storm-god returned to his house and took account of his land.
The fog left the window, the smoke left the house.

[On the pedestal the gods] were set straight,
in the fireplace the logs were set straight,
[in the fold] the sheep were set straight,
in the corral the cows were set straight.
[The mother] guided [her child],
the ewe guided her lamb,
the cow [guided her calf],
[the Storm-god] guided [the king and queen]
and took account of them for life and well-being [to the end
           of days].

As said before, various deities are cast in the role of the Vanished God. Telipinu and the Storm-god are the most prominent and happen to be those dealt with in the best-preserved texts. Similar myths about other deities are less intelligible, in part because of their bad state of preservation, in part because of philological difficulties. A story in which the Sun-god disappears and "Rigor" or "Paralysis" seizes all nature[8] belongs in the latter category. Some fragmentary texts contain a story similar to the Telipinu myth but dealing with Anzili and Zukki, deities of unknown linguistic background.[9] In a story that differs greatly in detail we find the Bee sent out to search for Inara, who is called the daughter of the Storm-god.[10] The motif of the fury of the deity, but without the description of the disappearance and its consequences, is found in texts dealing with the Storm-god of the town of Kuliwisna[11] and with the Mother-goddess, Hannahanna.[12] The rituals performed to appease these deities are very similar to, in part even identical with, those connected with the Telipinu and Storm-god myths. Whether these texts never had the mythological tale or whether it is only lost in the existing fragments remains an open question.

What matters is that in the texts mentioned so far the mythological tales are closely connected with ritual. The texts themselves were handbooks to be used whenever the occasion arose for the performance of the magic rites described in them. Thus they fall into a large group of magic rituals containing shorter or longer mythological tales. To mention only two examples for many: a ritual against paralysis contains the story of how nature was "bound," how the news reached Kamrusepa, the goddess of magic, and how she "'loosened" everything that was "bound."[18] In a ritual for the erection of a new palace, one of many mythological passages reads as follows:[14]

> When the king enters the house (the new palace), the Throne calls the Eagle: "Come! I send you to the sea. But when you go (there), look in the green forest (and see) who is sitting (there)!"
>
> The Eagle replies: "I looked! Istustaya and Papaya, the primeval Netherworld goddesses, are sitting there bowing down."
>
> The Throne answers: "And what are they doing?" The Eagle replies: "(One) holds a spindle, they (both) hold filled mirrors. And they are spinning the king's years. And of the years there is no limit or counting!"

The deified Throne is a Hattic goddess; Istustaya and Papaya are Hattic deities, too, who are elsewhere mentioned together with other Netherworld deities, the most prominent of whom is the Sun-goddess of the Earth. Here we get a glimpse of the Anatolian concepts of the Netherworld, which include goddesses spinning the thread of life like the Parcae. This similarity should, however, not be taken as evidence for Indo-European origin, since the goddesses are Hattic. Incidentally, the "filled mirrors" have been explained as flat pans filled with water that makes a reflection. The whole passage is typical of the device of using a brief mythological tale in a ritual: it is, of course, told in order to secure long life for the owner of the new palace; the tale itself has magic power here as in the other rituals.

Returning to the myth of the Vanished God, we saw that of the deities cast in that role, Telipinu has a Hattic name; Inara, too, is connected with the Hattic element, whereas "Storm-god" and "Sun-god" are universal great gods whose names are written with word signs. These gods existed also in the Hattic pantheon, where their names, Taru and Estan, respectively, are known, and there is nothing against the assumption that our stories deal with the Hattic Taru and Estan. Yet the texts are in Hittite, which means that the speakers of Indo-European Hittite adopted the myths together with the gods of their predecessors.

Among the Indo-European languages of Asia Minor there is one other that superseded a Hattic substrate: Palaic. One of the few Palaic texts known so far contains a mythological tale followed by a kind of hymn.[15] Although we still understand very little of the language we can see that here the tale contains the motif of the feast at which the gods "eat but cannot satisfy their hunger, drink but cannot satisfy their thirst." The town of Lihzina is also mentioned here. The hymnic part of the text contains the name of the god Zaparwa, the main god of the Palaians, who, as has been proposed, may well be a Storm-god. The two features mentioned remind us of the myth of the Vanished God, but the rest of the story, as far as it can be made out, seems to run differently.[16] Although we cannot, therefore, claim that the Palaic myth deals with Zaparwa as Vanished God, it is significant that it shares some motifs with the Hittite tales on that theme; these common motifs, at least, if not the whole stories, should then go back to the common Hattic substrate.

Luwian texts are almost exclusively of the magic type, either short spells or longer incantations inserted in ritual texts. Here again a myth is told in such a text.[17] Although very little of the story can as yet be understood, it seems to contain the motif of a feast prepared by the Sun-god, but in a completely different setting: this feast is closely linked with the cause of the illness which the ritual is intended to heal.

So far we have dealt with mythological tales written down in connection with magic rituals. There are, however, also tales connected with the cult. The best known of these is the myth of the fight between the Storm-god and the Dragon; *illuyanka*, thus far taken as proper name of the monster, is nothing but the common noun meaning "dragon" or "serpent." The text states expressly that the story was recited at the *purulli* festival of the Storm-god, one of the great yearly cult ceremonies.[18]

> *Thus speaks Kella, [the priest] of the Storm-god of Nerik:*
> "(These are) the words of the *purulli of the Storm-god of Heaven:*
> When they speak as follows:
> 'Let the land thrive and prosper
> and let the land be protected!'
> and if it, then, thrives and prospers,
> then they perform the *purulli festival.*"

The story itself, whose first version follows immediately, is well known and need not be repeated here in full. In a first round the Storm-god is defeated by the Dragon, so he asks the other gods for help. The goddess Inara helps him by preparing a feast and securing the assistance of a mortal man whom she promises her love. When the Dragon is drunk from the drinks offered him by Inara, the mortal helper binds him, whereupon the Storm-god returns and kills the Dragon. The story then goes on to tell the fate of the man who enjoyed the love of the goddess: He is told not to look out of the window, of course does so as soon as the goddess has left, longs for his family and, when he expresses the wish to go home, is punished in some way. The text is broken here, but we may assume that he was killed.

Unfortunately the break in the tablet makes it almost impossible to understand the passage immediately following the end of this version. In it the king and "the first *purulli*" are mentioned. The next paragraph reads:

> Mount Zaliyanu is the first of all!
> When it has apportioned rains to Nerik,
> the herald brings offering bread from Nerik.
> Mount Zaliyanu asked for rain:
> he brings [. . . . . .] bread to it.

Thereafter the tablet is broken again. Obscure as this passage may be, it somehow links the story with the important cult city of Nerik (whose priest was mentioned as author of the text in the introduction) and mentions the rain-giving, deified mountain, Zaliyanu, which is near that town.

Where the text becomes available after the gap we find the second version of the Dragon fight. In it, too, the Dragon at first defeats the Storm-god. Here he robs him of his heart and his eyes. The Storm-god then marries a mortal maid, daughter of a poor man, and has a son from her. When the latter grows up he wants to marry the daughter of the Dragon. His father instructs him to ask for the stolen heart and eyes when entering the house of the bride (the legal background is the Hittite custom that a wealthy father can get a husband for his daughter by paying the so-called bride price to the young man; the statement in the story that the lad's mother was poor thus gains perspective). The demand is met, the Storm-god regains his former stature and can engage in a new battle which, we are told, is to take place "by the sea again" (so it seems the first fight was by the sea as well; that passage is damaged). By marrying the Dragon's daughter, however, the son of the Storm-god has taken on an obligation of loyalty to his father-in-law; he therefore takes the latter's side and asks his own father not to spare him; whereupon "the Storm-god killed both the Dragon and his own son."

At the end of this second—and more sophisticated—version there is another gap, after which there follows a very difficult text, of which only one detail is of interest here: Zaliyanu, mentioned earlier in the text as a mountain, is here said to be the wife of Zaskhapuna. Zaskhapuna was once believed to be the Hittite name of the Storm-god, and I personally still consider this a possibility; at least it can be *one* name of the god beside others. According to its form it is a Hattic name. Our text calls Zaskhapuna "the greatest of all gods," a distinction certainly befitting a Storm-god more than any other deity.

We saw that the Dragon Fight Myth is linked to the city of Nerik by the office of its author and in the section following the first version. The Storm-god of Nerik himself, however, is not mentioned in the text. This young Storm-god, who was a son of the great Storm-god, had an important cult. There is a ritual aimed at bringing him back to Nerik from other towns to which he had gone.[19] This may be a mythological expression for the well-known historical fact that Nerik was for a time taken away from the Hittites by the Gasga people of the north but later regained. The text, however, explains the god's absence by his anger—a familiar motif. The god is called back to Nerik from wherever he may be. One passage (rev. 11–22) has a mythological flavor; it deals with the river Marassanta, the Halys of the ancients, now the Red River of Turkey:

> You, o Marassanta, are close to the heart of the Storm-
>   god of Nerik.
> The Marassanta formerly flowed astray,
> but the Storm-god turned it and made it flow toward the sun
> and (thus) made it flow near Nerik.
> The Storm-god said to the Marassanta river:
> "If some one infuriates the Storm-god of Nerik
> (so that) he walks away from Nerik and the couch,
> then you, o Marassanta, don't let him go to another river (or)
>   another spring!"
> The Storm-god of Heaven said to the Marassanta river:
> "(This) shall be (a matter of) an oath for you:
> do not alter your course!"
> The Marassanta did not alter its course.
> You, o gods, did it!
> Now let the river Nakkiliata call the Storm-god of Nerik.
> From under the sea (and) the [waves],
> from under the nine river-beds let it bring him back!

Other parts of this rather difficult text are prayer-like invocations directed to the Storm-god of Nerik himself, among other things asking him to "bring rain down from heaven" (rev. 60). The passage translated above, however, stands out as a rare Hittite example of an etiological myth: it was the great Storm-god of Heaven himself who diverted the course of the largest river of Central Anatolia so as to make it flow near the cult center of his son.

What we have surveyed so far does not cover all myths of Central Anatolia but may suffice to give a general picture of their character. Turning now to the myths of foreign origin, we may note in passing that the Hittites knew the Babylonian Gilgamesh Epic. The Akkadian version was treated in the scribal schools as is witnessed by a fragment of it found at Boghazköy. Beside it there are fragments of a Hurrian and of a Hittite version. The latter shows that the Hittites adapted the epic to their own sphere of interest by shortening those parts that dealt specifically with Uruk, the Sumerian home town of the hero.[20] And from the former, that is, from the very existence of a Hurrian version, we may gather that the Hittites became acquainted with the epic through the Hurrians; the same is true, as we shall see, of other Babylonian mythological concepts.

As stated at the outset, there is a whole epic literature in Hittite that deals with Hurrian and Canaanite deities or with human heroes bearing Hurrian names. In contrast to the Anatolian myths, which we found connected with rituals, these tales of foreign background are real literary compositions often called "songs" in the sense of "epics." Many of them can only be mentioned here very briefly. Among them there is, first, the epic of the hero Gurparanzakh. The name of the hero is Hurrian; it is derived from Aranzakh, the Hurrian name of the river Tigris, and this river, personified, plays a part in the story. The setting is, however, in Akkad, the famous north-Babylonian city; so this is another example of a Babylonian theme transmitted to the Hittites by the Hurrians, although no Akkadian prototype has yet been found. Second, there is the story of the hunter Keshshi, of which there are fragments of a Hittite and a Hurrian version, while an Akkadian version formed part of the reading material of the scribal school at Tell el-Amarna in Egypt. Third, the story of Appu and his two sons, Evil and Good, and fourth, a myth about the Sun-god and a cow, in which the cow bears a human child that is later found by a fisherman (possibly these two fragments belong to the same story as indicated by the end of the Appu text, where a cow is introduced and the Sun-god makes a prediction concerning it). Fifth, there is the myth about the serpent Hedammu, a voracious monster that is checked by the goddess Ishtar's womanly charms.[21]

Of Canaanite or Syrian myths we have Hittite versions of two: one deals with the god Elkunirsa and his wife Ashertu, that is, *El qônê ereṣ* "El the Creator of the Earth" and Asherah.[22] Of the existing fragments, one tells that a god whose name is written with the word-sign for the Storm-god but who must in this context be Ba'al-Hadad, visits his father Elkunirsa while the latter is camping out near the Euphrates; he tells his father that when he came to his house, Asherah made him advances which he refused. El advises him to go back and threaten her. In the second fragment a goddess called Ishtar, which again stands for the West-Semitic Astarte or 'Anat, in the guise of a bird overhears a bedroom conversation of El and Asherah and tells it to her brother, the Storm-god (Hadad).

The other Syrian myth in Hittite deals with an adventure of Mount Pishaisha. This mountain must be in Syria since it is mentioned in treaties among the deities listed as witnesses together with the equally deified mountains Lebanon and Hermos. In our epic fragment Mount Pishaisha rapes the goddess Ishtar, is threatened with punishment by her, and asks for mercy.[23]

The best preserved and, by their contents, most interesting Hittite epics reflecting Hurrian myths, however, are those dealing with Kumarbi, "the Father of the Gods." So far we have two, or perhaps three, such compositions. Of the first, the original title is lost; since its main theme is the sequence of gods who were kings in heaven, it has been called "The Kingship in Heaven."[24] The first part of this epic is preserved in a badly mutilated single copy; of other copies we only have one small fragment and possibly a second. The text begins with a proem:

[Let . . . . and . . . .] who are primeval deities hearken,
let [. . . . and . . .], the mighty gods, hearken!
Let Na[ra Napshara, Mink]i Ammunki hearken,
let Ammezzaddu [and . . . .], father and mother, hearken!
    Let [. . . .] and Ishkhara, father and mother, hearken,
let Enlil [and Ninlil], who are exceedingly mighty, ever-
        lasting deities, hearken,
let [. . . .] and [. .]ulkulimma hearken!

The story itself follows immediately:

    Formerly, in former years, Alalu was king in Heaven.
Alalu was sitting on the throne,
and mighty Anu, the first of the gods, stood before him.
He bowed down to his feet
and put the drinking cups into his hand.
    For nine "counted" years Alalu was king in Heaven.
In the ninth year Anu gave battle against Alalu.
He defeated Alalu,
and he (Alalu) fled before him
and he went down to the Dark Earth.
Down to the Dark Earth he went,
but on the throne Anu sat.
Anu was sitting on his throne,
and mighty Kumarbi gave him to drink:
He bowed down to his feet
and put the drinking cups into his hand.
    For nine "counted" years Anu was king in Heaven.
In the ninth year Anu had to give battle against Kumarbi:
Kumarbi, Alalu's offspring, gave battle against Anu.
Anu no longer withstood Kumarbi's eyes;
he slipped out of his hands and fled, Anu (did),
and went up to the sky.
After him Kumarbi rushed
and seized him, Anu, by his feet
and pulled him down from the sky.
    He bit his loins
(so that) his manhood united with Kumarbi's interior like
        bronze (i.e., as copper and tin unite to form bronze).

When it united,
when Kumarbi swallowed Anu's manhood,
he rejoiced and laughed.
Anu turned back
and to Kumarbi he began to speak:
"Thou rejoicest about thine interior
because thou hast swallowed my manhood!
    "Do not rejoice about thine interior!
Into thine interior I have put a (heavy) load:
First I have made thee pregnant with the weighty Storm-
            god;
second I have made thee pregnant with the river Aranzakh
            (Tigris), the irresistible;
third I have made thee pregnant with the weighty god Tash-
            mishu,
and two (other) terrible gods have I put as load into thine
            interior.
Thou shalt come to stop hitting the rocks of Mount Tassa
            with thy head!"
    When Anu had finished speaking
he went up to the sky.
But (Kumarbi) hid himself
and spat out of his mouth, he, [Kumarbi,] the wise king.
Out of his mouth he spat spittle [and the manhood] mixed to-
            gether.
What Kumarbi had sp[at] out,
Mount Kanzura . . . . fear.
    Kumarbi went in rage into Nip[pur, his town].
. . . . he sat down.
Kumarbi did not [. . . . .] count [the months].
The ninth month came, ... (rest of column lost).

Counting months is a common motif introducing childbirth.
In the second column of the tablet, where the surface is so
rubbed off that a satisfactory text cannot be established,
childbirth is indeed the theme, although it is of unusual
nature. It seems that here several deities who are in Kumarbi's
"interior" discuss with him through what opening of his body

they should make their appearance. Two of the deities
mentioned here are not among the three named by Anu: one
is Marduk (the god of Babylon, here represented by a rare
Sumerian name), the other's name is written with the word
sign KA.ZAL, meaning "lust." These may be the "two terrible
gods" mentioned without name by Anu. Only the last child
is one of those announced by name: the Storm-god. Although
the name of this god is here, as elsewhere, always written
with a word sign, we may safely call the god by his Hurrian
name, Teshub, in this Hurrian myth.

The third column is badly damaged, too, so that here
again a coherent text cannot be established. Following a suggestion made, we may insert in the gap between columns ii
and iii another fragment (which would be the third copy
alluded to above).[25] In it "the king of Kummiya," who can
only be Teshub (as we shall see from the Ullikummi Epic),
addresses Anu; he reminds him of the fact that "[Kumarbi,]
the Father of Gods, though a male, has given birth" to him;
he also mentions several hard tasks that his father gave him
(not otherwise known) and lists the divine powers with which
he was endowed (a passage similar to a listing of the powers
given Marduk in the second column). Following the same
scholar's suggestion we assume that, where the third column
of the main copy sets in with half-preserved lines, Teshub
asks Anu to kill Kumarbi.[26] In his reply Anu seems to dissuade Teshub from his plan of killing Kumarbi and speaks
of the kingship in terms that are too fragmentary for full
understanding. The suggestion that Anu proposes to make
Ea king[27] seems to agree with what can be gathered from the
following sections. After Anu's long speech one may restore
(column iii lines 19–22):

> When Teshub [heard these (Anu's?) words],
> [they] became loathsome to his heart,
> [and in anger] he spoke to the bull Sheri:
> "[. . . . .] are coming against [me] for battle!
> . . . . . "

Sheri is one of Teshub's sacred bulls. Several gods are mentioned in the fragmentary continuation; that Teshub pronounced a curse over them can be gathered from the reply (lines 31–32):

> The bull Sheri re[plied] to Teshub:
> "My lord! Why didst thou curse them? . . . . ."

Again the rest of the speech is beyond repair. After a gap the curse is still being referred to. This time it is Ea of whom we read (lines 67–72):

> When Ea had [hear]d those words
> they became loathsome to his heart.
> Ea began to reply these words to (the god) . . . -ura:
> "Do not pronounce curses against me!
> He who cursed me,
> [why] does he curse me?
> Now thou who [tellest me these words] again,
> thou art (thereby) cursing me.
> A dish [that . . . . . .] with beer,
> that dish will break to pieces!"

There follows another gap, after which there is childbirth again. This time it is Earth who gives birth to two children. Unfortunately we can tell neither who these children are nor who begot them. The logic of the story would require that we should hear what happened to the part of the seed that Kumarbi spat out, and Earth would be a good candidate for the one who received and bore it. In a fragment which partly restores the fourth column, however, mention is made of a "wagon," and a word that may be restored as "manhood" once follows "wagon" in an otherwise broken line. It has been suggested on these grounds that the children grew out of Wagon's seed and that with "the wagon" the constellation of the Great Wagon (or Great Dipper) is meant. To complicate things further, it is Ea who counts the months and to whom the news of the happy event is brought. Thus, the question of who is the father must be left open. Mention of a throne and the title king occurring in broken context in the vicinity of the name Ea might indicate that at this point it is indeed Ea who is king among the gods, which would agree with the tentative interpretation of the third column given above. It has to be stressed, however, that the present state of preservation of the tablet renders all these interpretations highly hypothetical. Shortly after the birth of Earth's two children the tablet ends.

Summing up the contents of this epic composition, we find that in its first part it tells how the celestial kingship passed from Alalu to Anu and from Anu to Kumarbi. Of these gods, Anu is, of course, the well-known Babylonian god whose name is Sumerian An "Sky"; a god called Alala is at least attested in a Babylonian list of gods as one of Anu's ancestors. That we are dealing with generations is stated in our text where Kumarbi is called Alalu's offspring. The name Kumarbi is Hurrian; Kumarbi is sometimes equated with the Sumerian Enlil, though—as we shall see—not consistently. The fact that in our text Kumarbi goes to Nippur seems to indicate that its author made that identification, since the Babylonian town of Nippur is well known as the cult city of Enlil. The parallels that exist between this story and both Hesiod's *Theogony* and the Phoenician mythology as related by Philo Byblius have often been discussed; a few remarks may therefore suffice here.

In Hesiod the sequence is Ouranos ("Sky")—Kronos—Zeus; the fight between Ouranos and Kronos includes the motif of castration as does the fight between Anu and Kumarbi in the Hittite text. There is in Hesiod no generation corresponding to Alalu. Philo Byblius, however, in the outline of Phoenician mythology which he ascribes to a certain Sankhuniaton, has that generation. Here the sequence is:

1. Phoenician Elioun, Greek Hypsistos "The Highest," corresponding to Alalu;
2. Greek Ouranos "Sky," Phoenician name not given, corresponding to Anu;
3. Phoenician El, Greek Kronos, corresponding to Kumarbi;

4. elsewhere Baʻal-Hadad is mentioned as the chief god, corresponding to Teshub and Zeus.

The fact that Philo knew of the first generation omitted by Hesiod is a point in favor of the authenticity of his account; similarly, the discovery of Ugaritic literature has shown that a complex mythology indeed existed in Syria some fifteen centuries before Philo.

What exactly followed Kumarbi's victory over Anu and his pregnancy incurred in this fight is not clear because of the deplorable state of the text. Teshub is born, somehow. That he became king in Heaven at some point of the story may safely be assumed because of his role as supreme god in the actual cult of both Hurrians and Hittites; but at what point of the story this happened we do not know. Nor is Ea's role too clear (Ea, the wise god, is a figure familiar from Sumero-Babylonian religion, too). We found some indications that he may have been made king (after Kumarbi?), but the bad state of the text does not allow for a definite statement. In another text, to which we shall presently turn, Ea rather is the one who appoints and deposes celestial rulers. This text[28] deals with the temporary rule of a deity whose name is written with the word sign KAL, which, unfortunately, is ambiguous. Neither the reading Sumerian *lama*, Akkadian *lamassu* "protective deity," nor the reading Inara— the name of an Anatolian goddess whom we met in the Dragon Fight Myth—fits the context which seems to deal with a rather unruly male god. So we shall simply use the form KAL instead of the unknown real name of the god. As far as the sequence of events is concerned, it would seem that KAL's rule interrupted that of Teshub, since it seems that KAL takes the rule from him at the beginning but has to recognize him as his master in the end.

The beginning of the text is lost and its first column badly mutilated. At one point one may restore (column i, lines 18–26):

> KAL [. . . . .] *and* to[ok] *the reins and* [*the* whip] *out of the Storm-god's hand.*

The [Storm]-*god turned back and* [*to KAL*] *began to speak:*
"[*My*] *re*[*ins and whip*] *thou hast taken from my hand
and* [*taken them into thine own*] *hand.
Those reins* [*are . . . . . .*]!
*Thou wilt be called to the . . . . house,
and the reins* [*. . . . . .*"].

There follow a few lines so fragmentary that they are beyond repair, and then a lacuna of some thirty to forty lines.
In it, it may have been told that Ea appointed KAL to be
king, if the following restoration is correct (ii 1–9):

> [*When*] *KAL* [*heard*] *Ea's words,*
> *he* [*. . . . .*]
> [*and*] *began to* [*rejoi*]*ce.*
> [*. . . . . .*] *he ate and drank,*
> [*. . . . . u*]*p to Heaven he went,*
> *up to Heaven* [*. . . . .*] *he* [*. . . .*]*ed.*
> [*In the years that*] *KAL* [*was king*] *in Heaven,*
> *in those years* [*. . . . . . .*].

Whether the following lines contained the description of a
time of disorder and distress or rather, as has been proposed,
of blessing, is uncertain because of their fragmentary state.
After another gap and some broken lines at the beginning
of the third column we read (iii 5–44):

> *KAL began to* [*reply*] *to . . . . . :*
> "[*. . . . . . .*] *I determine!*
> *These gods* [*grew*] *big,*
> [*they . . . . . .*] *and they arose,*
> (*but*) *I* [*do not fear*] *them at all;*
> *I shall not* [*put*] *bread into their mouths!*
> *The road they are to go*
> *and the road they are to come,*
> *those I, KAL, king of Heaven, determine for the gods!*"
> *The* impetuous *winds brought the* n[*ews*] (variant:
>   *KAL's evil words*) *to Ea* (*while he was*) *on his way.*
> (Variant adds: *When Ea heard KAL's* [*words*],
> *his* [mind became angry].)

Ea began to speak to Kumarbi:
"Come! Let us go back!
This KAL whom we made king in Heaven,
just as he himself is rebellious,
so he made the countries rebellious,
and no one any longer gives bread or drink offerings to the
          gods!"
    Ea and Kumarbi turned [their faces]:
Ea [went] to Abzuwa,
but Kumarbi went away to Du[. . .].
Ea made a messenger stand up in front [of himself]
and undertook to dispatch him to KAL (saying):
"Go, speak these words to [KAL]:
'Ever since we made thee king in Heaven
[thou] hast not done anything!
Never hast thou called [an assembly . . . .' "] *(end of*
          speech fragmentary).
The messenger departed
and recounted [Ea's words to KAL] exactly.
    When [KAL] had heard [Ea's words],
he began to [. . . . .].
Ea began to speak to Izzummi[, his vizier]:
"Go down to the Dark Earth,
and the words that I speak to thee,
go and tell them to Nara Napshara, my brother (saying):
'Take my speech and hearken to my words!
[KAL] has made me angry,
so I deposited him from the kingship in Heaven.
    " 'That KAL whom we made king in Heaven,*
just as he himself is rebellious,
so he made the countries rebellious,
and no one any longer gives bread or drink offerings to the
          gods.
Now, Nara, my brother, hear me!
And mobilize all the animals of the earth!
Mount Nasalma [. . . . . . .],
and unto his head [. . . . . !' "] (broken).

A small further fragment[29] seems to tell that Nara fulfilled Ea's wish. After another gap, someone (Ea?) gives orders on how to treat KAL, and the Storm-god and his vizier Ninurta carry that order out. It seems to consist of some bodily punishment involving mutilation. After it KAL speaks to the Storm-god, addressing him as "my lord" but apparently reminding him of the fact that he himself had been made king. The Storm-god gives a short reply most of which again is lost. There the tablet ends, and its colophon (the entry giving tablet number and title, always written at the end of a tablet) is broken in such a way that we learn neither the title of the work, nor whether this tablet forms part of the same epic as the one outlined before, nor whether the story continued.

The second (or, if the KAL text is a separate work, third) epic of the Kumarbi cycle is called "The Song of Ullikummi." Although it is a separate literary work its contents can be connected with the theme of the celestial kingship: Kumarbi tries to replace Teshub as king by the stone monster Ullikummi which he begets for this purpose.[30]

This epic also begins with a proem; its beginning is damaged, the fourth line reads:

Of Kumarbi, father of all gods, I shall sing.

There follows the beginning of the story:

Kumarbi takes wisdom unto his mind
and a bad "day" as evil (being) he raises.
Against Teshub he plans evil,
and against Teshub he raises a rival.
   Kumarbi [takes] wisdom unto his mind
and sticks it on like a bead.
   When Kumarbi had taken wisdom unto his mind,
he promptly rose from his chair.
Into his hand he took a staff,
upon his feet he put the swift winds as shoes.
He set out from his town Urkish
and came to (a place called) Cool Pond.

At Cool Pond a great Rock is lying:
Its length is three leagues,
but its width which it has below is [one] and a half leagues.
His (Kumarbi's) mind sprang forward,
he slept with the Rock,
and his manhood [flowed] into it.
Five times he took it,
[and again] ten times he took it.

Urkish, Kumarbi's home town, was in north Mesopotamia, the heartland of the Hurrians. After a gap there follows a passage in which Kumarbi is invited by the Sea; he follows the invitation and, after seven drinks, dispatches his vizier Mukishanu to the Waters with a message, the contents of which are lost. What this episode means in the story can only be guessed: presumably the two gods, Kumarbi and the Sea, agree that Kumarbi's future child should grow up in the sea. After another gap we read that the Rock bore a child:

[The midwives] brought him to birth,
and the Fate-goddesses and [Mother-goddesses lifted the child]
and placed him on Kumarbi's knees.
Kumarbi began to rejoice over his son,
he began to fondle him
and began to give him his dear name.
  Kumarbi began to speak to his own mind:
"What name shall I put on him,
on the son whom the Fate-goddesses and Mother-goddesses gave me?
Out of the body he sprang like a blade.
Let him go! Ullikummi be his name!
Let him go up to Heaven,
let him suppress Kummiya, the dear town!
Let him hit Teshub
and pound him like chaff
and crush him with his foot like an ant!

Let him break Tashmishu like a dry reed!
Let him scatter the gods down from Heaven like birds
and smash them like empty dishes!"

(Note the obvious etymological connection made here between the name given the child, Ulli-kummi, and the task given him, to destroy Kummiya, the city of Teshub. The following speech deals with the problem of letting the child grow up unnoticed.)

When Kumarbi had completed these words
he began (again) to speak to his own mind:
"To whom shall I give this son?
Who will [take] him and treat him as a gift?
[Who will . . . . .]
and [carry] him to the [Dark] Earth?
Let the Sun-god of Heaven [and the Moon-god] not see him!
Let Teshub, the brave king of Kummiya, not see him
and let him not kill him!
Let Ishtar, the queen of Nineveh, not see him
and let her not break him like a dry reed!"
Kumarbi began to speak to Impaluri:
"O Impaluri! The words which I speak to thee,
to my words lend thine ear!
Take a staff into thy hands,
put the swift winds as shoes upon thy feet!
Go to the Irshirra gods
and speak these strong words to the Irshirras:
'Come! Kumarbi, father of gods, calls you to his house!
The matter about which he calls you
[. . . . .].
Now come promptly!'
["Then the Irshirra]s will take the child,
and they [will carry] him to the [Dark] Earth.
The Irshirras [will . . . .],
but to the great [gods] he will not [be visible]."
[When] Impaluri [heard these words],
he took a staff into his hand . . . (etc.).

In true epic style the fulfillment of Kumarbi's command is
then told with identical words. The story continues:

When the Irshirras heard these words,
they [hurried], hastened.
[They rose from their seats]
and covered the way at once
and came to Kumarbi.
And Kumarbi began to speak to the Irshirras:
"Take [this child],
treat him as a gift
and carry him to the Dark Earth!
Hurry, hasten!
Put him on Ubelluri's right shoulder like a blade!
In one day he shall grow a yard,
but in one month he shall grow a furlong!
· · · · · · ·"

The Irshirras take the child, but first bring him to Enlil (who
is here taken as different from Kumarbi). Enlil sees that the
child's body is made of stone and immediately understands
the situation. He says:

"Of no one but of Kumarbi is this an evil plan!
Just as Kumarbi raised Teshub
so now he has raised this Stone as a rival against him."

Only after this interlude do the Irshirras put the child on
the shoulder of Ubelluri, who, as we learn later in the epic,
is a giant who carries Heaven and Earth, including the sea
(thus comparable to the Greek Atlas). There the stone child
grows up as fast as ordered. He grows in the sea, which
only comes to his waist, while his head reaches the sky. The
first among the gods to see him is the Sun-god, who decides
to break the news to Teshub.

When he saw the Sun-god coming
Tashmishu began [to speak to (his brother) Teshub]:
"Why does he come, the Sun-god of Heaven, the [king of]
*   the lands?*

The matter about which he comes,
that matter is [grave],
it is [not] *to be cast aside!*
Strong is it, the struggle,
strong is it, the battle!
Heaven's uproar it is,
the land's hunger and thirst it is!"

    Teshub began to speak to Tashmishu:
"Let them set up a chair for him to sit,
let them lay a table for him to eat!"

    While thus they were speaking
the Sun-god arrived at their [house].
They set up a chair for him to sit,
but he did not sit down;
they laid a table for him to eat,
but he did not reach out;
they gave him a cup,
but he did not put his lips to it.

    Teshub began to speak to the Sun-god:
"Is the chamberlain bad who set up the chair
so that thou sattest not down?
Is the steward bad who laid the table
so that thou atest not?
Is the cupbearer bad who gave thee the cup
so that thou drankest not?"

Here the first tablet ends. At the lost beginning of the second the Sun-god must have told Teshub and Tashmishu of the stone monster he had seen growing in the sea. Where the text becomes intelligible, the Sun-god finally is persuaded to take the food and drink offered him, and after the meal he returns to Heaven. After his departure the two brothers, Teshub and Tashmishu, decide to go and look for themselves; they are joined by their sister, Ishtar (Shaushga in Hurrian), who sees them leaving. All three ascend Mount Hazzi, a mountain on the shore of northern Syria known from Classical times as Casius and from Semitic sources as Zaphon.

They took one another by the hand
and went up to Mount Hazzi.
The king of Kummiya set his face,
he set his face upon the dreadful Stone.
He saw the dreadful Stone,
and from anger his [mind] was altered.
Teshub sat on the ground,
and his tears flowed forth like streams.
Teshub in tears spoke the word:
"Who will any longer endure this one's violence?
Who will any longer fight?
Who will any longer endure this one's fearfulness?"
Ishtar replied to Teshub:
"O my brother! He does not know . . . . or . . . . ,
but bravery has been tenfold given him!
. . . . . ."*

The continuation of Ishtar's speech is first fragmentary, then lost. Probably she tries to console and encourage her brother. After the gap we find her by the seashore, adorning herself and singing. She is told, however, (by a personified Wave?) that this is of no avail:

"In front of whom singest thou?
In front of whom fillest thou thy mouth with [songs]?
The man is deaf and hears not,
in his eyes he is blind and sees not!
And mercy he has not!
Go away, o Ishtar, and find thy brother
before the Stone becomes brave,
before the skull of his head becomes overwhelming!"

Ishtar takes the advice, throws away her ornaments and her musical instrument, and leaves, lamenting. After another gap we find Teshub giving Tashmishu orders for the preparation of battle. His war chariot and the two sacred bulls that are to pull it are to be readied. Furthermore,

"Let them call forth the thunderstorms,
let them call forth the rains and winds
. . . . !
The lightning which strongly flashes,
out of the bedchamber let them bring it!
And let them bring forth the chariots!
Now arrange, set them,
and word bring me back!"

The order is carried out; part of the preparations are lost at the end of the second tablet, as well as the beginning of the great battle in the following tablet. Obviously the "seventy gods" who participate in it on Teshub's side are unsuccessful against the Stone, who even overshadows Kummiya, Teshub's own town, where Hebat, his wife, is worrying about her husband's fate. A maidservant sent out by her returns without news. After another gap it is Tashmishu who, from the top of a tower, tells Hebat, who is on her roof, that her husband will have to give up his rule "until the years that have been decreed for him will be fulfilled."

When Hebat saw Tashmishu
she almost fell from the roof.
Had she taken a step,
she would have fallen from the roof,
but the palace women held her and let her not go.

Tashmishu then returns to Teshub and advises him to seek the help of the wise Ea. The two brothers go to Ea's abode where they approach him with great reverence. The passage in which they actually ask him for help is again lost, and so is Ea's reply to them. After the gap Ea goes to Enlil first and then to Ubelluri. He asks both whether they know of the stone monster created as a rival to Teshub. Enlil's reply is lost; the discourse with Ubelluri runs as follows:

Ea began to speak to Ubelluri:
"Knowest thou not, O Ubelluri?
Has no one brought thee word?

Knowest thou him not,
the swift god whom Kumarbi fashioned against the gods?
And that Kumarbi truly plans death for Teshub
and fashions a rival against him?
. . . .
Is it because thou art remote from the Dark Earth
that thou knowest not this swift god?"
        Ubelluri began to reply to Ea:
"When Heaven and Earth were built on me
I knew nothing.
But when it came to pass that Heaven and Earth were cut
                apart with a 'cutter,'
this, too, I knew not.
Now something makes my right shoulder hurt,
but I know not who he is, that god!"
        When Ea heard these words,
he turned Ubelluri's right shoulder:
there the Stone was standing on Ubelluri's right shoulder
                like a blade!

Ea then orders the Former Gods to produce the very tool with which once Heaven and Earth had been separated; now he will use it to separate the Stone from Ubelluri, on whom he has grown. This is obviously meant to break the Stone's power; for, after another gap, we find Ea telling Tashmishu:

> *"First I struck him, the Stone;*
> *now go ye and fight him again!"*

Delighted by this news, Tashmishu breaks it to the gods. Teshub mounts his chariot again, rides down to the sea with thunder, and engages in a fresh fight with the Stone. There follows an almost Homeric dialogue between the two adversaries, in which Ullikummi boasts of the role his father Kumarbi has assigned him. Thereafter the text is altogether lost, but we can safely assume that the outcome of this second battle was the final victory of Teshub. Such "happy end" is not only expected on the analogy of the Anatolian Dragon Fight story discussed above and of the Greek myth to be mentioned presently, but is required by the fact that in actual religion Teshub was the supreme god, so that the myth must have shown him victorious in the end.

The Greek parallel just alluded to is the story of Typhon. This monster arises as a new adversary to Zeus at the point of Hesiod's *Theogony* where Zeus has just gained power by his victory over Kronos and the other Titans. Later Greek tradition preserved details that fit our Hurro-Hittite myth even more closely. Thus one source says that Typhon grew out of an egg impregnated with the seed of Kronos. Other authors describe the first, unsuccessful battle as taking place at Mount Casius, that is, our Hazzi. Typhon himself was believed to have his home in Cilicia, and in an unpublished cuneiform text a mountain called Ullikummi is listed among the mountains of Kizzuwatna, that is, Cilicia.

Thus far the myths, to the extent that they can be understood or reconstructed. As said before, there are others, mostly in a bad state of preservation, and there probably were still others entirely unknown to us. From the foregoing excerpts the difference between Anatolian and foreign myths will have become clear. The Kumarbi cycle is a work of literature. Whether the existing Hittite version is a translation of a Hurrian original (as suggested in the past) or whether it is the creation of an author or authors who only drew their subject matter from Hurrian tradition but freely wrote the epic in Hittite, the literary language of the Empire, will remain an open question as long as we do not know more about a Hurrian version. The Hittite epics before us are not only written in a literary, truly epic, style; also their contents, the mythological concepts they represent, are very sophisticated. The question of whether these epics are translations or free adaptations thus becomes secondary: what matters is the fact that they reflect a very complex mythology whose elements can be traced back through the Hurrians to Babylonia. Not only such names as Alalu, Anu, and Ea with his vizier Izzummi (Akkadian Usmu) are Babylonian, but also the basic concept of generations of gods who successively ruled the universe goes back to Babylonia. Thus this Hurro-Hittite epic literature and the mythology contained in it are heirs to a long-established West-Asiatic mythological literature. The ties with the West-Semitic world, Phoenicia and Ugarit, are less obvious. Sankhuniaton as quoted by Philo Byblius only seems to reflect the same Hurrian mythology that underlies the Kumarbi epics; nevertheless it is interesting that in later times this mythology was simply considered Phoenician. The Canaanite myths preserved in Hittite, in turn, that is, the stories about Asherah and Mount Pishaisha, are too fragmentary to allow for detailed comparison. Yet it seems, even from these small fragments, that the tenor of these tales is very similar indeed to that of Ugaritic literature, although the particular stories have no counterpart there except for an allusion in the Pishaisha text to a victory of the Storm-god over the Sea, which may mean the victory of Ba'al over Yam "Sea" in the Ugaritic Ba'al cycle.[31] If we are permitted for a moment to look at Sankhuniaton, the fragmentary Hittite versions of Syrian myths, and the Ugaritic epics as one group, we may say that in complexity and sophistication it equals the myths of Hurro-Mesopotamian background.

In contrast, the Anatolian myths discussed in the first part of this survey seem to be much simpler. Although the Anatolian deities also form families, there is here no succession of rulers, nor do these myths contain Babylonian elements (the word signs used to write names of gods should not mislead us). It is true that the Storm-god who, as provider of rain, was the supreme god all over West Asia outside Babylonia proper, is the central figure in both the Anatolian and the Hurrian and Syrian myths. But the stories told about him show a marked difference: whereas in the Kumarbi cycle Teshub is the last king in a divine dynasty going back to the Sumerian Alalu, and whereas his struggle with the stone monster is a world-shaking battle involving all the gods, the Anatolian Storm-god is simply the great god of the land whose well-being and well-meaning are badly needed. If he goes into hiding because someone aroused his anger, he has to be propitiated. To tell, at the yearly festival, the story of how he ultimately overcame the Dragon is a means to secure the much-needed rain for the land. If a local Storm-god has left his cult city he can be brought back by a prayer containing the story of the river Marassanta that was especially made to flow nearby and charged with watching over him. It thus seems that these Anatolian stories are very close indeed to what is commonly called nature myths, although, perhaps, already one step removed from an hypothetical original form of such myths. We saw that the myth of the Vanished God is no longer connected with a seasonal ritual; and for the Dragon Fight story, which does belong to a seasonal festival, I doubt that the listeners "knew" that the Dragon "meant" drought: for them it was enough to hear that the Storm-god finally defeated his enemy. Yet the connection with seasonal phenomena is apparent.

Also the plots of the Anatolian myths are simpler than those of the foreign ones. To overcome the Dragon, simple ruses are used. None of the gods, not even the sharp-eyed Eagle, can find the Vanished God, but the Bee, dispatched by the Mother-goddess, finds him; to overcome his increased fury magic is needed. Family relations follow an all too human pattern. In the Telipinu version of the Vanished God myth, it is the Storm-god, Telipinu's father, who is concerned about his son's disappearance but unable to bring him back; old grandmother Hannahanna rudely tells him "do something!" but she herself has to take over by sending out the Bee. In the Storm-god version translated above the episode is added in which the Father first turns to the Grandfather for counsel, only to be reprimanded that it is all his own fault; here again it is Hannahanna who finds the solution after having reassured him.

I hope that in pointing out these differences we have done no more than bring into focus what seems obvious when the Anatolian and foreign myths are read. In doing this we have tried to bring out the fact that not all that is written in Hittite is just one "Hittite mythology" but that it is necessary to distinguish between genuine Anatolian myths and those of the

Hurrian-Mesopotamian-Syrian realm. That such different elements were brought together in the Empire and that the scribes of Hattusa included such diverse material in their writings only serves to illustrate the complexity of Hittite civilization. When the Hurrian or Kizzuwatnean element in the royal house and in the scribal schools imported Hurrian myths, the Anatolian tradition continued beside it; and whatever the ethnic background of the individual stories, they were written in the literary language in which the unifying power of the Hittite Empire manifested itself.

NOTES

For a general survey of Hittite history and civilization the reader is referred to:

  O. R. Gurney. *The Hittites* (Pelican Book, A 259. Harmondsworth: Penguin Books, 1952; 2nd ed. 1954).

Translations of Hittite texts by A. Goetze are found in:

  J. B. Pritchard, ed. *Ancient Near Eastern Texts Relating to the Old Testament* (Princeton: University Press, 1950; 2nd ed. 1955), which will be quoted in the notes as *ANET*.

  E. Laroche published a "Catalogue des Textes Hittites" in *Revue Hittite et Asianique* XIV (1956) 33–38; 69–116; XV (1957) 30–89; XVI (1958) 18–64, quoted hereafter as *Cat.* (with number). It contains references to the original publications of cuneiform texts and to translations and discussions. For the scholar, reference to *Cat.* will be sufficient in most cases; only a few texts are quoted below by the cuneiform edition, for which the following abbreviation is used:

    KUB: Keilschrifturkunden aus Boghazköi (Berlin, 1921–).

Other abbreviations used in the notes are:

  RHA: Revue Hittite et Asianique.

  ZA: Zeitschrift für Assyriologie.

Kum.: see note 21.

MGK: see note 24.

1. *ANET* p. 120.

2. For a sound warning against an easy application of the cliché of the "dying god" see the posthumous publication of a lecture by Henri Frankfort, "The Dying God," *Journal of the Warburg and Courtauld Institutes* XXI (London, 1958) 141–51.

3. For this character of Telipinu see H. G. Güterbock, "Gedanken über das Wesen des Gottes Telipinu," *Fest schrift Johannes Friedrich . . . gewidmet* (Heidelberg, 1959) 207–11.

4. Text: *Cat.* 261. For the distinction of the various versions of the myth see H. Otten, *Die Überlieferungen des Telipinu-Mythus* (Mitteilungen der Vorderasiatisch-aegyptischen Gesellschaft 46, 1, Leipzig, 1942); the Telipinu version used here for partial restoration is *Cat.* 258, translated in *ANET* pp. 126–28.

5. Otten, *op. cit.* pp. 55–56; *Cat.* 262, 1: *KUB* XXXIII 15.

6. Otten, *op. cit.* pp. 47–48; *Cat.* 262, 6: *KUB* XXXIII 33.

7. The ritual part of the Telipinu version is in *ANET* pp. 127–28.

8. The so-called Yuzgat Tablet with parallels listed *Cat.* 263; for a partial translation see Gurney, *The Hittites*, pp. 187–88.

9. *KUB* XXXIII 36 and 67, *Cat.* 264, 6, and 346, 2.

10. *Cat.* 267, 1 and 2; cf. *ibid.*, 6 and perhaps 3–5.

11. *Cat.* 342, 2–5.

12. *Cat.* 265, 5–9 and 16.

13. *Cat.* 332.

14. *Cat.* 308, *ANET* pp. 357–58; for the translation given here see H. G. Güterbock in *RHA* XIV/58 (1956) 22–23.

15. *Cat.* 438; A. Kammenhuber, "Das Palaische," *RHA* XVII/64 (1959) 1–92, section "Mythisches Fragment," pp. 40–63.

16. Cf. Kammenhuber, *loc. cit.,* p. 55 for contents, p. 91 for Zaparwa.

17. *KUB* XXXV 107–8, *Cat.* 452, 2; H. Otten, *Luvische Texte in Umschrift* (Berlin, 1953) pp. 97–99; P. Meriggi, "Zum Luvischen," *Wiener Zeitschrift für die Kunde des Morgenlandes* 53 (1957) 193–226; the myth on pp. 209–18; E. Laroche, *Dictionnaire de la langue louvite* (Paris, 1959) pp. 158–62.

18. *Cat.* 257; *ANET* pp. 125–26.

19. *KUB* XXXVI 89, *Cat.* 553, partly paralleled by *KUB* XXXVI 88, *Cat.* 290, 4.

20. *Cat.* 227–30. H. Otten, "Die erste Tafel des hethitischen Gilgamesch-Epos," *Istanbuler Mitteilungen* 8 (Deutsches Archäologisches Institut, Istanbul, 1958) 93–125, gave a translation of the first tablet including recently found fragments and showed where the Hittite version differs from the Akkadian (for which see E. A. Speiser's translation, *ANET* pp. 72–99). For the rest of the Hittite version cf. J. Friedrich, "Die hethitischen Bruchstücke des Gilgameš-Epos," *ZA* 39 (Neue Folge 5, 1930) pp. 1–82.

21. *Cat.* 232–37. An outline of these stories was given by H. G. Güterbock in an appendix to his *Kumarbi: Mythen vom churritischen Kronos* (Istanbuler Mitteilungen 16, Zürich-New York, 1946) pp. 116–22; full translations were published by J. Friedrich, "Churritische Märchen und Sagen in hethitischer Sprache," *ZA* 49 (N.F.15, 1950) 213–55 (Appu, Cow, Keshshi) and "Der churritische Mythus vom Schlangendämon Hedammu in hethitischer Sprache," *Archiv Orientální* XVII/1 (Prague, 1949) 230–54.

22. *Cat.* 231; H. Otten, "Ein kanaanäischer Mythus aus Boğazköy," *Mitteilungen des Instituts für Orientforschung* I (Berlin, 1953) 125–50; the same, "Kanaanäische Mythen aus Hattusa-Boğazköy," *Mitteilungen der Deutschen Orient-Gesellschaft* 85 (1953) 27–38; previously F. Hrozný, article "Hittites" in *Encyclopaedia Britannica* (Vol. 11, p. 607 of the 1956 edition).

23. *Cat.* 246; *Kum.* p. 122; J. Friedrich, "Zu einigen altklein-asiatischen Gottheiten," *Jahrbuch für Kleinasiatische Forschung* II (1952) 144–53, esp. pp. 147–50; Otten, in the article quoted last in note 22, pp. 35–36.

24. *Cat.* 238 (and possibly 244, see next note). First made known by E. O. Forrer in 1936. Translations: *Kum.*, Texts 1 a and b, pp. 6–10; Güterbock, "The Hittite Version of the Hurrian Kumarbi Myths: Oriental Forerunners of Hesiod," *American Journal of Archaeology* 52 (1948) 123–34, esp. pp. 124–25; H. Otten, *Mythen vom Gotte Kumarbi* (*MGK*) (Berlin, 1950) pp. 5–9; *ANET* pp. 121–22; P. Meriggi, "I miti di Kumarpi, il Kronos Currico," *Athenaeum* N. S. 31 (Pavia, 1953) 101–57, esp. pp. 110–29.

25. See Meriggi, *loc. cit.*, pp. 128–31, for the likely suggestion that *KUB* XXXIII 105 (*Cat.* 244; *Kum.* Text 1 b) belongs here.

26. Meriggi, *ibid.*, p. 123 to line 2 (p. 125).

27. *Ibid.*, p. 125 with n. 58 to lines 15–16.

28. *Cat.* 241 (and 251, see next note). *Kum.*, Text 1 c; Otten, *MGK* pp. 9–13; Meriggi, *loc. cit.*, pp. 133–47.

29. *KUB* XXXVI 3 (*MGK* No. 3), cf. Otten, *MGK* p. 12 n. 4; Meriggi, *loc. cit.*, p. 145; contrast *Cat.* 251.

30. *Cat.* 239; *Kum.*, Text 2, pp. 13–28; *MGK* pp. 13–25; *ANET* pp. 121–25; H. G. Güterbock, *The Song of Ullikummi* (New Haven: American Schools of Oriental Research, 1952); reprinted from *Journal of Cuneiform Studies* V (1951) 135–61; VI (1952) 8–42.

31. *Kum.*, p. 122; cf. the Ugaritic epic translated by H. L. Ginsberg, *ANET* p. 131.

Canaanite Mythology

BY CYRUS H. GORDON

Canaan is the Syro-Palestinian segment of the Fertile Crescent, between the Mediterranean and the desert. The people speaking the Canaanite dialects included the Hebrews and Phoenicians as well as a host of small kindred nations such as the Edomites, Moabites, and Ammonites. Canaanite paganism is of particular importance because Biblical religion in some ways continued it, and in others reacted violently and consciously against it. Our Judeo-Christian tradition harks back, both through borrowing and reaction, to its Canaanite substratum.

The Bible is a mine of information on Canaanite mythology and religion. The more limited corpus of Phoenician inscriptions provides some additional data. Much can be learned from numerous classical sources, such as Lucian's *Dea Syra*. But since 1929, mythological texts have been emerging from the soil at Ugarit, providing us with the texts of the myths that circulated in the fourteenth century B.C.[1] Any basic study of Canaanite mythology must therefore rest primarily on the Ugaritic mythological tablets. In the following pages we shall remain close to our Ugaritic sources, making only brief incursions into other material when the resultant comparisons are of special importance, or at least new.

The Ugaritic myths explain nature so as to satisfy man's craving for the answers to the universe, and to guarantee the regularity of the processes that result in fertility: fertility of mankind, animals, and plants. The content of the myths is conveyed through narrative full of action; the ancients were not interested in abstractions. Their thinking was concrete and their gods are portrayed as engaging in lively and significant action. For example, when Baal (the god of fertility and life) and Mot (the god of sterility and death) fight furiously, the action is not only interesting *per se*, but it is significant in that the outcome determines whether the land will be fertile or sterile for a prolonged period.

Fertility is the main concern of the Ugaritic myths. The fertility that the ancients aspired to was within the framework of nature; they wanted each manifestation of fertility in its due season. They wanted nothing (not even blessings such as rain and crops) out of season. What they dreaded was the failure of rain and crops in season. They desired the harvest of barley, wheat, tree fruits, olives, and grapes, each at its normal time. Fertility of the soil is an around-the-year affair without any necessary sterile season in Canaan. Only the component segments of Canaanite fertility (i.e., the successive harvests) are seasonal. Nor is precipitation as a whole seasonal in a good year; for when the winter rain ends, the summer dew begins. Rain is seasonal, and so is the dew. But since, as the texts tell us, Baal grants both rain and dew, he functions as the water-giving god during all twelve months of the year.[2] Dew (as the ancients knew) is necessary during the summer for the ripening of agricultural products such as grapes (which are harvested down to the end of the rainless summer). Accordingly, the great mass of scholarly writing on Baal, who is supposed to die for the rainless summer and return to life for the rainy winter, misses the point of ancient Near East religion as well as of Near East climate. The ancients wanted the regularity of the normal year, with everything including the rain and dew in its proper season. They dreaded rainless winters, dewless summers, and locust years. A succession of dry or locust years was the terrible scourge that they wanted to avert at all costs. We shall see that the theme of the dying and reviving gods is not seasonal but "sabbatical," having to do with seven-year cycles of fertility and sterility.

The fertility cult was not limited to Baal and his female counterpart Anath. It is true that our longest texts concerning the fertility myths are Baalistic, but it is also a fact that text #52, which deals specifically with this problem, never so much as mentions Baal. In that text El is the prime mover. The prominence of Baal and Anath in the fertility myths is simply a corollary of their general prominence as young, active, and appealing gods. Younger gods tend to be more popular than their elders. Zeus displaced his father Cronus, who had previously displaced his own father Uranus. In Iran, Ahuramazda with the passing of time yielded the limelight to Mithra and Anahita. Accordingly, the quantitative prominence of Baal and Anath vis-à-vis El in the fertility myths, is simply an aspect of their quantitative prominence vis-à-vis the older El in general.

Text #52 opens with the invocation: "Let me proclaim the Good and Gracious Gods," the heptad of fertility deities who are to be sired by El for the purpose of establishing seven-year cycles of abundance. The seven motif, as we shall see, permeates the text. The tablet is divided into sections by horizontal lines drawn by the scribe. The text is in dramatic form, with stage directions, giving the locale and *dramatis personae* for various scenes. The origins of drama are religious, and text #52 is a landmark in the prehistory of classical drama.

The prologue mentions the presence of the dignitaries of the community: civilian and military, ecclesiastical and lay: from the king and queen down. The note of abundance is sounded in line 6:

> *Eat of every food*
> *Drink of the liquor of every wine!*

The second section tells of the compound personage "Death-and-Evil," who holds two scepters: in one hand the staff of bereavement, in the other the staff of widowhood. They hack him down like a vine in its field. Thus section #2 is, so to speak, the reverse side of the coin: in #1 (the prologue) abundance is hailed; in #2 privation is banished.

Section #3 states that something is to be recited, or performed, seven times in keeping with the pervading heptad theme.

Section #4 opens by stating the locale:

> *The field is the field of the gods*
> *The field of Asherah and the Girl.*

The Elysian Fields of Ugarit are thus defined as the field of Asherah (consort of El) and the Girl (apparently Anath). There the "Lads" do something over a fire seven times. What they do is the subject of a considerable body of scholarly literature. The text states

> *They co[ok a ki]d in milk*
> *A young goat in butter.*

"Milk" and "butter" are certain and parallel each other perfectly. What is in brackets is broken away and restored. "Cook" is only half there, and most of "kid" is missing. Moreover, *"young goat"* is a *hapax legomenon*, with a conjectural translation that cannot be used to bolster the restoration of "kid." The restored passage has been used to establish the Canaanite custom of seething a kid in its mother's milk, against which the Biblical prohibition "Thou shalt not seethe a kid in its mother's milk"[3] may have been directed. This prohibition has given rise to the rabbinical insistence that milk and meat must not be eaten together. Since the separation of milk and meat is the cornerstone of Jewish ritual diet, the subject is of wide interest. The above restoration of the Ugaritic passage is possible, but it is so full of hypothetical factors that we will do well to move on without further ado.

The final line of section #4 parallels what we have just quoted, but "fire," written *'iššatu* (which is Semitic) the first time, is now paralleled by the Indo-European *agni* "fire," cognate with Latin *ignis*. The Ugaritic form beginning with *a-* is, however, closer to Sanskrit Agni (familiar to westerners as the Indian god of fire). This Indo-European word is a concrete reminder that Canaan was already influenced by Indo-Europeans prior to the Amarna Age. This is abundantly borne out by vocabulary, proper names, literature, and institutions as well as the mythology.

With section #5 we read that Rahmai "Lassie" (= Anath) goes and girds (= grapples with) a goodly hero. Anath's engaging in combat is in keeping with her bellicose character of slayer of dragons, game, and men.

Section #6 gives the scene as the Dwellings of the Gods, and specifies another sevenfold ritual.

Section #7 is an expression of zeal for the divine names of some deities called "The Sons of Sharruma," who apparently must be invoked to assure the success of the main section (#10), for which the first nine sections are the build-up.

Section #8 is the invocation to the Good and Gracious Gods who will be born and nurse at the breasts of Asherah. Dignitaries are on hand, bringing good sacrifices to the feast.

Section #9 brings the scene back to the Elysian Fields

> The field of the gods
> The field of Asherah and Rahmai . . .

and all is ready for the main scene.

Section #10 opens at the seashore where two women are to be created over a fire. El is the aged god, and it is a question whether he will remain impotent, so that the women will function as his daughters and remain childless; or whether he will rise to virility for the occasion so that the women may serve as his wives and bear offspring. The myth, and the drama whereby it was re-enacted, are full of suspense; for El's impotence would mean the onslaught of lean years, whereas his virility would herald the inauguration of a cycle of plentiful years.

El fashions the two women and puts them in his house. His staff (symbolizing his penis) is lowered, but he shoots heavenward, bagging a bird, which is plucked, cleaned, and roasted over the fire. He then tries to copulate with the two

women, whereupon the text brings us to a crisis of suspense,
for

> *If the women cry "O husband, husband!*
> *Thy rod is lowered*
> *The staff of thy hand has fallen"*
> *While the bird roasts over the fire*
> *Yea broils over the coals,*
> *Then the women are the wives of El*
> *The wives of El and his forever.*
> *But if the women cry "O father, father!*
> *Thy rod is lowered*
> *The staff of thy hand has fallen"*
> *While the bird roasts over the fire*
> *Yea broils over the coals,*
> *The girls are the daughters of El*
> *The daughters of El and his forever.*

Marriage and adoption could be on more, or on less,
permanent bases. A marriage contract could permit a short-
term union, or call for a permanent and indissoluable marriage. The same variation could hold for daughtership (called
mârtûtu in Babylonian), a legal state into which a girl could
be adopted. The permanence of whatever relationship emerges
between El and the two women, is in keeping with the seri-
ousness of the drama; on it depends the long-range fertility
of the land. What the women say will determine the future,
whether for good or for evil. To the relief and joy of the
populace, the women exclaim:

> *"O husband, husband!*
> *Thy rod is lowered*
> *The staff of thy hand has fallen"*
> *While the bird roasts over the fire*
> *Yea broils over the coals.*
> *So the two women are the wives of El*
> *El's wives and his forever.*

This guarantees a favorable outcome but not without further
suspense, for, as we shall now note, the first children to be

born of the union are not the Heptad but a pair of celestial
deities:

> *He bends, their lips he kisses*
> > *Lo their lips are sweet, sweet as pomegranates.*
> *From kissing, there is conception*
> > *From embracing, impregnation.*
> *They go into labor and bear Dawn and Dusk.*

Whatever importance Dawn and Dusk may have in the
fertility cult,[4] they are not the primary gods of fertility, whose
functioning is the goal of the text.

The birth of children was announced by messenger to the
fathers, who left obstetrics in the feminine hands of the mid-
wives and parturient women.

> *Word was brought to El:*
> *"El's wives have borne."*

But El knows the results without having to be told, for he
first asks and then answers his own rhetorical question:

> *"What have they borne?*
> *My children, Dawn and Dusk."*

Thereafter he joins his wives in conjugal love again. Then he
returns to his own abode till the women go into labor and
bear him another brood. Word is brought to him, and this
time the babes are the Good and Gracious Gods of fertility
who suckle the Lady's breasts thereby imbibing the nourishment that provides them with the power for their important
role. The newborn gods are voracious giants, with

> *A lip to earth,*
> > *A lip to heaven*
> *So that there enter their mouth*
> > *The fowl of heaven*
> > *And fish of the sea.*

El then addresses his seven sons and directs them to the
wilderness:

> *"There ye shall sojourn among the stones and trees*
> *Seven full years*
> *E'en eight circling (years)*
> *Till ye Good Gods walk the field*
> *E'en tread the corners of the wilderness."*

Long years of retirement to the wilds among the stones and trees is typical of Indic epic, where beloved heroes do this (often for expiation), pending a happy return to civilization. The seven ("e'en eight"[5]) years of sojourn in the wilderness mean that a bad sabbatical cycle has taken place and, by the process of alternation, a good sabbatical cycle is about to begin. It therefore is likely that text #52 is connected with a ritual to end a succession of lean years and inaugurate a cycle of fat years.

We now approach the happy ending. The seven lean years are over and the Good Gods are ready to enter the Sown, where the Guardian who is to let them in, is stationed.

They met the Guardian of the Sown
 And shouted to the Guardian of the Sown:
"O Guardian, Guardian, open!"
And he opened an aperture for them so that they entered.

They then ask for the entertainment due to strangers:

> *"If there is bread, give that we may eat.*
> *If there is wine, give that we may drink."*

The Guardian answered that there were both food and drink, and the text ends on the affirmation of plenty.

Text #52 thus reflects a religious ritual for initiating a seven-year period of plenty. The form is dramatic and was doubtless acted out. Our text is the libretto with stage directions. The authority that is invoked to produce the results is a myth: the story of how El procreated the Heptad who preside over the plenteous sabbatical cycle, and how they auspiciously entered the arable terrain bringing their blessings to it. The myth is the precedent to be invoked for re-establishing *in time* the *primeval* event. We thus have the myth, the verbal utterance and the act: the complete formula for agricultural prosperity (without any trace of the Baal cult).

Quantitatively the Baal and Anath texts form the bulk of the fertility myths from Ugarit, in keeping with the popularity of those younger gods in the religion of Canaan. About a dozen tablets deal with Baal and Anath myths, but there is no proof that they were intended to constitute a single composition. When we group them as parts of "The Baal and Anath Cycle" we do so as a matter of practical expedience. We must discuss them in some order, and we try to arrange them in the most meaningful sequence. And yet no sequence can claim to be the one and only sequence that a Ugaritic priest would have prescribed.

One of the main themes in the mythology is kingship among the gods. Just as Zeus wrested the kingship of the gods from Cronus, and the latter from Uranus, Baal wrested the kingship from the sea-god Yamm. Text #137 tells how the pantheon was assembled under the presidency of El, when Yamm sent his messengers with the insolent request that Baal be surrendered to him in bondage:

> *So says Yamm your lord*
> *Your master, Judge River:*
> *"O gods, give up him whom ye harbor*
> *Him whom the multitudes harbor;*
> *Give up Baal and his partisans*
> *Dagon's Son, that I may inherit his gold."*

The gods were seated for banqueting, when Baal spied the messengers coming. The gods, anticipating the unpleasant message, bent their heads in sadness; but Baal, showing the courage befitting the king-to-be, took his stand by El.

> *As soon as the gods saw them*
> *Yea saw the messengers of Yamm*
> *The emissaries of Judge River,*
> *The gods lowered their heads on top of their knees*
> *E'en on the thrones of their lordships.*

Baal rebuked them:
"Why have ye lowered, O gods,
Your heads on top of your knees
    E'en on the thrones of your lordships?
Let the gods twain read the tablets
    E'en the messengers of Yamm
        The emissaries of Judge River:
Lift, O gods, your heads
From on top of your knees
    From the thrones of your lordships
And I shall answer Yamm's messengers
    The emissaries of Judge River."

Baal's leadership commands the respect of the gods, who react by obeying him:

> *The gods lift their heads*
>   *From on top of their knees*
>   *From the thrones of their lordships.*

The messengers twain arrive and fail to pay obeisance to the head of the pantheon:

> *At the feet of El they do not fall*
> *Nor prostrate themselves in the gathered assemblage.*

Baal is already meditating violent revenge in his heart. He has a sharpened sword with flashing blade. Messengers (as in the Homeric world) had a kind of diplomatic immunity, so that no matter how great the provocation, Baal had no right to vent the violence of his feelings on them. The scene we are about to witness is a forerunner of an episode in the *Iliad* (1:188–222), where Achilles is about to slay Agamemnon because of Agamemnon's insolent demands, but two goddesses restrain him. Just as Achilles yields for the time being, so too does Baal. In fact El abjectly surrenders him:

> *El, Bull of his father, replies:*
> *"Baal is thy slave, O Yamm,*
>   *Baal is thy slave forever*
>   *Dagon's Son, thy bondsman*

> *He will bring thy tribute like the gods*
> > *Yea bring thine offerings like the sons of holiness."*

Thus betrayed by the cowardice of the venerable but senile
Father of the Gods, Baal flies into a rage and

> *[Seiz]es [a knife] in his hand*
> > *A butcher knife in his right*
> *To slay the messengers - - -*

whereupon

> *[Ana]th grabs [his right hand]*
> > *Yea Astarte grabs his left*

and tell him that he must not slay the emissaries of Yamm.
The text breaks off after a few fragmentary lines. It is pos-
sible that the goddesses told Baal to bide his time and things
would turn out in his favor, even as Hera and Athena advised
Achilles, who, in obedience to them, refrained from slaying
Agamemnon.

Baal's opportunity came. Text #68 tells how he vanquished Yamm and from him seized the kingship. The divine
craftsman, Kothar-and-Hasis, fashioned two clubs and gave
them to Baal for conquering Yamm. The need for two clubs
is a corollary of the ancient psychology that required climactic
action: the first club would strike a preliminary blow; the
second would deal the final and crushing blow. Kothar-and-
Hasis predicts to Baal the victorious outcome of the battle:

> *"Am I not telling thee, O Prince Baal,*
> > *Yea declaring, O Rider of Clouds?*
> *Lo, thine enemies, O Baal*
> *Lo thine enemies shalt thou smite*
> > *Lo thou shalt destroy thy foes!*
> *Thou shalt take thine eternal kingship*
> > *Thine everlasting sovereignty!"*

Then the divine craftsman gives the clubs their appropriate
names:

Kothar brings down two clubs and proclaims their names:
"*Thy name is Driver.*
  Driver, drive Yamm
    Drive Yamm from his throne
      River from the seat of his sovereignty!
Thou shalt swoop from the hand of Baal
  Like a falcon from his fingers!
Strike the shoulders of Prince Sea
  Between the hands of Judge River!"

Note that the imagery is in terms of falconry. The clubs will fly from the hand of Baal and strike his enemy Yamm, just as a falcon swoops from the hunter's hand to catch the prey. The expression "between the hands" means "on the back" in Hebrew as well as in Ugaritic. The "creative word"[6] of Kothar-and-Hasis is immediately translated into action:

    The club swoops from the hand of Baal
      Like a falcon from his fingers
    It strikes the shoulders of Prince Yamm
      Between the hands of Judge River.

But Yamm is not felled by the blow and still remains in the fray. So Kothar-and-Hasis names the next club "Expeller" and commands it to fly from the hand of Baal and deal Yamm the knockout blow on the head:

    So it swoops from the hand of Baal
      Like a falcon from his fingers.
    It strikes the head of Prince Yamm
      Between the eyes of Judge River.
    Sea sprawls and falls to earth - - -

Baal thus conquered Yamm and wrested from him the kingship of the gods.

Victory, however, often leaves a host of new problems in its wake for the victor. On this occasion, immediately after the victory, Astarte rebukes Baal for slaying Yamm. Baal is now king, but his future is fraught with vicissitudes as the mythology before us will bring out.

Text #75 tells of Baal's encounter with ravenous monsters in the wilderness. The weird creatures (part bovine, part anthropomorphic) are reminiscent of the Aegean Minotaur on the one hand and of the Mesopotamian Bull of Heaven on the other:

> On them are horns like bulls
> And humps like buffaloes
> And on them is the face of Baal.

The text is fragmentary with many of the line-ends missing. That the sabbatical cycle of fertility is an underlying motif is, however, clear from passages like the following:

> Seven years the god is full - - -
> Even eight circling years, till - - -

Then Baal perished and the years of sterility came on, for we read:

> Thus Baal fell - - - like a bull
> Yea Hadd collapsed - - - - - - - - - .

Baal had many ups and downs, slain for many a cycle of sterility and privation, and risen for many a cycle of fertility and plenty. The multiplicity of his ups and downs is required by nature itself in the Near East. Canaan is characterized by a succession of seasons that normally produce a fertile year. With some luck a number of such fertile years follow one after the other to form a fertile cycle. But unfortunately, rain does not always materialize in the rainy season; nor is there always sufficient dew in the summer. Moreover, locusts may plague the land and devour the crops. A series of bad years is the major natural catastrophe against which the fertility cult was directed. The meteorological history of Canaan, where Baal was pitted against Mot in the minds of the people, required the concept that the conflict between the two gods took place repeatedly. In the frame of reference of Canaanite religious psychology, each of the two gods was both vanquished and triumphant many a time in the course of any century.

One of the larger subdivisions of "The Baal and Anath Cycle" is called the "Anath" text, which opens with a banquet scene of the gods. Baal is honored on the occasion with roasted meat cut with a keen blade from the breast of a fatling. Also

> *A cup is placed in his hand*
> *An amphora in both his hands.*

Asherah, consort of El and mother of "the seventy gods," graces the occasion. Wine flows in profusion:

> *They take a thousand pitchers of wine*
> *Ten thousand they mix of its mixture.*

Like the Greeks in Homer, the Canaanites often cut their wine, and enhanced the pleasures of roast meat and mixed wine with music and song:

> *(A lad) began to sing and chant*
> *With cymbals, a goodly song*
> *The lad good of voice chanted.*

Thereafter

> *Baal went up into the heights of Saphon*
> *Baal viewed his girls*
> *He eyed Pidrai, Girl of Light,*
> *Also Tallai, Girl of Rain,*
> - - - - - - - - - - - - - - - - .

The daughters of Baal, as we know from several Ugaritic passages, are three in number: Pidrai, Tallai, and Arsai. They are appropriately nature goddesses: Pidrai symbolizing light; Tallai, dew and rain; Arsai, earth. Some scholars insist that they are not the daughters but the consorts of Baal. The texts call them Baal's *banât-*, which means primarily "daughters" and secondarily "girls." Since the triad of Baal's daughters is reflected in the triad of Allah's daughters according to the pre-Islamic Arabs,[7] there is some outside confirmation that the three goddesses are daughters of Baal. This does not rule out their serving as his consorts as well, because the ambivalence of relationships in an ancient pantheon may be remote indeed from the familiar patterns of human society.

Col. II begins with a reference to the scent of game, around the double doors of Anath's house. This is appropriate because she is a goddess of the hunt and of battle. Suddenly troops confront her:

> And lo Anath fights violently
> She slays the sons of the two cities
> She fights the people of the seashore
> Annihilates mankind of the sunrise.

The reference to the people of the west (seashore) and east (sunrise) is a common idiom called a "merism" or combination of antonyms to indicate totality (like our English "they came great and small," which means "everybody came"). Accordingly, Anath is said to be slaying "everyone." The scene we are about to witness is a parallel to the Egyptian (rather than Mesopotamian) story of the near-destruction of mankind. The Mesopotamians (followed by the Hebrews) conceived of the near-destruction of mankind at the hands of the god(s) in terms of a deluge. But the Egyptians had a myth about a brutal goddess, Sekhmet, who went berserk and would have exterminated the human race had she not been stopped before it was too late. Ugaritic mythology, confronting us with a variant of this tradition, tells of how the violent Anath slew men and exulted as their cut-off heads and hands flew through the air:

> Under her (flew) heads like vultures
> Over her (flew) hands like locusts.

Again, note the merism; "under" and "over" indicate "everywhere" about her. The ancient Near Easterners used to cut off heads and hands to count, and boast of, their victims slain in battle. Heads and hands are therefore symbols of victory, figuring in the art as well as texts of the Near East. Our present text is paralleled by Syrian seal cylinders of the Amarna Age, showing the victorious goddess with heads and hands filling the atmosphere.

Sekhmet of Egypt was stopped by flooding the area with beer dyed blood-red with ocher. The bloodthirsty Sekhmet, mistaking the reddened beer for blood, drank her fill and was put to sleep by the beer. Anath, somewhat similarly, is depicted as wading in the blood of her human victims:

> She plunges knee-deep in the blood of heroes
> Neck-high in the gore of troops.

She battles on with club and bow until she reaches her palace. At this point we are confronted with a typical feature of the literature. All the fighting so far is merely the first round. Another scene, paralleling this one, will come later and tell of the climax (i.e., final victory). So our text states that on this first round "she was not sated." She thereupon renews the battle, adding new tactics:

> She fights violently
> Battles the sons of the two cities
> She hurls chairs at the soldiers,
> Hurling tables at the armies
> Footstools at the troops.

Brawl tactics, specifically the throwing of furniture, are famous from Odysseus' battle against the suitors in his halls at Ithaca. In Psalm 23:5, "Thou preparest a table before me in the presence of mine enemies" may mean that God provides His own with ammunition.

With her tactics in the second round, Anath scores the victory and is overjoyed at the massacre she has wrought:

> Much she fights, and looks;
> Slays, and views.
> Anath swells her liver with laughter
> Her heart is filled with joy
> For in the hand of Anath is victory.
> For she plunged knee-deep in the blood of soldiers
> Neck-high in the gore of troops.
> Until she is sated
> She fights in the house
> Battles between the tables.

The parallel with the *Odyssey* is many-sided. Anath is depicted returning from the hunt, trying to enter her own palace, which is occupied by intruders. Her first battle, out of doors, does not end with her in full possession of her premises. But the second battle, concluded indoors, leads to her repossessing her palace. Both the tactics of furniture throwing, and the massacre of the intruders to repossess one's own palace, jibe with Odysseus' victory in his halls. After her victory Anath first

> *Washes her hands in the blood of soldiers*
> *Her fingers in the gore of troops.*

But the blessings of peace follow the ravages of war:

> *She draws water and washes:*
> *Dew of heaven*
> *Fat of earth*
> *Rain of the Rider of Clouds.*

All of the myths we are discussing lead up to the theme of nature functioning with regularity and benevolence to bless mankind with fertility. The formula "dew of heaven and fat of earth" recurs in the blessings of Isaac. "Rider of Clouds" refers to Baal in Ugaritic, but to Yahwe in Psalm 68:5.

The acts of Anath bring on the corresponding functions of nature:

> *Dew that the heavens pour*
> *Rain that the stars pour.*

The text goes on to tell of the abundance of game too.

Baal next dispatches his messengers to Anath, telling her to lay aside warfare and establish peace, promising her to reveal the secret of nature if she will come to his mountain abode:

The message of Aliyan Baal
* The word of Aliy the Mighty:*
" - - - - - - - - - - - - -

(Bury) enmity in the earth of battles

> Put mandrakes in the dust
> Pour (a) peace (offering) into the midst of the earth,
> Conciliation into the midst of the fields

- - - - - - - - - - - - - -

> To me let thy feet race
> To me let thy legs hasten,
> For I have a word to tell thee
> An utterance, to declare unto thee:
> The word of the tree and the whisper of the stone
> The sound of the heavens to the earth
> Of the Deeps to the stars.
> I understand lightning which the heavens do not know
> The word which men do not know
> Nor the multitudes of the earth understand.
> Come and I shall reveal it
> In the midst of the mountain of me, God of Saphon
> In the sanctuary, in the mountain of mine inheritance
> In the Good Place, on the Hill of Power."

When Anath beholds the messengers coming she is stricken by misgivings that some ill may have befallen Baal. Before they have time to deliver their joyous message Anath

> Lifts her voice and shouts:
> "Why have Gupan and Ugar come?
> What foe has risen against Baal
> Or enemy against the Rider of Clouds?"

Anath then recounts her past victories over Baal's enemies. Those battles symbolize the triumph of the forces of good (or life) over the forces of evil (or death).

> "Have I not crushed Yamm, El's Darling,
> Nor annihilated the great god River?
> Have I not muzzled the dragon
> Nor crushed the crooked serpent
> Mighty monster of the seven heads?
> I have crushed Mot, darling of the earth gods

- - - - - - - - - - -

I have destroyed the house of El-Zebub
I have battled and gained possession of the gold of those
*   who (once) drove Baal from the heights of*
*   Saphon - - - - ."*

The sea-gods figure prominently among the foes of Baal, lord
of earth and fertility. The dragon (*tannîn*) is well known
from Scripture. The crooked serpent is none other than
Leviathan, who is actually named as such in other Ugaritic
texts that we shall presently examine. His seven heads give
the number of the heads that God crushed according to
Psalm 74:14 ("Thou hast crushed the heads of Leviathan").
In Revelation 12:3 ff. the seven-headed monster of evil that
emerges from the sea is a reflex of the old Leviathan myth
and symbolized the evil to be vanquished by God. Later still,
in the Aramaic incantation bowls (from about A.D. 500 in
Babylonia), magicians invoked the precedent of God's conquest of Leviathan, to dispel the forces of evil from the homes
of their clients.[8] All this has a bearing on New Testament and
various forms of Jewish dualism (N.B. the Qumran Scrolls[9]),
whereby the forces of good (or light or God) are pitted
against the forces of evil (or darkness or Satan). This is
frequently attributed to borrowing from Zoroastrianism. But,
as we now see, the myth of the dualistic battle was deeply
entrenched in Canaan from pre-Hebraic times. The myth
of the conflict was absorbed by the Hebrews along with the
language, literature, and lore of Canaan from the very start of
Hebrew history in Canaan. We know the parallel (and related) myth of the Greeks, about the seven- (or nine-) headed
Hydra slain by Heracles. The earliest attestation of the myth
is a seal cylinder from Mesopotamia of the third millennium
B.C. (Dynasty of Akkad) showing heroes vanquishing the
seven-headed monster.[10] Accordingly, all the available evidence points to the spread of this dualistic myth from the
Semitic to the Iranian sphere, not vice versa. That Iranian
back-influence may have heightened the already existing
dualistic tendencies in the Semitic world is quite likely, starting with the Achaemenian Conquest and continuing into

Roman times; but that is very different from attributing the origin of Christian dualistic tendencies to non-Jewish sources.

Mot ("Death") is the most prominent adversary of Baal. He appears often enough in Hebrew poetry, and his cult is reflected in the early Hebrew name Az-mawet[11] ("Mot-Is-Strong"). Appeasing the forces of evil, as well as adoring the forces of good, is familiar in many religions (cf. the cults of the lethal Nergal in Mesopotamia, and of the evil Seth in Egypt).

El-Zebub, as we have noted above, is already an evil deity. He reverberates as Baal-Zebub,[12] the prince of the demons in the New Testament.[13]

The gold guarded by dragons on mountains is a common motif in Indo-European epic.

Anath ends her address to Gupan and Ugar by concluding her tale of conquests over Baal's foes, who had once

Driven him from the seat of his kingship
  From the dais, from the throne of his sovereignty . . .

and she asks

> *"What enemy has arisen against Baal*
>   *Or foe against the Rider of Clouds?"*

The messengers allay her fears:

> *"No enemy has arisen against Baal*
>   *Nor foe against the Rider of Clouds."*

Then they deliver the message and invitation, repeating the very words put into their mouths by Baal, as quoted above.

The secret that Baal offers to reveal to Anath is the word of nature. The passage describing it is one of the finest in Ugaritic, anticipating the Scriptural formulation of the same idea: "The heavens declare the glory of God, yea the firmament tells of His handiwork. Day utters word to day; and night imparts knowledge to night. There is neither utterance nor words whose sound is unheard. Throughout all the land their sound goes forth; at the end of the world are their

words" (Psalm 19:2–5). In Canaan, whether at Ugarit or in
Israel, the poets heard the voice of nature; heavens and
earth talked to them, revealing the glorious mystery of the
god(s) and creation. For those ancients, nature was animate;
with the segments thereof conversing in words that the
initiated could understand.

Anath accepts the invitation, and instead of wasting time
sending further messages back and forth, she decides to race
ahead of Gupan and Ugar.

> *Then she sets face toward Baal*
> *On the heights of Saphon*
> *By the thousand acres*
> *Yea myriad hectares.*

This formula expresses the speed at which gods travel.
All too prosaically, it could be rendered "by leaps and
bounds."

Baal entertains Anath, upon her arrival, with roasted ox
and fatling. She draws water and washes with

> *Dew of heaven, fat of earth*
> *Dew that the heavens pour*
> *Rain that the stars pour . . .*

and game abounds because of her felicity; for she is the
Lady of fertility and of the hunt.

Baal's invitation is not without ulterior motive. In exchange
for his secret he wants Anath to intercede on his behalf to
get a palace. Diplomacy in divine circles is as devious as
among men. Baal's tactics were to get Anath to appeal to
Asherah to ask El, the head of the pantheon, to authorize
Kothar-and-Hasis to construct a palace for Baal. Baal was
the only important god without a palace of his own. His
newly won kingship required his possessing one. His plea
included the statement that just about all the gods had
palaces:

> *"There is the dwelling of El, the shelter of his sons*
> *The dwelling of Lady Asherah of the Sea*

> *The dwelling of Pidrai, Girl of Light,*
> > *The shelter of Tallai, Girl of Rain,*
> > > *The dwelling of Arsai, Girl of Y°bdr*
> *The dwelling of the famed brides."*

Anath assures Baal that she will, if necessary, compel El to grant the request, by dire threats of violence.

> *"And the Virgin Anath declared:*
> *'The Bull, God of my father, will yield*
> *He will yield for my sake and his own*
> *For I shall trample him like a sheep on the ground*
> > *Make his gray hair flow with blood*
> > > *The gray of his beard with gore*
> *Unless he grants Baal a house like the gods*
> > *Yea a court like the sons of Asherah!' "*

Anath then departs for the abode of El where the two cosmic rivers, the sources of the Two Deeps, have their origin. There she threatens her aged sire with physical violence. El, afraid of his brutal daughter, has hidden in the innermost chamber: the eighth chamber within a chamber.

> *El answers from seven chambers*
> > *Out of eight compartments:*
> *"I know thee to be impetuous, O my daughter,*
> > *For there is no restraint among goddesses.*
> *What dost thou desire, O Virgin Anath?"*

Now that El has been cowed into granting whatever she wants, Anath can afford to be filial and give up her crude tactics:

> *And the Virgin Anath replied:*
> *"Thy word, O El, is wise*
> > *Thy wisdom, unto eternity*
> > > *Lucky life is thy word.*
> *Our king is Aliyan Baal*
> > *Our judge, above whom there is none."*

Anath's appeal was carefully planned. Asherah and her brood were already there to add their voices to Anath's in getting El's authorization for building Baal's palace:

> There shout Asherah and her sons
> The Goddess and the band of her kin:
> "Baal has no house like the gods
> Nor a court like the sons of Asherah."

Vociferously they remind El that practically every god except Baal, who is now king, has a palace. El has no choice but to authorize the construction.

Asherah's messengers, Holy and Blessed, are dispatched to Caphtor, where Kothar-and-Hasis has his atelier. They are to convey to the divine craftsman El's orders to erect the palace.

Text #51 takes up the story. Like Hephaistus busy at his forge when Thetis comes to request armor for Achilles, so too Kothar-and-Hasis is described at work making fine objects in his atelier:

> The skilled one went up to his bellows.
> In the hands of Hasis were the tongs.
> He pours silver
>   Casts gold
> He pours silver by the thousand (shekels)
> Gold he pours by the myriad.

The text then enumerates the handsome creations he is making: a table, a footstool, shoes, a bowl, etc.—all fit for the gods.

The construction of Baal's mythical house is a forerunner of the erection of Yahwe's historical First Temple in Jerusalem. The two accounts are organically related because of common background and attitudes. In both cases the god's interests had grown to a point where he could not condignly go on any more without a house. The Bible tells that it was no longer fitting that Israel's king should dwell in a cedar palace while God still lived in a tent (The Tabernacle). Times had changed; Israel had arrived; with the added

stature of Israel among the nations, the cultic requirements
for Israel's God rose. We have seen how Baal's rise to kingship required the building of a palace for him. The Biblical
and Ugaritic accounts of the building materials (cedars of
Lebanon covered with metal) also link the mythical and
historic houses of Baal and Yahwe, respectively.

The definitive authorization is sent through Anath to Baal
with instructions to invite certain creatures (their identity
is not yet clear, for we cannot translate their names) whereupon nature itself will fetch the building materials for him.
Anath, overjoyed, darts through space to the heights of
Saphon to tell the good news to Baal:

> "Be informed, O Baal!
>   I bring thy tidings.
> A house will be built for thee like thy brethren
>   Even a court, like thy kin.
> Invite - - - - into thine house
>   - - - - in the midst of thy palace
> So that the mountains will bring thee much silver
>   The hills, the choicest of gold
> And build a house of silver and gold
>   A house of lapis gems."

The combination of silver, gold, and lapis lazuli is familiar
from Egyptian and Sumerian mythological texts, too. It is a
reflection of actual art that gloried in the color scheme
produced by the three materials.

Baal now summoned the divine builder.

> After Kothar-and-Hasis arrived
> He set an ox before him
>   A fatling in the midst of his presence.
> A throne was set so that he might sit
>   At the right hand of Aliyan Baal
> Until he had eaten and drunk.

After wining and dining the guest Baal got down to business
and instructed Kothar-and-Hasis to build the palace promptly

"in the midst of the heights of Saphon.
The house shall comprise a thousand acres
The palace, ten thousand hectares."

But a major disagreement arose between Baal and Kothar-and-Hasis as to whether the palace should have a window. A new type of building was coming into vogue: "the window house" (called *bît-ḫi(l)lâni* in Babylonian). The divine architect recommended this new type of building with a window; Baal, however, stubbornly objected to windows. Finally the architect prevailed, with the consequence that Baal's adversary Mot entered Baal's palace through the window. Mot's (i.e., Death's) entrance through windows is a theme reflected in Jeremiah 9:20. The dialogue between Baal and Kothar follows:

And Kothar-and-Hasis declared:
"Hear, O Aliyan Baal,
* Perceive, O Rider of Clouds!*
Shall I not put a window in the house
* A casement in the midst of the palace?"*
And Aliyan Baal replied:
"Do not put a window in the house
* A casement in the midst of the palace!"*
And Kothar-and-Hasis replied:
"Thou wilt come around, Baal, to my word."

Kothar then repeated his advice, but Baal would not be budged and added that he had three girls (Pidrai, Tallai, and Arsai), whom he presumably did not want to expose to any outsider through windows.

From the majestic trees of Lebanon, and the choicest cedars of Antilebanon, the palace was erected. Then a mighty conflagration (which we are to compare with the "fire of Hephaistus") is applied to the house for a week, at the end of which the palace emerged resplendent with gold and silver. This may reflect a process of melting and applying precious metal to sheath the wood and bricks, giving the illusion of a house built of solid gold and silver. When the process was completed

> *Aliyan Baal rejoiced:*
> *"I have built my house of silver*
> *Yea made my palace of gold."*

Thereupon Baal made a great feast to commemorate the event, slaughtering bulls, sheep, and goats, fatlings and yearling calves to regale his guests.

> *He invited his brethren into his house*
> *His kin into his palace.*
> *He invited the seventy sons of Asherah.*

He also invited specialized deities: personified animals and objects, some of which are paralleled in other literatures of the East Mediterranean. Homer tells of animated tripods that come to, and go from, the banquets of the gods, automatically. This parallels the deified pithoi in the following passage. In Hittite rituals, thrones are personified quite as in the following:

> *(Baal) caused the ram gods to drink wine;*
> *Caused the ewe goddesses to drink wine.*
> *He caused the bull gods to drink wine;*
> *Caused the cow goddesses to drink wine.*
> *He caused the chair gods to drink wine;*
> *Caused the throne goddesses to drink wine.*
> *He caused the pithos gods to drink wine;*
> *Caused the jar goddesses to drink wine.*

Note how each category comes in parallel pairs, male and female, giving poetic form to what would otherwise be a prosaic list. The text adds that the wining and dining continued

> *Till the gods had eaten and drunk*
> *And the twain who suck the breast had quaffed.*

The twain are the two deified kings. As in Homer, the kings at Ugarit were accorded divine status. Note that dyarchy existed at Ugarit, somewhat as at Sparta. The institution at both sites would appear to be the legacy of a common Aegean heritage. On a carved panel on the royal bedstead from Ugarit, two princes or kings are depicted sucking the breasts of a goddess, thereby imbibing the milk that imparts divinity to them.[14] The kings of Ugarit therefore have a place in the pantheon. It is part and parcel of the epic that kings should move in divine as well as in human circles; cf. Homer, the Gilgamesh Epic, and the Patriarchal Narratives in Genesis.

After the banquet, Baal sallied forth and captured ninety cities. His conquests inspired him with so much confidence that he felt secure enough to have a window installed in his house.

> *And Aliyan Baal declared:*
> *"I'll install (it), Kothar son of Yamm,*
> *Yea Kothar, son of the Assemblage.*
> *Let a window be opened in the house*
> *A casement in the midst of the palace."*

Thus Baal did come around to following Kothar's advice.

> *Kothar-and-Hasis laughed.*
> *He lifted his voice and shouted:*
> *"Did I not tell thee, O Aliyan Baal,*
> *Thou wouldst come around, O Baal, to my word?"*
> *He opens a window in the house*
> *A casement in the midst of the palace.*

All this is connected with the functioning of Baal as the storm-god, because a rain- and thunderstorm ensue. Perhaps it is somehow connected with the "windows" of heaven mentioned in Genesis 7:11 as the source of rain.

At this seemingly happy juncture, trouble looms ominously for Baal. His foes seize the forest and mountainsides, and his archenemy Mot resolves on wresting the kingship for himself, saying

> *"I alone am he who will rule over the gods*
> *Even command gods and men*
> *Dominate the multitudes of the earth."*

Baal is obliged to communicate with Mot in the underworld, but warns his messengers, Gupan and Ugar, to beware of Mot lest he swallow them alive:

> "Do not draw near to the god Mot
>   Lest he make you like a lamb in his mouth
>   Yea like a kid in his gullet."

The negotiations end in the confrontation of Baal and Mot in the underworld as we read in text #67. Mot's summoning of Baal is connected with Baal's conquest of the seven-headed Leviathan. Perhaps Mot felt sympathy for the forces of evil, since he was after all destructive like them. On being summoned, Baal is terrified of Mot, and all nature becomes, as a result, unproductive.

> Aliyan Baal feared him
>   The Rider of Clouds dreaded him.
> Word went back to the god Mot,
>   Was relayed to the Hero, El's beloved:
> "The message of Aliyan Baal
>   The reply of the Mighty Warrior:
> 'Hail, O god Mot!
> I am thy slave, e'en thine forever.'"
> The two (messenger) gods departed
>   Nor did they sit.
> Then they set face toward the god Mot
>   In the midst of his city Hamrai.
> Lo the throne on which he sits
>   Is the land of his inheritance.
> The twain lift their voices and shout:
> "The message of Aliyan Baal
>   The reply of the Mighty Warrior:
> 'Hail, O deity Mot!
> I am thy slave, e'en thine forever.'"
> The deity Mot rejoiced.

The capitulation of Baal is complete, since he becomes by his own declaration the slave of Mot in perpetuity. In the Old

Testament there are two kinds of slaves: the native (Hebrew) slave who has the right to go free in the seventh (or sabbatical) year; and the eternal slave, who never becomes free of his master.

Baal's capitulation meant his descent to Mot and to death. But before doing so, Baal copulated with a heifer who bore him a tauromorphic son. Then we find Baal fallen dead on the earth. When a pair of messengers bear the sad tidings to the head of the pantheon (El, or Latpan):

> Thereupon Latpan god of mercy
> Goes down from his throne
>   Sits on the footstool
>   And from the footstool sits on the earth.
> He pours the ashes of mourning on his head
>   Yea the dust of scattering on his pate.

El also dons a special garb for mourning and lacerates himself, wandering in grief through mountains and forest. Anath too wanders in grief until she comes upon the corpse of Baal lying on the earth. With the help of the sun-goddess, Shapsh, Anath removes the corpse to the heights of Saphon for burial with numerous sacrifices in his honor.

Anath then proceeds to the abode of El and Asherah, and (in text #49)

> She raises her voice and shouts:
> "Let Asherah and her sons rejoice
>   E'en the goddess and the band of her kin
> For Aliyan Baal is dead
>   The Prince, Lord of Earth, has perished."

It will be noted that this mythology is cosmic, not local. Baal is the Lord of the entire Earth, not the Baal of Ugarit, Byblos, Tyre, or Sidon. El and Asherah are the chief god and goddess of the whole pantheon. Baal and Anath are the universal gods of fertility. And so forth.

The news that Baal is dead meant that another god would have to be appointed king in his stead. El and Asherah finally

decide on their son Athtar the Terrible as king to replace
Baal:

> Thereupon Athtar the Terrible
> Goes up into the heights of Saphon
>   Yea sits on the throne of Aliyan Baal.
> His feet do not reach the footstool
>   His head does not reach its top.
> So Athtar the Terrible says:
> "I cannot be king in the heights of Saphon."
> Athtar the Terrible goes down
>   Goes down from the throne of Aliyan Baal
> To be king over all the grand earth.

Though Athtar became king of the earth, he was unequal
to the magnitude of Baal's kingship in Saphon, as the in-
adequacy of his physical stature indicated.

Meanwhile Anath nursed her desire for vengeance on
Baal's slayer. Eventually she asks Mot for her brother Baal
and Mot admits his guilt, whereupon

> She seizes the god Mot
> With a sword she cleaves him
> With a fan she winnows him
> With fire she burns him
>   In the millstones she grinds him
>   In the field she plants him.

Mot is thus destroyed, but his being planted in the ground
is somehow connected with the future growth of the soil.
Perhaps the fact that he had swallowed Baal explains why
Mot's body can function as seed giving rise to life.

The planting of Mot is the prelude to the resurrection of
Baal. El himself anticipates the joyous moment, but even
the chief of the pantheon depends on dreams for information. When El dreams of nature functioning with abundance,
he will know that Baal has come back to life:

> In a dream of Latpan god of mercy
> In a vision of the Creator of Creatures

The heavens rain oil
  The wadies flow with honey.
Latpan, god of mercy, rejoices
His feet on the footstool he sets
  He cracks a smile and laughs
He raises his voice and shouts:
"Let me sit and rest
  So that my soul may repose in my breast
Because Aliyan Baal is alive
  Because the Prince, Lord of Earth, exists."

Shapsh, the sun-goddess who sees all, is dispatched to find Baal. When she finds him, he is battling once more with Mot. Baal had attacked Mot, knocked him to the ground, and forced him from the throne of his kingship for seven years. And now, in the seventh year, Mot accuses Baal of having subjected him to seven years of annihilation. From Mot's words, he apparently is referring to what Anath did to him to avenge Baal:

"On account of thee, O Baal, I have seen shame
  On account of thee I have seen scattering by the sword
On account of thee I have seen burning by fire
  On account of thee I have seen grinding in the millstones
- - - - - - - - - - *."*

Soon Mot and Baal are again locked in mortal combat:

    They tangle like hippopotamuses
      Mot is strong, Baal is strong.
    They gore like buffaloes
      Mot is strong, Baal is strong.
    They bite like serpents
      Mot is strong, Baal is strong.
    They kick like racers
      Mot is down, Baal is down.

As the fight is thus fought to a draw, Shapsh arrives and intimidates Mot with the threat of El's punishment on Baal's behalf:

"Hear, O god Mot!
How canst thou fight with Aliyan Baal?
How will the Bull, god of thy father, not hear thee?
Will he not remove the supports of thy seat
  Nor upset the throne of thy kingship
    And break the scepter of thy rule?"
The god Mot was afraid
  The Hero, beloved of El, was scared.

There are other Baal and Anath fragments. As long as nature continues to function and to malfunction, the conflict of Baal and Mot continues. The aim of the cult was always to secure the victory of Baal over Mot, to usher in a seven-year cycle of plenty, so that the populace may enjoy the blessings of abundance.

As we have already noted, the fertility cult transcended Baalism. Text #77 is lunar, dealing with the marriage of Yarih ("Moon") with the Mesopotamian lunar goddess Nikkal (from Sumerian Nin-gal). The wedding is to result in fertility symbolized as the child that the bride will bear to the groom. The text is divided by a scribal line into two sections. The first part is essentially of masculine interest, and deals with the groom's courtship and payment of the marriage price. The second part has to do with the ladies and the bride's dowry. We may close our discussion of Ugaritic mythology with Yarih's proposal of marriage:

"I shall pay her bride price to her father:
A thousand (shekels) of silver
  E'en ten thousand of gold.
I shall send jewels of lapis-lazuli.
I shall make her fields into vineyards
  The field of her love into orchards."

The handsome price is of course beyond the range of normal human ability to pay, but the term *muhr* ("bride price") is taken from real life. Moreover, his promise to make her fertile reflects the real attitude toward marriage, whose purpose was human fertility. A husband was like a farmer who cultivates the soil so that it yields a harvest. A woman, like a field, needs the seed and cultivation of a husband, if she is to be fertile. Our text is therefore a *hieros gamos:* a wedding of the gods, whose fertility brings on terrestrial abundance for mankind.

The mythology of Canaan is important in more ways than one. Its chief significance lies in its effect on ancient Israel. Both where the Old Testament incorporates it, and where the Old Testament reacts against it, Canaanite mythology continues to exert its impact upon us through the Bible.

NOTES

1. The translations in the following pages have been newly made from the Ugaritic texts in my *Ugaritic Manual*, Rome, 1955. Some additional mythological fragments have since appeared in Ch. Virolleaud, *Palais royal d'Ugarit* II, Paris, 1957.
2. *Ugaritic Manual*, pp. 269–70 (§20.766).
3. Exodus 23:19; 34:26; Deuteronomy 14:21.
4. Šaḥar ("Dawn" or "Morning Star") is also connected with the rains of fertility in Hosea 6:3. The imagery of text #52, wherein God impregnates two human wives, reverberates in the Hebrew prophets; cf. Ezekiel 23 (N.B. v. 4) and Hosea *passim* (e.g., 1:2 followed by 3:1). Hosea connects this theme with agricultural fertility; for depending on the relationship of the women to Him, God either gives or withholds food and drink (Hosea 2:10–11).
5. These numbers are not used as loosely as meets the eye. For while ordinarily there is no eighth year in the sabbatical cycle, twice in a century there is in a peculiar way. Each jubilee ends with a sabbatical cycle in which the seventh year thereof (= the forty-ninth of the jubilee cycle) calls for the land to lie fallow; and then that year is followed by another in which the land is again to lie fallow. Accordingly the worst sabbatical cycle is a sterile seventh cycle the seventh year of which is climaxed by the eighth sterile year. See Leviticus 25.

6. The concept of the creative word is familiar from the first chapter of Genesis. The Creation was effected neither by work, nor with materials, nor by tools. God simply says, "Let there be x," and x comes into existence.

7. See *Moslem World* XXXIII, No. 1, 1943, for "The Daughters of Baal and Allah."

8. See *Orientalia* XXII, 1953, pp. 243–44.

9. I have surveyed the basic ideas and bibliography of the Scrolls in *Adventures in the Nearest East,* London, 1957, pp. 132–43; and "Selected Books on the Dead Sea Scrolls," *Jewish Book Annual* XVII, 1959–60, pp. 12–18.

10. See my *The Living Past,* New York, 1941, Chapter VI, seal #14.

11. II Samuel 23:31; I Chronicles 8:36; 9:42; 11:33; 12:3; 27:25.

12. II Kings 1:2, 3, 6, 16.

13. For Beelzebub, see Matthew 12:24.

14. See *Antiquity* XXIX, 1955, pp. 147–49, and Plate VII.

BIBLIOGRAPHY

Aistleitner, J. *Die mythologischen und kultischen Texte aus Ras Schamra*, Budapest, 1959.

De Langhe, R. Chapter in S. H. Hooke's *Myth, Ritual and Kingship*, Oxford, 1958.

Driver, G. R. *Canaanite Myths and Legends*, Edinburgh, 1956.

Gaster, T. H. *Thespis*, New York, 1950.

Ginsberg, H. L. Translations of Ugaritic literary texts in J. B. Pritchard's *Ancient Near Eastern Texts*, 2nd ed., Princeton, 1955.

Gordon, C. H. *Ugaritic Literature*, Rome, 1949.

———. *Ugaritic Manual*, Rome, 1955.

Gray, J. *The Legacy of Canaan*, Leiden, 1957.

Kapelrud, A. S. *Baal in the Ras Shamra Texts*, Copenhagen, 1952.

Pope, M. H. *El in the Ugaritic Texts*, Leiden, 1955.

Van Selms, A. *Marriage and Family Life in Ugaritic Literature*, London, 1954.

Virolleaud, Ch. Numerous articles in *Syria* since 1929, and books including those currently appearing in the series *Palais royal d'Ugarit*, Paris.

Mythology of Ancient Greece

BY MICHAEL H. JAMESON

In recent years Greek mythology has suffered from being too plentiful and too familiar. For most of the western world mythology is *Greek* mythology—read to children, taught in school, and dreamt, we are told, by the clients of certain psychoanalysts. No wonder that it has become simplified and sugar-coated and, perhaps worst of all, taken for granted. By default, the interpreters who speak to the laymen have come to be those who seek for secret systems and hidden meanings and whose often considerable learning is used to construct impregnable castles of mythological fantasy. And yet it is true that much of the interest in the ancient world and in mythology in general probably has its beginnings in an early acquaintance with Greek mythology. Unfortunately, this acquaintance is often with a form of myth that never existed outside of the handbooks, ancient as well as modern, namely as an orderly and unified system into which the intractable material of living myth is forced to fit.

To give Greek mythology its due we need to see it in the forms in which it was known and used by the Greeks, that is, in their poems, plays, and works of art. And we need to see it in the constantly changing social and historical context of the Greek world. Our understanding of a mythology increases with our understanding of the history and culture of the people to whom it belongs and of their contacts with the cultures around them. For the Greeks this will be especially true of those formative centuries from the Mycenaean to the Archaic periods during which the Greeks received and assimilated impulses from neighboring peoples and fashioned them together with their own experiences and the products of their own imagination into stories that continued to provide stimulus for further creation.

Greater and more accurate knowledge of other ancient mythologies, such as is to be found in the other essays in this volume, not only adds to our understanding of myth in general but also permits us to distinguish the characteristic qualities of Greek mythology. In the past, attempts to do this have tended to the smug conclusion that Greek mythology was more humane, spiritual, and rational than others. Even the most sober and respected of contemporary scholars in this field has congratulated Greek rationalism on rejecting the common folk-tale theme of casting objects behind one while fleeing, which then turn into mountains, rivers, and lakes and impede the pursuers; instead we have the more "rational" device of Medea, which is best told in the form of a modern parody: "Having fetched the [Golden] Fleece, Jason fled with Medea in a small boat accompanied by Medea's small brother Absyrtus. The father of Medea pursued them . . . Medea therefore made a *beautiful plan*. She took her small brother Absyrtus and CUT HIM INTO SMALL BEAUTIFUL ABSYRD PIECES, which she strewed in the wake of the boat with the object of detaining her father. In this she was entirely successful, her father stopping his boat and spending day after day in mid-ocean trying to fit the small absyrd pieces together in order to see whom they would make." (W. C. Sellar and R. J. Yeatman, *And Now All This* [London 1932], pp. 87–88.)

If the Greeks, in fact, did not give much place to the more fantastic themes of folk tale, the explanation is to be found elsewhere than in any innate rationalism. The earliest and largest body of myth known to the Greeks of the historical period were the Homeric poems in which the actions and sufferings of mortal men were the chief subject. In the sketch of Greek mythology that follows we shall first consider the prehistoric background of Greek culture and then give a major share of our attention to these poems which affected so much of Greek art and thought that came after. We shall see the differences in the post-Homeric stories of men, especially the increase in the amount of folk tale, and shall describe a few of the more important groups of stories. Finally, we shall turn to the gods and their stories, with special attention to the generations of gods in Hesiod's *Theogony* and in Homer and their connection with oriental myths. The reader may find it useful to refer to the brief historical table and the list of principal gods at the end of this essay.

A word is needed on what is understood here by the term "mythology." We commonly include persons, relationships between persons, and stories about persons; and these are all found, to a greater or lesser degree, in popular belief, in cult, and in art, in the widest sense. The persons of Greek mythology are both gods and men, more specifically "heroes," great men of the past, who come to form an intermediate category between ordinary men of the present day and the gods proper. The concept of these persons—something of their character, local connections, or sphere of influence—and the simplest relationships between them is often all that popular belief required. Cult in Greece required more, but still limited, relationships, and some few stories. But it is to art, poetic and visual, that the stories properly belong, and art was generally independent of cult and unhampered by belief while drawing on both for persons and some relationships. All three—persons, relationships, and stories—were enormously affected by the persistent particularism of the many small and fiercely independent communities that made up classical Greece. In mythology the common ground between them was largely the result of the circulation of art from at least the beginning of the Archaic period. Art tended to regularize local stories and even cult. In turn local stories were constantly finding their place in the body of pan-Hellenic art. But Greece as a whole never had an official, fixed, or "correct" mythology, or, for that matter, religion. Here we shall be chiefly concerned with stories and hence

with art, but it will be clear that we must constantly refer
to belief and cult.

PROLOGUE

The Greeks, like the Hittites, the Iranians, and the Indic
speakers, to the east, and the Italic, Celtic, and Germanic
speakers to the west, spoke one of the Indo-European family
of languages. Very little of the religious and mythical ideas
from a time before the differentiation of these various languages can be detected even in our earliest glimpses of the
Greeks at least a thousand years later. Partly this is because
the Greeks, like other Indo-European peoples to the east,
had entered regions where more complex societies were already well established and had learnt much from them;
partly it is because in myth and religion the originally Indo-
European ideas appear to have been relatively simple. Nonetheless, the greatest single figure belongs to the Indo-European inheritance—Zeus, who is the Indic Dyaus pitar, the
Latin Iuppiter, known by the phenomena of the sky and
described as "father" (so *Zeus pater*). For the Greeks he
seems always to have been the supreme god and in some
contexts he is just "God," divinity in general. There was a
constant tendency in Greek religious thought for God
(*theos*), the gods (*theoi*), and a named god, especially Zeus,
to be used as equivalent terms, the particular term used
depending on the context of thought. If this is an early and
basic tendency it is not surprising that little or no mythology
would attach to such concepts of the divine: there are no
persons and no relationships, no stories to be told. Earth
(Gaea), Dawn (Eos), Sun (Helios), and Moon (Selene) are
among the few Greek gods with names which are also common nouns, or at least which were so recognized by the
Greeks and by us, and it is not unlikely that some vague

divinity attached to them from Indo-European times. The vagueness persisted and only Earth, whose name does not yield a sure Indo-European etymology, had much cult. The "Sons of Zeus," the two Dioscuri, also have an understandable title and may be compared to the twin Ashvins of Indic mythology. When we first see the Dioscuri they have taken their place in heroic legend, have a putative mortal father, and separate heroic names, Castor and Polydeuces. Hearth (Hestia) ought to belong here too. She should be very old since she is the center of family religion, the fire on which family sacrifice is made, and she is, in fact, very holy, but hardly a personality separate from the material fireplace, and so ignored in mythology. In brief, just as the Indo-European heritage, for all its obscurity, is important for understanding Greek social structure, ritual, and theology, so the supremacy of Zeus the father is the primary datum for mythology as well; but of itself this heritage does not seem to have been productive of much mythology.

Sometime after 2000 B.C. the Greeks began to enter the mainland of Greece and to settle the Aegean shores of the Mediterranean. Almost everything beyond the strictly material culture of the so-called "Helladic" people the Greeks conquered can only be guessed at, though the Greeks no doubt derived much from them. The Minoan culture of the island of Crete remained independent for some five hundred years. Its art and probably something of the thought behind that art came to influence the Greeks profoundly in the course of the second millennium before Christ. Gods, daemons in partly human form, men and animals are vividly depicted, but what persons and stories these scenes may represent we cannot tell: no theme of later mythology has been securely identified. And yet Crete left a deep impression on the Greek imagination. A series of distinct, rather sinister stories were later told of the kings of Crete. Zeus in the form of a bull swam to Crete carrying the daughter of the king of Phoenician Tyre upon his back. There Europa became his bride and bore him Minos, very likely a dynastic title of the kings of Crete. The bull, so popular in Cretan art, appears again when the king's wife, Pasiphaë, falls in love with a magnificent bull and gives birth to the Minotaur monster, half man and half bull. Minos's master craftsman, Daedalus, "Cunning Artist" (a common noun), builds a maze, the Labyrinth of Cnossos, to keep the monster in. In Homer, far earlier than our witnesses for these other stories, Daedalus is said to have built a dancing place at Cnossos for the king's daughter Ariadne. In later sources, the king's daughter helps a Greek hero, Theseus, to kill the Minotaur and escape from the Labyrinth together with the rest of the seven youths and maidens, annual tribute to Minos from Athens on the mainland, by following a thread he had unwound on his way in. Daedalus himself escapes from Minos by making wax and feather wings. He and his son Icarus fly to Sicily but Icarus suffers the fate of the sorcerer's apprentice: he flies too high, comes too close to the sun, the wax melts, and he falls into the sea. Minos pursues Daedalus to Sicily but is killed by the natives.

In these stories we see the impression made upon the Greeks by the brilliant, exotic life of the Minoan palaces— the ties with the Orient, the omnipresent bull, the daemon attendants of the gods, the maze named after the sacred double-ax (the *labrys*), the skilled craftsmen, the youths and maidens who performed as acrobats in the dangerous bull games, the far-reaching navigation of the Cretans. There is no reason, however, to think that the stories themselves are Cretan myths; for most of the sources are not early and the stories include widespread folk-tale types, such as the hero who kills the monster with the help of the king's daughter and wins her as his bride, and the culture hero the "Cunning Artist."

Some elements, atypical by normal Greek standards and found in early sources, may be Cretan: in Homer's *Odyssey*, King Minos and his brother Rhadamanthys live among the dead in the paradise of the Elysian plain, dispensing justice as they did in life. There too, since he married Zeus's daughter Helen, will go the hero Menelaus instead of dying, a unique privilege though not undeserved in view of the merry chase she led him in life. We must not be too hard on the mortal Helen, the fallible heroine of legend, for, to judge by customs at Sparta and Rhodes, she may be only acting out the part of her prototype, a prehistoric tree goddess, a type of vegetation deity that exists to be abducted and recovered, as Helen so conspicuously was in the Trojan cycle of stories. In Hesiod, Zeus is said to have been born in a cave on Crete where he was identified with the chief male god of the Minoans who seems periodically to have been born and died, and the grave of Zeus was also said to have been on Crete; neither birth nor death agrees with the normal Greek view of Zeus. These are only scraps of stories and much more is likely to have come from the Cretans and the pre-Greek Helladic mainlanders, but so thoroughly assimilated in Greek tradition and reported so late as to be beyond detection. What is certain is the imaginative stimulus and the image of Crete that persisted throughout Greek history.

About 1500 B.C. the Greeks of the mainland seized Cnossos and ruled Crete. From 1400 B.C. on, though their captured palace at Cnossos had been destroyed, the Greek lords of such palaces as those at Mycenae, Pylos, and Thebes enjoyed wealth and a common culture not to be equaled in the Aegean for many centuries. They were the contemporaries and very likely the correspondents of Hittite kings, their ships traded at Ugarit on the Syrian coast, and brought in alternation tribute and rapine to Egypt. The Mycenaean age (roughly 1600 to 1100 B.C.), which owes its name to its richest site, traditionally the home of the most powerful kings, was the formative period of Greek myth. One has only to consider the coincidence of Mycenaean sites and the locale of the chief Greek myths: Mycenae and Tiryns, insignificant in historical times, were the homes of Agamemnon and Heracles; Thebes, which continued to be important, had a Mycenaean palace with frescoed walls; Troy across the Aegean had contact with Mycenaean sites and was destroyed toward the end of the Mycenaean period. For the myths themselves we have no witness earlier than Homer (in the eighth century B.C.). The clay tablets found in and near the palaces, some five hundred years earlier than Homer, provide us with no literary texts, unlike those of Sumer, Akkad, of the Hittite and the Canaanites. The common occurrence of names later restricted to mythology applied on the tablets to ordinary men shows only that these particular names had not yet become fixed in those stories to which they were later confined, for Greeks generally avoided naming their children after figures of myth. The gods are another matter. Many of the gods of Homer and later Greece—Zeus, Hera, Poseidon, Athena, Artemis, Hermes, for example— were already worshiped, the majority having been acquired or developed since the Greeks separated from the other Indo-Europeans; but for their relationships to one another and for the stories told about them we must look first to Homer. Mycenaean art adds little. If scenes from myth are represented at all they cannot be securely identified with stories we know. The most convincing series of mythical representations is found on large vases from Mycenaean Cyprus whose subjects lie rather in the realm of an oriental mythology that was not incorporated, recognizably, into the body of story common to all the Greeks.

THE HEROES

Although the form in which we have them cannot be much earlier than the second half of the eighth century B.C., Homer's two poems have their genesis at the courts of Mycenaean kings. The *Iliad* and the *Odyssey*, thanks to their metrical formulae, to the exigencies of the old stories basic to their structure, and to a conscious archaism when contemporary facts (as of geography and the use of metals) obviously clashed with traditional stories, preserved not a little of the language, the detail, and the spirit of the distant past. They are the only survivors of a rich tradition of oral poetry whose early vigor may partly explain the absence of literary texts from Mycenaean times. Their length (15,695 and 12,110 lines, few of which can safely be attributed to later additions), their complexity, and the miracle of their survival may be due to the reintroduction of writing, from the east after the long isolation of the early Iron Age that followed the fall of the Mycenaean palaces, but still early enough to permit the dictation of genuinely oral poems before the techniques and the traditions were destroyed by the changing conditions of social life and the widespread use of writing itself.

Both poems have man in the foreground acting out a stern and even tragic part in a world whose mechanism can be understood in purely natural and human terms. We shall see later that this is only part of the story, but for the present let us consider the human side. In the *Iliad*, before the walls of Troy (Ilion), Achilles, a king in his own right, quarrels with the supreme commander, Agamemnon, when tactlessly he takes the lead in forcing Agamemnon to give up his prize of war; Agamemnon retaliates by taking Achilles' prize, another captured girl. Achilles' enormous and ruinous anger is the subject of the poem. He will not fight, and the Greeks suffer at the hands of the Trojans. Achilles' comrade, Patroclus, cannot bear to see his friends defeated and gets Achilles' permission to fight in his armor and in his place. He is killed by Hector, the Trojan champion. Achilles makes up with Agamemnon and transfers his anger to Hector, whom he kills in single combat. He mistreats the body and will not give it up for burial. So long as he has the body his anger need not turn against himself, the true cause of his comrade's death. Finally Hector's father comes to him with ransom; in him Achilles sees his own father; they weep; Achilles gives up the corpse and rejoins humanity.

Clearly, this is already a sophisticated work of art. Though it is long, its subject is but a single incident in a long war which is itself the center of a long cycle of stories. It is not "the story of Achilles"—his death is alluded to but is no part of the poem. To be sure, Homer uses the luxury of leisurely dictation to include a remarkable amount of detail. He conveys a feeling of the whole war in all its weary length and he makes sure that the principal actors in the war are distinctly identified—the Greeks by Helen, who waits nine years before providing the indispensable score card! But in the last analysis it is the poet's frugality that is striking. His is not a compilation of Achilles stories or stories of the Trojan War; it is a brief moment in a man's life through which the whole world is seen. And this is characteristic of the form in which the Greeks knew their myths—not through ritual recitations, though poems were recited as part of the artistic, secular entertainment of festivals, nor from collections of tales, and not even very much, in historical times at least, from the popular retelling of old stories, but from individual works of art. For the Greeks not only was myth a form of art, but the reverse was also true: literature, and to a great extent the visual arts as well, was myth. Before the Hellenistic period (some five hundred years after Homer) only in comedy was there a non-mythic imaginative literature, and even comedy often consisted of mythological burlesque. One cannot properly speak of Greek mythology apart from Greek literature, and the history of the use of mythology and the place of mythology in Greek life is the history of artists and the public they honored and entertained, a public which might, indeed, include the gods. Myth was neither sacred nor secular; it was, like art, simply a necessity of life.

Homer's other poem, the *Odyssey*, is more inclusive than the *Iliad*, but it too restricts its subject. The famous wanderings of Odysseus on his way home from Troy are confined to a relatively short section. Of the twenty-four books, books Nine to Twelve contain most of the adventures, told in Odysseus's own words: the land of the lotus-eaters whose fruit makes a man forget about home—ultimate madness for the Greeks!—and that of the one-eyed Cyclops giants, cannibals from whom Odysseus escapes by blinding his captor and identifying himself as "No-one"; the island of the king of the winds who shuts the unfavorable winds in a bag which his foolish sailors open in sight of home, hoping for treasure;

the Laestrygonians, violent giants; the witch Circe, who turns men into animals; the land of the dead, which gives an opportunity for the mention of many heroes and stories; the sweet-singing Sirens who lure sailors onto the rocks; Charybdis and Scylla, the twin terrors of whirlpool and polyp monster; the three hundred and fifty untouchable cows of the Sun, some of which the crew kill—with the result that only Odysseus reaches the island of the immortal Calypso, who keeps him as her lover and would make him immortal too; his release by the gods and his coming to the land of the Phaeacians, marvelous sailors, to whom he tells his story and who finally convey him home. And yet the bulk of the poem is about the troubles that face a hero of the Trojan War once he gets home—young stay-at-homes who would take over his wife and property, and a wife and son to recover after a twenty-year absence. The manner of presentation is more complex than in the *Iliad*, with the focus shifting from son to father, and from the fantastic storytelling of Odysseus to the harsh realism of what he does at home to greedy suitors and treacherous servant girls.

Some features of these stories are at home only in the Mycenaean age when chiefs from all over the mainland and islands could sail under the leadership of a king of Mycenae to seek a rich city overseas. And the conflict between Agamemnon and Achilles may be based on the clash of civil king and military war-leader, distinct offices in the complex Mycenaean system. Odysseus's seamanship may owe as much to Mycenaean enterprise as it does to the navigation of the eighth century, just as the great hall in which he traps his wife's suitors, the bow with which he shoots them down, and even their seemingly presumptuous claim to be some kind of "king" (*basileus*) are all old. Troy itself flourished and was destroyed at that time. It has been suggested that some heroic themes came to Greece from the Orient in the Mycenaean period: Achilles and Patroclus are compared to Gilgamesh and his comrade Enkidu, the wanderings of Odysseus with those of Gilgamesh; the theme of the valued wife who is lost and must be recovered (Menelaus in search of Helen—the reason why the Greeks came to Troy; Odysseus and Penelope) is known from Hittite and Canaanite poems. No doubt the life and interests of the court nobility of the eastern Mediterranean in the late Bronze Age had much in common, and in the present state of our knowledge it is this common atmosphere rather than any specific borrowing that seems to be reflected in the stories of the Homeric poems. In the realm of divine story the influence may have been greater.

But the chief Mycenaean contribution is the concept of a heroic age, of great deeds done in the past that cannot be duplicated today, but in a real, not a fantastic, past, set by Greek tradition in a few generations of what archaeologists today recognize as the late Bronze Age; the scenes are the cities and palaces of that time, the actors are conceived of as historic dynasts, sometimes claimed as ancestors by later nobles. The sober historian Thucydides did not doubt the fact of the Trojan War but clarified the logistic problems involved. Myth was used to back claims to territory: the Athenians supported their claim to the island of Salamis by the place of the Salaminian hero Aias's ships next to those of the Athenians in the *Iliad*. The sure reality of the age and its heroes led eventually to euhemerism, the interpretation of the gods too as powerful rulers of the past. The disorganization and poverty that followed the fall of Mycenaean civilization made its wide range and wealth seem all the more wonderful. The stories with their heroes became fixed in the ensuing "Dark Ages" and ever afterward the image of Mycenae dominates and dazzles the Greek imagination. The Spartan king Agesilaus, in the fourth century before Christ, thought of himself as another Agamemnon when he sacrificed at Aulis before embarking against Persia; neither his sacrifice (broken up by local authorities) nor his expedition were much of a success, but at least he did not sacrifice his daughter or return home to be axed by his wife. He left it for Alexander the Great to conquer Asia with the *Iliad* under his pillow. In times when monarchs were overthrown and strong individuals suspect, all drama continued to concern itself with the doings of royal families of the heroic age.

Many stories of a completely different origin found their way into the heroic age, became attached to its heroes, and took on something of its character.

The result was that the mythical basis of Greek art was essentially human and historical, though we cannot trust its details, but with an exaggerated, extreme humanity, larger (if not always better) than life: there was no anger to equal Achilles', no endurance or cleverness like that of Odysseus. Heroic myth provided familiar symbols, names whose merest mention invoked vivid associations: Odysseus, patient, shrewd, a devastating speaker, the prototype of the politician —a part which most Greeks would willingly have played; Achilles, wholly committed to an ideal of excellence. When Socrates tried to convince the Athenian people that he would not give up philosophy for fear of losing his life, he reminded them of Achilles' answer to his mother's warning, that if he killed Hector his own death would quickly follow: more than death he feared to live as a coward and not avenge his friends, sitting by the beaked ships, a useless weight on the earth. How different are their goals—the search for truth, and blood vengeance, and how different, at first sight, are the two men. What they have in common is absolute courage in the service of their own highest value.

In the course of the two centuries of the Archaic period that followed Homer (the seventh and sixth centuries B.C.) the bulk of the raw material for Greek literature and art was brought together and put in writing, which is to say that Greek mythology received what measure of standardization it ever had at that time, if we exclude the scholarly and editorial efforts of the Hellenistic age. The main vehicle of Greek myth from then on was literary. In the earliest representations in art that are not simply genre scenes most subjects are drawn from folklore and need not have been affected by epic: battles with centaurs (half men, half horse), with the twin Molione who were physically joined together; "Heracles," if it is he, fighting a lion or birds. But after the early seventh century the literary influence is strong and folklore themes, when they occur in art, assume the guise of established heroic myths and are attached especially to the hero Heracles, who is represented with both heroic armament and the club and bow essential to the tales in which he appears. Local variants, or rather local folk tales attached to figures of myth, continue to enter the main body of myth, and provide the means for variation and experiment, for satisfying new interests without losing the strength of the traditional and the familiar. No Greek writer or artist was ever afraid to deviate from the dominant tradition. Achilles could not be cowardly nor Odysseus a fool, though often a knave, but even Helen might prove faithful—it was a fraudulent substitute that slept in the bed of Paris, according to the lyric poet Stesichorus. So he said in his recantation after Helen had struck him blind for subscribing to the usual slander, if we are to believe the story. The attitude of the user of myth may be compared to that of a historian who is convinced of the outlines of the history he is studying but feels free to rearrange, reject, and add to the incidents and persons reported by tradition in order to make sense of his subject. The analogy is cogent since, as we have seen, for the Greeks myth was in fact a kind of history. The originality of the Greek artist lay in the sense he made of his material.

The stories that clustered around the Trojan War were far and away the most influential in classical times—they account for three out of the seven extant plays of both Aeschylus and Sophocles, and ten out of nineteen of Euripides. Direct reuse of the *Iliad* and *Odyssey* was often avoided, partly because their subjects were so apt for the medium of epic poetry and had received from Homer an expression that continued to be valid. The earliest versions of the other Trojan stories known to the Greeks were a series of poems in the language and meter of Homer that supplied the events before, between, and after the *Iliad* and *Odyssey*. Although they have not survived we have a good idea of the contents of these so-called "Cyclic Epics."

The *Cypria* in eleven books told of the wedding of Peleus and Thetis, the mortal father and sea-nymph mother of Achilles, attended by the gods who failed to invite the goddess Discord; she threw a golden apple among the gods inscribed "For the Fairest" and set the gods to quarreling. Three of the goddesses, Hera, Athena, and Aphrodite, asked Paris, a son of the king of Troy, to choose between them. He chose Aphrodite and was rewarded with the most beautiful of mortal women, Helen. Since Helen was already married to Menelaus, the king of Sparta, she had to be taken away; Menelaus with his brother Agamemnon, and the other Greek kings who had been suitors of Helen and had sworn to support Menelaus against abduction, came to Troy to fetch her back. Thus arose the Trojan War. The oath of the suitors is unknown to Homer, and it seems to be an explanation of how Agamemnon could have commanded an army of all the Greek kings when the supremacy of Mycenae had come to seem incredible.

After the events of the *Iliad* came those of the *Aethiopis* (in five books) in which Achilles kills the queen of the Amazons, warlike women, and Memnon, the son of Dawn, both fighting for Troy, and is himself killed by Paris. The four books of the *Little Iliad* told of the rivalry between Aias (Ajax) and Odysseus for the arms of Achilles; Odysseus wins, and Aias goes mad, slaughters the flocks of the Greeks, and kills himself (the story is told in Sophocles' *Aias*). The bowman Philoctetes, wounded by a snake and abandoned on the island of Lemnos on the way to Troy, is brought to Troy and kills Paris. Neoptolemus, Achilles' son, is also brought to Troy. The palladium, a statue of Athena, vital to Troy's safety, is stolen from the city by Odysseus and Diomedes. The wooden horse in which Greek warriors hide is built and drawn into Troy while the rest of the Greeks pretend to leave for home. Here several keys to Troy have been combined—the sick and despised warrior, the son of the dead champion, the magical statue, and the practical trick of the wooden horse. The *Sack of Troy* (*Iliu Persis*), in two books overlapping somewhat the *Little Iliad,* described the excesses of the Greeks, including the murder of old king Priam at the altar of Zeus by Neoptolemus, which came to stand for all cruelty in war. They divide the loot and sail for home, while Athena prepares trouble for them. The *Nostoi* are the *Returns* of the heroes other than Odysseus, told in five books. The *Telegonia* followed the *Odyssey* and told of Odysseus's son Telemachus, and Odysseus's death at the hands of his bastard son by Circe, Telegonus.

Unlike the *Iliad* and the *Odyssey,* these later poems were more in the nature of compilations of stories than independent works of art. Though all were much shorter than the Homeric poems, each of the later poems included many stories and consequently served as a useful quarry for later writers. Some themes may have been the subjects of old heroic poems contemporary with the Homeric poems and their predecessors: for instance, the rivalry between Aias and Odysseus as to which was the most worthy to succeed Achilles presupposes the heroic world of Homer and may reflect the struggle to fill the Mycenaean post of war-leader. On the other hand, some of the stories referred to in the Homeric poems, such as the quarrel of Odysseus and Agamemnon, are not known later or not in the same form: there was an old tale of the great boar of Calydon and the heroes who hunted it down under the leadership of Meleager. In the *Iliad* we hear that Meleager quarreled with his mother because he killed one of her brothers in a fight. She cursed him and he retired to sulk. He ignored all pleas to help his countrymen in war until his wife persuaded him, too late to receive the gifts that had been offered. The moral is made clear to the sulking Achilles.

We do not have the whole story, but there is nothing here that might not have been told in a heroic poem. But from later sources we hear that Meleager's life depended on a brand that was burning in the fire when he was born. So long as the brand was intact he lived. When his mother quarreled with him she threw the brand on the fire and his life burnt out. This is the familiar folk-tale motif of the "life index," the implication that the hero was invulnerable and potentially immortal is completely contrary to the ideas of heroic epic. The story that Achilles had been dipped at birth in the waters of Styx which made him invulnerable except where his mother held him by the heel is inconsistent with the *Iliad* where the fact that Achilles' mother is a goddess of the sea does not affect his own mortality. The heroes are mortal and vulnerable; they may suffer pain or death each time they take the field of battle, and in this lies the power of the stories.

Here we see the difference between the heroic themes and the folk tales with their predilection for the miraculous and the monstrous. It is not a matter of the one being early and the other late. To judge from the fifth-century history of Herodotus, history based on oral tradition tends to fall into the patterns of folk tale. This means that although Agamemnon and Achilles, Paris and Helen, were characters out of a real historical period and were generally thought of as historical persons, most of the *stories* told about them are likely to have had their origin in the themes of folk tales—so Odysseus is the husband who returns in the nick of time to prevent his wife's remarrying. But the tradition of epic poetry transformed stories that may have had such origins and kept contemporary folk tales for the most part out of sight.

We may believe that parallel to epic there were other tales and songs in a less formal and courtly oral tradition. In the *Odyssey* something of this is evident: Circe is a witch who turns men into animals and Odysseus's only protection is a magic plant; Scylla, Charybdis, the Sirens, the giants, are out of a sailor's tall story; the bag of winds is magic; Calypso is a fairy with the gift of immortality and Odysseus reaches safety in the land of the marvelous sailors thanks to a magical veil that keeps him afloat in the sea. But all except these last were in a story told by Odysseus, who did not always tell the truth. The real story is resumed when Odysseus lands on Ithaca, and has to do with kings, their families, and their retainers. But by the time of the post-Homeric cycle, society has changed; epic poetry has come to be the possession of the public at large, and the tastes of the public admitted material from various sources, especially folk tales, in the guise of heroic epic.

The process is well seen in the story of the voyage of the ship Argo to fetch the golden fleece, a story almost as famous as the travels of Odysseus. The most complete version is the long *Argonautica* in four books by the third-century Hellenistic poet, Apollonius of Rhodes. The leader, Jason of Thessaly, had his characteristically Mycenaean protecting goddess, in this case Hera, just as Achilles and Odysseus had Athena, and we know that Iolcos from which he sailed was a Mycenaean center. Thus there seems to have been a core of old legend, very likely the subject of heroic poetry, that told of the hero's travels and adventures. But their setting in the Black Sea and its approaches cannot have preceded by many years the Greek exploration of the area starting in the late eighth century. Magic and romance, the latter as early as the seventh century, in the Ionian poet Mimnermus, are in the foreground of the versions we know. Jason wins the golden fleece, itself a miraculous object, by passing various ordeals with the help of the "ogre's daughter," Medea, a folk-tale theme we have already seen in the story of Theseus and Ariadne. Medea herself is a potent witch who continues to ply her craft on her arrival in Greece with Jason. The most familiar story was that popularized in the late fifth century by the tragic poet Euripides, who presented the Athenians with some of the problems involved in marrying, or rather in trying to divorce, a witch, while at the same time suggesting that a close community may call a witch any woman that is strange and clever. At any rate, Euripides was probably the first to have Medea deliberately kill her own children when Jason deserts her, transforming her from a fairy ogress with a bag of tricks into a violent actor of domestic drama. In the Archaic period the fantasies of folk tale and the appeal of strange places and peoples dominated the old heroic story. For the fifth-century theater it yields particularly gruesome domestic tragedy. In the Hellenistic age a craving for the exotic restores the fantastic and magical and elevates a thorough-going romanticism. The modern spoof with which this essay began catches exactly the incongruity of the heroic and the fantastic—Jason triumphantly returning with the golden fleece, while Medea scatters her small brother behind.

Within the large body of material of non-heroic origin that makes its way into heroic myth in the course of the Archaic period we can distinguish two broad categories: the more purely magical and fantastic, fairy tale or *Maerchen* (to use the technical term), and, secondly, themes arising out of the kinship and social structure of Greek society. Of this latter class a sure sign are the Furies (Erinyes): they are the frightful females that bedevil Orestes because he killed his mother and Oedipus because of his patricide and incest with his mother. They operate against crime or sin inside the family unit. Unlike bloodshed between different families and clans, where the society divides along kinship lines to provide prosecution and defense, there is no such way of handling bloodshed within the family. In the Greek cognatic system kin who are related to Orestes' mother are equally related to Orestes and the kin of Oedipus's father are also the kin of Oedipus, so that human action is impossible and the supernatural must intervene.

The Furies are mentioned incidentally in Homer: a single Erinys is said to have heard Meleager's mother's curse upon her son but it is not evident to what effect, and Phoenix attributes his sexual sterility to the Furies summoned by his father's curse when, at his mother's urging, he had seduced his father's concubine—both examples coming from a single speech; Oedipus's mother is among the famous women Odysseus sees in the underworld and we hear that Oedipus suffered from his mother's Erinyes. All these are examples of non-heroic plots, of which we are provided glimpses thanks to the vast bulk of Homer. They are not yet admitted to the forefront of action. However, their place in normal belief is revealed by other passages that speak of impersonal, automatic divine intervention—in support of the rights of the elder brother, against oathbreakers, and against the unnatural speech of Achilles' horse. By the fifth century they are seen in their full force only in Aeschylus's *Eumenides* (their euphemistic name) and the play shows how, in fact, they have been tamed. But stories involving violence and continuing disaster within a family were still the most popular in the theater and through drama received their best-known forms —indeed, the theater came to be the most popular source of myth after the fifth century, to judge by its effect on painting. Aristotle pointed out that the plots of tragedy came to be drawn from the history of only a few families whose domestic violence he and the Greek audience evidently regarded as providing the most satisfying tragedy, emotionally and intellectually, for there is a sure fascination in seeing the most basic rules one lives by violated, for whatever reason, and in contemplating the inevitable reaction. We shall restrict ourselves to the troubles of two families—that of Agamemnon and that of Oedipus.

Agamemnon's fate is mentioned several times in the *Odyssey* as a warning to Odysseus, an example to his son Telemachus, and a foil to his own good fortune with Penelope; and it was described at greater length in the cyclic *Nostoi,* an important source for the dramatists. In the *Odyssey* Agamemnon's wife Clytemnestra conspires with his cousin Aegisthus to murder him at a banquet on his return home. His son Orestes returns from abroad to take vengeance on Aegisthus and probably kill his mother as well, though this is not said explicitly, and there is no mention of the Furies. Also un-Homeric are the sufferings of his sister Electra, who helps him against Aegisthus and their mother (Aeschylus's *Libation Bearers,* Sophocles' *Electra,* Euripides' *Electra* and *Orestes*) and the other sister, Iphigenia, whom Agamemnon sacrificed at Aulis in order that he might sail to Troy (the cyclic *Cypria* and Aeschylus's *Agamemnon*). In Homer a daughter Iphianassa is mentioned; on the other hand, Iphigenia is known to be a title of the goddess Artemis and in Euripides' play, *Iphigenia among the Taurians,* Artemis rescues her from the altar, substituting a stag, and spirits her away to be a priestess among the far-off Taurians in the Black Sea where she is found by her brother years later. They bring back the Taurian statue of Artemis to Attica where Iphigenia continues to be her priestess. Thus local traditions of Attic cult have been brought into the myth and produced a melodrama to the taste of Euripides and the public that came after him. A feint toward the stuff of tragedy is made when Iphigenia almost sacrifices her unrecognized brother according to Taurian custom. For Aeschylus, Iphigenia stayed sacrificed and her death was one reason for her mother's hatred of her father; the rescue at the altar was described in the cyclic *Cypria* (or at least in the text known to late antiquity) but was a turn in the story Aeschylus felt free to ignore. A charmingly romantic treatment was also given by Euripides to the story of how Iphigenia was brought to Aulis for the sacrifice under the pretense that she was to be married to Achilles (in his *Iphigenia at Aulis,* the motif already in the *Cypria*). Here we are at the further limits of the heroic tradition.

The family's troubles had already begun with violence in the generation before Agamemnon when unpleasantness between his father Atreus and his uncle Thyestes over Atreus' wife culminated in the grisly story of Thyestes' feast where his children (except, of course, for the unsavory Aegisthus) were served up to him, a folk-tale motif that recurs in Herodotus's history of the Persian Wars, told of the Mede Astyages. Aeschylus and Herodotus also share an interest, foreign to heroic epic, in recurring or delayed disaster in a family, that may be expressed in the form of a curse, ending in extinction, as in the family of Oedipus, or absolution, as in the case of Orestes. Aeschylus's sequence of three plays to be performed successively on the same day, *Agamemnon, Libation Bearers,* and *Eumenides,* explores the violence of father to child, wife to husband, and children to mother against the backdrop of long smoldering evil and with the prospect of continuing disaster; he saves Orestes from the Furies and rejects the inevitability of violence by the means of man's rational judgment passed on a crime in a court of law, the ancient Areopagus of Athens, with the assistance of the god Apollo's rites of purification. Incidentally, this shows the use of myth to comment on current political issues for the function of a court of homicide was precisely that which had been left to the Areopagus after recent controversial reforms.

Two of the oldest poems that came after Homer had nothing to do with Troy. The once powerful Mycenaean city of Thebes in Boeotia is said to have taken no part in the Trojan War because of its destruction by Argives, including Diomedes and Sthenelus who fight under Agamemnon in the *Iliad.* The story of the Theban kings was told in the *Thebais* (7000 lines long) and the *Oedipodia* (6600 lines), and by the somewhat later poem, the *Epigoni,* "The Successors," who succeeded in destroying Thebes. Oedipus ("Swell-foot" and possibly "Foot-wise") unknowingly killed his father Laius, married his own mother (Epicaste in Homer, later Jocasta), again unknowingly, and became king of Thebes; he suffered his mother's Furies when she killed herself on learning the truth; so much was already known in Homer, though in a passage of cataloguing poetry of no great antiquity. The basic story is a non-heroic folk tale, and in time it was filled out with other folk-tale elements, notably Oedipus's encounter with the Sphinx, a monster that devastated Thebes and could only be mastered by answering the riddle about the feet—"What goes on four feet in the morning, two at midday, and three in the evening?" Oedipus ("Foot-wise") knew the answer: "Man."

Oedipus's discovery of the truth is the subject of the *Oedipus the King* of the tragic poet Sophocles, who no longer works in trilogies nor is interested in continuing disasters but views each disaster separately. Oedipus was supposed to have been abandoned at birth on the mountain so that he might not live to kill his father and so fulfill an oracle; instead he had been saved and brought up as the son of the king of Corinth. He left Corinth forever when he learned from the oracle of Apollo at Delphi that he was to kill his father and marry his mother. On the way from Delphi he had quarreled with and killed a stranger who tried to force him off the road. Then he defeated the Sphinx, was made king of Thebes, and married the previous king's widow. This is the background which is gradually revealed as the play progresses. Sophocles shows a city that because of an unknown crime is suffering plague, an old alternative to the Furies as supernatural intervention for a crime without a social solution. Oedipus's relentless search, first as a good king to find the truth for his city and then as an individual, to find the truth of his own identity forces into the open the patricide and incest. His mother kills herself and Oedipus blinds himself with the pins of her dress and begs to be cast out of the city. The conventions are those of the fifth-century theater—Mycenaean royalty, plagues, and oracles; the intellectual context is that of Athenian democracy in the age of Pericles; the appeal of the basic motif, it need hardly be said, is universal.

In his *Oedipus at Colonus,* produced some twenty years later, Sophocles shows Oedipus's arrival in Athens after years of wandering with his daughter Antigone, his welcome by King Theseus, his hatred and rejection of his sons who had failed to help him, and finally his disappearance and death in a grove of the Eumenides, a miraculous and holy event that will benefit Athens. Much of the force of the play comes from blending in one person the figure of the horrible, blind beggar and a mysterious, beneficent power. This was not part of the old stories; instead, in the *Iliad* he had a grave and funeral games at Thebes, the marks of a normal royal death.

The struggle of Oedipus's two sons, at first not always regarded as of incestuous birth, to possess the throne of Thebes is old and may have been the subject of heroic poems; for the poet Hesiod the war over "the flocks of Oedipus," their inheritance, was the other great war of the heroic age. The brothers quarreled, Eteocles ("True Renown") remaining in Thebes while Polynices ("Much Strife") led an army of Argives against his own city. The *Seven Against Thebes,* the last and only surviving play of Aeschylus's trilogy on the family, tells of that war. Thebes is victorious, but the two brothers meet and kill each other, as in folk tale they must; part of Aeschylus's achievement is to make it seem inevitable before our very eyes. He shows a conscientious king arranging for the defense of his city against the enemy and trying to control hysterical civilians. Each admirable measure, as Eteocles tells off Theban champion to face Argive champion, makes it more certain that only he will face his brother, and so leads to the elementary horror of brother killing brother.

In Sophocles' *Antigone,* the earliest in production of his three, we see the efforts of Oedipus's daughter for the proper burial of both brothers against the orders of her uncle Creon, now king. For attempting the burial of the traitor she is condemned to be buried alive. Creon is convinced by the seer Teiresias that he is wrong, but by then Antigone and his own son, Haemon, betrothed to her, have killed themselves, as has his wife on hearing the news. Sophocles' treatment is not romantic, as was Euripides' in a play that has been lost. The opposition of Antigone to the demands of state policy and the ruler's edicts owes more to the intellectual currents of the fifth century than to folklore or heroic epic. However, Oedipus's own story, and that of his sons, illustrates the powerful hold those folk-tale motifs that are shaped by the relationships within the basic family continue to have on the imagination, especially when they have passed through the hands of such writers as Aeschylus and Sophocles.

The greatest collection of folk tales gathered around the name of Heracles, the most popular single figure in Greek mythology. He too was placed in the Mycenaean age, before the generation of the Trojan War, but all that is left of what may have been his role as a Mycenaean king is his connection with the Mycenaean sites of Tiryns and Thebes (which at an early date identified him with a hero Alcides), his name "Renowned of Hera" which looks like a normal man's name, and his death, so certain that Achilles in the *Iliad* can cite it as proof that even the most favored men must die. As a Mycenaean hero, one would expect him to have his protecting goddess, as Jason had Hera, Odysseus and Achilles Athena, and for an Argive hero it should surely be Hera. But instead he is the victim of Hera, who is the cause of all his labors. Her hostility comes from his being the son of her husband Zeus by a mortal wife. He is forced to serve a cowardly king who sends him off on impossible tasks, all of which he accomplishes—he kills the Nemean lion, the Lernaean hydra monster, the Erymanthian boar, the Cerynitian hind, the Stymphalian birds; he battles the centaurs; he cleans the stables of Augeas of acres of manure. These are Paul Bunyan exploits. He is more of a folk hero than a Mycenaean lord: most of his battles are with animals, monsters, and giants, not men. His habits are coarse, his lust and appetite enormous—at Thespiae in a single night he fathered fifty children on the fifty daughters of the king: when hungry he robs a plowman of his ox and eats it on the spot. One wonders if Hera's hostility is not that of the wicked queen of fairy tale, perhaps the inversion of the original patronage his name and his home at Tiryns suggests.

A number of his exploits show him in another of the folk hero's roles: he battles and defeats Death—literally, to restore Alcestis to her husband (as in Euripides' *Alcestis*), and symbolically when he goes to the underworld and drags up the Dog of Hell (Cerberus) or to the West of the world and brings back the golden apples of immortality; and in a version that cannot be traced back earlier than the fifth century he burns himself on a funeral pyre and is transported as a god to Olympus, where he had been brought without the help of the pyre as early as Hesiod's *Theogony* (c. 700 B.C.); there he is given immortal youth by marriage with Hebe, "Youth" herself. Heroes of mythology often received some form of cult, but only he was worshiped as a god as well as revered as a great, dead man. He had, indeed, conquered death.

So numerous and varied are the stories attached to his name that there is some truth in almost every theory of his origin, including that which looks to the Orient. We shall not go far wrong in understanding Heracles if we realize how close to the ordinary man he was, despite, or perhaps just because of, his ultimate divinity. In his popular guise, and as culture hero, benefactor of mankind, he was not fit for the old heroic epic, but lost poems of the Archaic period and the early fifth century told his adventures, and to the story in Hesiod's *Catalogue of Women* of how Zeus slept with Amphitryon's wife and she bore a mortal and immortal son there was attached a description of his heroic combat with Cycnus, a brigand son of Ares (see *The Shield of Heracles* attributed to Hesiod). Tragedy could use his predictable triumphs only to save plots in which he had played no part, as in Sophocles' *Philoctetes* and Euripides' *Alcestis*. When he himself was the subject, tragedy looked to stories of family violence—the sudden madness in which he killed his wife and children (Euripides' *Heracles*), or, in Sophocles' *Women of Trachis*, a different wife's fatal use of love magic, the gift of a dead enemy. Deianira smeared poisonous ointment on his shirt to win back his love; in his agony he relives all his battles with the monsters and ends by turning the weapon of fire against himself; Sophocles ignores Heracles' destined immortality and uses the fire of his funeral pyre, elsewhere a step to immortality, by itself as the end of an utterly human and once again heroic Heracles. But on the whole Heracles was more at home in comedy—boasting, feasting, and lusting, or achieving the pose of nobility in the sculptured decoration of temples.

THE GODS

In describing the action of Homer's *Iliad* we said its mechanism could be understood in purely natural and human terms. To make the Greeks realize that they cannot do without him Achilles need only stay out of battle. Patroclus's death is not surprising when, wearing Achilles' armor, he becomes overconfident, carries the fight to the walls of Troy, and exposes himself to an admittedly superior fighter. Hector's death, in turn, could come about as the natural consequence of his being ashamed to avoid Achilles, the best warrior at Troy. But as Homer actually describes them, none of these events are free from supernatural intervention: Achilles begs his mother, Thetis, to intercede with Zeus, king of the gods; Zeus tricks Agamemnon into attacking without Achilles and when even so the Greeks get the better of the fighting (Homer after all had a Greek audience) he intervenes to guarantee Trojan success. Patroclus's downfall begins with a mighty blow on the back by the god Apollo, and Hector is only a poor third in killing him. Achilles misses Hector with his spear throw, but the goddess Athena retrieves it for him when Hector in his turn has missed. As Achilles himself had said: "The goddess Athena will kill you by my spear."

Behind the seemingly human actions the gods are operating. This is not the fantastic and magical, the supernatural as we see it in fairy tales or in parts of the *Odyssey* and in the adventures of the Argonauts where nothing in normal human experience can account for what happens, and there would be no story at all without the miraculous; nor is it the almost impersonal, automatic intervention of the supernatural when the core of morality is endangered by family murder, incest, etc. Here the poet has deliberately added a new dimension, that of the divine, to what one would otherwise describe as purely natural and human.

The gods are seen in a fictional world of their own as well which is in a sense the explanation of their intervention on the human plane. They have favorites among men and are hostile to the favorites of their enemies among the gods. That world is a storyteller's fancy, a deathless, painless reflection of the world of men, whereas their intervention is a fact of human experience common to the poet and his audience: when Agamemnon apologizes to Achilles he attributes his foolish behavior to Zeus who "took my wits away from me," a notion which in no way prevents him from making good his apology with ample gifts. When, earlier, Achilles had been tempted to draw his sword against Agamemnon, Athena, sent by Hera, had appeared to him, unseen to the others, and promised a better way to protect his honor. To the rest it seemed that Achilles was on the point of drawing his sword, but (as we might say) "He thought better of it,"

"He had second thoughts," or (as the Greeks would have said) "Some god intervened." That "some god" is here Athena, and that she was sent by Hera, the chief of staff of the pro-Greek gods, is due to the particular fictional context of this poem. In the manner of epic every detail is spelled out, everything is named and given its epithet; so too the anonymous supernatural becomes a named god playing a part in a story.

Like the heroes, the gods live at a Mycenaean court, as tradition remembered and distorted it. Brothers and sisters, sons and daughters of Zeus, they feast in his great hall in heaven, Olympus, which is also conceived of as Mt. Olympus, the highest peak in Greece. They eat gods' food (ambrosia) and drink gods' drink (nectar). Apollo, the patron god of music, plays the lyre. The Muses dance. Zeus sleeps with his wife Hera in his palace. The others have their own homes built by the craftsman-god Hephaestus. In comparison with the life of men that of the gods seems gross and trivial. They are jealous and quarrelsome, reluctantly keeping the peace under the threat of simple violence. Zeus tells his wife Hera: "All the gods on Olympus will not be able to help you if I lay my hands on you," and her crippled son, Hephaestus, reminds her of the time he tried to help her but Zeus caught him by the foot and threw him out of the house, and he fell the whole day before he touched land—one of the drawbacks, it would seem, of living in heaven. No hero spoke to or treated his wife and children like that, or if he did no one thought to make it the subject of "a song for men who come hereafter." The problems of the gods are trivial. Achilles accepts death to avenge his friend and protect his self-respect; the immortals have no such opportunities and inevitably their motives are petty. When Aphrodite exchanges the boudoir for the battlefield and is wounded by Diomedes her tears over the spilt *ichor* (god's blood) are a joke among gods and men.

In the *Odyssey*, Odysseus's last stop before coming home is at the court of the king of the Phaeacians. There he is entertained with epic poetry telling of the quarrel of

Odysseus and Achilles and of the Trojan War, which brings tears to his eyes. He is also entertained by young men dancing to a song about the gods: the lame smith Hephaestus takes a trip and leaves his wife Aphrodite at home. She welcomes the handsome war-god Ares into her bed, but her husband has contrived a trap of invisible chains that holds the lovers fast. On word from Helios, the all-seeing Sun, Hephaestus hurries home, calls the gods to witness, and demands his bride price back. The gods laugh uproariously, and those young bucks, Hermes and Apollo, nudge each other and agree they would like to be in Ares' place, with chains, audience, and all. Clearly this story gave delight to men and gods, but mark that in poetry about men and women adultery leads to war (Helen and Paris) and murder (Clytemnestra, Aegisthus, and Agamemnon); among the gods all the realistic details of the spy, the bride price, the guarantee which Poseidon gives in case Ares jumps bail, simply add to the joke.

Only when the gods have mortal children are their feelings serious: Zeus is tempted to save his son Sarpedon and weeps tears of blood upon the earth when he must let him be killed—he *could* save him but the other gods would not like it; it would be breaking the rules of the game. And there are few more moving passages in Greek literature than that in which Thetis, seated in the depths of the sea by her father and her sea-nymph sisters, hears the cries of her son on the death of Patroclus:

> *"Hear me, Nereids, my sisters; so you may all know well all the sorrows that are in my heart, when you hear of them from me.*
> *Ah me, the sorrow, the bitterness in this best of child-bearing,*
> *since I gave birth to a son who was without fault and powerful,*
> *conspicuous among heroes; and he shot up like a young tree,*
> *and I nurtured him, like a tree grown in the pride of the orchard.*

I sent him away with the curved ships into the land of
*   Ilion*
to fight with the Trojans; but I shall never again receive
*   him*
won home again to his country and into the house of
*   Peleus.*
Yet while I see him live and he looks on the sunlight,
*   he has*
sorrows, and though I go to him I can do nothing to
*   help him.*
Yet I shall go, to look on my dear son, and to listen
to the sorrow that has come to him as he stays back
*   from the fighting."*

(Iliad 18. 52–64, transl. Lattimore)

Only through men can sorrow, and nobility, come to the gods. There was a story, told in Hesiod's *Catalogue of Women*, that Zeus sent the great flood to destroy mankind and free the gods of sorrow.

For some cultures mythology consists of the stories of the gods. This is not true of the Greeks, and for that reason their stories have purposely been postponed in our discussion. Their stories neither played as large a part in the imagination of the Greeks nor possessed the same degree of historical conviction. The reality of the gods was something few Greeks ever called into question; what men said about the gods was another matter. "Homer and Hesiod have attributed to the gods everything that for men is disgraceful and blameworthy —stealing, adultery, and the deception of one another," wrote the philosopher Xenophanes. The grounds of his complaint are the product of the Ionian enlightenment of the sixth century B.C., but the feeling that it is the poets who are responsible could be as old as the first folk tale which raised the question: "Did that really happen?" and the answer: "Well, that is what the poets say." Even when not being critical the Greeks realized how much the common picture of the gods was due to the poets (see Herodotus 2. 53 on Homer and Hesiod).

It would be easy and wrong to suppose that the human fallibility of the gods, their immorality toward one another, their amorality in dealings with men, showed lack of respect for the gods' reality or power. On the contrary, as we have seen, the men of the poems are all too well aware of the gods' strength: all the destruction and suffering of the *Iliad* was simply the accomplishing of the will of Zeus (*Iliad* 1. 5) and Achilles in answer to Agamemnon's apology remarks that "Zeus somehow wished that death should befall great numbers of the Achaeans." But of the stories about the gods and of the particular motives for their actions the men show little awareness; they come from the storyteller's imagination and are modeled on the world of men—stories of immortal men and women at an immortal court. The gods are characters in a story, actors in a play, but for the most part in the background while man is in the foreground. The stories are independent of the worship of the gods, even if some features were originally suggested by facts of cult, such as the worship of a divine couple called Zeus and Hera in those areas where epic developed, or the stories of Zeus's philandering originating from his being linked with other goddesses elsewhere; a man did not pray or sacrifice or conceive of the place of the divine in his life any differently because of these stories.

Some of the Homeric gods we know from Mycenaean tablets were already the objects of cult in Mycenaean times—Zeus, Hera, Poseidon, Athena, Hermes, Artemis—and most of the others too were probably worshiped though their names have not yet been found in texts. All received cult in post-Homeric times, with the exception of Iris, "Rainbow," the messenger who passes between heaven and earth and who, like other phenomena of Indo-European name and origin, has little more than this metaphorical function. But they are only a few out of many more figures that were the object of cult, a far larger number than at first appears since many an "Athena" or "Hera" or "Demeter" on examination is seen to be rather a god of the type of Athena and the rest who has come to receive the more widespread name, often preserving the old name only as a title. Some important gods such as Demeter and Dionysus, though mentioned in Homer, are not among the divine actors in the poems. What we have is a selection that forms the cast of divine characters, with limited and clearly defined personalities which have only a tangential relationship to their qualities in cult, some of which have been generalized while others have been ignored. One would never guess, for instance, the important agricultural aspects of Poseidon's cult; in Homer he is almost exclusively the god of the sea.

Thanks to the prestige of epic, the gods henceforth retain essentially the conventional roles they had acquired through centuries of storytelling (and which I have set out in a table at the end of this essay). The Aphrodite of Euripides' *Hippolytus* is a larger and more considerable concept than the foolish creature who complained of Diomedes and was caught in her husband's chains, but the notion of an irrational, imperious power, working a woman's destruction, had already appeared in the figure that in the *Iliad* led Helen to Paris's bed when, as she thought, she felt only shame and regret after he had escaped from Menelaus on the battlefield. The gods of Homer, if not the stories about them, had their effect on cult. In the absence of dogma, priestly caste, holy books, or a single, dominant center, this process—what we might call the Homerization of the gods—did much to impose a pan-Hellenic order on the diverse elements that the Greeks had taken to themselves from the time they first came to the Aegean. And that the Greek gods were predominantly anthropomorphic, that is, conceived of in human (sometimes all too human) shape, is largely due to their familiar place in epic where men were the chief actors.

As for the stories themselves, rather than the characters in them, in Homer they often seem to be the unheroic doings of men, a sort of caricature of heroic epic. In the *Odyssey* and in the cyclic epics we can detect an increase in the element of folk tale, as we did in the myths about men: Poseidon has the function of a wicked king who keeps Odysseus wandering for ten years, and the story of the uninvited guest at the wedding of Peleus and Thetis (in the *Cypria*) is introduced to explain the vague "will of Zeus for the destruction of many men" in the *Iliad*. Other stories centered around noble genealogies with a divine connection brought in, so to speak, by the back door. To make the sons of Tyndarus Dioscuri and to make Heracles the son of Zeus, the poor mortals Tyndarus and Amphitryon, had to be cuckolded. The *Catalogue of Women*, probably begun by Hesiod around 700 B.C. but which by its very nature attracted many additions, gathered together and organized various heroic genealogies while telling stories about famous women whose fame often consisted in their connections with gods. The origins of these stories were diverse—noble claims to divine origin, a desire for genealogical tidiness, the variety of the supreme god's consorts in local cult or the concept of a god's relationship to his priestess as that of groom and bride. But the net result was that the Greeks possessed many stories of the beautiful and terrible love of the gods for particular men and women, not mankind as such, and we must suppose that this represented for the Greeks a way of conceiving of the intervention of the divine in human life. This view of the world has its finest expression in the brilliant, allusive poems of Pindar, the fifth-century writer of lyric poems for choruses.

Other stories arose from local cults and traditions though few became universally known. A widespread story told of the wanderings of the goddess Demeter in search of her daughter Kore, "The Maid," also known as Persephone (perhaps a separate figure at one time); she had been kidnapped by the god of what lies beneath the earth, Hades or Pluto, again probably separate conceptions in origin. Demeter's special province was the grain, the staple of ancient life, and in her sorrow the grain did not grow and men suffered. Zeus pities Demeter and mankind and arranges that Kore will pass part of the year with her mother, when the grain grows, and part of the year with her husband below the earth, when the grain is stored away. This is not a sacred story in that it was indispensable to cult and ritual or that it was the property of a priesthood. Rather it is the imaginative complement to a common ritual whose main concern was the continued fertility of the seed sown in the autumn after the dry, dead summer. The version of the story told at the most famous site of this cult had Demeter coming in disguise as an old woman to Eleusis, near Athens, where she was welcomed by the king's family and made the nurse of the king's son, whom she tries to make immortal by passing nightly through fire. She is discovered doing this and reveals herself to be the goddess but rewards the Eleusinians with the establishment of her cult and its secret rites, the "mysteries."

The Eleusinian version is told in one of the so-called "Homeric Hymns," poems never longer and usually shorter, than a single book of Homer in the epic language and meter, most of which were written in the Archaic period (from about 700 to 500 B.C.); the form at least originated as preludes to recitations of epic at religious festivals. The great sanctuaries at Delos and Delphi each accounted for a poem about their god Apollo, telling of his birth on the tiny island of Delos which welcomed his mother Leto when all other places rejected her for fear of Hera's anger (Zeus was Apollo's father), and how Apollo killed the serpent Pytho and established his own cult at Delphi. The gods come off much better in the Homeric Hymns than in Homer. They are kept in the foreground and do not simply form a backdrop to heroic action. Though all storytelling must be in human terms, here their humanity is pathetic rather than ludicrous—a mother who searches for her child, a mother who looks for refuge in which to bear her child. Greek religion made little use of the emotional power of such stories, but at least the pride of the great sanctuaries insured that their gods would be noble and beneficent.

The hymns to Aphrodite and Hermes celebrate their gods in more ambiguous terms and are less likely to be connected with cult places. Aphrodite is caught by her own magic and falls in love with a mortal man, the Trojan Anchises, father of Aeneas. Hermes, the messenger, the patron of the roads, is the god of those who use the roads—travelers, merchants, and thieves, who are not always clearly distinguished. The very day on which he is born he steals out of his cradle, rustles a herd of cattle from his brother Apollo, drives them (backward, so as to confuse pursuers) halfway across Greece, and invents the lyre with which he buys off the angry Apollo who threatens to bring him to court before their father Zeus. And yet the poet's obvious affection for the impudent wonder child of the gods should remind us that raillery and even insult is in no way inconsistent with an active cult of the god. So Dionysus, in his own great festival at Athens, appeared in Aristophanes' comedy, *The Frogs*, as a cowardly aesthete made doubly ridiculous by trying to pass himself off as Heracles.

These and other stories show the special powers of particular gods. Demeter's sorrow reveals her power over the grain. Aphrodite's power over love is seen in what happened to Helen, and to Phaedra, who longs for her stepson Hippolytus and, because she cannot have him, kills herself while accusing him of trying her virtue. The motif is that of Potiphar's wife and also appeared in a story about the hero Bellerophon mentioned in the *Iliad*. Phaedra's story is best known from Euripides' *Hippolytus* where Aphrodite uses Phaedra against Hippolytus because he discounts and despises the power of love. The myths of Dionysus show him a stranger, despised and rejected, or returning home from abroad unrecognized by his relatives, until his opponents succumb to the madness of his cult willy-nilly, without his having to make an effort. In Euripides' *Bacchae*, the god, in the guise of a leader of oriental women, devotees of his cult, is imprisoned by his cousin Pentheus, king of Thebes, but then is miraculously released. Meanwhile Pentheus has become fascinated by the cult and in order to spy upon the maenads (women affected by the god's madness) he disguises himself as a maenad. But he is caught and torn limb from limb by his own mother and other Theban converts who in their hallucination mistake him for an animal (a young lion) to be torn apart in their rites. These stories are often seen as a memory of historical opposition to the introduction of his cult from abroad, and Euripides' version as referring to the ecstatic, foreign cults introduced into Athens in the late fifth century. Whatever the truth in this, it may be wondered if the stories would have been so persistent through the centuries—Dionysus's name has been read on a Pylos tablet of the thirteenth century B.C., and the first known story is as early as the *Iliad*—had they not expressed a feeling that the god's cult was always something foreign and dangerous—fascinating, liberating, and wild, and so forever threatening reason and social order but, like the god, not to be denied.

When stories about the gods did not serve the interests of particular cults they are free to reflect how men emotionally if not literally conceived of the gods. In Homer's *Iliad* we found a sense of the gods' basic, incomprehensible hostility to man against which the depiction of their ignoble behavior may be something of a defense. In Hesiod's *Catalogue of Women* (whom gods loved) Zeus's ill will is made explicit:

> . . . and already Zeus who thunders on high
> was planning monstrous events; to blast a confusion of
> tempests over the endless earth; for he was now urgent
>   to
> obliterate the great race of mankind; and the end in
>   view
> was the destruction of the lives of the demigods,
> so the children of the gods might no longer mate with
>   wretched mortals,
> and so look forward to doom; so the blessed ones might
>   hereafter,
> as in the past have their own life and their own ways,
> apart from humanity . . .

(transl. Lattimore)

In Hesiod's *Theogony* the story of Prometheus's deception of Zeus is usually taken to be an explanatory ("aetiological") myth of how normal sacrifice originated: gods and men met together and Prometheus killed and divided an ox in two parts, keeping the meat and the inwards hidden in the skin and stomach while attractive rolls of fat covered only the white bones. Zeus is asked to take his pick and, though he knows better, he chooses the worthless fat and bones, which men ever afterward have burnt on altars for the gods. The story does not, in fact, explain why the Greeks sacrificed in this way. To the end of antiquity the Greeks continued to sacrifice like this, convinced that it was their major act of piety. But the underlying feeling of the gods' hostility had long interpreted a step in the sacrificial procedure as a deception of the gods that earned their anger—a deception and a hostility that are constantly renewed in the very act of honoring the gods. Prometheus himself is easily recognized as a figure of folk tale, the master trickster "for-seer," whose every victory against the gods brings compensating misery as much to mankind as to himself, whose creation of man may have been his first and greatest trick. The dramatic and intellectual implications of this conflict were explored by Aeschylus in a group of plays of which only the *Prometheus Bound* survives—the supreme example of the hostility of the divine, directed this time against man's champion, Prometheus.

Many stories tell of individual instances of the gods' hostility, of the fate of mortals who thought to rival the gods and so incurred their anger. A people whose imagination was dominated by the deeds of great men of the past, "demigods," as they came to be called after Homer, and whose gods so easily appeared in story as less noble but more durable men, had constantly to remind themselves of the gulf between man and god. When men were too successful and so tempted to think themselves the equals of the gods, the gods felt resentment. Some men challenged the gods: for example, Eurytus, the bowman, is killed when he challenges the archer god Apollo to a contest, as Aeneas's trumpeter Misenus is killed when he challenges the sea-god Triton in the Roman Vergil's *Aeneid*. Niobe, the proud mother of many sons and daughters (six, seven, or ten of each), boasted that she was a more successful mother than Leto, the mother of only two, the gods Apollo and Artemis, who promptly shot all the children. Sudden death, incidentally, in men was attributed to Apollo's invisible arrows, in women to those of Artemis.

In general it can be said that the stories of the gods when they are not modeled on or appended to the heroic myths have their own reality, unlike the historical reality of the heroic stories: their truth is that they reveal the nature of divine intervention in human life, and in this they resemble the myths of family violence and its consequences. When myth loses even this degree of reality and comes to be synonymous with falsity, as in popular use today, the creative era of myth is over.

THEOGONY

We have left until near the end that part of mythology which in some cultures would be primary and central—the origin of the world and the origin, history, and the generations of the gods. Most of the gods of cult, being presently manifest and potent, were conceived of, when need to relate them to one another arose, as more or less contemporary members of two generations of a single family, that of Zeus, Hera, Poseidon, Demeter, etc., and their children, Athena, Aphrodite, Hermes, Apollo, etc. This is not to say that they were always so conceived even in the Classical period or originally had this or any relationship at all to one another. For example, Aphrodite, the daughter of Zeus and Dione in Homer, and Eros, later commonly conceived of as her son, are both generations older than Zeus in Hesiod's *Theogony*, whereas it is now generally believed that the figure of Aphrodite is among the surest importations from the Near East and thus that she is relatively a late-comer. Eros, on the other hand, with his meaningful Greek name "Love," could be as old as the language itself. By and large, we can say that these questions of the genealogy and relationships of the gods simply did not arise for the Greeks in the ordinary course of life or even in their normal religious activities. Some need to relate one god to another no doubt was felt in local cults when more than one god was worshiped at a single shrine, and the analogy of the human family was at hand to formulate the relationship if not, indeed, to initiate it; human marriage, we take it, was prior to the joining of a god and goddess in cult. If the local gods happened to have the same designations or to be similar in important features to gods who were characters in more than local myth, this could lead to contradictions in the usual scheme: so, for instance, Poseidon and Demeter were husband and wife only in Arcadian cult. The trend was for these inconsistencies to be ironed out, especially in literature. Pan-Hellenic myth even came to introduce its own associations into cult; there was a tendency at shrines to fill out the divine families by recognizing other members with altars, with or without statues, and sacrifices or libations in conjunction with the principal cult of the shrine.

The one constant feature of Greek popular theogony, independent of cult and local schemes, is the place of Zeus as father of gods and men. It is with him that the Muses "begin and end their strain" in Hesiod's *Theogony*, the earliest Greek example of the type we have, and very likely the earliest worked out in detail and put into writing, as well as the most influential. Hesiod begins with the fact of Zeus and the divine order of which he is the paramount ruler. In popular thought the present dispensation may sometimes be seen as a time of labor and suffering and its character contrasted with a better age before it without toil and trouble, a time of the former ruler of the gods, Kronos, and his fellows; this is a theme treated by Hesiod in his other completely surviving poem, the *Works and Days,* concerned with man's place in the present scheme of things. The previous age is necessarily vague, for it is no more than a construct to show up our present condition, an Eden from which we have been banished. Kronos and his generation are vague figures with only the slightest traces of cult or independent existence apart from their place in this scheme. There is no reason to believe that Kronos was the chief god worshiped before

Zeus, or that he was "before Zeus" in any historical sense, because he is placed before him in divine genealogy.

This is about as far as common Greek tradition went in conceiving the past that lay behind the present order. But both in the Mycenaean age, the sixteenth to twelfth centuries B.C., and then again in the late eighth and seventh centuries B.C., Greece was in close touch with the cultures of the Near East and shared in their myth as well as their art. In the account of origins in Hesiod's *Theogony* there are too many resemblances to the oriental myths described elsewhere in this volume for all to be attributed to a parallel development. When we consider that in no case do we have models from which Hesiod's account could possibly have been descended in a direct line but at best distant cousins at least six centuries earlier or later than Hesiod, the similarities are all the more striking. The oriental versions with which the Greeks actually came into contact could have been considerably closer to the resulting Greek versions. This contact need not have been confined to one place or one time, though a major source of influence is likely to have been Cilicia and Canaan, where there were settlements of Greeks in the Bronze Age and also at Al Mina in Canaan in the Iron Age, not to mention what could have been learned through the Minoans of Crete and the Greeks and Semites of Cyprus. In the present state of our knowledge it is all too likely that we shall be tempted to count as oriental themes that are simply common to Greece and the Orient, but equally that we are overlooking genuinely oriental material. However, for the study of Greek myth, the admission of oriental influence is only the starting point. What matters is how and with what effect this new material was used, and it is with this justification that we shall draw on and add to the parallels presented in the essays on Hittite and Canaanite myth.

There is a distinctive passage of divine narrative in the *Iliad* (14. 153 ff.) which is not likely to be free of some form of oriental influence. Hera borrows Aphrodite's seductive girdle, claiming that she must go and reconcile the primeval father and mother of the gods, Ocean and Tethys, who "now for a long time . . . have stayed apart from each other and from the bed of love, since rancor has entered their feelings." Tethys, we hear, had taken Hera into her house from Rhea her mother, when Zeus fought Kronos. Hera wins the help of Sleep by promising him one of the Graces to wife and swears on the waters of Styx, calling to be her witnesses the Titans, the generation of gods before Zeus who are said to be below Tartarus (a region of the underworld). Her real purpose is the seduction of Zeus so that the Greeks may prosper on the battlefield while he sleeps. Though strictly subordinate to the larger pattern of heroic action the whole passage has the flavor of quite a different kind of poetry comparable only to some parts of the Homeric Hymns:

> . . . the son of Kronos caught his wife in his arms. There
> underneath them the divine earth broke into young, fresh
> grass, and into dewy clover, crocus and hyacinth
> so thick and soft it held the hard ground away from them.
> There they lay down together and drew about them a golden
> wonderful cloud, and from it the glimmering dew descended.
>
> (Iliad 14. 346–51, transl. Lattimore)

The points of similarity here with oriental myths include the comparison of Ocean and Tethys with Apsu and Tiamat of the Babylonians—a stage that is not found in the nearer Hittite sources. The gods around Kronos, "the Titans," may be compared to the former gods who are in the nether world in Hittite myth. There is also the theme of divine seduction in Hittite myth in Ishtar's attempted seduction of Ullikummi, as she had once seduced a dragon, and in the female sent by Ouranos to ensnare El-Kronos in Philo of Biblos's version of Canaanite myth (first or second centuries, A.D.). In a passage that is the sequel of the one just described in which Zeus and Poseidon expostulate with one another through a messenger we learn that Zeus claims the supremacy as the oldest brother while Poseidon reminds Zeus that he is his equal in rank and that he, Zeus, and Hades divided the world by lot between them: Zeus got the sky, Poseidon the sea, and Hades the dark underworld, while earth and Olympus were to be common to all three. This tripartite division does not really work in Greek cult and belief: instead of Hades we sometimes find "Zeus of the Underworld" and, as we have said Poseidon is often a god of agriculture rather than the sea. Consequently a comparable threefold division in Canaanite myth may be more than just a parallel. The Homeric interlude is narrative rather than theogonic or genealogical, but enough is seen incidentally to show the likelihood that oriental divine myths had reached the composers of Ionian heroic poetry, and in a form in some ways substantially different from the Hesiodic.

In Hesiod's *Theogony* (1022 lines) the contrast between the present dispensation and the past is extended back in the form of three generations whose main outlines can be paralleled in the Near East, where, however, four generations are more usual. Corresponding to the first generation Hesiod has a period of cosmic evolution in which he places the coming into being of various natural phenomena and barely personalized concepts, using the same word ("came into being"— *egeneto*) when no source is given as he uses when there is a source of parent ("came into being out of"—*exegeneto*) or as when male and female "mingle in love," in the epic formula for human marriage, and the metaphor of birth is explicit. First came Chaos, "void," "emptiness," and then Gaea, "Earth," and Tartarus "in the pit of the wide-wayed earth," and Eros, "Love," "handsomest among all the immortals, / who breaks the limbs' strength, who in all gods, in all human beings / overpowers the intelligence in the breast and all their shrewd planning." Out of Chaos came Darkness (Erebus) and Night, who mate and produce Air and Day. A long series of "children of Night" without father are of the same order of creation, meaningful names without cult or myth: Death, Sleep, Dreams, several different names of fate or doom, Misery, Deception, Friendship, Old Age, and Discord who, in turn, without husband, produces another long series of forces that affect man's life, including Toil, Hunger, Murder, Battles, etc. Earth brings to birth without husband Heaven (Uranus), the Mountains, and Sea (Pontus). With Sea she mates to produce various beings of the sea.

With Earth and Heaven's mating we are at the first generation of the line of descent of the rulers of the gods. In a widespread myth heaven covers earth and their separation permits the coming into being of all other things. A number of features show that even if this myth had once been native to the Greeks, with Zeus perhaps as the sky father, the version we have has a number of oriental parallels: Heaven is the grandfather of the present ruler of the gods, Zeus, just as, in the Babylonian and Hittite myths, he is two generations back. He keeps his children by Earth hidden within her. She conspires with her youngest, Kronos, who, as his father, Heaven, lies upon Earth, castrates him with a sickle. From Heaven's blood and members various creatures are born— the Furies (Erinyes), the Giants, and the Nymphs of the Ash Tree from the blood, and Aphrodite out of the sea foam that gathers around the members. The Hittite Kumarbi castrates Anu, but with his teeth, and there are creatures born of the seed; the sickle corresponds to the ancient tool with which Heaven and Earth were separated. In Canaanite myth, as recorded by Philo, El-Kronos castrates Heaven and the blood and the severed members fall into springs and streams. Kronos and his sister Rheia are parents of the Olympian gods, the present generation of powers. Kronos fears that one of his children will overthrow him and swallows each one as it is born: for Zeus, the last-born, his wife substitutes a stone which Kronos swallows. Thus Zeus escapes and is hidden by his grandmother Earth in a cave in Crete—here the Minoan myth of the divine child has been brought in to identify the chief male god of the Minoans with that of the Greeks. Somehow Zeus forces his father to disgorge his brothers and sisters; Zeus's triumph makes him the king of the gods and the Titans are confined to the underworld. Their collective confinement is clear, but several of them individually are seen to be part of Zeus's dispensation; in fact in the Greek scheme the Titans have no other function than to be the previous generation of gods, and their presence in the underworld could well be part of the oriental borrowing. The swallowing of the stone and perhaps the intention, at least, of swallowing his son is found with Kumarbi, the Hittite equivalent of Kronos.

Greece's geographical position, close but not immediately adjacent to the main centers of Near Eastern civilization, meant, first, that though she profited from contacts with the Orient she was never under its cultural domination and so was free to develop her own cultural resources; and, second, it meant that her contacts were intermittent. The strong contacts of the Mycenaean age, for instance, a period of trade and expansion, were followed by internal disruption and international isolation, which in turn gave way to the revived movement of trade and art in the eighth century B.C. The Greeks were always prone to identify foreign gods with their own, and the absorption of oriental mythological material once again in the eighth century would have been all the easier if similar material had been received and identifications made in the Mycenaean period and thoroughly assimilated in the succeeding centuries. However, after an interval of four or five hundred years, the new influences are not likely to have been identical, though similar, and we would expect that inconsistencies and even contradictions would be found, as they most certainly were in the native mythology. We have seen, for instance, in Homer the role of Ocean and Tethys as the primeval father and mother with its Mesopotamian parallels, but this is not their role in Hesiod. Even as the introduction of the elements of the alphabet, of mathematics, of large-scale sculpture and a multiplicity of decorative motifs from the Orient stimulated many aspects of Greek creativity so the myths of Greece's eastern neighbors served as a catalyst to her own mythical thought.

The details of this process are lost to view, but it is possible that we can see something of its operation in the work of Hesiod and in his reaction to a theme whose oriental source is assured. He lived at a time when the horizons of the Greek world were being rapidly and immensely enlarged and was a poet concerned with the organizing and cataloguing of tradition. In the *Catalogue of Women* he organized the raw material of his poet's craft under the genealogies of famous women. In the *Works and Days* he organized views on morality, farming, and various lucky and unlucky days and actions. In this organization he had, by his own account, a personal stake. Society was in crisis, old values were threatened, as he knew from his troubles with the local lords and with his own brother. The poem was to teach his brother, Perses, and others like him to forego cheating and to learn instead how to earn an honest living while staying on the right side of the gods. The reality of the authority of Zeus and of the divine order he represents are important to Hesiod as guaranteeing that the traditional powers still support the morality he propounds—Hesiod is right and his brother must pay attention. The urgency of the emphasis on Zeus is understandable, though there is nothing new to Greek thought in his paramount position nor even in a rather monotheistic conception of him. In the *Theogony*, however, where Hesiod organized traditions about the gods and especially about previous generations of the gods, the reasons for the insistence on the fact of Zeus's present power are less obvious. There is less interest in the character and realms of the various Olympians than in their victory over the previous gods, and Zeus is not so much the god of justice as the god who is presently and completely in control. Yet, one would have thought, for the Greeks this was never in doubt.

The explanation may be found in the need to reconcile conflicting traditions and identifications resulting from renewed contacts throughout Greece and with the Near East. For instance, if a sequence similar to the Hittite-Hurrian one of Heaven, Kumarbi, Storm God with the final victory of the latter had come to Greece, it could have been absorbed without difficulty, the Storm God being identified with the Greek god of weather, thunder, and lightning—Zeus. The present order is that of Zeus and agrees with the facts of cult and belief. However, a sequence such as is found among the Canaanites would cause trouble, for although after Heaven comes El, who is identified with Kronos by the Greeks and who castrates Heaven, the figure the Greeks equated with Zeus (explicitly in Herodotus 3. 158) is Baal, and Baal does not completely displace El. El continues to be father of men and gods, which is Zeus's title in Greece, and, in theory at least, the supreme authority. Of course we do not have the immediate oriental sources or the first Greek versions, but some such violation of a basic Greek view would have been quite enough to set Hesiod composing his vast hymn to Zeus where the previous generation of the gods are assigned their proper places and the true facts presented—after all, the Muses know also how to lie, as they told Hesiod himself on Mt. Helicon.

But if the occasion for the poem was the need to assimilate and reconcile oriental materials, old and new, Hesiod does much more than that. The awareness of the operation of the divine in man's environment which, in narrative myth was expressed by means of unseen intervention or dramatic epiphany, in Hesiod is revealed through a process of naming (with a minimum of dramatic character drawing) and relating through genealogy to describe the world as it is under Zeus —which means the world as it is. There are few stories here but the evocation of a world through names and their relationships. Earth, Sea, and the vast array of lesser figures— such as the sea children of Nereus, the children of Night and Discord, who are "old gods" in terms of theogony, continue to be effective forces in the world of Zeus. In contrast, Aeschylus, some two hundred and fifty years later, had learned Hesiod's lesson when he wrote of the former ruling gods who are gone forever:

> He who in time long ago
> was great
> throbbing with gigantic strength,
> shall be as if he never were, unspoken.

He who followed him has found
his master and is gone.
Cry aloud without fear the victory of Zeus,
you will not have failed the truth.

(*Agamemnon* 167–75, transl. Lattimore)

The use of divine genealogy to describe the world was for long the dominant, and always a popular, mode of speculative and moral thought. Except for sectarian versions, such as those of the so-called Orphics, designed to promote abnormal views and cults, Hesiod's version of the succession of generations remained standard, but not official, for most people even after its crudities were attacked by the philosophers. It may be doubted that many Greeks took such misty figures as Uranus or Kronos very seriously and only an utter crank like Euthyphro, in Plato's dialogue of that name, would think to justify his prosecution of his father by Zeus's unfilial treatment of Kronos.

It is curious that there is no mention of the origin of mankind either in the *Theogony* which, in the form we have it, leads by way of mortal brides of the gods through heroes born of divine mothers to the *Catalogue of Women,* or in other early sources, although Hesiod twice tells of the creation of women as a punishment for already existing man. The closest thing is the story in the *Catalogue* that only Deucalion and Pyrrha (daughter of Prometheus) survived the great flood, and all men are descended from them or from the stones they were told to throw behind them. Prometheus's role as the creator of man, though very likely an old folk tale, is not mentioned in our sources until the fourth century B.C. Partly this may be because of the particularism of the different Greek peoples who claimed to be "autochthonous" with ancestors born from earth itself (e.g., the Thebans born from the dragon's teeth sown in the ground by Cadmus and the Arcadians descended from earth-born Palasgus). Partly it may be that the old Greek view was that implicit in the description of Zeus as "father." "Father Zeus

. . . you do not pity men when you beget them to mix with misery and harsh pains" (Homer's *Odyssey* 20. 201–2).

To sum up, the dominant character of Greek mythology is given it by the paramount influence of heroic stories associated with the Mycenaean age and known through the Homeric poems and later poems modeled on them. Later, folk tales were widely admitted but in the guise of heroic or divine stories. The stories of the gods are also affected by the dominance of stories about heroic men, but they generally reflect the Greek view of the intervention of the divine in human life. Historically the Greeks derived little more than Zeus from their Indo-European heritage, various divine and heroic persons from the pre-Greek cultures of the Aegean, and the setting and action of their heroic stories from their own Bronze Age—the Mycenaean period. The influence of the Orient is strongest in their theogony, serving as a stimulus to organizing and thinking through their normally unexamined ideas about the origins and relationships of the gods. Finally, it may be suggested that the particular richness and persistence of mythology throughout the more isolated and, many would say, golden phase of Greek history, up to the Hellenistic age, comes from their developing from a simple peasant culture to an urbanized and sophisticated civilization at a certain distance from other comparable cultures so that while learning much from the Orient classical Greece was never culturally under its dominance, and thus had to exploit its own resources of language and symbol to the fullest extent. The Greeks did not have, as we do, a Greece and Rome to provide them with a technical vocabulary and a secular symbolism, nor a Jerusalem for their religion.

EPILOGUE

Through the classical period myth continues to be the main channel of artistic imagination. In the Hellenistic period when the small city-states and the few great sanctuaries were no longer the centers of artistic and intellectual life, and their institutions and traditions no longer the framework of all social life, then variety, originality, the unusual and exotic, learning and polish came to be prized. Peculiar local myths furnished much of the material for numerous local historians; literary historians made commentaries on earlier literature, giving variant versions of myth, and handbooks in which stories were set out systematically, in this respect continuing the efforts of the earliest historians. The local historians are preserved only in quotations; of their myth and religion we get a good idea from that ancient Baedeker, Pausanias, who visited old Greece in the second century of the Christian era. The literary commentaries are known to us mostly through the excerpts we call "scholia" that were copied as notes on the medieval manuscripts of ancient texts. Of the handbooks the best preserved is itself only a digest of Roman imperial times, that which is wrongly called the *Bibliotheca* ("Library") of Apollodorus. All are extremely useful for what they can tell us of myth in earlier writers. But outside of an artistic, cult, or social context myth is flat and meaningless, like the compendia used in modern times, where the only flashes of life come from the persistence even in disguise of that spirit which mythmakers had once infused into their stories—or from that new mythology in the form of interpretations by the modern compiler.

The creative writers of the Hellenistic and Roman periods also continued to use myth to speak of their own concerns, though the concerns and the myths chosen by learned and cosmopolitan writers were very different from those of an earlier time. Callimachus, the most remarkable of the Alexandrians, used curious local myths in his ingenious and sophisticated accounts of the origins of strange customs, the *Aetia*, and in mythological hymns on various gods which served as an occasion to exercise his versatility and show the breadth of his interests—myth, history, and political, literary, and personal comment. Romance has been mentioned in connection with the *Argonautica* of Callimachus's rival, Apollonius, and is the predominant function of myth in many elegiac poems, Greek and Roman; for a Roman poet's use a collection of erotic myths was compiled by the learned Parthenius. An interest in astronomy, and even more in astrology, led to a mythology of the stars in which constellations and stars came to be the ultimate form of many a star-crossed lover. Romance and fantasy gathered together and multiplied stories of transformations into plants or birds or stars where in a make-believe world there may be sadness and regret but nothing of any magnitude can happen to the characters or stir the reader profoundly. This is a world far removed from the strong realism of Greek mythology in its prime. It is not only, as is sometimes said, that Greek mythology loses power when men no longer believe in the gods but rather when men are spared the fate of men that myth is no longer capable of being the vehicle of the most serious thought and feeling, and even burlesque and parody lose their bite. Such art has its own charm and beauty, recognized, recaptured, and created anew from Roman times to the Renaissance and beyond. The greatest of the latter-day mythologists was the Roman poet Ovid, and I would let Gilbert Murray's description of his mythological world stand for the fate, at its best, of Greek mythology:

> *A world of wonderful children where nobody is really cross or wicked except the grown-ups; Juno for instance, and people's parents, and of course a certain number of Furies and Witches. I think among all the poets who take rank merely as story-tellers and creators of mimic worlds, Ovid still stands supreme. His*

criticism of life is very slight; it is the criticism passed by a child, playing alone and peopling the summer evening with delightful shapes, upon the stupid nurse who drags it off to bed. And that too is a criticism that deserves attention.

(in *Tradition and Progress* [Boston and New York, 1922] 117)

CHRONOLOGY

		GREECE	CRETE
	3000 B.C.		
BRONZE AGE		*Early Helladic Period*	*Early Minoan Period*
	2000 B.C.	coming of the Greeks	
		Middle Helladic Period	*Middle Minoan Period*
	1600 B.C.	*Late Helladic =* *Mycenaean Age*	*Late Minoan Period*
		about 1500 B.C., Greek possession of Cnossos on Crete	
———	1100 B.C.	Dorian invasion	
		Geometric Period	
IRON AGE	750–700 B.C.	Homer's *Iliad* and	
		Odyssey	
	700 B.C.	Hesiod	
		Archaic Period	
	500 B.C.	*Classical Period*	
		Aeschylus	
		Sophocles, Herodotus	
		Euripides	
	323 B.C.	death of Alexander the Great	
		Hellenistic Period	
		Callimachus,	
		Apollonius Rhodius	
	146 B.C.	sack of Corinth	Roman domination
		Ovid (43 B.C.–A.D. 17?)	
		[Apollodorus] *Bibliotheca*	

THE MAJOR GREEK GODS

ZEUS, son of Kronos. Latin Jupiter or Jove, King of the Gods, "Father of Gods and Men," "the Olympian." Symbol = thunderbolt, eagle.

HERA. Latin Juno, Zeus's Queen (and sister), patron goddess of Argos, Samos; goddess of marriage. Symbol = crown, veil.

POSEIDON. Latin Neptune, brother of Zeus; god of the sea, earthquakes, horses, and much more. Symbol = trident, horse.

HADES or PLOUTON. Latin Pluto, brother of Zeus, sometimes "Zeus of the Underworld," ruler of the dead, husband of Kore (Persephone).

DEMETER. Latin Ceres, sister of Zeus, goddess of grains, of agriculture; the sorrowing mother of Greek myth, mourning her daughter, Kore, abducted by Hades. With her daughter, goddess of the Eleusinian mysteries. Symbol = torch, ear of wheat.

KORE ("The Maid") or PERSEPHONE. Latin Proserpina, daughter of Demeter, abducted by Hades; Queen of the Dead.

ATHENA (ATHENE). Latin Minerva, daughter of Zeus (no mother), virgin, warlike; also goddess of crafts. Patron goddess of Athens. Symbol = owl, helmet and spear.

HEPHAESTUS (HEPHAISTOS). Latin Vulcan, son of Zeus and Hera, god of the forge, of industry. Lame. Symbol = hammer.

HERMES. Latin Mercury, son of Zeus and nymph Maia. Messenger of the gods, god of roads, commerce, doorways, luck; conductor of the Dead, patron of shepherds, athletes. Symbol = the caduceus (herald's staff).

APOLLO. Son of Zeus and Leto; god of the oracle at Delphi, of purification and music. Symbol = lyre, bow.

ARTEMIS. Latin Diana, sister of Apollo, goddess of the hunt, protectress of wild animals, of women; chief of the Nymphs. Symbol = bow.

DIONYSUS. Latin Bacchus, son of Zeus and Semele, god of emotional release, of drama, of vine; accompanied by Satyrs and Sileni (half-horse or half-goat), worshiped by Maenads (wild women). Patron of Thebes. Symbol = the vine.

APHRODITE. Latin Venus; also "Cypris," "Cytherea"; sometimes daughter of Zeus, goddess of love, beauty.

EROS ("Passionate Love"). Latin Cupid, son of Aphrodite.

ARES or ENYALIUS. Latin Mars, god of carnage.

In the spelling of Greek proper names often k = c; kh = ch; ai = ae; -os = -us.

In translation, Greek Odysseus is often rendered by the Latin Ulysses, Aias by Ajax, Heracles by Hercules, and Achilleus by Achilles, which last has also been used in this paper.

BIBLIOGRAPHY

The finest general account, magnificently illustrated, is in French: M. P. N. Nilsson "La Mythologie," in *Histoire Générale des Religions*, II, *Grèce—Rome* (Paris, 1948), pp. 150–289. The same author's *The Mycenaean Origin of Greek Mythology* (Berkeley, 1932) is the major work for the early period.

H. J. Rose, *A Handbook of Greek Mythology* (London, 1953 or New York, 1959, both essentially the edition of 1927) is the most useful, concise manual. Rose's *Gods and Heroes of the Greeks* (London, 1957) is a simplified account without reference to sources. Rose is also the author of most of the articles on mythology in the *Oxford Classical Dictionary* (Oxford, 1949) which is especially to be recommended since it provides brief articles on the geographical places and on the history and literature, all of which need to be consulted in connection with the myths. (I have followed the *Oxford Classical Dictionary* in the transcription and spelling of names.)

Among larger studies the standard work is by L. Preller, revised by C. Robert, *Griechische Mythologie*, part I (Berlin, 1894) and II (1920–26). The fullest dictionary, valuable especially as a collection of sources, is edited by W. H. Roscher, *Ausführliches Lexikon der griechischen und römischen Mythologie* (Leipzig, 1884–1937). Both works are in German.

Translations of ancient sources: Homer, *The Iliad*, translated with an introduction by Richmond Lattimore (Chicago, 1951). There is no comparable translation for the *Odyssey* until that in preparation by Robert Fitzgerald appears. Meanwhile one may read the translations of G. H. Palmer or W. H. D. Rouse.

Hesiod, *The Works and Days, Theogony, the Shield of Herakles,* translated by Richmond Lattimore (Ann Arbor, 1959).

For the Homeric Hymns and the fragments of Hesiod and Cyclic Epic see *Hesiod, the Homeric Hymns and Homerica,* translated by H. G. Evelyn-White with additions by D. L. Page (Loeb Classical Library; Cambridge, Mass., 1936).

Tragedy: The *Complete Greek Tragedy,* edited by D. Grene and R. Lattimore (Chicago, 1959).

[Apollodorus] *Bibliotheca* translated (with very useful notes) by J. G. Frazer (Loeb Classical Library; Cambridge, Mass., 1921).

(NOTE: the quotations I have given from the *Iliad,* Hesiod, and the *Agamemnon* are by R. Lattimore in the editions cited above.)

Mythology of India

BY W. NORMAN BROWN

1. VARIETIES OF RELIGIOUS MYTHOLOGY IN INDIA

There are at least three well-distinguished varieties of religious mythology native to India. One of these is that of tribes still living in a preliterate condition, either not yet absorbed in Hinduism or else only in the early stages of acculturation, recognizing their own local deities and largely unaware of the great Hindu gods and their mythology. These tribes' religious conceptions and myths are known to us from investigations made in modern times by ethnologists, folklorists, missionaries, administrators, educators, and others. Their mythology is only with difficulty capable of systemization. It is fragmentarily reported and the ideas are hard for field workers to identify and assess, often varying widely within a single language group or even a single tribe. Nearly always this mythology shows some relationship to classical Hindu mythology, but it also shows a great deal of independence. It will not be discussed in this chapter, which the terms of assignment restrict to the ancient.

The second kind of mythology is that which is attached to faiths founded by known persons; Buddhism and Jainism are in this category. In Buddhism the mythology is centered on the historical Buddha, and while there exists a good deal of Buddhist mythology which is not Buddhacentric, it is of less

importance in the faith. We may compare the mythology of
Buddhism in this respect to that of Christianity, which is
chiefly Christocentric. Jainism has a mythology which treats
almost exclusively of the twenty-four Tirthankaras or Saviors,
all but the last two of whom are without historical basis, and
with ancillary figures associated with them, the whole well
enough articulated for their mythology to have been compiled by the medieval monk Hemachandra (1089–1173) in
a single large work known as the Trishashtishalakapurusha-
charita or *Adventures of the Sixty-three Outstanding Personages.*

Standing in contrast to such relatively unified and articulated mythologies is the third variety, that of Hinduism, which
can in no way be given a unity. Hinduism is much more than
a religion; it is a total way of life, incorporating the customs,
beliefs, practices, institutions of peoples in all parts of the subcontinent developed at all periods of human settlement there.
As a religion Hinduism has set side by side in peaceful co-
existence every shade of belief ranging from the most primitive sort of animism to a highly sophisticated philosophical
monism, and with this has gone a corresponding range of
worship or practice extending from the simplest sort of effort
to propitiate fertility or vegetation or disease spirits to the most
concentrated meditation designed to produce knowledge of
abstract impersonal reality. The whole is a conglomerate,
a chaotic chance association, at best a loose confederation.
Theologically Hinduism is not a single religion but many religions, tolerating one another within the shifting social framework of caste. To see them as a unified and coherent whole
would be as difficult as to find unity and coherence in the
total landscape of the subcontinent.

It would not be possible to survey all of India's immense
mythology within the compass of this chapter, but a few
parts will be discussed which have a special interest as
symbolizing ideas which have been important in the development of religious thought there.

2. THE PROCESS OF CREATION

Our oldest literary records of India lie in the *Rig Veda*, composed in an archaic form of Sanskrit by Aryans who entered India from the northwest probably between 1500 and 1200 B.C. This work was presumably compiled by 1000 B.C. and consists of 1028 hymns by various priestly authors for use in the public Vedic sacrifice, through which the Aryan gods were gratified and strengthened and in return aided the patron of the sacrifice to achieve his legitimate aims. In this way men and gods collaborated to keep the universe operating smoothly and thwart the machinations of demons and their misguided human allies. There is a vast amount of mythology in the *Rig Veda* and the other closely allied and slightly later texts which all together constitute the body of Vedic literature, not presented in clear direct narrative or discussed in systematic exposition, but only indicated, hinted at, alluded to, or implied in terms that make its reconstruction a complicated and difficult procedure. The problem is somewhat like that which would face an investigator trying to reconstruct Christian mythology from church hymnals. The chief figure in the Rigvedic pantheon, however, is Indra—many more hymns are addressed to him than to any other deity—and his myth is the work's central theme. That myth largely concerns creation, and in brief form it is as follows.

In the beginning, before our universe existed, there were beings called Asura, a name which means something like "living power." One of these was a demon named Vritra, a masculine form beside which there is a neuter stem *vṛtra*, meaning "covering." We can see that Vritra the demon is a personification of *vṛtra*, the covering. Vritra is called a Danava, that is, "descendant of Danu, something having the character of Danu." This last is a feminine stem, derived from a root *dā*, "bind, restrain," and *dānu* means, therefore, "bondage, restraint." As such Danu is Restraint personified, and when Vritra is called a Danava, the meaning is that he too personifies restraint. Though Vritra has a mother named Danu, there is no father mentioned for him. The reason is simple; he is the manifestation of an abstraction, and when that abstraction is expressed as a feminine stem, the feminine gender of the stem furnishes a basis for giving him a mother. The metaphor, in short, is taken literally. But there was no metaphorical use of a masculine stem to provide him a father as well; hence the question of his paternity can be ignored. In post-Rigvedic times there are other Danavas besides Vritra; that is, the name Danava is applied to allies or subordinates which Vritra is said to have. In the *Rig Veda*, as in later times, they are called rakshas or rakshasa "demon," or sometimes Vritras. Also in later times they are called Daitya, which is a derivative from another feminine stem *diti*, meaning "bondage, restraint," coming from the same verbal root *dā*, "bind." Vritra is the archdemon of the *Rig Veda*, and he and his cohorts represent evil.

Besides Vritra and the Danavas there are other Asuras called Aditya. This is a derivative from a feminine abstract stem *a-diti*, meaning "non-bondage, non-restraint, release," and *āditya* means both "pertaining to release" and "descendant of Aditi." Thus the Adityas, too, have a mother, named Aditi, so that they are called outright "sons of Aditi" (*aditeḥ putrāḥ*) and their mother figures frequently in the *Rig Veda* as a benevolent feminine divinity, but again nowhere is a father mentioned for them. The chief of the Adityas is Varuna, whose name has so far defied all attempts to find it a convincing etymology. The Adityas represent good in the *Rig Veda*.

The Adityas and the Danavas were in a state of active hostility with each other; it might be right to call it a state of war. The Adityas were being worsted or at least were having no success against the Danavas. They needed a champion. This they got in the person of Indra, another Rigvedic figure whose name has never been satisfactorily explained in spite of many efforts, though his character and quality seem indicated by the epithets "son of might" (*sahasaḥ putraḥ*) or "lord or husband of might/Might" (*śacīpatiḥ*). Indra's parentage is uncertain, but perhaps the best deduction is that he was the son of Heaven and Earth, conceived and born at a time when these two were living together or had a common house. The birth was miraculous, apparently from his mother's side, as in later times was that of the Buddha. When first born, Indra remained in concealment, but he shortly got a drink of a powerful beverage called soma, which in one version of the legend he found on his mother's breast and in another got when it was brought him by an eagle, possibly the moon. The drink caused him to swell to an enormous and terrifying size, so terrifying that Sky and Earth flew apart, to stay so forever, while he filled the space between them, whence it can be said that he made his mother a widow and so is "the youngest or last [child]," while his realm of activity was the atmosphere, lying between heaven and earth, the region in which both gods and men move and act. He was not himself normally called Asura; rather he was called *deva,* "god," a term applied to the original children of Sky and Earth, namely the Dawn Ushas, etymologically equivalent to Greek Eos and Latin Aurora, and the two Ashvins or Sons of the Sky (*divo napātā*), a name corresponding in meaning to their Greek counterparts, the Dioskouroi.

The Adityas, and with them presumably the other gods, besought Indra to be their champion, but he, though young, was no innocent, and before accepting he stipulated that he should become their king. To this they had to agree. He now went forth to do battle with Vritra. Tvashtri, the artificer of the gods, had forged for him a weapon called vajra, which tradition regularly identifies as the lightning bolt, and when he had fortified himself with three great beakers of soma and thus increased his size and strength he attacked Vritra, whom the text describes as a serpent lying upon the mountains. The battle was fierce. Sometimes the hymns tell us that Indra fought alone; sometimes they say he had helpers consisting of Rudra and the Maruts, understood to be storm gods. Vritra was not only mighty, but crafty and full of magic wiles. Nevertheless neither his might nor his magic availed him. Indra finally brought down his vajra on him and broke his back, or, as is also said, burst his belly, or, as is still further said, split open the mountains. In the conflict he slew Danu as well, and the stricken mother lay upon her dead son.

When the fight was over it became apparent what the Adityas and the Danavas had been quarreling about. For out of the shattered mountains, or out of a cave, or variantly out of Vritra's belly, emerged the cosmic Waters, motherly females who had longed to escape confinement. They came out now like lowing cattle, flowing over the prostrate body of their former restrainer and lord Vritra, to acknowledge Indra as their new lord. And, astonishingly, the Waters were pregnant, and their embryo was the Sun.

All that was needed to construct the universe was now at hand: sky, earth, the atmosphere—the three parts of Vedic man's world—moisture from the Waters, heat and light from the Sun. Creation consisted first in differentiating the Sat from the Asat. Sat means the Existent, that is, the world of the Existent, the universe in which men and gods move. The Asat is the Non-Existent, the region of the demons, which lacks heat and light. The Sat, we are informed in the *Rig Veda*, was born from the Asat (10.72.2,3), which latter is described as now situated below the earth and reached by a great chasm, a place of terror, where the demons carry and destroy the wicked. The Sat was established with its three parts, and a pathway was made in the undersurface of the vaulted stone sky to be a course for the Sun to travel. The cosmic Waters took their abode in the sky, whence they let down moisture to the earth. Everything was put in order and set operating under rules devised for control, and different deities had separate departmental functions for supervising the operation. All this systemization and regulation was known as rita (*rta*), which means etymologically "set in motion" and has the idea in the *Rig Veda* of cosmic truth or order. Over the rita presided Varuna, the leader of the Adityas, seated in heaven and ever watching to see that no one violated any of the laws that together constituted the rita. Some passages in the *Rig Veda* say that Indra, or Indra and the gods, celebrated creation or even effected creation in a dance, where they "raised the dust."

In some other passages the gods are pictured as co-operating to institute the first sacrifice, at which time they pronounced the names of things and creatures, whereupon these came into existence. Later, the first man came into existence as a son of Vivasvant "the Wide-shining [Sun]," his function being to perform the sacrifice on earth and so strengthen the gods for the maintenance of the rita through the execution of their duties and the frustration of their demonic and human opponents.

How are we to interpret this myth? That is, what are the ideas which are symbolized in this story of anthropomorphic and theriomorphic beings? What had been going on in Vedic man's mind? We do not need to resort to psychoanalytic speculations; we can instead deal with material which seems to lie on the surface or at least not very far below it. The answer seems to be somewhat as follows. In the beginning was chaos. To be sure, all the elements needed to produce our universe existed in that chaos, but they were not in an ordered and operating state. Some of them, essential ones, were held or restrained within a hard covering, where they could not be used. Heaven and earth existed, too, though they were then joined together. Forces of expansion and release were present, however, tendencies conducive to the ordered arrangement and setting in motion of the parts of the universe, but their activity was insufficient to overcome inertia. There was a deadlock until power was generated of heaven and earth. This first drove heaven and earth apart, filling the space between them. Then, with the use of mobile fire, it overcame inertia, piercing the hard covering and releasing the reservoirs of water and the sun. The parts of the cosmos were now put into order or harmony and set in motion, to run like a machine. All, however, remained subject to power. Continued harmonious operation of the cosmic machine depended upon the performance of the sacrifice by men and gods in collaboration, each strengthening the other. This last was a never-ending process. Trends toward disorder were not completely eliminated when power set everything going. Every day the sun sinks and must be brought up again out of the black space below the earth; water must fall from heaven to nurture plants and provide food; and man must do his part in producing these phenomena. And everywhere the resistance of inertia must unceasingly be obviated.

We cannot say, because we have no direct evidence, that the impersonal and abstract basis is either older or younger than the concrete anthropomorphic myth. It is possible that the substance of the myth once existed without any kind of metaphysical rationalization such as is here suggested. Further, the myth, which is not Indo-European in character in spite of some echoes and parallels in Iranian mythology contemporary with it, also has wider affinities to the even older Sumerian and Assyrian mythology. This last may have reached the Indo-Iranians when they arrived in northern Iran. There the two parts of their community appear to have handled the Mesopotamian material in different ways, and the version developed by the Indo-Aryans acquired the particular form which we find in the *Rig Veda*. Though this theory is not implausible, it contains a good deal of the speculative and cannot be affirmed as a certainty.

It does seem certain, however, that the myth had a metaphysical meaning to some thinkers toward the end of the Rigvedic period, for we see it being challenged or being displaced by other explanations, which nevertheless reveal their subsurface relationship to the Indra-Vritra myth. These present some of the same problems, sometimes using the same verbalisms, but offering more sophisticated answers. They question and even reject outright the myth of an anthropomorphic demiurge imposing his righteous will upon an evil, resistant demon, and instead they substitute another kind of personal deity differently conceived or an impersonal force of some sort. There is a well-known pair of hymns which bear upon this point. In one of them (2.12) the power of Indra is affirmed and his qualities and deeds are extolled, with an implicit warning to people not to doubt him. The other (10.121) does not refer to Indra by name, but recites powers and deeds regularly ascribed to him, and in each case, in successive stanzas, asks who the god is whom men should worship with oblation, obviously meaning that the god is not Indra. In the final stanza the hymn gives the answer. The god, up to this point unmentioned and unidentified, is there named as Prajapati, "Lord of Creatures." This god is a kind of abstraction with no particular personality in the *Rig Veda*, who becomes a prominent figure not long afterward in the Brahmanas, where he is a supreme overseer god. A further implied denial of Indra appears in connection with an epithet given him in effecting creation when he is called the All-Maker (*viśvakarman* 8.98.2; 9.63.7). But elsewhere a separate deity is posited called Vishvakarman (10.81; 10.82), who proceeds in quite a different way than by slaying a demon and himself creates all, including the gods. Another kind of repudiation of Indra appears in connection with the feat of separating the Sat from the Asat. This it is stated Indra accomplished (6.24.5), but in another hymn (10.72) the feat is ascribed to the gods, after they had been brought into existence, when they performed the first sacrifice. That is, power lies in the sacrifice, not in Indra. The power of the sacrifice is indeed considered by some late Rigvedic sages to be supreme, and the final word respecting it in that work appears in the celebrated Purushasukta (10.90). There the gods effect creation by celebrating the first sacrifice with all the unordered elements of the cosmos being contained within the body of the sacrificial victim conceived as a gigantic anthropomorphic male (*puruṣa*), who encompasses all the universe which we know and extends beyond it.

The best known of the so-called "philosophical hymns" of the *Rig Veda* (10.129) shows us that work's most transcendent adaptation of the Indra-Vritra myth. In the beginning there was neither the Asat nor the Sat, neither the Non-Existent nor the Existent. There was no sky nor heavenly vault beyond it. What covered all? Where? What was its protection? Was there a fathomless depth of the waters?

For "covered" the text uses the verb *vṛ*, from which is also derived the name Vritra. The hymn goes on to say that there was then neither death nor immortality nor distinction between day and night. The first existent, called That One (*tad ekam*), though uninspired by any outside breath, breathed through its own potentiality, that is, came into existence spontaneously. Besides it nothing existed. There was darkness hidden by darkness at the beginning. This all was an undifferentiated flood. That which had the potentiality of becoming was hidden by a shell and was born through the power of its own heat. In the beginning desire came upon That [One], which One became the first seed of mind. The sages searching in their hearts with pious insight (that is, by introspection) found the relation of the Sat (the Existent) with the Asat (the Non-Existent). A line of demarcation was extended horizontally for them. What was below it, what above it? There were seed depositors, there were powers; there was potentiality here below, there was emanation above. Who is there who knows, who here can tell whence the origin, and whence this creation? The gods are on this side of the creation of the universe (that is, they too were created by something superior to themselves). Who knows then whence it came into being? This creation, whence it came into being, whether it placed itself (that is, was spontaneous, not created) or not—he who is its overseer in highest heaven, he surely knows, or perhaps he knows not. From this final statement we may infer that the author of the hymn thinks even Prajapati is ignorant of his origin and the origin of the universe; only the sages by mystic introspection have been able to discover the truth.

From then on in Brahmanical speculation on cosmogony the anthropomorphic figures of Indra and Vritra are absent, but there remain the concepts of material in chaos and will-directed power to give it order. The prevailing notion is of a primeval state in which the elements of the material universe are undiscriminated. Some force, often said to be soul or souls, moves in the mass and so differentiates the phenomenal universe. Or the souls may be quiescent until set into activity by the accumulated karma (force generated by their actions in previous existences) associated with them and so produce differentiation. The universe thus comes into existence. It passes through successive stages of deterioration from perfection until it finally reaches a state of maximum evil, whereupon it dissolves into nothingness or quiescence, to remain so for an astronomical period of time, after which a new creation takes place. The process has gone on and is to go on indefinitely in a cycle that reaches backward beyond our imagining and will extend forward beyond it also. This is the viewpoint roughly of the Sankhya, Yoga, Nyaya, and Vaisheshika philosophies, of the epics, and of the Puranas. Varying somewhat from this are the conceptions of the Former Mimansa system, and the still different ones of the Later Mimansa, which is generally known as the Vedanta. At almost all points the thinking is in terms of the impersonal, both with respect to the inert material of the universe and to the effective power that moves it, differentiates it, gives it form. The myth which symbolized the earliest Brahmanic philosophizing had by this time ceased to serve a purpose for those who were in the stream of speculative philosophical development, yet it was part of the hidden foundation on which their systems were erected.

3. THE CULTURE HERO AS DEITY

Modern Hinduism is for the most part divided between those sects devoted to the worship of Vishnu and ancillary figures and those devoted to Shiva and figures associated with him. Each of these two great gods is a syncretic deity, combining in his over-all self many different separate deities who have become blended with the capital figure, while their names have also become his names. Further, Shiva has a wife and Vishnu has two wives, and each wife is a syncretic deity as well, uniting in her person more than one female deity and bearing the names of all. It is admittedly impossible to identify the original figure in either the Shiva or the Vishnu complex. We find both the name Vishnu and the adjective shiva (*śiva*, "kindly") in the *Rig Veda*, but this fact does not necessarily mean in either case that the element in the syncretism denoted by the word is the god's oldest or original element. There may be other elements, coming from non-Aryan sources, of equal or even greater antiquity, possibly autochthonous in contrast to the Aryan element, which last may not have been known in India until the arrival of the Aryans in the second millennium B.C.

The god Vishnu combines in himself an unusually large number of forms. He may be conceived as Vishnu embodying the totality of his various elements, or as the striding, ascending, conquering hero sun (Vikrama or Vishnu) or as the brilliant shining sun (Surya), or as any one of his ten major avataras or incarnations—the word *avatāra* means "descent [from his supernal form in heaven] to earth"—or in any one of his lesser avataras, sometimes enumerated as twenty-two, to which we may add the further statement that his incarnations are really innumerable. His magnetic capacity to attract other figures to himself is a dynamic one; all over India there are shrines to local godlings whom worshipers characterize as aspects of Vishnu. At the beginning of the present century there were Hindus who expected, and Christians who feared, that Christianity in India might be absorbed in Hinduism through an identification of Christ as an avatara of Vishnu.

Not all the forms of Vishnu receive much worship; for example, the historical Buddha is the ninth of Vishnu's ten major avataras, but he has no cult of any note. The two most popular aspects of Vishnu are the seventh and eight avataras as Rama Chandra and Krishna. Each of these, like every other form of Vishnu, has his own separate mythology, and each of these mythologies is in its turn a blend of mythologies about separate elements that have come to constitute the whole composite figure. We may consider here certain features of that which aureates Rama Chandra, commonly known simply as Rama, whose story is narrated in the Sanskrit epic *Ramayana* (Tale of Rama).

Rama is, first, the pattern of the temporal aristocracy, the group of castes known as Kshatriya. As a prince his character is represented as without reproach; as a ruler he was the ideal king, and *rāmarājya*, "rule of Rama," is a synonym for the lost Golden Age and for the future Utopia. He seems also to have been a vegetation deity, perhaps representing the fertilizing function of the sky, while his wife Sita, whose name means "Furrow," symbolizes the productive earth. Their fate is interwoven with that of the demon Ravana, the archvillain of the *Ramayana*, perhaps originally some malevolent power of nature that opposed the fecundating mission of Rama and Sita. Third, Rama is the mythic agent for spreading Aryan (that is, Brahmanic or Sanskrit) culture to the then un-Aryanized south of India, where even now Aryan culture is primarily a possession of the Brahmans overlying a substratum which is chiefly Dravidian. These three strains of his character seem to have been fused by the fifth or fourth century B.C. in an early form of the *Ramayana*. Later, other elements were added: an introductory narrative explaining that Rama is an incarnation of Vishnu, while Sita is an incarnation of Lakshmi, Vishnu's consort, and a conclusion telling of her banishment and life with her two sons in the hermitage of Valmiki, the traditional author of the epic.

The received text of the total *Ramayana* begins with the theme of Ravana, demon king of Lanka (Ceylon), who had once received a promise from the god Brahma that he should not be killed by god or demon. In his overweening insolence he was oppressing the world, above all interfering with the sages' holy sacrificial rites, necessary to both men and gods. At about this time King Dasharatha of Ayodhya, in northern India, had been performing a horse sacrifice that he might continue his line; for, though he had three wives, none had borne him a son. The gods had come to get their share of the offerings, and, pleased with the sacrifice, they promised that the king would have his wish. Then they went to Brahma to ask for some remedy of the evil he had caused by his criminal generosity to Ravana. Brahma, realizing that Ravana had left himself vulnerable in not demanding that he be immune to man as well as to god and demon, advised the gods to beseech Vishnu that he incarnate himself for the purpose of slaying the demon. The gods made the request and Vishnu consented. To fulfill his promise Vishnu caused himself to be incarnated as four sons of King Dasharatha, that is, as Rama and his brothers Lakshmana, Shatrughna, and Bharata. At the same time, at Vishnu's request, the gods mated with various kinds of non-human, semi-divine females, such as apsarases, kinnaris, and others, to produce in swarms the vanaras (monkeys) and other creatures that were to be Rama's allies in the future war with Ravana.

Before Rama was sixteen years old he went out on a series of adventures, in the course of which he married the peerless Sita, daughter of King Janaka, won when he bent a bow that no one else could master. Shortly after he got back home, King Dasharatha decided to abdicate and nominated Rama as heir apparent, but Queen Kaikeyi, mother of Rama's half-brother Bharata, by now claiming a boon granted her long before by the king and since then held in reserve, had Bharata nominated in Rama's place and Rama sent into exile for fourteen years. Rama set forth accompanied by Sita and his brother Lakshmana. They wandered in the forest, dwelling at the hermitages of various sages, and at last settled down at Panchavati beside the river Godavari, on the northern edge of the Deccan plateau, where they built a hut and lived in happiness.

While they were dwelling there, a loathsome demoness Shurpanakha ("she who has nails like winnowing baskets"), sister of Ravana, chanced to see Rama and made advances to him, which he repulsed. She complained to Ravana, who sent out fourteen demons to slay Rama, and then 14,000, all of whom were defeated, but one named Akampana escaped to Lanka, Ravana's capital, to report the affair. Enraged, Ravana vowed to slay Rama but was advised by Akampana not to attack him; rather he should abduct Sita, whereupon Rama would quickly pine away to death. The plan was for one of Ravana's warriors named Maricha to take the form of a golden deer with silver spots, show himself near Rama's hut, and beguile him into pursuit. Rama slew Maricha, but as Maricha died he emitted a great cry in a voice exactly like Rama's, "Sita! Lakshmana!" Sita compelled Lakshmana to go to Rama's aid. This was Ravana's chance. In the form of a wandering mendicant he came to Sita and got her to tell her story. Then he revealed himself as Ravana and offered her himself and his kingdom. She rejected him, he took his true form and violently put her in his ass-drawn air-traveling chariot and headed for Lanka. On the way he was attacked by a giant vulture which destroyed the chariot, but Ravana beat him down and continued to Lanka. There he installed Sita in his palace and renewed his suit, but again he was repulsed.

Meanwhile Rama and Lakshmana, distraught at the loss of Sita, wandered about until they chanced upon the vulture, which with his dying words told them of his battle with Ravana. They went south in their search, met a headless monster who was under a curse, and Rama cut off his arms, whereupon he was released from his curse. He advised them to get aid from Sugriva, rightful king of the vanaras (monkeys) but now ousted by his usurper brother Valin. Rama slew Valin, restored Sugriva to his throne, and won him as ally. The rainy season now came on, and when it was over, Rama and his allies set out to find Sita. Sugriva's general, a monkey named Hanuman, discovered from the dead vulture's brother that Sita had been taken to Lanka, a hundred leagues (*yojana*) across the sea. With one gigantic leap Hanuman crossed the water and came to the magnificent city of Lanka. There at night he reduced himself to the size of a cat, entered the city, conquered its guardian spirit, and came unobserved to Sita's presence in time to hear her again refuse Ravana. When Ravana had left he revealed himself, showing a ring Rama had given him for identification, and offered to take her to Rama, but she declined on the ground that as a faithful wife she could allow no male to touch her but her husband. Hanuman left her, destroyed a temple, and was caught by the demons with the aid of a magic charm. He was taken to Ravana but escaped a sentence of death on pleading that he was an envoy and therefore inviolable. However, he was punished for the harm he had done by having an oil-soaked cloth tied to his tail and ignited. The fire did him no harm, thanks to a Truth Act Sita had performed by her chastity, and he leaped from place to place in Lanka setting houses on fire, and then leaped back to the Indian mainland.

To get to Lanka, Sugriva's forces built a bridge of trees, stones, and mountains. The battle was long and fierce. Rama accomplished nothing by shooting at Ravana's ten heads, for as fast as a head was shot off another grew in its place. Finally he discharged a heavenly arrow which he owned, and this pierced Ravana's heart and the victory was won.

Hanuman now brought Sita in a palanquin, but when she approached, Rama made her dismount. Surprised at this conduct, yet enraptured to see her lord, she did so. Then Rama told her that he had fought the war and killed Ravana, not for love of her but to avenge his honor and restore broken laws. But for her he had no further use: Ravana had thrown his arms about her; she was stained forever. Vainly she protested her fidelity and at last asked Lakshmana to prepare a funeral pyre. Then she made another Truth Act by her chastity, to the effect that if she had always been a true wife, the fire should not injure her body. She entered the circle of flame, and the crowd shrieked. Then the god Brahma rolled back the flame, and Sita emerged unscathed, led out by Agni, god of fire, who restored her to Rama. Rama now declared that he had insisted upon such a test of Sita, not because he had any doubt of her, but because appearances were against her and he could not risk letting the folk think he would live with an impure woman as his wife.

Indra now restored the dead vanaras to life, and Rama returned to Ayodhya in a magic chariot. There Bharata gave back the throne, for he had all along acted only as regent.

Rama now ruled for ten thousand years. There was no death in his kingdom, no disease, no crime; the earth yielded abundantly; peace was unbroken. At the end of this period Rama returned to his form as Vishnu, transporting all the inhabitants of Ayodhya to Brahma's heaven without suffering death.

In the final (seventh) and later book of the *Ramayana*, Rama, bothered by gossip in the city, exiled Sita again, now pregnant, and she took refuge in the hermitage of Valmiki. There Rama one day discovered her and her twin sons, when as he was passing by he happened to hear the latter reciting his deeds as narrated by Valmiki, then in the process of composing the epic. He begged Sita to return to Ayodhya and reaffirm her purity. This ordeal, however, she could not endure. She made still another Act of Truth by her chastity, this time asking her mother, the Earth, to receive her. The ground opened, a throne appeared, the Earth placed her on it, and then it descended underground amid a rain of heavenly flowers.

No section of Hindu mythology is more deeply venerated than the tale of Rama and Sita. There are countless small shrines to Rama and others to Hanuman throughout India. Every autumn in most parts of India their story is enacted in a ten-day celebration. On the last night huge bamboo and paper figures of Ravana and his chief adjutants are burnt in a noisy and joyous conflagration, often with explosions of gunpowder that has been placed inside them. Thus righteousness triumphs again over evil.

The name of Rama is blessed throughout India, for one who calls upon Rama will not be refused. This is understood literally. For example, a story tells of a thief who was being punished with death by impalement. As he was dying he kept repeating the word *marā* (dead), but as he kept saying "*marā, marā, marā*" again and again, the syllables inadvertently came to form the name "*rāma rāma rāma*" and when he died he went to Rama's heaven. When Gandhi was assassinated, he died saying, "*He rām*" (O Ram), which words are inscribed today on his memorial at Delhi. The final

stage in the evolution of the Rama myth came with the great
Hindu poet Tulsi Das (1532–1623), who composed a version
of the *Ramayana* in which he describes Rama as the supreme
soul and constantly, after relating each single incident in
the story, invokes Rama in mystically phrased thought and
prayer.

In this composite figure of Rama, which blends mighty
warrior, forest-wandering pioneer, and carrier of culture—
a kind of George Washington, Daniel Boone, and Hernando
Cortez in one—the element which I would stress in this study
is that of culture hero. Two names figure in Aryan mythology
as carriers of Aryan civilization to South India. One of these
is the doughty sage Agastya, a well-known character, who
once swallowed the ocean and at another time caused the
then lofty Vindhya Mountains to bow down before him when
he was on his way to the south, to stay prostrate until he
returned, but since he never returned they still lie low,
unlike the towering Himalayas to the north of them. Agastya
carried the *Veda* and the sacrificial fire to the south, which
is a symbolic way of saying he civilized the region. Rama,
the warrior, is represented in the *Ramayana* as having gone
to visit Agastya some ten years or more after he went into
exile, and at that time Agastya presented him with a bow
that once belonged to Vishnu, an inexhaustible quiver, a
javelin that had been Shiva's, and a sword. Rama's conquest of
the south is by force of arms, as we have seen. He is thus
represented as having brought culture and light to the
aborigines, who when intransigent are called demons and
when willing converts monkeys and bears. The social stigma
of their state as something less than men, though possessing
some human characteristics, is hardly removed by the later
rationalization recorded in the *Ramayana* that gives them
descent from the lesser gods and semi-divine females, a
rationalization doubtless less inspired by a wish to soften
Brahmanical Aryan contempt of non-Aryans than by a desire to give appropriate status to the allies of incarnate godhead in the battle of righteousness. It is possible and not
implausible that the culture hero is the first element in the

Rama constellation, though we cannot prove it to be. His tale might even have a historical basis, and some scholars have endeavored to date it, but without getting general credence. There are other Aryan culture heroes, who are stated in varying terms to have civilized non-Aryan regions, such as Mathava Videgha, who followed the sacrificial fire Agni into Bihar, according to the *Shatapatha Brahmana*. But none of these has become identified with one of the great gods. Rama's elevation remains something of a mystery. Was it some other element in the complex that elevated the total? Or was it only when the full complex had come into existence that its importance caused it to be assimilated to Vishnu? We cannot say, but we may surmise that the latter is the more likely.

4. GOD IS LOVE

Krishna, the eighth avatara of Vishnu, encloses within himself two dissimilar personalities of probably separate origin, both of which were doubtless once conceived only as human beings. One presents Krishna as a bucolic hero living in the forests beside the Yamuna (Jumna) River near the city of Mathura (Muttra). His legend is widely familiar all over India; its best versions are in the tenth chapter of the *Bhagavata Purana*, a work possibly as old as A.D. eighth century, and in the *Vishnu Purana*, an earlier work. The other personality is as a warrior in the much more ancient epic, *Mahabharata*, who recited the celebrated mystic poem known as the *Bhagavad Gita* (Song of the Blessed One). The story attached to the first personality is briefly as follows.

In Mathura ruled the wicked King Kansa, who had been born to the queen of King Ugrasena but was not Ugrasena's son. A demon had seduced the queen by impersonating Ugrasena. Kansa had usurped the throne and was ruling with such unprecedented tyranny that the earth, in the form of a cow, besought aid of the god Indra. The latter, accompanied by the other gods, went to Brahma for relief. Brahma sent them to Shiva, and Shiva sent them to Vishnu, who promised to have a portion of himself incarnated as Krishna to destroy Kansa. Another portion of himself or of the endless serpent Shesha, on which he reclines and which is also sometimes considered to be a part of himself, was to be incarnated as Balarama, Krishna's older brother, to be his companion and helper. Not long after this it was prophesied to Kansa that he would be slain by a child of his female cousin (or sister) Devaki and he was about to have her killed, but her husband Vasudeva persuaded him to spare her on condition that Vasudeva make over her children to him as fast as they were born. In this way Devaki's first six sons were destroyed, but the seventh, Balarama, was transported while still a fetus to the womb of Rohini in Gokula, across the river from Mathura, where he was born and raised in safety. Kansa held Vasudeva and Devaki in prison under strong guard. Devaki's eighth pregnancy was with Krishna. When born, he revealed himself to his parents as the Primeval Being Adipurusha, dark-colored, wearing his crest and necklace, bearing ornaments, four-armed, with the attributes of Vishnu in his hands, namely, conch, discus, mace, and lotus. All the gods came to adore him. Then he erased the memory of this vision from his parents' mind so that they thought him only a mortal child, which they feared Kansa would slay. But miraculously Vasudeva was enabled to escape from prison and ford the river Yamuna, which subsided when Krishna's foot touched the water, and with his infant son in his arms he carried him to Gokula, there to substitute him for the newborn daughter of the herdsman Nanda and his wife Yashoda, who in turn miraculously lost all recollection of the fact that the child actually born to them had been a girl.

Now follows in Krishna's life a large number of infancy and youth stories, some indicating his divine powers, some depicting his irresistible charm. In the first category are his triumph over creatures sent by Kansa to destroy him or over jealous gods who try to humble him. For example, Kansa sent a demoness named Putana, who smeared her breasts with poison, arrayed herself in her finery, went to Yashoda, took up the infant Krishna, and started to nurse him. But Krishna sucked the very life out of her so that she fell down dead, while no harm came to him. At another time Kansa sent a demon to ambush him in the forest when he was tending cattle, but Krishna grasped the demon by the foot, swung him around his head, and threw him to the ground and so killed him. At another time a demon in the form of a crane tried to swallow Krishna, but Krishna promptly defeated him. Once a huge serpent swallowed Krishna, his fellow cowherds, and their cows, but Krishna swelled in the serpent's belly until he burst it. Again, in the river Yamuna dwelt a noxious serpent named Kaliya, which harassed the people living nearby until Krishna fought with it, grasped it by the tail, whirled it about his head, and is represented either as slaying it or as sparing it at the intercession of its wives on condition that it and they leave the Yamuna to live in the ocean. Again, he slew a demon named Panchajana and won from him the conch Panchajanya, which is one of his attributes. Once the god Brahma stole the cows and cowherds, but Krishna, that great illusion-maker, made others that were exactly like those which had been carried off. On still another occasion the rain-god Indra and Krishna were engaged in a contest because Krishna advised the cowherds not to worship Indra. Indra sent a great flood of rain to wash aways the herdsmen and their cattle, but Krishna raised Mount Govardhana over them and supported it on the tip of his finger, thus sheltering them beneath it for seven days and nights until Indra acknowledged Krishna's superiority and stopped the deluge.

Of the incidents which illustrate Krishna's charming childish and youthful behavior, some may be mentioned. At one time Yashoda discovered him eating dirt. She reproved him and commanded him to open his mouth so that she could remove it, but when she looked inside she saw there the entire three worlds. He used to interfere with the milkmaids (*gopī*) when they were churning butter, or steal and eat the butter. Once for his pranks he was tied to a post or a mortar. He pulled this mortar along until it stuck between two trees, and then by the exercise of divine strength he uprooted the trees, whereupon there stood forth two beautiful young men, sons of the god Kubera, who had been cursed by the sage Narada to become trees until Krishna should release them. When Krishna was five, Nanda and Yashoda went to live in the forest of Vrindavana (Radha's forest), and there Krishna insisted upon becoming a cowherd. He grew up in the forest, ever playing his flute, with which he charmed the cowherds, the milkmaids, and the cows alike. Once he came upon a party of milkmaids while they were bathing and he stole their clothes and took them to the top of a tree, making them beg for their return. Later, in the month of Karttika (October–November), he called them to the dance he had promised when he stole their clothes. They came deserting their husbands, longing for Krishna. He at first danced with them in the circle dance called the rasalila, then abandoned them, and they searched for him in despair; then he returned and danced with them again, exercising magic yoga power to multiply his body so that each girl thought she had him as a partner. Of all the girls his favorite was Radha, who is considered to be an incarnation of Lakshmi, Vishnu's consort, and it was with her that the real Krishna danced. The love of Krishna and the milkmaids (gopis) and especially his love of Radha are celebrated in lyrics, paintings, sculpture, and there is a whole body of erotic literature and even of erotic cult practice connected with this aspect of the Krishna myth. He dances with the gopis; he swings with them, above all with Radha; he is shown with the god of love Kama in company with them; he and Radha have their separations, their misunderstandings, their ecstatic reunions. Through all these adventures as the darling of the milkmaids he never incurs the jealousy of their husbands, who view these affairs with no dismay, for they too are under the spell of Krishna's charm. Even the matrons of Mathura cannot resist him. When he went to that city to beg food of the

Brahamans, the latter refused him but they were foiled by their wives, who gave it and reaped the reward.

When the right time came, Krishna went to Mathura, where after a number of adventures he slew the wicked King Kansa and restored Ugrasena to the throne, while he and his brother Balarama took up their residence in that city. Later, when other enemies appeared, Krishna built the citizens of Mathura a new and safe city called Dvaraka on the western coast of the peninsula of Kathiawar. Finally, when his mission was accomplished, he and his brother Balarama died and were reabsorbed in the godhead of Vishnu and the endless serpent Shesha.

The character of Krishna in the epic *Mahabharata* is quite different from that of Krishna in Gokula, Vrindavana, and Mathura. In the *Mahabharata* he is chiefly represented as a warrior, a mighty fighter, who uses guile as well as skill in arms. He worships Shiva and befriends Arjuna, the commanding field general of the Pandavas, representatives of righteousness, in the war with their cousins the Kauravas, who represent evil. It is as counsellor of Arjuna that he recites the *Bhagavad Gita*.

The setting of the *Bhagavad Gita* is dramatic. The physical scene is the field of the impending battle, with the rival armies drawn up opposite each other. Arjuna, the beau ideal of warriors, goes in his chariot with his charioteer Krishna to the no man's land between the two armies. There he surveys the enemy whom he is bound to slay, and sees in their ranks kinsmen, friends, his teacher; and his heart fails him. His limbs sink down, his irresistible bow falls from his hand, his mind is distraught. No longing for victory does he feel when it has to be won at such expense. World rule would be only a grief. Moreover, by destroying his own family, he would undermine the very structure of society. He would produce lawlessness, from which would come corruption of the women, and this would lead to caste mixture. Only hell could be the fate of him and his followers. Better would it be for him to let the other side slay him unresisting. Unnerved, he collapses in the pit of the chariot.

But Krishna, to whom Arjuna has told his despondency, is no mere charioteer but an incarnation of Vishnu. Though born a warrior, he is by force of circumstances obligated to abstain from fighting in the great battle. However, he has associated himself with the side of righteousness and become Arjuna's charioteer in a status that might be called benevolent non-belligerency. Arjuna has some measure of awareness of Krishna's high origin, though far from a complete one, and so he puts the problem before him, asking for instruction. Little does he suspect how full an answer he is to get. For Krishna in the remaining seventeen chapters of the *Bhagavad Gita* deals with the structure of society, the duties of its respective parts, including that of the warrior caste (Kshatriya), to which Arjuna belongs, cosmogony and cosmology, man's psychological organization, the nature of god, the goal of human existence, the ways to reach that goal.

Krishna is called the Exalted or Blessed or Adorable One (*bhagavat*) and he begins his discourse, called *gītā* (song) by answering Arjuna's immediate question. But in doing so he almost at once touches upon most of the other topics. In fact, he touches upon many topics wherever else in the *Gita* he deals with any single one as a starting point. For all the topics are interrelated, and the *Gita* is meant to be a "practical" work, aiming to give an exposition of all important matters of life and religion.

Krishna tells Arjuna that as a Kshatriya he has a duty to fight. Especially, in a war of righteousness he should not withhold his hand. But he need not fear real harm in the highest sense; for the only real part of man is the soul, which is unitary in all men, is indestructible, and is in fact unknowable except by itself. This is the monistic idealism of the Upanishads. Under further questioning, Krishna goes on to explain the purpose of life, which is to know God. He announces himself as God, and in the climax reveals himself to Arjuna in all his majesty and glory. The ways to God are various. One is by works, doing one's duty fully but doing it selflessly, without attachment, that is, seeking no end except the performance of duty for its own sake. Another way is by knowledge, seeking and attaining perfect knowledge by means of intensive concentrated meditation, a way of the greatest difficulty, which only the rarest of men is capable of pursuing successfully. There is, however, still another way, which is easier and better, namely, that of loving devotion (*bhakti*) to God. One who adopts that will be accepted by God; Krishna will always receive the true seeker. Devotion is thus the way by which all men can reach God. They need not be profound metaphysicians or iron-willed adherents to duty. The simple, but devout and loving, heart is enough. By means of it one can gain the fullest knowledge, can know God, can win to Him. Such a one, in fact, has a special advantage: "I am the same to all beings," says Krishna. "There is no one either hateful to Me or dear; but those who adore Me with loving devotion, they are in Me and I too in them." (9.29)

Arjuna absorbs all the teaching, acknowledges Krishna as God, is heartened, and prepares to enter the battle, which his side is destined to win. Meanwhile the teaching of the *Bhagavad Gita* has let him and the world know that God can be reached by man's effort, and that the best means of reaching God is by loving devotion to Him, for God himself is Love.

In the two personalities united in Krishna the common theme is love, love which runs the gamut from the simplest to the highest. The infancy legends show Krishna as the charming child of destiny, adored by all good creatures, aided by them when he needs help and in his turn aiding them in their need, a child full of heart-enthralling tricks, lovable and loving, reciprocating love with the maximum capacity of which a child is capable. In his youth he is the lover whom none can withstand and whom none envies. Playing the flute, dancing with the gopis, he lives a life of untrammeled joyousness with his companions in a never-never land, where they prove all the simple pleasures. He is India's apotheosis of infancy and youth. But this is far from all. In his relations with Radha and his mass love affair with the gopis he symbolizes the relation of god with the human soul; he is the individual god of each human being, yet really one and indivisible, whom all reach. This is also the teaching of the

Bhagavad Gita. Through many ways all come to the same goal; deliverance follows merely because of the search. One may even seek him as enemy and still win him, for in some of the legends those who attack him and are slain by him nevertheless are taken by him into his heaven. This all-encompassing love of God is then the central theme of the Krishna legend, which has both endeared the bucolic hero to millions of worshipers and at the same time has made the *Bhagavad Gita* the favorite book of other millions, including Gandhi. The mythology of Krishna is a mythology of a natural human emotion, which is complex in its many manifestations, yet simple in its need of gratification. When recognized and gratified it is man's best hope—or so, at least, the followers of Krishna maintain.

5. THE MEDITATIVE ASCETIC GOD

Among the remains of the prehistoric Harappa civilization which flourished in the valley of the Indus during the third and second milleniums B.C. are representations on seals and pottery of a human figure seated in a posture later used by practitioners of the yoga system of meditation or flanked by worshipers. In one case the figure is accompanied by serpents; on two seals it is three-faced and on one of these it is surrounded by various animals. These figures are generally interpreted as representing a deity, and the resemblances between them and aspects of the god Shiva, as he is known in historical times, were pointed out in 1931 by the late Sir John Marshall in the book *Mohenjo-daro and the Indus Civilization.* We cannot categorically affirm that these figures represent Shiva or even an older form of some one of his constituent elements, but there is a *prima facie* case in favor of such an identification, while no other suggestion has been offered that is as plausible.

The implication of such an identification, if correct, would be momentous. It would mean that those aspects of Shiva which associate him with serpents, know him as Pashupati, "Lord of Creatures," and connect him with the practice of asceticism and the use of yoga postures and conventionalized gestures of the hands and fingers (*mudrā*), which are among the oldest known religious phenomena of India. There is even more. In the historic period Shiva is, and for two thousand years has been, commonly worshiped with a representation of the phallus as his symbol, while his wife Parvati is symbolized by the female generative organ. Unmistakable examples of the phallus have also been found in the Harappa culture, while other objects have been found which may represent the vulva, though the latter identification has been questioned. The problem presented by these items is one of the most fascinating in the history of Indian religions. The answer to it would presumably illuminate many other features of Harappan civilization besides the religious and would help to clarify the relationship of that civilization to later historic Indian civilization.

Shiva, like Vishnu, is a syncretic god with many strands woven together to compose his total self. He is the Vedic storm-god Rudra, "the Roarer." He is the Mountain-born One (*girija*), whose home is in the Himalayas. There on Mount Kailasa he and his wife Parvati live in perfect marital happiness. He is the righteous avenger, shocked at evil in high places, who punishes the god Brahma for incest with his daughter. He is Nataraja, "Lord of the Dance," who when the demon Muyalaka attacked him pressed his toe upon his back and broke it, and then with him underfoot danced the cosmic dance of creation, maintenance, and destruction, wherein his four arms and his feet are posed by Indian sculptors to represent that cyclic flux in what is one of the world's greatest plastic conceptions. He is the generative principle of the universe, the gigantic phallus which Brahma going upward and Vishnu going downward to seek its tip and its root tried in vain to measure. He produces the angry fire of dissolution at the end of an aeon, in which the universe is consumed, to be re-created when he so wills. He and his wife Parvati lead a kind of nomadic camping-out life, often being shown with their two children, Ganesha, god of wisdom and remover of obstacles, and Karttikeya, god of war and patron of thieves, and accompanied by his vehicle, the bull Nandi, and her vehicle, a lion. They give succor to the poor and unfortunate, provided only the latter are pure of heart and devoted worshipers. He is a frequenter of isolated spots, a cave or a mountain height or a cremation ground strewn with half-consumed human corpses, infested with scavenging jackals, and haunted by man-destroying witches and demons. There he practices meditation, his body smeared with ashes, his hair uncut and heaped upon his head in a tangled mass.

The side of Shiva which commands our attention for the moment is that as the meditative ascetic. Just as archaeological remains of India's oldest civilization illustrate a yoga pose, so the oldest literature of India also records some notions and practices later associated with yoga. There is a Rigvedic hymn (10.136) which tells of ascetics (*muni*), wind-girdled, wearing soiled yellow garments, who follow the course of the Wind, when the gods have entered them. The ascetic flies through the air, the text goes on to say, "looking upon forms of every sort, the muni, incited by the gods . . . the long-haired one drank from the cup of poison with Rudra." The muni and the sun are being compared in this hymn, and in the comparison we see some of the ways by which the mystic experience of visiting the world of the gods, of practicing levitation, may be induced: leaving the body behind, the muni ascends in spirit, being under the influence of some poison, that is, some drug. In post-Vedic times Shiva is frequently represented as using a narcotic drink, made of hemp, and he is sometimes shown in eighteenth-century paintings in a Himalayan setting with his family, accepting such a drink from Parvati, who has just brewed it for him; it is evidently not the first he has had on that occasion, for his eyes are already glazed and rolling. The orders of ascetics, called sadhus or yogis, vowed to his service, have long been notorious for their use of drugs to induce mystic sensations. The fullest mastery of yoga, Sanskrit texts tell us, can be won only when sought in intense asceticism, and the highest knowledge can be won only with the aid of yoga practice; hence Shiva, the practitioner of yoga, has also become the archetype of ascetic. He is described in a well-known poem called *Hymn of Praise to the Greatness of Shiva* (Śivamahimnastava, stanzas 9, 24) as follows:

A mighty bull, a skull-shaped club, an ax, a tiger's skin, ashes,
　　serpents,
And a skull—this, and no more, is your chief paraphernalia;
But the gods possess their separate powers, entrusted to them
　　by a flicker of your eyebrow;
For a mirage of objects of sense does not delude that one
　　(Shiva) whose delight is in his soul.

Your sport is in burning grounds, O destroyer of Smara (god
　　of love); pishachas (demons who devour the flesh of
　　human corpses) are your companions;
For ointment on your body you use ashes from funeral pyres;
　　your garland is a string of human skulls—
Let your character and your name as well be wholly in-
　　auspicious,
Yet, O gift-bestower, to those who call you to mind you are
　　the supreme auspicious sign.

Though Shiva frequents macabre spots, his preferred place of meditation is the Himalaya. There in his devotion to the quest of knowledge of the Self he practiced meditation so devotedly and successfully that he conquered himself (*svaṃ jitavān*). But since his self is the Self, in conquering himself he won the greatest victory of all time. One time, however, he himself was vanquished, though the victor paid a penalty for his temerity. The familiar story was narrated fifteen hundred years ago by the great dramatist and poet Kalidasa in his *Ode in Celebration of the War God's Nativity* (*Kumārasaṃbhava*).

Once the universe was troubled by a noxious demon, so

powerful that even the gods were helpless before him. They learned, however, that if the god Shiva could be persuaded to have a son, he would be able to destroy the demon. This seemed difficult to manage; for Shiva was grieving for his wife Sati, who had recently died in consequence of slights heaped upon Shiva by her own father; and, further, he was in the high Himalaya absorbed in meditation. But it happened that the beauteous daughter of the Himalaya, Parvati by name, who was none other than a reincarnation of Sati, was seated nearby practicing austerities to win him as husband. The gods, therefore, delegated Kama (Desire), the god of love, also known as Smara (Memory), to take care of the affair. Kama set out accompanied by his wife Rati (Passion) and his adjutant Vasanta (Spring). When they reached the Himalaya, the snow and ice melted, soft breezes blew, flowers blossomed, all nature was filled with life and joy. Kama watched his opportunity, his bow of sugar cane full-drawn, a flower-tipped arrow in the string which was made of honey bees. At a moment when Shiva relaxed the intensity of his meditation, Kama let fly. The arrow struck home, and when Shiva felt it he glanced around, saw Kama, and flashed a fierce flame from his third eye, which utterly consumed Kama's body. But being a god and immortal, Kama did not die; only his body was consumed; hence he is often known as the Bodiless One (Ananga). But Shiva had glimpsed Parvati; the arrow did its work; a marriage took place; a son was born called Karttikeya or Kumara; and in due season the demon was slain and the universe saved.

Sects of wandering ascetics or sadhus devoted to Shiva go about India, practicing tapas (austerity), which an eminent Sanskrit scholar used to define as a "stunt" with a religious or quasi-religious end in view, and visiting the shrines sacred to Shiva that are dotted all over the subcontinent. They dress in ragged garments, often no more than the scantiest G-string, their bodies are smeared with ashes, their uncut hair is piled in snarled coils on their heads, their ears are pierced to hold great earrings. They go with staff in hand, or with Shiva's weapon and emblem, the trident, selling charms, professing to perform miracles, sometimes accompanied by a female ascetic of similarly unkempt appearance. Unfortunately, these ascetics have an unsavory reputation. They are generally ignorant, seldom practice meditation, are economically unproductive, are held responsible for much mischief and crime, and the literature of India for almost two millenniums has testified to this record. Ascetic wanderers they may be, but seekers of the Self by conquering themselves through meditation they all too often are not. Sometimes they may be sincere devotees of asceticism and meditation for true religious ends, but sometimes they may be cultivating yoga for base purposes, seeking only to gain the magic powers that may be acquired at an advanced stage in the progress toward complete mastery. And frequently, of course, they are only charlatans. Nevertheless to the folk, and doubtless to themselves as well, the mythology of Shiva is accepted as basic fact, and this belief gives status to ascetics using his name. The average person, who may have his doubts about a sadhu arriving in his community, also feels that he lacks sound criteria for distinguishing between the true seeker and the pretender, and does not want, does not dare to risk offending one who may possess supernatural and dangerous powers. Such is a consequence of the aura emanating from asceticism and yoga practice, whose mythology is part of that clustering around the mighty figure of Shiva.

6. THE GREAT MOTHER

Though we cannot be absolutely certain that some predecessor of Shiva or aspect of his being was a god in the times of the Harappa civilization in the third millennium B.C., we seem to have almost unarguable assurance that one of the many strands comprising the composite character of his wife Parvati has such an age. This is her role as the Great

Mother, one of her most important roles, and Sir John Marshall has pointed out the probable relationship. There have been found at Harappa sites many pottery figurines of pregnant females, corresponding in general appearance to figurines found to the west in Baluchistan, Elam, Mesopotamia, Egypt, Cyprus, Crete, the Cyclades, the Balkans, chiefly in the second millennium B.C. It is considered that in Western Asia these are representations of the Mother Goddess, or the Great Mother, or the Earth Mother, whose worship was generally observed throughout all this region, and it is assumed therefore that the same worship existed in the Indus Valley.

Unfortunately, it is not until long after the period of the Harappa civilization that we get literary records in India expounding beliefs about the Great Mother, and relating mythology connected with her. We hear of her in literature of the middle and late classical periods, especially in the Puranas, from A.D. sixth century on, and also in the Tantras, whose dates are indeterminable though probably later than those of the Puranas. She appears as a part of the syncretic deity Parvati, known also by the names Uma, Gauri, Ambika, Durga, Kali, Chamunda, Minakshi, and many others, including especially the name Devi (goddess), that is, *The* Goddess par excellence. The reason why we do not hear of her sooner doubtless is that the Great Mother is not Aryan in origin and was late in getting Brahmanic recognition. She is quite different from any of the female deities of the *Rig Veda*. It is true that in early post-Rigvedic times we find literary allusions to ideas similar to some associated with Devi, such as the lotus on the waters, symbolizing the earth in the cosmic ocean, while in early Buddhist sculpture of the second and first centuries B.C. we see vegetation rhizomes and lotuses, which as the late Dr. A. K. Coomaraswamy pointed out are assimilated to representations of the deified earth, but these items become associated in Brahmanic Hinduism with Lakshmi, wife of Vishnu, rather than with Parvati, and though originating in a popular sphere are elevated in Brahmanic thinking to the realm of symbolized metaphysics.

The Great Mother goddess, the Earth Mother, is widely worshiped in India today in non-Aryan circles; in South India every village has its collection of Ammas, or Mothers, and their worship is the chief religious exercise of the village. Frequently one of these is the head of the sorority, while the others are local deities manifesting particular powers or having control over limited subjects. The priests of such deities are not Brahmans, as are those serving other aspects of Parvati in the great temples, but are members of lower castes, thus indicating the pre-Aryan, or at least non-Aryan, worship of these goddesses. Mother Goddess worship is also prevalent in the north, and sculptures of the Mother Goddesses appear in India in mediaeval times. Gradually such deities, and especially the Great Mother goddess, make their way into Brahmanical Hinduism, to become best established in Tantric literature. But the Scriptures dealing with them and with Parvati as the Great Mother are Agamic or non-Vedic, as contrasted with the Vedic or Nigamic. The Great Mother conception still has a dubious position in Brahmanic circles.

It is not easy to tell what aspects of Parvati's multiple person are outgrowths of her character as the benevolent Great Mother and what aspects belong to figures developed apart from the Great Mother. There is the horrific form of Ambika, created with the most powerful qualities of all the gods, who slew the otherwise invincible buffalo demon Mahishasura; there is Chamunda, who destroyed the demons Nishumbha and Shumbha. There is Kali, who in her elation at annihilating demons danced until the earth rocked and the gods feared for its safety, whereupon they called upon Shiva to intercede, and he lay down before her until she danced on his body and then in shock stopped. In such forms she rides upon a terrifying lion, and has many arms carrying an immense array of weapons. These sides of her godhead demand bloody sacrifices, the usual victim being a goat, but legends tell of human victims as well. It is hard to reconcile these fierce figures with the kindly, benevolent parts of the complex. Her mythology also tells us that by practicing intense asceticism she won as her husband Shiva, the great lord of procreation. Once she had won him, she remained ever true, but not always the eternal homebody taking care of their two sons and running the household, though paintings and stories may show her in such guise. Rather than a Griselda, she is a demanding, quick-tempered wife, quite ready to resent a real or fancied slight, or be jealous of some other of Shiva's ladies, such as Sandhya, the Twilight, or the heavenly river Ganga (Ganges), who has lived in Shiva's hair ever since he caught her there when she descended from heaven and would have overwhelmed the earth.

The final word in Parvati's history was reached when she was identified by followers with the all-powerful feminine principle considered to be the fundamental and dominant element in the universe. In this phase of her character she is generally called Devi (The Goddess), though her other names are applicable as well, and many words meaning mother are applied to her, such as matri, janani, amba, and others. The feminine principle is known as Shakti (śakti, a feminine abstract noun meaning "power"), and worshipers of that principle as the supreme principle are called Shaktas (śākta). Such worship is part of the whole large section of Hinduism known as Tantrism, because its texts are called Tantra. It is centered around Shiva and Devi, though every god has his Shakti, without which he is powerless. As a much esteemed mediaeval ode to Devi (Saundaryalaharī) says, "If Shiva is united with Shakti, he is able to exert his powers as lord; if not, the god is not able to stir." He is, in short, in the latter case only unrealized potentiality. In Shakti worship the feminine principle far outweighs the masculine. So dominant is it that it is only through Devi's grace that all the various other gods have their powers. If Devi were to close her eyes for but an instant all the cosmos would disappear including the gods. Her motherly concern keeps her from doing so and preserves the universe with all its helpless and dependent creatures. When the cyclic great dissolution finally comes, all does disappear except Shiva, whom she saves out of wifely devotion.

Devi's supreme position among the gods as the first principle of the universe is forcefully affirmed in Shakta texts. The *Saundaryalahari* (Flood of Beauty) tells much about her. The Scriptures (*śruti*) wear her feet as their crest. She is mind and the five material elements, namely ether, air, fire, water, earth. She is also the supreme and unseconded Intelligence and pure Bliss. Anyone who really comes to understand her complete nature can master the whole universe, apparently because he becomes one with her. The gunas, or strands of the material universe, which are white, red, and black, are hers and their colors are the colors of her three eyes; for, like her husband Shiva, she has an additional eye. In her lies all love. She inspires Kama, god of love. Let a worn-out old man, unattractive and long since become incapable in the art of love, but chance to fall in one of her side glances, and he is transformed into an irresistible youth, whom bevies of young women pursue, their hair flying loose, the bodices slipped from their swelling breasts, their girdles burst, their garments dropping down. One who worships Devi throws a spell over the heavenly nymphs, and even the triple universe, conceived as a woman with the sun and moon as her breasts, is agitated by him. She embodies the whole power of creative love, from which everything springs. But besides this kind of love, she also embodies motherly love. To her devotee she is all grace and maternal concern. He calls upon her as a child addresses its mother, and she cherishes him, taking him to herself, so that he at last becomes one with her, experiencing a flood of supreme joy, tasting boundless intense bliss. Thus he wins to salvation and life everlasting.

At some time, date unknown but probably before A.D. 1000, the Shakti cults accepted the notion that there resides within the human being a power known as kundali or kundalini, which normally lies asleep in the form of a serpent in three and a half coils surrounding a penis in a mythical center or circle (*cakra*) or nerve plexus at the base of the spinal column. By the use of yoga techniques one can awaken this power and cause it to ascend to five other mythical centers lying one above the other along the spinal column. As one becomes more adept, he can cause it to rise ever higher until at last, when his mastery is complete, he can cause it to pass above the sixth center and reach the thousand-petaled lotus (*sahasrāra*) assumed to exist at the top of the cranium. The six centers are described in various texts in terms which indicate that they represent in the human being as microcosm similar centers in Devi's body as macrocosm, while the thousand-petaled lotus represents her residence in her essential and non-material form. From there, having Shiva as her mate, she evolves into the six elements of the material universe in stages. In the highest of them she produces mind, then in the one below ether, in the one below that air, and in the remaining three fire, water, and earth. This completes the evolution: the world is thus born having Devi and Shiva as mother and father.

When a human being causes his kundalini power to ascend he is retracing within his microcosmic self the steps of macrocosmic creative evolution, and when he causes it to reach the thousand-petaled lotus he has reached the state of non-material unevolved and unmodified first principle. This is man's highest good, and it constitutes indescribable bliss, for he has attained to pure being.

There exist a number of Shakta cults, falling into two fairly distinct groups. One is the Samayin or dakshinachari (right-hand) school and the other is the Kaula or vamachari (left-hand) school. The latter has various kinds of extreme practices, including the erotic. Of these the most notorious is that of the pancha-ma-kara, use of the five essentials of worship, the word for each of which begins with the sound of the letter *m*, namely wine (*madya*), meat (*māṃsa*), fish (*matsya*), finger-gestures (*mudrā*), and sexual intercourse (*maithuna*).

Tantrism as a whole and Shakta cults as a part of it have a large place not only in Hinduism, but also in the varieties of Buddhism existing in northern Bengal, Nepal, and Tibet, and in certain cults of Jainism. Their beginnings we cannot see, but they may be of the greatest antiquity. Though we cannot say categorically that they existed in the Harappa civilization 4200 years ago, representations there of the phallus (*linga*) and possibly the vulva (*yoni*), in form much like the representations in historic India, constitute presumptive evidence that they did. In that case the mythology of sex power would have existed then too, probably in association with the whole generative process as symbolized by the notion of the earth as the Great Mother, and so we may not unreasonably say that this aspect of religion was the earliest in civilized India, as indeed it may well be thought to have been in many other parts of the world.

7. THE HUMAN TEACHER AS SAVIOR

Two of the great religions of India are recognized by their adherents as well as by Western scholars as having been founded by human beings. These are Buddhism and Jainism. Buddhism was founded by Siddhartha Gautama, the Buddha, who probably lived 563–483 B.C., though the traditional Sinhalese dates are equivalent to 624–544; Jainism was being preached at the same time by Vardhamana Jnataputra, generally known as Mahavira, whose dates are given by the Jains as corresponding to 599–27 B.C. or variantly by modern scholars as 539–467 or 549–477 B.C. He taught a doctrine in the tradition of a predecessor named Parshva, who, the Jains say, died two hundred and fifty years before him. Parshva was probably the founder of the faith, Mahavira a preacher who added or modified a few points and popularized it. Both Mahavira and the Buddha carried on their activities in the present Bihar and the eastern part of Uttar Pradesh in northern India.

The sixth century B.C. was a time of great religious and philosophical creativity and also of economic expansion in that region. Commerce was thriving, large cities were coming into existence, trade routes to both East and West had become important, a wealthy aristocratic land-holding group had established itself, a rich merchant middle class was rising in the urban centers. Presumably the population was increasing, too. Small states were developing, out of which grew larger ones until in the latter part of the fourth century B.C., Chandragupta Maurya created the first great Indian empire with its capital at Pataliputra (modern Patna) on the Ganges in Magadha in Bihar. Conditions were favorable in this region for a revolt, or any rate a protest, against the Brahmanism of the late Vedic period. The latter frankly regarded cities as places of evil and taught that the religious life could be cultivated only in forests. It affirmed also the overriding power of the elaborate Vedic sacrifice performed by Brahmans according to an ancient ritual of the greatest complexity and carrying unrivaled authority. The Brahmans arrogated to themselves, as custodians and sole competent officiants of this all-important ritual, a position of moral and social superiority to both the old temporal military and governing aristocracy and the newly developing merchant middle classes. At the same time, this region had been only imperfectly Aryanized. The river Gandak, which enters the Ganges hard by Pataliputra, had not many centuries before been regarded as the eastern boundary of the Aryans, and Magadha and the regions beyond it had been looked upon with contempt by the authors of the sacred Brahmanic texts. Hence it was only natural to find the powerful nobility and the rich middle classes there restive before the Brahmans' pretensions.

Even within orthodox Brahmanic circles there, that is among those who acknowledged the authority of the Vedas, there were some with a skeptical attitude toward the excessive Brahmanic ritualism. Videha, adjacent to and north of Magadha, was the scene of some of the most important speculative discussions recorded in the Upanishads. These works as a class recognize validity in the ritual, but, having given it that much service, go on to teach a higher knowledge concerning the soul and the reality in the universe. Janaka, king of Videha, was himself an inquirer, who welcomed philosophers to his court that he might discuss ultimate truth with them. As there were seekers who honored the Vedas, so there were others who had no reverence for those works, and side by side with Upanishadic speculation there existed unorthodox inquiry and teaching. Thus the gentle and moderate Buddha and the austere Mahavira shared something despite their anti-ritualism with the rather crabbed Yajnavalkya, who is pictured in the Brahmanic texts as philosopher and ritualist alike.

It was to the landed aristocracy and the rich urban merchants that Jainism and Buddhism made their appeal. Both faiths denied the validity of the Vedic ritual; both rejected the claims of Brahmans to the maximum holiness and the highest social status merely by reason of birth, proclaiming on the contrary that one is a Brahman only by reason of his conduct. Such teaching made them heretics (*pāṣaṇḍa*) in Brahmanical eyes, but it gained them the patronage of the politically and economically powerful. Each faith also, in promulgating its doctrine, abstained from using the Brahmanic language, Sanskrit, which at that time had its center to the west of Bihar, and instead used dialects locally current, Pali for Buddhism and Ardhamagadhi for Jainism, which became the vehicles of their canonical texts. Still further, each preached a new ethical doctrine, that of Ahinsa (*ahiṃsā*) or non-injury of living creatures. This was not known at all to early Vedic literature; the word appears only once in the older Upanishads and there most inconspicuously; even the *Bhagavad Gita*, though employing it four times, again does so without any emphasis or elaboration, so that Professor Franklin Edgerton can say of the doctrine in the *Gita* that "some lip-homage is paid to it. But it is never definitely and sharply applied in such a form as 'Thou shalt not kill.'" In fact the *Bhagavad Gita's* immediate aim is to inspire the reluctant Arjuna to do his duty as a Kshatriya and fight the battle of righteousness, destroying evil without feeling qualms at slaying those who support it. To Jainism and Buddhism, however, Ahinsa was the first of all ethical principles. They preached it constantly in a thou-

sand ways and with such success that it made its way into
Hinduism as well and was firmly established there early in
the Christian era.

Buddhism and Jainism represent their great teachers or
Saviors as being born in Kshatriya families, not Brahman,
and in this respect they remind us of the parentage of Rama
and Krishna. Jainism goes even further, for it maintains that
when the soul of Mahavira descended from the Pushpottara
heaven to be born on earth it was first conceived in a Brahman
woman's womb. But the god Indra, becoming aware of this,
reflected that all Saviors (*tīrthaṃkara*)—Jain mythology
recognizes a series of twenty-four—were born in Kshatriya
families, not Brahman. To prevent this latest Savior from
being born of a Brahman woman, he sent the general of his
army, Harinaigameshin, a deer-headed fertility deity, to transfer the embryo from her womb to that of the pregnant Queen
Trishala, and this he did, putting both women into a deep
sleep, and then exchanging the two embryos. Thus Mahavira
had a prenatal history not unlike that of Krishna and
Krishna's older brother Balarama.

In Buddhism and Jainism an extensive mythology has developed around the great teachers who became Saviors,
much richer than the brief credible data we have concerning
them and far more significant to Jains and Buddhists, just
as the legend of Christ has meant more to Christians than
have the bare historical facts. In each religion, also, the legend
has expanded as the centuries have passed. The lives of the
two masters have a good deal of similarity along broad lines,
although details differ, as if there had been in India an
informally accepted pattern of myth appropriate to great
teachers. The mythic conception of each teacher has echoes of
Vedic myth, as in employing some of the characteristics and
epithets of the Vedic idea of the sun as conquering hero.
Jain mythology also has many points of contact with the
mythology of Krishna; of the sixty-three "outstanding personages" in Hemachandra's great work, twenty-seven have
been shown to be associated in one way or another with

Krishna. There is, in short, a certain degree of relationship between Buddhist, Jain, and old Brahmanic mythology.

Before their historical and final existences the Buddha and Mahavira had had innumerable others as many kinds of beings. Buddhism recounts far more of these than does Jainism, and one Buddhist work alone (*Jātaka*) deals with 547 of them. With each of these teachers the last life before the historical life was one of great duration spent in a heaven. Conception is accompanied by wondrous dreams; Mahavira's mother sees fourteen (a variant account makes the number sixteen); Siddhartha's mother sees a white elephant entering her side. Marvelous dreams regularly accompany the conception of a Great Person (*mahāpuruṣa*). Shortly after conception both fathers have the dreams interpreted by wise men, who announce that the child is destined to be either a universal emperor or a world savior; in the case of the Buddha a second prediction is made after the birth, when the sage Asita, who has seen a host of divine beings in the sky rejoicing that a future savior has been born, goes to the place they indicate, looks at the babe, sees it has the thirty-two characteristic bodily marks of a Great Person, and then, like the Christian Simeon, prophesies its destiny and at the same time is saddened that he himself will not live to see the prophecy fulfilled. Siddhartha's mother gives birth standing up and the child comes forth from her side, while she dies seven days later, as do the mothers of all Buddhas; but Mahavira's mother produces her child lying down and in the usual manner, and does not suffer premature death. Gods attend the infants at birth. There are various legends of childhood and youth concerning both, especially in noncanonical texts, recounting the schooling, the selecting of a bride (or brides), encounters with friendly and unfriendly superhuman creatures. These legends are different from those relating to Krishna's infancy and youth, while one of the two great divisions of Jainism, the Digambara (Sky-clothed) Jains, whose monks go naked, deny that Mahavira ever married. Each future teacher lives in his father's palace, sheltered from the world, gently nurtured, enjoying luxury and all possible pleasures, and the father of each wishes the worldly career of universal emperor for his son. Buddhist legend tells that Siddhartha is awakened when the gods give him successively sight of four premonitory signs, heretofore never seen by him—an old man, an ill man, a dead man, who together illustrate the misery of life, and finally a monk, who illustrates the method of finding release from that misery. In the Jain legend the gods come to Mahavira when he is thirty years old, adjuring him, "Propagate the religion which is a blessing to all creatures in the world!" Mahavira then resolves to leave the world, gives away his possessions, goes forth in a palanquin, which he presently has stop under an ashoka tree. There he dismounts and dismisses it; then he removes all his ornaments and plucks out his hair in five handfuls, which the god Indra receives. Siddhartha, however, having first viewed his young son and disgustedly looked at the women of his harem, repulsive in their sleep, goes forth secretly in the dead of night, riding his horse Kanthaka, with his charioteer Channa holding on to its tail, while gods keep its feet from striking the ground and the city gate rolls back for him. Thirty leagues away he reaches a river, which the horse leaps across; then the prince dismounts, gives his ornaments to the charioteer, and cuts off his hair with his sword. Each of the two great beings thus renounces the world to undertake the religious quest.

Mahavira's search was one of unrelieved austerity and meditation lasting for twelve years. The texts recount his many sufferings, the hardships from cold, hunger, attacks of wild beasts, the rage of a fierce poisonous serpent whose very look carried death, the hostility of barbaric folk who sicked the village dogs on him; the seductions of women. At length during the thirteenth year he obtained omniscience, while deep in meditation, standing in the body-abandonment posture, and so became a Conqueror (*jina*), and the gods descended from heaven and ascended in honoring him. Then, as they always do for Saviors, they prepared the ground for his first sermon, cleansing it for the space of a league, erecting three walls, the first of jewels, outside it one of gold, and outside that one of silver, with each wall having four jeweled gates. In the center was a tree, and under the tree four lion thrones. Mahavira occupied that on the east, and duplicates of him occupied the others. There he preached to gods, men, animals.

Siddhartha's course was very different. He first went to two religious teachers, whom he found unable to give him the answers to his search, though they taught him how to achieve certain states of concentration in meditation. Then for six years he practiced rigorous asceticism, in company with five disciples, until his body wasted away to unbelievable thinness and he all but died. But still he did not win enlightenment. He therefore gave up asceticism, ate normally, and step by step gained enlightenment, winning in trance knowledge of his previous existences and the means of destroying the defilements, with final realization of truth. Thus he became the Buddha (Enlightened One). Later accounts add incidents of his approach to the meditation spot and a lurid description of his temptation by Mara (the Evil One) as he sat under the Tree of Enlightenment (*bodhi*). When he had won the victory, he decided that he would first preach it to his five disciples, who were still practicing austerities. They, when they saw him approaching, determined not to rise and greet him, since he had abandoned the life of mortification, but, as he drew near, the glory acquired in his achievement could not be withstood and they arose involuntarily. Thereupon in a deer park at Sarnath, just outside Varanasi (Banaras), with them as audience, he preached his first sermon, by which he set rolling the wheel of the Law, and they became his first converts.

The teachers now both set forth on a long career of preaching, wandering through the countryside and visiting towns and cities, and the texts relate many marvelous and miraculous incidents, astonishing conversions of great rulers and rich merchants, defeats of hostile superhuman adversaries, victories over rival teachers. Each established an order of monks and an order of nuns and corresponding groups of laymen and laywomen, thus leaving a fourfold congregation.

Mahavira died at the age of seventy-two and his liberated soul went to the Siddhashila, or Ishatpragbhara, which is at the top of the universe. This resembles an inverted white parasol, being made of pure white gold, 4,500,000 leagues in diameter, eight leagues thick at the middle, but tapering off till at the edges it is thinner than a fly's wing. All varieties of perfected beings (*siddha*) go there; of these the Saviors (*tīrthaṃkara*) are the foremost. There they dwell in omnipotence and omniscience, perfectly blissful, and with no contact with the material universe.

The Buddha was eighty when he died. He had already realized that the time for his death was at hand, and he was ready. In his wanderings he came to a village, where he stopped in a mango grove belonging to a smith named Chunda. This pious follower provided a meal of many kinds of food, including a good deal of something called sukaramaddava, sometimes understood by commentators to mean pig's flesh and sometimes understood to mean something which pigs eat, such as a vegetable, mushrooms or truffles. The Buddha would not allow his disciples to eat this dish, for when he examined it, he saw that only a Buddha could digest it, but even at that it brought on his final illness. He traveled on ill, but as the end approached he gave his followers various sorts of instruction, including a charge that no blame should be attached to Chunda. At last, after passing through the various trances, he attained final Nirvana.

The lives of the historical Saviors have stimulated a vast mythology of other, non-historical and purely mythical, Saviors, thought to have existed in remote ages before them. In Buddhism we find first that there was a doctrine of six preceding Buddhas; later the number was increased to twenty-four; elsewhere there is a list of fifty-four, then one of more than a hundred; still later the number is considered in some sects to be unlimited. Among the mythical Buddhas is reckoned Dipankara (the Lightmaker), to whom the historical Buddha, at that time a child, offered a handful of dust, making a resolution that he would himself in some future existence attain enlightenment. Further, Buddhism in one of its two great divisions, the Mahayana, has cultivated a notion of Bodhisattvas, beings whose designation means that they have enlightenment (*bodhi*) as their essence (*sattva*); this was the designation of the historical Buddha up to the moment when he actually won enlightenment. The Mahayana sects consider that the Bodhisattvas have reached such a stage of spiritual development that they could, if they wished, attain Buddhahood, but they prefer not to do so, since a Buddha can have no contact with the world. They therefore remain Bodhisattvas, performing good works so that the benefit from these may accrue to other beings and help them on the road to salvation.

In Jainism the two historical Saviors have been multiplied to twenty-four. That number, however, is only for the cycle in which we now live. Jainism teaches that the universe has already gone through a beginningless series of similar cycles, each of an astronomical length of years, and will go through an endless future series. The movement of cycles is like a hand traveling incessantly around the face of a clock. When it is at the top, the world is in the best of conditions; from that state it steadily deteriorates until it reaches the lowest point, one of maximum evil; then it starts to improve and so ascends again by stages to the best of states. At a certain point in the deterioration conditions become so bad that rulership is needed; men can no longer digest uncooked food; learning becomes necessary. Then the first Savior appears, who is also the first king. He teaches the arts, such as pottery making, cooking, writing, arithmetic. He also preaches the Law. He is succeeded in the rest of the downward or deteriorating period of the cycle by the other twenty-three. All twenty-four Saviors are very real to the Jains; their achievements are honored; images are carved to represent them and temples are dedicated to their memory. Each cycle has such a series, born to preach salvation for souls wandering in the otherwise beginningless and endless round of rebirth.

The tendency to translate teacher to supernatural Savior or deity is not without existence in India today. It would not be irrational to suppose that neither the Buddha nor Mahavira thought of himself as anything more than a human being who had found an answer to life's great problem and was preaching it to those who would listen. But their followers, perhaps within their teachers' own lifetime, were magnifying them, ascribing to them supernatural powers, possibly making deities of them. Great teachers or leaders are sometimes so treated by their immediate disciples in modern India, but rarely do they become the founders of a continuing religious order. That seems, in part at least, to be a matter of chance. When Gandhi died in 1948 there were many people in India ready to deify him. This would have been abhorrent to Gandhi himself, a man as humble as he was sincere. It was, in fact, a dread of some of Gandhi's closest friends and most devoted admirers, who spoke publicly against the tendency. There now seems to be no likelihood that he will ever become an object of worship, the resort for salvation of hundreds of millions of Indians. But for a time in 1948–49 it looked like a close thing. If it had happened, he would have been in our time a successor to the tradition of the Buddha and Mahavira, the human teacher become Savior.

8. THE USES OF MYTHOLOGY IN INDIA

The different varieties of mythology treated here show it serving a variety of uses as well. It has, in the first place, represented man's natural wish to have an explanation of his environment—how did the universe come into being and how does it operate; where did man come from; what are the functions and the relationships of the various parts of nature, the sun, the moon, the wind, storms, drought, floods; what is the source and cure of disease? Mythology thus embodies India's most primitive scientific ventures.

Out of this develops the second use of mythology, that is,

as a stimulus to metaphysical speculation. In the symbols of mythology we find the earliest recorded efforts of Indians to explain the universe as a whole, to find the first cause. For the intellectually unsophisticated the myth may be reality, but to the sophisticated it is only symbol, from which they pass on to exact and rational investigation. Mythology is in this way the portal to philosophy. And as in India philosophy and religion have never been separated, but both have been wedded for a teleological purpose, so mythology has expressed man's religious desires, above all that of gaining future happiness in another existence, in a word, salvation, however that may be imagined.

Third, mythology, such as is attached to Rama or as appears in the *Mahabharata*, has served the purpose of history. In the culture of India, more than in that of the Greeks and the Chinese, mythology is almost the only sort of history the traditional literature presents.

Fourth, mythology has provided expression for the basic human emotion of love. This includes love for children and love by children, love between man and woman, love of the human being by God, and love for God by the human being. It even includes love of the animal creation.

In the fifth place mythology in India symbolizes the study by man of himself, the winning of self-knowledge and self-mastery, as by Shiva. It translates to a divine sphere the need of such mastery, won by renunciation and mental application. We might say that India has used mythological symbolism as psychology.

The myths that have accumulated around the figures of Mahavira and the Buddha illustrate its sixth use, which is to establish human capacity as unlimited, to teach the dignity and worth of man.

Seventh, mythology has been used to satisfy the human craving for entertainment and edification. Its tales have given to people a mirror of their own hopes, fears, gratifications, disappointments, heroism, baseness. The oldest preserved narratives in India are mythological; the oldest hints we have of drama are in the dialogue hymns of the *Rig Veda*. Mythological themes have been the subject matter of literature, have suggested plots, have led to the development of narrative frankly conceived as fiction.

Finally, mythology has been used to inspire aesthetic expression. It has given subject matter for most of the traditional sculpture and painting; it has inspired the building of noble temples.

Put in another way, we may say that in India man has found mythology a vehicle to carry him to the exploration of science, philosophy, religion, history, sex, love, his own psychology, literary entertainment and edification, creation of art.

For us, looking in from outside, acquaintance with India's mythology can be a first and easy step in the study of that land's culture.

SOME BIBLIOGRAPHICAL NOTES

Section 2, "The Process of Creation"

W. Norman Brown. "The Creation Myth of the Rig Veda," *Journal of the American Oriental Society*, Vol. 62, 1942, pp. 85–97.

A. B. Keith. *Religion and Philosophy of the Veda*. Harvard Oriental Series, Vols. 31–32. Cambridge, Harvard University Press, 1925.

A. A. Macdonell. *Vedic Mythology*, in Grundriss der Indo-Arischen Philologie und Altertumskunde, III Band, 1. Heft B. Strassburg, 1897.

Sections 3 and 4, "The Culture Hero as Deity" and "God Is Love"

E. Burnouf. *Le Bhāgavata Purāṇa, ou Histoire Poètique de Krichna*, 5 Vols. Paris, Imprimerie Royale, 1840–47.

R. T. H. Griffith. *The Ramayan of Valmiki*. Benares, E. J. Lazarus and Co., 1895.

E. Washburn Hopkins. *Epic Mythology*, Grundriss, III Band, 1. Heft B. Strassburg, 1915.

Protap Chandra Roy (or Pratapa Chandra Ray). *The Mahabharata*, translated into English prose, 12 Vols. Calcutta, 1884–86.

H. H. Wilson. *The Vishnu Purana*, translated . . . London, Oriental Translation Fund, 1840 (republished in various editions).

Sections 5 and 6, "The Meditative Ascetic God" and "The Great Mother"

Arthur Avalon (Sir John Woodroffe). *Shakti and Shakta,* 2nd ed. London, 1920 (also Madras, 1929).

R. G. Bhandarkar. *Vaiṣṇavism, Śaivism, and Minor Religious Systems,* Grundriss III, 6. Strassburg, 1913.

W. Norman Brown. *The Saundaryalaharī.* Harvard Oriental Series, Vol. 43. Cambridge, Harvard University Press, 1958.

John Dowson. *A Classical Dictionary of Hindu Mythology and Religion, Geography, History, and Literature.* London, Kegan Paul, Trench, Trübner and Co., Ltd., 1928.

J. N. Farquhar. *Outline of the Religious Literature of India.* Oxford University Press, 1920.

Sir John Marshall. *Mohenjo-daro and the Indus Civilization,* 3 Vols. London, Probsthain, 1931.

Section 7, "The Human Teacher as Savior"

Hermann Jacobi. *Gaina Sūtras, translated from Prakrit.* Part I. *The Ākārānga Sūtra; the Kalpa Sūtra.* Sacred Books of the East, Vol. 22. Oxford, Clarendon Press, 1884.

Edward J. Thomas. *The Life of Buddha as Legend and History.* New York, Knopf, 1927.

PRONUNCIATION AND TRANSLITERATION OF WORDS FROM SANSKRIT AND RELATED INDIAN LANGUAGES

In pronouncing Sanskrit and other words from the languages of India and Ceylon appearing in this essay, speakers of English should accent the next to the last syllable when it is long, and otherwise put the accent on the nearest long syllable before it. A long syllable is one which contains:

a vowel marked long: $\bar{a}$, $\bar{\imath}$, $\bar{u}$; or

a diphthong: *e, o, ai, au* (in Sanskrit *e* and *o* are always diphthongs and long; in most words from other languages appearing in this essay they are also long); or

a vowel followed by more than one consonant, but note that *h* following a consonant usually represents an aspiration of the consonant, not a second consonant, and therefore does not serve to make the syllable long.

The pronunciation of vowels is approximately as follows:

a like *u* in English but   *e* like *ai* in English chair
$\bar{a}$ like *a* in English far   *ai* like *ai* in English aisle
i like *i* in English pin   *o* like *o* in English go
$\bar{\imath}$ like *i* in English machine   *au* like *ow* in English how
u like *u* in English pull $\underset{\cdot}{r}$ like *ri* in English river
$\bar{u}$ like *u* in English rule

The following remarks apply to consonants:

c like *ch* in English church $\acute{s}$ and $\underset{\cdot}{s}$ like *sh* in English rush
g like *g* in English go

The sounds represented by *t, d, n,* are made with the

tongue farther forward than in the pronunciation of English *t, d, n,* while *ṭ, ḍ,* and *ṇ* are made with the tongue turned farther back, but casual users of words may in both cases employ the English sounds.

The aspirates *th, ph, kh* may be pronounced like the *t, p,* and *k* in tin, pin, kin; the nonaspirates *t, p, k* may be pronounced like the *t, p, k* of English stun, spin, skin. The aspirates *dh, bh,* and *gh* may be approximated by imitating the combinations of *d, b,* and *g* with *h* in English roundhouse, clubhouse, doghouse. Otherwise the consonants are to be pronounced like the English consonants.

Mythology of Ancient Iran

BY M. J. DRESDEN

MOTTO

. . . . *Ere Babylon was dust,*
The Magus Zoroaster, my dear child,
Met his own image walking in the garden.
That apparition, sole of men, he saw.
For know there are two worlds of life and death:
One that which thou beholdest; but the other
Is underneath the grave, where do inhabit
The shadows of all forms that think and live,
Till death unite them and they part no more.

(Shelley, *Prometheus Unbound*)

INTRODUCTION

Understanding of the mythology of ancient Iran requires a number of prefatory remarks. A substantial body of linguistic, religious, and social evidence warrants the assumption that, at one time, the bearers of the two cultures, which find their expression in the Indian *Rigveda* on the one hand and in parts of the Iranian *Avesta* on the other, formed a unity. In the following the term Indo-Iranian will be used to refer to the language, religious beliefs, and social institutions of this unity.

Evidence for the emergence of the Indo-Iranian type of language is found as early as 1800 B.C. in the Kassite word *šuriaš* (Indian *sūryas*) for the sun god and, further, in a number of proper names from Anatolia of about the same time. Some four centuries later, around 1400 B.C., the names of four divinities, *Mitra, Varuṇa, Indra,* and the two *Nāsatyas,* all of whom appear in the *Rigveda,* occur in a treaty between a Hittite king and a ruler of the Hurrian kingdom of Mitanni in northern Mesopotamia. Passages from a Hittite treatise dealing with the training of horses contain technical terms such as *wartana,* "turn, lap," from Indo-Iranian *vart,* "to turn," in combination with the Indo-Iranian numerals for one (*aika*), five (*pantsa*), and nine (*nawa*), in order to indicate the number of rounds to be made in horse-racing contests. In addition, Indo-Iranian *ašva-šama,* "horse attendant, groom," Greek *hippokómos,* appears in Hittite as *aš-šušanni,* a term which designates the same profession.[1] The full significance and implications of these scattered materials remain to be assessed. They are at least the oldest direct testimony for the existence of the Indo-Iranian type of language and of a number of divinities belonging to the Indo-Iranian pantheon at an early date.

Records for the time in which the Indo-Iranian unity was broken up (after 1500 B.C.?) are absent. The routes taken by the Iranian groups on their way to the Iranian plateau and its surrounding areas are obscure. Such groups as the Scythians, Sarmatians, and Alans in the north, the Sogdians, Šakas and Parthians in the east, and the Medes and Persians in the west, are attested in a direct way only several centuries later.

Our main source of information for Iranian mythology and religion is the *Avesta*, a collection of canonical sacred scriptures ascribed to Zarathuštra (630–553 or 628–551 or 618–541 B.C. according to different computations), which in its actual form constitutes only a relatively small part of the original corpus. Among other texts the *Avesta* comprises: (1) *Yasna*, "worship, adoration," texts of liturgical character. Chapters 28–34, 41–51, and 53 are known as *Gāthā*, "chant," Zarathuštra's own meditations and preachings, written in verse form and in a language, known as *Gāthic*, which differs from the language of the rest of the *Avesta;* (2) *Yašt*, "sacrifice," hymns of sacrificial character devoted to individual deities; (3) *Vendīdād*, "law against the demons," by and large a book of religious and ritual law which, in addition, contains mythological and legendary materials.[2]

Not one but two forms of religion are represented in the Avestan writings. The first is reflected in Zarathuštra's own words as expressed in the Gāthās and will be called *Zarathuštrianism*. It posits an ethical dualism between "Truth" (*Aša*) and "Falsehood" (*Drug*) which is regulated and topped off by a monotheism expressed by *Ahura Mazdā*. On another level is the opposition between "the Augmentative Spirit" (*Spenta Mainyu*) and "the Wicked Spirit." Ahura Mazdā is the father of Spenta Mainyu (*Yasna* 47. 3) and through him he is the creator of all things (*Yasna* 44. 7). Of a somewhat similar nature is the relationship between Ahura Mazdā and the six "Augmentative Immortals" (*Ameša Spenta*). These entities, organs or aspects of Ahura Mazdā, are known as "Good Mind" (*Vohu Manah*), "Truth" (*Aša*), "Power" (*Xšathra*), "Devotion" (*Ārmaiti*), "Wholeness" (*Haurvatāt*) and "Immortality" (*Ameretāt*), each of which is connected with one of the elements: cattle, fire, metal, earth, water, and vegetation, respectively.

In the second form of religion represented in the *Avesta*, which has been termed *Zoroastrianism* after the later form (*Zoroaster*) of the name of Zarathuštra, several components are present. Besides Zarathuštrianism proper, the texts, which were composed by authors who wrote in the centuries following Zarathuštra's death, recommend the cult of both Indo-Iranian divinities such as *Mithra* (Indian *Mitra*) and *Haoma* (Indian *Soma*), who have their replica in the *Rigveda*, and of others such as the goddess *Anāhitā*, who do not have their counterpart in the Indian scriptures and, therefore, seem to be purely Iranian.

Centuries later, at the time Zoroastrianism had become the official state religion of the Sassanian empire in the third to seventh centuries A.D., it found its expression in theological books which were written in an idiom commonly referred to as *Pahlavi*, the local language of southwestern Iran of the time. In most cases where a precise date for the composition of any one of these books can be given, they seem to have been written after the Islamic conquest of Iran in the middle of the seventh century. There can be little doubt, however, that they are based on a tradition which goes back to the fourth century when Zoroastrian orthodoxy was established in a definite form. Two of the most important Pahlavi books are the so-called *Bundahišn*, the correct title of which is rather *Zandāgāhīh* or exposition of the information as provided by the Pahlavi version of the *Avesta*, and the *Dēnkart*. The first is a work on cosmology, the second an encyclopedia of religious lore.[3]

Another, later source for Iranian mythology is epic tales written in classical Persian among which the *Šāh-nāma* or

Books of Kings, the great national Iranian epic, written by *Firdausī* around the year A.D. 1000, ranks foremost. This epic literature will be used only sporadically, since it contains tales about mortal heroic personalities rather than narratives in which the gods are the major protagonists.[4]

Elements of Iranian mythology are, further, among those which were known to and incorporated by *Mani* (216–77) into the system known as *Manicheism.*[5]

A complete account of Iranian mythology is not intended here. Limitations of space have imposed restrictions on the extent of the materials which are presented. The following headings offer a list of selected topics of essential interest:

1. The world and its origin
   a. Zarathuštrian — b. Zoroastrian — c. Manichean
2. The origin of man
   a. *Gayōmart* — b. The first human couple — c. *Yima*
3. The gods
   a. Preliminary remarks
   b. Individual gods
      i. *Mithra* — ii. *Haoma* — iii. *Verethragna* —
      iv. *Vayu* — v. *Anāhitā* — vi. *Tištrya* —
      vii. *Xvarenah* — viii. *Zurvān*
4. Demonology
5. Eschatology
   a. Paradise — b. Judgment of the dead — c. Final resurrection

1. THE WORLD AND ITS ORIGIN

a. Zarathuštrian

No precise and comprehensive account of the ancient Iranian concepts and theories regarding the creation of the world is preserved in the *Avesta.* According to the usual interpretation a famous Gāthic passage (*Yasna* 30. 4) mentions the two twin primordial spirits, the "better" and the "evil" one, a basic theme of Zarathuštra's philosophy, as engaged in the creation of "life" and "non-life." This passage, however, permits more than one interpretation.[6] In another, equally famous, passage (*Yasna* 44. 3–5) a series of questions is addressed to Ahura Mazdā: "Who . . . (is) the primordial father of Truth? Who has set the path of the sun and the stars? Who (is he) through whom the moon waxes and wanes? . . . Who holds the earth below and the clouds from falling down, who (upholds) waters and plants? . . . Which skillful (craftsman) created the lights and darknesses, which skillful (craftsman) created sleep and awakeness? Who (is he) through whom morning, noon and evening (exist) which remind the sensible (person) of his duty?" The answer to these obviously rhetorical questions is implied. It is Ahura Mazdā who is the author of all these performances and who is at the origin of the world and its organization. In a similar way the inscriptions of the Achaemenian kings, in the sixth and fifth centuries B.C., open with the statement, "A great god is Ahura Mazdā, who created this earth, who created that sky, who created man . . ." It should be noted that in both cases the term for the verb "to create" is *dā*, Indian *dhā*, Latin *facio, fēci*, "to put, make, create," and also that details as to the precise way the act of creation was performed are absent.

b. Zoroastrian

In the Pahlavi books the world's creation is discussed in great detail. The fullest account is contained in the first chapter of the Bundahišn while further details and variants are provided by other texts. In brief outline the Bundahišn account runs thus: "Thus it is revealed in the Good Religion. Ohrmazd [the later form of Ahura Mazdā] was on high in omniscience and goodness. . . . Ahriman [Angra Mainyu], slow in knowledge, whose will is to smite, was deep down in darkness . . . Between them was the Void . . . Ohrmazd in his omniscience knew that the Destructive Spirit [Ahriman] existed, that he would attack and . . . would mingle with him . . . (and he knew) with what and how many instruments he would accomplish his purpose. In ideal form he fashioned forth such creation as was needful for his instrument. For three thousand years creation stayed in this ideal state . . . . The Destructive Spirit . . . was unaware of the existence of Ohrmazd. Then he rose up from the depths and went to the border from whence the lights are seen. When he saw the light of Ohrmazd intangible, he rushed forward . . . he made haste to destroy it. Seeing valour and supremacy superior to his own, he fled back to the darkness and fashioned many demons . . . . Then Ohrmazd . . . offered peace to the Destructive Spirit."[7] After the offer was rejected, Ohrmazd thought of a strategem to avoid an endless struggle and he proposed a period of nine thousand years, since he knew that "three thousand (years) would pass entirely according to the will of Ohrmazd, three thousand years in mixture would pass according to the will of both Ohrmazd and Ahriman and that in the last battle the Destructive Spirit would be made powerless."[7] This time, in his ignorance, the Destructive Spirit accepted Ohrmazd's proposal ". . . just as two men who fight a duel fix a term (saying), 'Let us on such a day do battle till night falls.' "[7] The motif of the nine-thousand- or twelve-thousand-year cycle occurs with variations in other Pahlavi texts.

More than one version of the creation of the material world is handed down in the Pahlavi sources. The same first chapter of the *Bundahišn* proceeds to say that, after the conclusion of the agreement between Ohrmazd and Ahriman, Ohrmazd "first created the Amahraspands [the later form of the Ameša Spenta], six originally . . . and the seventh is Ohrmazd himself . . . . Of material creation (he created) first the sky, second water, third the earth, fourth plants, fifth cattle, sixth man; the seventh was Ohrmazd himself."[7] A little further in the same text again, it is said with regard to each one of these six creations: "Now I shall describe their properties. First he created the sky, bright and manifest, its ends exceeding far apart, in the form of an egg, of shining metal . . . The top of it reached to the Endless Light; and all creation was created within the sky—like a castle or a fortress in which every weapon that is needed for the battle is stored, or like a house in which all things are present."[7] Elsewhere, it should be added, the sky is described as "pillarless" or "supportless" and the earth is conceived to be in the center of the sky "like the yoke of an egg in the center of the egg." The *Bundahišn* account, then, continues: "Second from the substance of the sky he fashioned water . . . . Third from water he created the earth, round . . . poised in the middle of the sky . . . . And he created minerals within the earth and mountains which afterwards sprang forth and grew out of the earth . . . . Beneath this earth there is water everywhere . . . . Fourth he created plants . . . . Fifth he fashioned the . . . Bull . . . . Sixth he fashioned Gayōmart [the first man] . . . . He fashioned Gayōmart and the Bull from the earth . . . . And from the light and freshness of the sky he fashioned forth the seed of men and bulls . . . and he put (it) in the bodies of Gayōmart and the Bull that from them there might be progeny abundant for men and kine."[7]

Among the more unorthodox attempts to explain the genesis of the world is the one contained in the so-called Pahlavi *Rivāyat* ("tradition") to the *Dātastān i dēnīk*, a theological work of miscellaneous character. In anthropomorphic fashion it is said that the various creations evolved from a manlike body. First the sky was created from the head, then the earth from the feet, the waters from the tears, the plants from the hair, the bull from the right hand and, finally, fire from the mind. Whatever the precise interpretation of the intricate Pahlavi passage and in spite of considerable variations in detail, a similarity of a general nature seems to exist between this myth and the contents of the well-known *Puruṣa* hymn of the *Rigveda* (X. 90). In this hymn certain parts of the body of Puruṣa, who has been sacrificed by the gods, are said to correspond, among other things, to parts of the cosmos. In itself, given the actual presence of representatives of Indian religious sects in Iran in

Sassanian times and the occurrence of references to products of Indian thought in scattered passages in the Pahlavi books, the assumption of a direct relation between the Iranian and the Indian myth could be argued for. Caution, however, is needed before reaching the conclusion of mutual influence or borrowing. A case in point is the discussion started by A. Goetze who compared two passages, one in the *Bunda-hišn* and one in a Greek medical text, both providing a description of the cosmos in terms of a human body, and decided for an Iranian origin of the Greek doctrine.[8] Further research has, in fact, shown that the chances are that the *Bundahišn* account owes its existence to foreign, either Greek or Indian, sources.[9]

As to the creation of the sky, stars, etc., the importance of the account found in the second chapter of the *Bundahišn*, which contains materials from periods as far apart as pre-Achaemenian and late Sassanian times, warrants a lengthy quotation. "Ohrmazd created the lights and set them between the heaven and the earth: the fixed stars, the non-fixed stars, then the moon, then the sun. After he had first created a sphere, he set the fixed stars in it, in particular the following twelve (constellations) whose names are: Lamb, Ox, Two Pictures, Crab, Lion, Spica, Balance, Scorpion, Centaur, Goat, Pail, Fish . . . Over the fixed stars Ohrmazd appointed four generals . . . As he [Ohrmazd] says: *Tishtrya* (Sirius) is the general of the east, *Sadwēs* (Antares) is the general of the south, *Wanand* (Vega) is the general of the north, *Haftōreng* (Great Bear) is the general of the north, and *Mēx-ī Gāh* (Polaris) also called *Mēx-ī miyān āsmān* (the peg in the center of the sky), is the general of generals . . . Ohrmazd created the moon . . . Over the moon he created the sun . . . He appointed sun and moon to the chieftainship over the stars . . . Between the earth and the (lower) sphere Ohrmazd placed the winds, the clouds, and the lightning-fire so that . . . Tishtrya . . . could take the water and cause the rain to fall . . . etc."[10]

c. Manichean

More space than is available here would be needed to explain in detail the Manichean position on the genesis of the world. Therefore, only its most essential and relevant features will be indicated. To the Manichean theologian the present status of man is the unfortunate result of a state of mixture between, what may be called in different terms, Mind and Matter or Good and Evil or Light and Darkness. The explanation of this situation in terms of an appeal to "rational" understanding can be considered as the main purpose of the Manichean cosmogonic hymn.

In former times, the two realms of Light and Darkness, which were ruled by the Father of Greatness and the Prince of Darkness, constituted a complete and balanced duality. This equilibrium was disturbed when the Prince of Darkness became attracted by the splendor of the realm of Light. Before the threat of his onrush the Father of Greatness evoked a number of hypostatic powers of light. Their defeat and subsequent disappearance into darkness lies at the origin of the state of mixture. A reminiscence of a by and large similar situation with regard to the beginning of the struggle between Ohrmazd and Ahriman will come to mind. The deliverance of the light particles of which the vanished powers of light consist is the main theme of the remainder of the myth.

Among the first hypostases which were absorbed by darkness was Primeval Man or *Ohrmizd*, as he is known in the Iranian sources. Another entity, known as the Living Spirit or *Mihryazd* ("god Mithra"), then set out to punish the demoniacal powers of darkness. From the skins of the defeated demons the skies, usually ten in number, were made, from their bones the mountains and from their flesh and excrements the earths, four or eight in number. In addition, the ten firmaments, the zodiac ("Within the zodiac he fettered those of the demons of Darkness that were most iniquitous, vicious and rebellious."), the constellations and planets ("The twelve constellations and the seven planets they made rulers over the whole Mixed World . . .")[11] were created. Sun and moon were fashioned out of uncontaminated light particles, while the stars originated from only partially contaminated substance. Finally, the vegetable and animal worlds, both of which because of their origin contained undelivered light particles, came into existence.

2. THE ORIGIN OF MAN

a. Gayōmart

In the Bundahišn account from which passages were quoted above, Gayōmart appears as the sixth in the list of Ohrmazd's creations: "Sixth he fashioned Gayōmart, shining like the sun, and his height was about four cubits and his breadth equal to his height." Gayōmart's name can be traced back to an older form *Gaya maretan* (nominative singular *Gayō mareta*) which occurs in a number of Avestan passages. In a *Yašt* passage (*Yašt* 13. 87) worship is paid to the *fravaši* (approximately "soul") of Gaya maretan "who as the first heard the thought and teachings of Ahura Mazdā, (and) from whom he (Ahura Mazdā) fashioned the family of the Aryan lands, the seed of the Aryan lands." Elsewhere, his fravaši is mentioned, together with the fravaši of Zarathuštra, of Vištāspa (Zarathuštra's protector) and of a son of Zarathuštra, as worthy of worship because of their victory for the sake of Truth (Aša) (*Yasna* 26. 5). These data leave room for considerable variation in interpretation.

The later sources, however, provide a much clearer picture. In them Gayōmart appears as the prototype of mankind as is, for instance, indicated in the phrase ". . . My stock and lineage is from Gayōmart . . ." which occurs in a Zoroastrian catechism of probably post-Islamic date. An echo of the prototype of mankind motif is heard in the Manichean *Gēhmurd,* the name of First Man. Another similar indication is the fact that in the lists of kings of Iran as found, for instance, in Firdausī, the name of *Kayūmarth* comes first. No certain argument, however, can be adduced for the assumption that Gayōmart as First Man has a counterpart in *Jēh,* the (primeval) whore, as First Woman. The passage in question, from the Pahlavi book known as *Zātspram* (34. 30–31): "In the scriptures it is thus revealed, that when Ahriman rushed into the creation, he had the species of the demon Whore of evil religion as companion, even as a man may join a whore-woman . . . And he appointed the demon Jēh . . . queen of her species, that is chief of all whore-demons . . . And he joined himself with the [demon Whore] . . . , for the defilement of females he was joined with (her), that she might defile females, and the females, on account of their defilement, might defile men, and they might turn from their duty" seems to state, in a general way, only what is known from elsewhere, namely that woman because of her subservience to Ahriman is the cause of the defilement of man.[12]

b. The first human couple

Mašya and *Mašyānag* in Avestan or *Mahlya* and *Mahlyā-nag* in Zoroastrian parlance, the first human (male and female) couple, originated from the seed of Gayōmart, who had died after having been slain by Ahriman. "When Gayōmart passed away and let fall his seed . . . one part (of it) was received by Spandarmat (the earth). For forty years it remained in the earth. When the forty years had elapsed, Mašya and Mašyānag grew out of the earth in the form of a rhubarb plant," as the *Bundahišn* relates the story.[13] After they had assumed human shape, Ohrmazd addressed them: "You are human beings, the father (and) mother of the world. Do your work in accordance with righteous order and a perfect mind. Think, speak and do what is good. Worship not the demons."[13] By acts contrary to these precepts, however, they fell short of the performance expected of them and it was after fifty years only that they begot offspring.

In Manicheism the names of the first man and first woman, *Gēhmurd* and *Murdiyānag,* the Adam and Eve of other sources, not only are the exact verbal correspondences of Gayōmart and Mašiyānag, but the myth of their origin and nature shows features, which because of their technical character will not be discussed, similar to those of the Zoroastrian myth.

c. Yima

Domination of the world, in what may be termed a golden age, is one of the chief characteristics of Yima in the Iranian tradition. He is said to have been born as a son to *Vīvahvant* as a reward for the latter's performing the act of pressing the *haoma* (Indian *soma*) plant (*Yasna* 9. 4). In the next paragraph the same text introduces Yima as a ruler during whose reign no cold, heat, old age, or death existed. The latter statement is more fully developed in the second chapter of the *Vendīdād.* After having accepted Ahura Mazdā's proposal to become the protector and ruler of a world in which there will be no cold wind nor hot, nor disease nor death, Yima is presented by Ahura Mazdā with two golden implements, a whip and a goad. Prosperity becomes so abundant that the earth can no longer hold all "small and large cattle, men, dogs, birds, and red flaming fires." At the instigation of Ahura Mazdā, Yima resorts three times, after periods of three, six, and nine hundreds years, to the procedure of extending the earth "by one third more than it was before" by using the instruments given to him.

In the next episode (*Vendīdād* 2. 20–41) a different theme is struck. After Ahura Mazdā has warned Yima that destruction in the form of winter, frost, and floods, subsequent to the melting of the snow, are threatening the sinful world, he proceeds to instruct him to build a *vara,* "fortress or estate," in which specimens of small and large cattle, human beings, dogs, birds, red flaming fires, plants and foodstuffs will have to be deposited in pairs.

One more feature of the Iranian Yima is that he is known for having sided with Drug (Falsehood) against Aša (Truth), thus becoming a sinner (*Yasna* 32. 8; *Yašt* 19. 31–36). Reminiscences of this feature are found in the later literature as, for instance, in the Šāhnāma episode in which *Jamšēd* (the later form of Avestan *Yima xšaēta*, "Yima the lordly") falls victim to his own *hybris*. The same source, however, also depicts Jamšēd as the inventor of a number of arts and crafts in line with the motif of the golden age.

More than one parallel exists between Yima in the Iranian and *Yama* in the Indian tradition. The latter, whose father is *Vivasvant* (*Rigveda* X. 14. 5), the Avestan Vīvahvant, and whose twin sister is *Yamī* (*Rigveda* X. 10)—the Avestan *yēma* like the Indian *yama* also has the meaning "twin" (*Yasna* 30. 3)—is, however, primarily spoken of as a king who rules the dead (*Rigveda* X. 16. 9) and, in general, is connected in the Rigvedic and later Indian tradition with death.

3. THE GODS

a. Preliminary remarks

In recent years attempts have been made to discover a common structure of an exclusive nature in the religious traditions of the peoples who as a vehicle of expression used a language of the Indo-European type. Since the methods used and the conclusions reached by G. Dumézil, the initiator of these recent investigations, concern Indo-Iranian and Iranian religion and mythology—in fact, a number of them were inspired by a comparative study of Indian and Iranian materials—attention has to be given to his approach and its results.

As a starting point can be taken Dumézil's statement that "The Indo-Europeans possessed a concept of the social struc-

ture which was based upon the distinction and hierarchiza-
tion of the three functions."[14] This social structure of the
three functions (priests, warriors, and herdsmen, or: priests,
warriors, and producers) is next taken to be reflected in Indo-
European theological and mythological concepts. In more
specific terms: "The first rank is occupied by two antithetic
and complementary divine rulers, of whom the one (represented for example by the Rigvedic Mitra . . .) is the divine
jurist, contract personified, 'rassurant, bienveillant, protecteur
des actes et rapports honnêtes et réglés;' while the other
(exemplified by Varuṇa . . .) is 'un maître inquiétant, terrible, possesseur de la *māyā*, c'est à dire de la magie créatrice
de formes, armé de noeuds, de filets, c'est à dire opérant par
saisie immédiate et irrésistible.' II [the second function]
represented by Indra (also Vāyu) . . . calls for no special
comment; while III [the third function] is particularly represented by the twin deities, the Aśvins."[14] And further: "In
addition to dominating these main provinces, triplicity can
be traced in a host of other places. Thus, we find triads of
calamities (e.g. I injustice; II war; III famine) and of wrongdoing (I harming by charm; II physical violence; III theft);
three types of medicine (I healing by charm; II surgery; III
herbs); tripartite eulogies of kings; triple juridical mecha-
nisms."[14]

The validity of the claim laid by Dumézil to the exclusively
Indo-European character of the trifunctional structure was
recently investigated by J. Brough, who was able to show
that the same tripartition is also present in the Old Testament.[14] It is likely that further application of the same general, wide and elastic notions to other social structures and
religions will yield similar results. A healthy dose of skepticism is, therefore, recommended with regard to a table of
the Iranian pantheon such as:

God of beginning: Vāyu or Vāta, god of the wind
    I. Function of sovereign: Ahura Mazdā and Mithra
       (surrounded by Sraoša and Rašnu) both accompanied
       by Airyaman.

II. Function of warrior: Indra Verethragna

III. Function of nutrition and collectivity: the two Nāha-
ithya and the goddess Ardvī Sūrā Anāhitā.[15]

The same trifunctional pattern has been used for the purpose of explaining the Zarathuštrian Ameša Spenta in terms
of Indo-Iranian gods:

First function	Varuṇa	Aša
	Mitra	Vohu Manah
Second function	Indra	Xšathra
Third function	2 Nāsatyas	Haurvatāt
		Ameretāt

In this case, too, the data do not quite seem to fit the table.[16]

To sum up, caution is needed when it comes to accepting
any one of the definitions of individual Iranian gods or groups
of gods which is derived from the trifunctional pattern. The
safest way to arrive at such definitions is, rather, unbiassed
analysis of the available evidence in each individual case.

b. Individual gods

Earlier in this survey attention has been drawn to the
existence of non-Zarathuštrian, or Zoroastrian, divinities of
Indo-Iranian inheritance. The following gods of such origin
will be dealt with, (i) *Mithra,* (ii) *Haoma,* (iii) *Verethragna,*
(iv) *Vayu.*

i. *Mithra:* The result of recent investigations into the nature
of Mithra on the basis of the evidence contained in the Avestan *Mithra Yašt* is that both in origin and in essence Mithra
is the god of contract. He is "the punisher of wrong . . . whose
perception is thousandfold, who rules as an all-knowing
potentate" (*Yašt* 10. 35); he "has a thousand ears" and "ten
thousand eyes" and is "sleepless, (ever-)waking" (*Yašt* 10.
7); he is "Mithra the strong, whose spies are ten thousand"
(*Yašt* 10. 24). Although he is connected with light and is
said to be "the first . . . god to approach . . . in front of the
immortal swift-horsed sun" (*Yašt* 10. 13), he is by no means

identified with the sun. Another aspect of Mithra is expressed in the statement that he is the one "who dispenses fat and herds, who gives power and sons, who bestows life and comfortable existence" (*Yašt* 10. 65). These qualifications can be considered the natural outcome of Mithra's role as a maintainer of law and order. Finally, from his function as "punisher of the wrong," another secondary aspect, that of a militant and well-armed defender of the "contract" originated.

Mithra's companions are, among others, *Sraoša* and *Rašnu* (*Yašt* 10. 41). The triad of Mithra, Sraoša (who is the personification and genius of "obedience" and "discipline") and Rašnu, or of *Mihr, Srōš,* and *Rašn,* as they are called in Pahlavi, acts throughout the Zoroastrian tradition as the judges of the souls of the dead at the *Činvat* bridge. Another companion is *Apąm Napāt* (Indian *Apāṃ Napāt*), or "grandson of the waters," a deity of Indo-Iranian inheritance, of whom it is said among other things that he "will further all supreme authorities and hold down (the countries) that are in turmoil" (*Yašt* 13. 95).

In Manichean theory the role assigned to Mithra was that of the Living Spirit or demiurge, as was pointed out above. Little if any evidence for this feature can be gathered from the *Avesta.* The Third Messenger (*Tertius Legatus*), on the other hand, who according to Manichean beliefs is going to complete the salvation of the lost light substance and who is a sun god, is also known under the names of *Mihryazd,* "god Mithra" (in the Parthian language), and of *Myšyy,* "Mithra" (in the Sogdian language). From this it appears that to the Parthian and Sogdian Manicheans Mithra represented the sun. This is obviously a later development only the very beginning of which is present in the *Avesta.*[17]

Coming to the Roman *Mithras,* it will be found that in his make-up both ancient Iranian elements as attested in the *Avesta* and elements of non-Iranian origin can be distinguished. The former, such as Mithras' relation to light, the representation of the ocean (*Apąm Napāt*) on Mithraic reliefs, the technical term *Persa,* "Persian," for a grade in the Mithraic mysteries, the use of the Iranian term *nama,* "homage," in a Mithraic formula of worship, are too strong to lend support to the recently suggested non-Iranian origin of the Roman Mithras.[18] Among the latter, such frequent and essential scenes on Mithraic reliefs which represent the slaughter of a bull by Mithras, the subsequent ejaculation of the animal's sperm and the sprouting of ears of corn from its tail, can only be traced back indirectly and incompletely to the account of the killing of the primordial bull by Ahriman as provided by the Pahlavi books.

ii. *Haoma:* Among the Indo-Iranian gods there is hardly one of whom the characteristics in both the Iranian and the Indian tradition show so many similarities as Haoma (Avestan)-Soma (Indian). All the evidence points to the fact that haoma-soma, a plant (perhaps the rhubarb)[19] termed *zairi.gaona,* "golden-colored," in the *Avesta* and *hári,* "yellowish," in the *Rigveda* and growing on a particular mountain or mountains in both texts, the juice of which possesses intoxicating qualities, was already known, used and prepared for sacrificial purposes and worshiped as a god (Haoma-Soma) in the Indo-Iranian period. To Haoma-Soma the features of a provider of health and long life and of a remover of death (the standing epithet of Haoma in the *Avesta* is *dūraoša* which, with some reservation, may be translated as "keeping death far") are attached. While Zara-thuštra in the Gāthās does not mention Haoma except for an indirect reference strongly condemning the "detestable fluid of that liquor" (*Yasna* 48. 10) for its evil effect, other passages praise its qualities (*Yasna* 10) and describe the legendary first occasions on which Haoma-haoma was pressed (*Yasna* 9, known as *Haoma Yašt*). In *Yasna* 9 it is told that *Vīvahvant, Āthwya, Thrita* (the Indian *Trita,* with or without the epithet *Āptya,* is also connected with the preparation of soma in the *Rigveda*) and *Pourušāspa* performed the first four successive pressings of haoma. As a result and reward each one of them begot a son. *Yima* was born to Vīvahvant and *Thraētaona* (the hero *Ferīdhūn* of the Šāhnāma), "who killed the dragon *Dahāka* [*Daḥḥāk* is slain by Ferīdhūn in the Šāhnāma] who has three mouths, three heads, six eyes . . ." (*Yasna* 9. 8), to Āthwya. One of the two sons of Thrita was *Keresāspa* (the later *Karsāsp*) who "slew the horned dragon, who devours horses and men, (who is) poisonous, yellow . . ." (*Yasna* 9. 11). As a result of the last soma pressing Zarathuštra was born to Pourušāspa.

Another theme is struck in the Mithra Yašt (10. 88–90) in which Ahura Mazdā installs Mithra as a "promptly-sacrificing, loud-chanting priest" and as "the first mortar-priest [a priest using mortar and pestle to press the haoma] to elevate the . . . haoma stalks on the high *Harā* [mountain]." In addition, Haoma is introduced as paying worship to Mithra "with immaculate Barsman [sacrificial] twigs, immaculate libation, immaculate words." This situation in which Haoma acts as a priest who performs the haoma sacrifice himself and in doing so combines the functions of god, priest, and sacrificial substance became a significant part of later Zoroastrian ritual and liturgy.[20]

iii. *Verethragna:* The etymological connection between the Iranian word *verethragna* and the Indian *vṛtrahán* has since long been noticed. In India the killing of a dragon or demon *Vṛtra* is attributed to the god Indra and his specific epithet is *vṛtrahán* or "slayer of Vṛtra." In fact, the Vṛtra myth is an essential feature of Indra. Although the etymological representative of the Indian Indra occurs in the *Avesta*, it is only the name of a demon who both in character and in importance is far removed from the Indo-Iranian and Indian Indra. The counterpart of the demon Vṛtra is totally absent. Instead, there is a common noun *verethra*, the exact meaning of which ("defense, hostility"; "attack, victory"; "strength, valor") is still under discussion. By and large two main positions have been held in the face of this evidence. One, assuming the Iranian tradition to have stayed closer to the Indo-Iranian than the Indian, maintains the existence of an Indo-Iranian *vṛtraghan*, a reconstructed form explaining both the Iranian and the Indian phonological development, with the meaning "smasher [*ghan*] of hostility [*vṛtra*]." In India this word would, then, have been identified with the slaying of the dragon by Indra and wrong interpretation of *vṛtra* would have resulted in a dragon or demon called Vṛtra. The other position holds that Indo-Iranian *vṛtraghan* already had the meaning "slayer of Vṛtra." In that case, the Iranian development would be secondary and the Indian tradition would have preserved the original Indo-Iranian concept.

A number of interesting features of Verethragna, which may be taken as the hypostasis of the noun *verethragna* in the sense of "victoriousness," is contained in Yašt 14. In the first part of that text (14. 1–28) ten incarnations (wind, bull, horse, male camel, boar, young man, falcon, ram, male antelope, warrior) of Verethragna are listed. Next (14. 29), the gift of virile potency, strength of arms, vigor of body, and sharpness of vision as presented by Verethragna to Zarathuštra is mentioned.

Most of the evidence contained in the later Zoroastrian sources confirms the general character of Verethragna as a god of victoriousness, who is then known as *Varhrām, Vahrām,* or *Bahrām*. Testimony from outside the boundaries of Iran is to be found, for instance, in the Armenian *Vahagn,* a destroyer of monsters, in Mithraic reliefs showing Verethragna-Heracles next to a boar, in proper names of the Šakas in eastern Iran from the first through third centuries, and in the Sogdian *Vašagn,* the name of the twentieth day of the month over which Verethragna similarly presides in the Zoroastrian calendar.

iv. *Vayu:* In recent years much effort and ingenuity has been spent on the interpretation of the god *Vayu,* "wind, air," who in form corresponds to the wind god *Vāyu* of the *Rigveda*. In Yašt 15, devoted to him, it is first said that Ahura Mazdā worshiped him (15. 2–4), a characteristic which he shares with other gods such as Mithra (Yašt 10. 123), Anāhitā (Yašt 5. 17), and Tištrya (Yašt 8. 25) to whom also worship is paid by Ahura Mazdā. Then follows a series of mythical heroes who sacrificed to Vayu and finally comes a list of qualifications, epithets, and names (15. 43–48) by which Vayu is to be invoked. On the basis of these data and of the evidence of the later Sassanian Zoroastrian sources the suggestion has been made that already in ancient times Vayu possessed a "good" and an "evil" side. In addition, the double-natured Vayu was promoted to the function of initial god as shown in the table reproduced above (p. 346). Finally, he was compared with and transposed into the Zarathuštrian Spenta Mainyu and Angra Mainyu. At the moment such a genetic analysis of Vayu does not seem to be borne out by the available data.

In the Pahlavi texts a clear distinction exists between the personal deities which are referred to as the good Vāy and the evil Vāy. The first assumes the protection of the righteous Zoroastrians in that he takes the souls of the departed by the hand and leads them across the Činvat bridge toward their determined place. His evil counterpart, identified with the demon of death, fills the opposite role of being harmful to the soul. Of a different nature is another aspect of Vāy which also appears in the Pahlavi sources. "Vāy, once the god of the wind that blows between heaven and earth, has now become the intervening space between the Kingdom of Light above and the Kingdom of Darkness below. Within this impersonal element the struggle between the principles of Light and Darkness takes place . . . Vāy . . . has become a place of mixture between the powers of good and the powers of evil."[21] Further research will be necessary before the precise connections of these various functions of Vayu can be established.

Coming now to the non-Zarathuštrian, or Zoroastrian, divine entities of non-Indo-Iranian origin, the following will be briefly discussed, (v) Anāhitā, (vi) Tištrya, (vii) Xvarenah, and (viii) Zurvān.

v. Anāhitā: Information with regard to the goddess Anāhitā is found in Yašt 5, which is devoted to Aredvī Sūrā Anāhitā, as her full name goes. In it she appears as "the goddess of sacred waters; her dwelling place is amongst the stars. Full of strength and courageous nobility, she advances on a four-horsed chariot and crushes the demons, the tyrants, all hurtful beings. Ahura Mazdā has entrusted her with the care of watching over creation. All the gods invoke her and ask of her glory and riches. She assures the fecundity of nature and living creatures, extends her protection to the flocks and pastures . . . she is a slender maiden with noble bearing, who wears a crown of chased gold adorned with stars, ear-rings and a golden collar. She has a very trim waist, an ample bosom, and white arms adorned with bracelets. She has golden shoes on her feet, and a sumptuous cloak of otter skin embroidered with gold envelops her."[22] In terms of Avestan literary technique, this is an unusually rich and vivid description which has been traced to the possibility that the author of the Yašt had a statue of the goddess before him or in mind. Furthermore, there is reason to believe that this statue was of foreign origin.

Other indications also point to Anāhitā's foreign (Western) origin. Her name (Aredvī "humid"?, Sūrā "strong," Anāhitā "immaculate") resembles and may be an adaptation of the Greek Anaïtis, a goddess who was the object of worship in Asia Minor. Her name does not appear in the inscriptions of the Achaemenian kings until the first half of the fourth century, when she is mentioned by Artaxerxes Mnemon (405–359 B.C.) in the stereotype phrase, "May Ahura Mazdā, Anāhitā, and Mithra protect me." In the famous inscription of Paikuli of the end of the fourth century A.D. it is said that King Narseh set out from Armenia "in the name of Ohrmizd, all the gods and Anāhit the Lady." Both instances, far apart as they are in time, mark the stature of Anāhitā in the official pantheon.

vi. Tištrya: Concern with the way in which Tištrya (Sirius) produces rain is the reason behind the myth related in Yašt 8. After three metamorphoses, each lasting for ten days, into a young man, a golden-horned bull and a beautiful white horse, with yellow ears and golden bit (Yašt 8. 13–18), Tištrya in the last shape meets with the demon Apaoša (older form *Apavṛta,* perhaps "he who retains the waters") in the form of a black horse, with bald ears, back and tail (*Yašt* 8. 21). As the result of a fierce battle, which lasts for three days and three nights, Apaoša chases Tištrya from the Vourukaša sea. Tištrya, then, turns to Ahura Mazdā, who gives him the strength of ten horses, ten camels, ten bulls, ten mountains, and ten rivers. Once more battle rages between the two opponents and this time Tištrya is the winner (*Yašt* 8. 28–29). As a result the waters are released and rain starts to fall.

Among the companions of Tištrya is *Satavaēsa* (Antares). Manichean theology assigned to *Sadwēs* the function of the Maiden of Light, an evocation of the Third Messenger. She is a rain goddess who causes rain, hail, frost, snow, thunder, and lightning to come from the clouds in a way which is reminiscent of the role assigned to Satavaēsa in *Yašt* 8. 33.[23]

vii. *Xvarenah:* Significant progress in the understanding of the Avestan *xvarenah,* corresponding to *farnah* in proper names of the Achaemenian period and to *farrah* in Middle and *farr,* "splendor," in modern Persian, was achieved by H. W. Bailey.[24] From his study it appears that from the well-attested concrete meaning "good things, riches" of xvarenah, a hypostasis with the sense "(Good) Fortune" was developed to which was attached the power to grant good fortune, success, and victory to kings, finally developing into the symbol *par excellence* of legitimate royal authority, as well as to heroes and men.

As to the myths which were developed concerning xvarenah once it was drawn into the sphere of divine hypostases, the Avestan texts know of three such myths. In one the "xvarenah of the Aryans" (*airyanem xvarenō,* nominative singular) is mentioned. Its function is among other things to assist in gaining victory over the non-Aryan lands (*Yašt* 18. 2). In the second, the "xvarenah of the Kavis" (*kavaēm xvarenō,* roughly corresponding to "royal xvarenah") is in Yima's possession. After Yima has sided with Falsehood the xvarenah disappears from him in the shape of a hawk

(*Yašt* 19. 34–35). Mithra, Thraētaona, and Keresāspa each obtain one third of it and as a result Thraētaona and Keresāspa are enabled to perform the heroic deeds for which they are traditionally known. Yet another kind is Zarathuštra's xvarenah which in the *Dēnkart* (600. 20 ff.) is said to have descended in the likeness of fire into the body of his mother whence it became part of his own. This account introduces a new element into the xvarenah concept although the connection of xvarenah with fire is already attested in the *Avesta*.[25]

viii. *Zurvān:* Explicit textual or other confirmation for the existence of *Zervanism*, the essential feature of which is the cult of *Zurvān* (Avestan *Zrvān*), the god of time and fate, in early times is hard to find. The evidence which has been produced for the thesis that Zervanism is an old Iranian cult is not convincing. The same uncertainty as to its validity applies to the further thesis, which was developed by H. S. Nyberg,[26] that all of the *Avesta* has to be viewed against the background of a cult of which Zurvān was the supreme god. The likelihood seems to be rather that "Zervanism, with its speculations on Time, its apparatus of numbers, and the idea of the world-year, is the outcome of contact between Zoroastrianism and the Babylonian civilization. It originated in the second half of the Achaemenian period."[27] However this may be, direct evidence for Zervanism does not appear until Sassanian times, when Zervanism and Zoroastrianism probably were two branches of the official church. This differentiation may have originated in regional sectarianism with Zervanism prevalent in southwestern and orthodox Zoroastrianism in northern and eastern Iran.[28]

The main tenets of the Zervanite myth of the origin and genesis of Ohrmazd and Ahriman, which is preserved in both non-Iranian (Armenian and Syriac) and Iranian (Pahlavi) sources, where it is embedded in and between passages of an orthodox Zoroastrian nature, have been expertly described and studied by R. C. Zaehner.[29] In outline the story runs thus: "When nothing at all existed, neither heaven nor earth nor any other creature which is in heaven or on earth, there existed one, Zurvān by name . . . For a thousand years he sacrificed that perchance he might have a son whose name should be Ohrmazd, who should create heaven and earth and all that is in them. After having thus sacrificed for a thousand years he began to ponder, 'Are these sacrifices which I offer of any use, and shall I have a son Ohrmazd, or do I strive in vain?' And while he considered thus, Ohrmazd and Ahriman were conceived in their mother's womb [perhaps to be interpreted as the female half of Zurvān himself, who was considered to be of hermaphrodite nature] . . . Now Zurvān . . . made a vow that whichever should come into his presence first should receive the kingdom from him. Ohrmazd . . . divined his thought and somewhat guilelessly divulged it to Ahriman . . . Ahriman . . . ripped the womb open . . . and presented his detestable person to his father Zurvān . . . When Ahriman came into the presence of Zurvān, he said: 'I am thy son, Ohrmazd.' . . . Zurvān, however, denied him because he belonged to darkness, was stinking and loved to do harm. He wept: and even as he talked to Ahriman, Ohrmazd was born, bright and sweet-scented; and Zurvān knew that it was his son Ohrmazd . . . Ahriman approached Zurvān and reminded him of his vow, addressing him thus: 'Take care, didst thou not make that vow, "To the first to come I shall give kingship."' And Zurvān replied: 'Begone, Satan; I have made thee king for nine thousand years, and I have made Ohrmazd to rule above thee, and after the allotted time Ohrmazd shall reign and order all things to his will.'"

Elements of similarity, all the details of which are not clear, between Zurvān and the Manichean Father of Greatness (the ruler of the realm of Light) must have been responsible for the selection of the designation *Zrwā* for the Father of Greatness by the Sogdian Manicheans. The Buddhist Sogdians, on the other hand, used the name Zrwā to translate the name of the Indian god *Brahmā*.

Some doubt exists as to whether the lion-headed figure of Mithraic art represents Zurvān or Ahriman. It can, perhaps, be argued that the former, traditional hypothesis is still more acceptable than the latter.[30]

4. DEMONOLOGY

Characteristic of the *daēvas*, the powers considered as hostile by Zarathuštra and, therefore, roughly corresponding to "demons," is, in Zarathuštrian parlance, that they choose wrong, when it comes to making up their mind whether to stand with the "good" or the "evil" side (*Yasna* 30. 6). Elsewhere in the Gāthās they are called, together with those who pay them worship, "the progeny of Evil Thought, of *Drug* (Falsehood), and of arrogance" (*Yasna* 32. 3).

Reflections of the Zarathuštrian attitude toward the daēvas are to be found in the Yašts, the *Vendīdād*, and the Pahlavi books. It can also be seen from these sources that the number of daēvas gradually increases along with the more and more dogmatic and schematic character of the Zoroastrian opposition between the powers of good and evil. By and large, it will be found, there is little significant change in their individual features which, in fact, are not too distinct to begin with. Their general *raison d'être* is to act as assistants to Ahriman in one function or other.

As for individual demons, two cases may be singled out. First, a group of five demons which are known from the *Vendīdād* and frequently occur as archdemons in the Pahlavi books. The names of three of this group, *Indra, Sauru,* and *Nānhaithya,* correspond in the Indian tradition to *Indra, Śarva* (an epithet or other name or consort of the god *Rudra*), and *Nāsatya* (an epithet of the twin *Aśvins*). In addition, it will be remembered that two of them, Indra and Nāsatya, are known as early as 1400 B.C. Secondly, the demon *Āz*, who appears in the *Avesta* as a masculine demon of relatively little importance. In the Pahlavi books, however, *Āz*, a female demon, is known as the prototype of lust, greed, and "wrong-mindedness" in the Zoroastrian sense of the word. Of a similar nature is the role assigned to *Āz* in Manicheism. She is the personification of concupiscence and greed and she corrupts the soul of man so that he becomes blind to his divine origin.[81]

In both Manicheism and Persian epic literature borrowings from and continuation of the Zoroastrian tradition with regard to demons is evident. In Manicheism, *Ahrmēn* (Ahriman) is the opponent of Primeval Man (Ohrmizd); *dēv* (daēva) is the general designation for "demon" and *parīg* (Avestan *pairikā,* "witch") for "witch," *perī;* *xēšmān* (Avestan *aēšma*) is used for the demons of wrath; the *mazan* (Avestan *māzanya* "Mazanian demon") are demonic creatures; the *druxšān* (*drug* "falsehood") are female demons. In the epic tales, the *dīvs,* cruel, strong and wicked demons, and the *perīs,* who by a reversal of the original meaning are charming and pleasant females instead of hideous and wicked creatures, are frequently mentioned.

5. ESCHATOLOGY

a. Paradise

"Paradise" or, perhaps, rather "heaven" is referred to in the Avestan texts in different ways. One expression is *vahišta ahu,* literally "best existence," which later in the Persian language became *bihišt* with the meaning of paradise. The connotations attached to this expression are clear from the following passage, "The radiant quarters of *Aša* [Truth] we worship, where dwell the souls of the dead . . . the Best Existence of the *ašavans* [possessors of Truth] we worship, (which is) light (and) affording all comforts" (*Yasna* 16. 7). In a similar way the Indian *r̥tá,* which etymologically corresponds to the Avestan *aša*, is connected in a number of passages with the idea of heaven. This seems to point to a possibly Indo-Iranian origin of the concept that paradise or heaven is the abode of or at least thought of as being related to *Aša-Rtá*.[32]

Another designation of paradise-heaven is Avestan *garō nmāna*, which has been rendered as "house of praise," "house of treasure," or "house of reward." *Garō nmāna*, often with the epithet *raoxšna*, "shining," is the abode of Ahura Mazdā and the Ameša Spenta (*Vendīdād* 19. 32). It has recently been argued that it was thought of as situated above mount *Harā*, the first mountain created (*Yašt* 19. 1), which itself was part of it.

b. Judgment of the dead

In spite of some variations in detail the Zoroastrian doctrine on what happened to the individual's soul after death was consistent and uniform. Though well-known, an outline of this doctrine as it appears in the Pahlavi text known as *Mēnōk ī Xrat* deserves to be quoted. "For three days and nights the soul sits beside the pillow of the body. And on the fourth day at dawn (the soul) . . . will reach the lofty and awful Bridge of the Requiter [*Činvat* bridge] to which every man whose soul is saved and every man whose soul is damned must come . . . and it will (benefit by) the mediation of Mihr, Srōš, and Rašn, and will (needs submit) to the weighing (of his deeds) by the righteous Rašn . . . And when the soul of the saved passes over that bridge, the breadth of the bridge appears to be one parasang broad . . . And his own good deeds come to meet him in the form of a young girl, more beautiful and fair than any girl on earth . . . Then with his first step he bestrides (the heaven of) good thoughts, with his second (the heaven of) good words, and with his third (the heaven of) good deeds; and with his fourth step he reaches the Endless Light which is all bliss . . . And for ever he dwells with the spiritual gods in all bliss for evermore." In the case of the soul of the damned his body, after three days and three nights, is carried off and dragged

to the Činvat bridge by a demon and thence to hell. He is
met by "a young girl who has no semblance of a young girl,"
passes through the three hells of evil thoughts, words, and
deeds, and ends with his fourth step in the presence of
Ahriman and the other demons.[33]

c. Final resurrection

In the *Avesta* the term *frašō.kereti* (Pahlavi *fraškart*), of
which the exact translation ("rehabilitation" or, perhaps,
"miraculization," if any weight can be put on the Armenian
loanwords *hrašk°* and *hrašakert*, "wonder" and "wonderful")
is uncertain, is used to refer to the final miraculous transformation and consummation which the world will experience. This
transformation is described as "ageless, immortal, undecay-
ing, not-rotting, ever-living, ever-prospering, self-sufficient"
(*Yašt* 19. 11).

What is meant, becomes clear from the Pahlavi books. The
fraškart is both a final judgment, different in character and
purpose from the judgment of the individual soul of the
deceased, and it also represents the ultimate victory of Ohrmazd over Ahriman. The whole dramatic event, therefore,
falls into two main acts. In one of them the final defeat and
doom of Ahriman and each of his assistants is enacted, while
the other deals with the resurrection of the bodies of the
dead. This resurrection is brought about by the Sōshyans
(Avestan *saošyant*), a term which refers to each of the three
posthumous sons of Zoroaster, who appear, at intervals of
1000 years, during the last period of 3000 years. After the
bodies of the dead have been raised and have been reunited
with their souls, both the saved and the damned have to
suffer an ordeal by molten lead for a period of three days.
The ordeal is the final punishment for the damned, but to
the saved it "causes no discomfort . . . for the surging
metal seems to them like warm milk." Finally, the Sōshyans
insure the immortality of the resurrected by preparing "the
white Hōm (Haoma), (the drink of) immortality," and "the
material world will become immortal for ever and ever."[34]

NOTES

1. H. W. Bailey. "A problem of the Indo-Iranian vocabulary," *Rocznik Orientalistyczny* XXI (1957), pp. 64–66.

2. These and other parts of the *Avesta* were translated by F. Wolff, *Avesta, Die heiligen Bücher der Parsen* (1910; reprinted in 1924). The *Gāthās* were translated by Chr. Bartholomae, *Die Gāthā's des Awesta* (1907); by J. Duchesne-Guillemin, *Zoroastre, étude critique avec une traduction nouvelle des Gāthā* (1948), rendered into English by Mrs. H. Henning, *The hymns of Zarathushtra* (1952); and by H. Humbach, *Die Gathas des Zarathustra* I–II (1959). Of the *Yašts* there exists a translation by H. Lommel, *Die Yäshts des Avesta* (1927).

3. An up-to-date translation of neither of these works is available. The *Bundahišn* was translated by E. W. West, *Pahlavi Texts* I (1880); for its first and third chapter, R. C. Zaehner, *Zurvan, a Zoroastrian dilemma* (1955), pp. 276–336; for its second, W. B. Henning, "An astronomical chapter of the Bundahishn," *Journal of the Royal Asiatic Society* (1942), pp. 229–48. The contents of the *Dēnkart* are surveyed by J.-P. de Menasce, *Une encyclopédie mazdéenne, le Dēnkart* (1958).

4. A translation in French accompanies J. Mohl's edition of the *Šāhnāma* (1838–78); this translation was also published separately (1876–78). There exists also an English translation by A. G. and E. Warner (1905–12).

Th. Nöldeke's "Das iranische Nationalepos," in *Grundriss der iranischen Philologie* III (1896–1904), pp. 130–221, of which an English translation was made by L. Bogdanov (1930), is still an excellent introduction to the Persian national epic. A. Christensen, *Les gestes des rois dans les traditions de l'Iran antique* (1936) will also be found useful.

5. The literature on Manicheism is extensive. H.-Ch. Puech, *Le Manichéisme, son fondateur, sa doctrine* (1949), is the best and most recent introductory book. It gives excellent references to primary and secondary sources.

6. H. Humbach. "Zur altiranischen Mythologie," *Zeitschrift der Deutschen Morgenländischen Gesellschaft* 107 (1957), pp. 367–71.

7. R. C. Zaehner. *Zurvan, a Zoroastrian dilemma* (1955), pp. 312–20.

8. A. Goetze. "Persische Weisheit in griechischem Gewande," *Zeitschrift für Indologie und Iranistik* II (1923), pp. 60–98.

9. J. Duchesne-Guillemin. "Persische Weisheit in griechischem Gewande," *The Harvard Theological Review* XLIX (1956), pp. 115–22.

10. W. B. Henning. "An astronomical chapter of the Bundahishn," *Journal of the Royal Asiatic Society* (1942), pp. 230–33.

11. W. B. Henning. "A Sogdian fragment of the Manichaean cosmogony," *Bulletin of the School of Oriental and African Studies* XII (1948), p. 313.

12. M. Boyce. "Some reflections on Zurvanism," *Bulletin of the School of Oriental and African Studies* XIX (1957), pp. 313–14.

13. R. C. Zaehner. *The teachings of the Magi, a compendium of Zoroastrian beliefs* (1956), pp. 75–76.

14. J. Brough. "The tripartite ideology of the Indo-Europeans: an experiment in method," *Bulletin of the School of*

Oriental and African Studies XXII (1959), p. 70; the article covers pp. 69–85.

15. G. Widengren. "Religione dell' Iran antico," *Le Civiltà dell' Oriente* III (1958), p. 536.

16. J. Duchesne-Guillemin. *The western response to Zoroaster* (1958), p. 40.

17. I. Gershevitch. *The Avestan hymn to Mithra* (1959), pp. 40–41.

18. S. Wikander. *Vetenskaps-Societetens i Lund, Årsbok* (1950).

19. G. Morgenstierne. *Sarūpa-Bhāratī, Dr. Laksman Sarup Memorial Volume* (1954), pp. 30 ff.

20. R. C. Zaehner. *The teachings of the Magi, a compendium of Zoroastrian beliefs* (1956), pp. 126, 129.

21. R. C. Zaehner. *Zurvan, a Zoroastrian dilemma* (1955), p. 85.

22. E. Benveniste. *The Persian religion according to the chief Greek texts* (1929), pp. 61–62.

23. M. Boyce. "Sadwēs and Pēsūs," *Bulletin of the School of Oriental and African Studies* XIII (1951), pp. 908–15.

24. H. W. Bailey. *Zoroastrian problems in the ninth-century books* (1943), pp. 1–51.

25. The numerous cognates of *xvarenah* outside the Zoroastrian tradition are discussed by H. W. Bailey in the same book (note 24), pp. 52–77.

26. H. S. Nyberg. *Die Religionen des alten Iran* (1937).

27. W. B. Henning. *Zoroaster, politician or witch-doctor?* (1951), p. 49.

28. M. Boyce. "Some reflections on Zurvanism," *Bulletin of the School of Oriental and African Studies* XIX (1957), pp. 308–9.

29. R. C. Zaehner. *Zurvan, a Zoroastrian dilemma* (1955), pp. 419–28.

30. J. Duchesne-Guillemin. "Ahriman et le dieu suprême dans les mystères de Mithra," *Numen* II (1955), pp. 190–95.

31. On Āz, R. C. Zaehner, *Zurvan, a Zoroastrian dilemma* (1955), pp. 166–83.

32. I. Gershevitch. *The Avestan hymn to Mithra* (1959), p. 154.

33. R. C. Zaehner. *The teachings of the Magi, a compendium of Zoroastrian beliefs* (1957), pp. 133–38.

34. For Manichean eschatology, A. V. Williams Jackson, "A sketch of the Manichaean doctrine concerning the future life," *Journal of the American Oriental Society* L (1930), pp. 177–98.

BIBLIOGRAPHY

In addition to the literature given in the notes the following selective list may prove of use and profit for further reading.

A survey of ancient Iranian religion with special attention to its main problems and to topics deserving further investigation was written by G. Widengren in two articles, which also appeared together in separate form, published in the periodical *Numen* I (1954), pp. 16–83 and II (1955), pp. 47–132 under the title "Stand und Aufgaben der iranischen Religionsgeschichte." A valuable book on Zarathuštra's religion is H. Lommel, *Die Religion Zarathustras* (1930). A recent work on Zarathuštra, besides J. Duchesne-Guillemin's *Zoroastre* (1948) and W. B. Henning's *Zoroaster* (1951), is E. Herzfeld's *Zoroaster and his world* (1948). The main theses of G. Dumézil are to be found in *Les dieux des Indo-Européens* (1952) and *L'idéologie tripartite des Indo-Européens* (1958). A good survey of Pahlavi literature is J. C. Tavadia, *Die mittelpersische Sprache und Literatur der Zarathustrier* (1956).

Of monographs the following deserve to be mentioned: A. Christensen, *Les types du Premier Homme et du Premier Roi dans l'histoire légendaire des Iraniens* (1919), on Gayōmart and Yima; S. S. Hartman, *Gayōmart, étude sur le syncrétisme dans l'ancien Iran* (1953), on Gayōmart; I. Gershevitch, *The Avestan hymn to Mithra* (1959), on Mithra; E. Benveniste and L. Renou, *Vṛtra et Vṛθragna* (1934), on Verethragna; S. Wikander, *Vayu* (1941), on

Vayu; A. Christensen, *Essai sur la démonologie iranienne* (1941), on demonology.

M. J. Dresden

Myths of Ancient China

BY DERK BODDE

I. INTRODUCTION

The student of Chinese religion quickly learns that there is a world of difference between the gods of classical China (ending with the fall of the Han dynasty in A.D. 220) and those of post-classical times. The latter are large in number, diverse in origin (Buddhist, Taoist, or numerous local cults), have clearly defined anthropomorphic traits, and belong to a spiritual hierarchy which, in its gradations, closely parallels the terrestrial hierarchy of bureaucratic imperial China. These gods are portrayed for us in art, described in religious literature, and even satirized in works of fiction such as the great sixteenth-century novel *Hsi yu chi* (translated by Arthur Waley as *Monkey*). It is notable that relatively few of them are known as early as the classical period. This means that though several compendia have been published under such generalized titles as "Chinese mythology," they are of little relevance for the study of *ancient* Chinese myth since, despite their titles, they limit themselves very largely to these later gods.*

The gods of ancient China, by comparison, are fewer in

---

* For these compendia, see the Selected Bibliography under Ferguson, Maspero, and Werner. In this bibliography will be found all modern studies mentioned in this essay, as well as others not mentioned. Primary Chinese sources, however, are not listed, since for the specialist this is unnecessary, whereas for the general reader it has little purpose.

number, appear very rarely or not at all in art, and are commonly described so vaguely or briefly in the texts that their personality, and sometimes even their sex, remains uncertain. Side by side with them, on the other hand, appear a good many figures who, at first sight, seem to be human beings, yet on closer examination are found to display more than ordinary human qualities. They are gods or demigods who, through a process to be discussed presently, have been largely stripped of their divine attributes and transformed into men.

It would be tempting but erroneous to conclude from this that there are no myths in ancient China. More accurate would be the statement that individual *myths* certainly do occur, but not a systematic *mythology*, meaning by this an integrated body of mythological materials. On the contrary, these materials are usually so fragmentary and episodic that even the reconstruction from them of individual myths—let alone an integrated *system* of myths—is exceedingly difficult. Before discussing the myths themselves, we shall in the following section elaborate on some of the factors which may throw light on this peculiar situation. First of all, however, some definitions and explanations are in order.

In this essay we shall confine our attention to the field covered by what Stith Thompson calls a "minimum definition" of myth. "Myth," he has written (in an article appearing in *Myth: A Symposium,* 1955), "has to do with the gods and their actions, with creation, and with the general nature of the universe and of the earth. This is a minimum definition." Even within this minimum definition, moreover, reasons of space will compel us to limit ourselves still further to myths of a cosmogonic nature. This means that, aside from their mention in connection with cosmogonic phenomena, we shall be obliged to disregard the much larger category of ancient Chinese *hero* myths: those of the culture hero who enjoys supernatural birth, is sometimes aided by protective animals, becomes a sage ruler or otherwise performs great deeds for mankind, and so on.

Chronologically, our attention will be focused for the most

part on myths believed to have existed during the pre-imperial epoch of Chinese "feudalism," in other words, during the Chou dynasty (ca. 1027–221 B.C.). (For the preceding Shang dynasty, trad. 1766–ca. 1027, the extant inscriptional material is unfortunately too limited to be serviceable for our subject.) This means that whenever possible we shall base ourselves on texts belonging to the Chou dynasty itself. Because, however, these are often inadequate, we shall in case after case supplement them with the more abundant sources dating from the Han dynasty (206 B.C.–A.D. 220)— an age of empire which, though still forming a part of China's "classical" period, differs in many respects from the pre-imperial Chou dynasty. The question of textual chronology is an exceedingly complicated one, on which we shall have more to say in a later section (II, 3).

Finally, a word about the seemingly precise dates given for many of the personages to appear in these pages. These dates, when marked as "trad." (traditional), should not, of course, be accepted literally, nor even as necessarily signifying that the personages in question ever historically existed. They derive from the traditional chronology formulated by Chinese historians of a later time, and as such are indicative of that same euhemerization about which we shall speak in a moment. We give them here, therefore, simply to show how the Chinese historians have tried to fit their ancient traditions into a chronological framework.

II. THE PROBLEMS

Though ancient Chinese myths have been studied by some of the best known scholars of East and West alike, the nature of the available data has prevented anything like a generally accepted consensus from emerging. What we have, instead, are diverse theories which, though often ingenious, are rarely conclusive and sometimes exceedingly fanciful. In writing a brief essay such as this, therefore, we are at once confronted by an almost impossible task: that of synthesizing and simplifying where no really reliable basis exists for so doing; of compressing into a few pages what would ideally require a good-sized volume of analysis and exposition. The manifold factors responsible for this situation can perhaps be summarized under three main headings: those of euhemerization, of fragmentation and language, and of chronology.

1. The Problem of Euhemerization

The theory to which Euhemerus has given his name maintains that the origin of myth is to be found in actual history, and that the gods and demigods of mythology were, to start with, actual human beings. As commonly used by writers on Chinese mythology, however, "euhemerization" denotes precisely the opposite process: the transformation of what were once myths and gods into seemingly authentic history and human beings. Unquestionably, a fair amount of what purports to be early Chinese history has been subjected to this kind of euhemerization, the literal acceptance of which by most people until recent years has led to gross misunderstandings concerning the beginnings of Chinese civilization. Not infrequently, to be sure, the literalists might encounter certain mythological elements not wholly concealed beneath their euhemerist dress, but when this happened, these could always be explained as mere later accretions to what in essence was genuine history. Henri Maspero, in the opening paragraph of his notable study, "Légendes mythologiques dans le *Chou king*" (1924), has vividly described the situation as follows:

> Chinese scholars have never known more than one way of interpreting legendary accounts, that of euhemerization. Under the plea of recovering from such accounts their historical kernel, they eliminate those elements of the marvellous which seem to them improbable, and preserve only a colorless residue, in

which gods and heroes are transformed into sage emperors and sage ministers, and monsters into rebellious princes or evil ministers. Such are the lucubrations which, placed end to end according to a sequence imposed upon chronology by various metaphysical theories, especially that of the five elements, constitute what is called the history of Chinese origins. In this there is nothing but the name of history; actually there are only legends, sometimes mythological in origin, sometimes coming from the ancestral temples of the great families, sometimes emanating from local religious centers, sometimes the accounts—more or less learned—which have been elaborated to explain a rite, sometimes simple stories borrowed from folklore, etc. All these phantoms ought to disappear from the history of China, whose origins they encumber; rather than persist in the search for a non-existent historical basis beneath the legendary form, we should seek to recover the mythological basis or the popular story beneath the pseudo-historical account.

It should be added that since 1924, when this was written, the Chinese scholars themselves have done wonders along these lines. In many cases, indeed, they have been more iconoclastic toward their own early history than have the Western scholars—sometimes, one might add, overly iconoclastic.

That euhemerization was already a recognized process in Chou dynasty China, and that it was then viewed with skepticism by some, is clearly indicated by several amusing anecdotes preserved in literature ranging from the fourth to around the first century B.C. In all of them, significantly, Confucius (551–479 B.C.) is made the exponent of euhemerism. The first story (contained in *Ta Tai li-chi,* ch. 62; compiled i cent. B.C. from earlier materials) concerns the legendary sage ruler Huang Ti, the "Yellow Lord" or "Yellow Emperor" (trad. xxvi cent. B.C.). "Was the Yellow Lord a man or was he not a man?" asks a disciple of Confucius.

"How is it that he reached (an age of) three hundred years?" To which Confucius is made to reply that this is a misunderstanding: what is actually meant is that during the Yellow Lord's own life of one hundred years, the people enjoyed his benefits; during the first hundred years after his death, they revered his spirit; and during the next hundred years after that, they continued to follow his teachings. "And this is why there is mention of three hundred years."

The next anecdote, also about the Yellow Lord, is based on a double meaning of the word *mien,* primarily signifying "face," but also meaning a "side, direction, quarter." In a passage from the fourth century B.C. *Shih-tzu* (now missing from the text, but quoted in a later encyclopedia), another disciple asks Confucius: "Is it true that the ancient Yellow Lord had four faces [*ssu mien*]?" To which Confucius replies that this is not at all true. What is meant is that the Yellow Lord used four officials to govern the four quarters (*ssu mien*) of his empire, so that he was "four faced" in the sense that the four "faces" or "sides" of his empire were controlled by these officials on his behalf.

The third anecdote again rests on a double meaning, this time of the word *tsu,* ordinarily meaning "foot" but in some contexts meaning "enough." This anecdote (recorded in *Han Fei-tzu,* ch. 33, and *Lü-shih ch'un-ch'iu,* XXII, 6; both iii cent. B.C.) has to do with a curious being called K'uei. In the euhemerized histories he is the human Music Master of the sage ruler Shun (trad. xxiii cent. B.C.), but from other scattered references we can see that he was actually a mythological creature having only one foot. In the story, the ruler of Confucius' native state of Lu is made to ask Confucius: "I have heard that K'uei was one-footed [*yi tsu*]. Is this really so?" To which Confucius replies: "K'uei was a man, so why should he have one foot?" Then he goes on to explain that because K'uei's royal master Shun was greatly pleased with K'uei's musical ability, he once exclaimed of him: "As to K'uei, one (like him) is enough [*yi erh tsu*]." By later people, however, this saying came to be misconstrued as meaning that K'uei had but one foot (*yi tsu*).

These anecdotes are surely apocryphal, yet the fact that they all center around Confucius is no accident. For it is precisely the Confucianists who, more than any other school of thought, were historically minded and assumed prime responsibility for conserving and editing the ancient texts which eventually became the Chinese classics. In so doing they were, on the one hand, always intensely interested in the search for historical precedents which would confirm their own social and political doctrines; on the other hand, their strong humanism tended to make them either indifferent toward supernatural matters, or to seek to explain them in purely rationalistic terms. The results have been disastrous for the preservation of early Chinese myth, for they mean that it is precisely in those classical texts which might otherwise be expected to be prime repositories of myth, that such myth has either vanished entirely or (more probably) suffered grievous distortion.

Obviously, therefore, our search for myth must go beyond the Confucian-dominated classics to include the writings of the several non-Confucian schools. Among such writings, those of the Taoists, because of their iconoclasm toward Confucian tradition, their greater interest in popular beliefs, and their richly imaginative mode of expression, are by far the most promising. Here again, however, there is a limitation imposed by the philosophical assumptions of Taoism: its denial of teleology and anthropocentrism, and insistence upon a natural rather than a supernatural explanation for the universe. This in practice means that though mythological allusions abound in Taoist writings, they are introduced as a rule only for philosophical or literary effect, and not because the Taoist authors actually believe in them themselves. Rarely, therefore, do these authors bother to narrate at length the myths to which they allude. Rather, they take from them those elements which can be used for allegories of their own invention, thereby to express the philosophical ideas in which they themselves are interested.

A good example is the conversation in the seventeenth chapter of the *Chuang-tzu* (iii cent. B.C.) between a centipede

and that same K'uei whom we have just encountered in
Confucian dress. There is no doubt that Chuang Tzu's K'uei
is a mythological creature, for he is made to complain to the
centipede about his own difficulties in hopping around on
one foot, and to ask the latter how he succeeds in controlling
those many feet of his. The allegory's purpose, however, is
not at all mythological but philosophical. From it we learn
the Taoist moral that every creature should be satisfied with
his own native endowment, but nothing whatsoever concerning the K'uei himself, other than the basic fact that he is
one-footed.

2. The Problems of Fragmentation and of Language

Not only does pre-Han literature lack any separate genre
which might be called myth, but within any single literary
work it is not easy to find a myth recorded in consecutive
entirety. All that we have are casual references and tantaliz-
ing fragments, widely scattered among texts of diverse date
and ideological orientation. No wonder then that scholars can
rarely agree as to how to fit these pieces into some kind
of unity.

This fragmentation is characteristic even of what is probably the richest single storehouse of Chou mythological lore:
the anthology of imaginative and sensuous poems known as the
Ch'u tz'u or Songs of Ch'u (wherein, however, are to be found
Han as well as Chou poems). A striking example, to which
we shall refer many times, is the T'ien wen or "Heavenly
Questions" (prob. iv cent. B.C.), whose 185 lines are packed
with mythological allusions, all, however, presented in the
form of enigmatic riddles. Typical are the following lines
(as translated by David Hawkes, Ch'u Tz'u, the Songs of the
South, Oxford, 1959, pp. 49, 56):

> Where is the stone forest? What beast can talk?
> Where are the hornless dragons which carry bears
>   on their backs for sport? (ll. 47–48)
> P'eng Chien made a drink-offering of pheasant's
>   broth. How did the Lord eat of it?

*He received the gift of long-lasting life. Why
then was he still sad?* (ll. 171–72)

Other than that P'eng Chien may be identified with fair
certainty as the Chinese Methuselah, P'eng Tsu, practically
nothing is known of what is here alluded to (aside from the
very uncertain guesses of much later commentators).

The difficulties produced by such fragments are enhanced
by linguistic difficulties inherent in the Chinese classical
language. In the first place, its many homophones and characters easily confused for one another make very tempting the
search for new readings and identifications, usually based on
such arguments as: character X of text A appears as character
Y of text B; character Y appears in turn as character Z in
text C; hence character X of text A and character Z of text C
are equivalents. This kind of work, brilliantly performed by
a long line of Chinese scholars, has done wonders in eluci-
dating the ancient texts. On the other hand, conducted too
exuberantly it can lead to quite startling results.

In the second place, the telegraphic brevity of classical
Chinese, coupled with its inflectional inability (without the
use of added words) to indicate gender, number, or tense,
makes it often possible to translate a small fragment in several
ways, with no assurance as to which is correct unless a larger
clarifying context can be found. A good example is the fifty-
sixth line of the *T'ien wen* poem, wherein most scholars see
an allusion to the myth of the shooting of the ten suns by
Archer Yi (see III, 4 below), and therefore translate: "Why
did Yi shoot down the suns? Why did the ravens shed their
wings?" Bernhard Karlgren, however (in his encyclopedic
"Legends and Cults in Ancient China," 1946, p. 268), believes
that the motif of *ten* suns came to be associated with Archer
Yi only in Han times. Therefore he translates in the singular:
"Why did Yi shoot at [and not "down"] the sun? Why did
the raven shed its feathers?" Either translation is grammati-
cally possible; which one we accept, however, determines our
entire decision as to whether or not the two themes originally
formed a single myth.

3. The Problem of Chronology

The year 221 B.C., because it saw the final unification of "feudal" China into a truly centralized empire, is the great watershed of early Chinese history. Before that year, the country was divided into mutually warring, independent states, each ruled by a hereditary house and divided in turn into lesser domains also held by noble families. Politically, most of this pre-imperial age was covered by the Chou dynasty (ca. 1027–221 B.C.). Following 221, on the other hand, the next several centuries saw the consolidation of a new form of centralized empire, in which an official bureaucracy which was non-hereditary and centrally appointed took the place of the landed aristocracy of Chou times. The patterns of empire then laid down remained the norm until the present century, but the classical phase of Chinese history came to an end with the disintegration of the Han dynasty (206 B.C.–A.D. 220).

Culturally speaking, the Chou dynasty was the creative age of China's great classical and philosophical literature, whereas the Han dynasty, though also notably creative, was at the same time the first age when the writings of the past were systematically collected, edited, and commented upon. It was likewise the epoch which saw the appearance (ca. 100 B.C.) of China's first "universal" history. To what extent the Han scholars changed the texts they edited, sometimes introducing (perhaps quite unconsciously) ideas reflecting their own environment, and to what extent they may even have forged works which they then attributed to Chou or earlier times, still remains a subject of great controversy. Fortunately, much has been done by Chinese and Western scholars alike in recent decades to clarify the situation. Nonetheless, many points of uncertainty still remain.

In the field of mythology, the differences between the two dynasties are equally striking. Thus what, in the Chou literature, is fragmented and frequently euhemerized, often becomes, in Han times, so greatly elaborated that though the personages in the myths remain in large part the same, what is said of them may be totally new. It would seem, in many cases, that the Han writers were tapping new sources of living popular tradition, hitherto neglected by the more aristocratically oriented writers of the Chou. Likewise, for the first time, a very few of the mythological figures are portrayed in sculptured reliefs. A notable example of the new imaginative trend is the *Shan-hai ching* or *Classic of Mountains and Seas* (trad. ascribed in part to the Chou, but probably all of Han date), wherein not only the lands of China proper, but those extending to the far reaches of the earth, are populated by hundreds of strange new gods and monsters. So fantastic and prolific, indeed, are the beings of this book, that one may fairly ask whether many of them are not simply the fanciful creations of their author (or authors), rather than based upon actual popular belief.

On the other hand, we can also often see the Han scholars manfully grappling with a body of older tradition which apparently has lost its living reality. They strive to reconcile seeming differences, to fill in lacunae, to put into order (according to their own ideological preconceptions) matters that they no longer truly understand. These efforts are particularly conspicuous in the disagreements often found among the Han commentators on the Chou classics.

All these developments, it should be kept in mind, are entirely distinct from the phenomenon noted at the very beginning of this essay: the gradual fading, in post-Han times, of most of the ancient gods from popular consciousness, and their replacement by a new and more clearly defined pantheon (no doubt stimulated in part by the advent of Buddhism).

What, then, is the scholar of early Chinese myth to do when confronted by these two very different bodies of literature? Two general approaches are possible, one of which we may term the "historical," the other the "sociological." As respective examples of these approaches, let us briefly contrast the theories of Bernhard Karlgren (expressed in his large "Legends and Cults in Ancient China," 1946), and of Wolfram Eberhard (expressed in several works, notably his two-volume *Lokalkulturen im alten China,* 1942, which, however, covers much else besides myth proper).

According to Karlgren, the main reason for the recording of ancient Chinese traditions in Chou literature is the fact that the personages in these traditions were regarded by the many grandee houses of Chou times as their ancestors. As a consequence, their memory was kept alive in the ancestral cults maintained by these houses. This, Karlgren believes, explains why they are portrayed neither as outright gods nor yet quite as ordinary mortals, but rather as "supermen," that is to say, as cultural heroes who are definite historical figures, but who at the same time possess something more than purely human characteristics. With the destruction of the old social order at the end of the third century B.C., however, the ancestral cults of these grandee houses lost their social significance, with the result that the memory of the ancient legends and heroes became divorced from living tradition. Thus was the way paved for the fanciful elaborations or antiquarian speculations of the Han writers.

In discussing these legends and heroes, therefore, Karlgren distinguishes sharply between what he calls the "free" texts of Chou times (texts in which the legends and heroes appear casually, without any tendentious purpose), and the fanciful or "systematizing" texts of Han times (in which materials are arranged according to set systems and theories, notably that of the five elements; among these "systematizing" texts Karlgren would also include a few late Chou works). For the study of genuinely early myth and legend, therefore, Karlgren believes that only the pre-Han "free" texts have any real validity.

Eberhard, on the other hand, sees the rise of Chinese civilization as resulting from the interaction and intermixture of various cultural components which, he believes, were in early times ethnically and regionally distinct from one another. Therefore, though by no means indifferent to the problem of historical development, his main interest lies in trying to isolate (regionally rather than chronologically) what he believes to be these basic cultural components. For his purposes, therefore, what is recorded in a Chou text, and what may be said by a writer many centuries or even a millennium later, may both be valid provided they both point toward a common cultural cluster. Basing himself on this standpoint, Eberhard, in a lengthy review (1946), has severely criticized Karlgren's methodology on several counts, two of which in particular may be mentioned:

(1) The mere fact that version A of a given myth happens to appear in an older text than version B, does not necessarily mean that *developmentally* speaking version A is the earlier or more primitive. On the contrary, as Eberhard points out, the Han writers could and did utilize long-existent popular oral tradition to a greater extent than did the more aristocratically oriented writers of the feudal age. (2) Karlgren's belief that most of the beings in the myths were originally human heroes, who only later, in some cases, acquired the attributes of gods or even animals, is at variance with modern ethnological and sociological theory. "If this opinion were correct, Chinese mythology would be the greatest exception hitherto known in the whole field of ethnology: the Chinese would first have created heroes and later only have made them into gods or even animals!"

Karlgren's strictly historical approach does indeed seem overly mechanical when, for example, he accepts or rejects a text simply according to whether it happens to have been written before or after the dividing line of 221 B.C., instead of evaluating, in each case, the particular ideology and other individual circumstances of the text itself. Furthermore, his rigid approach would seem to overlook the possibility of persistence or recurrence of a given motif (perhaps in varying forms) over a very long period of time.

On the other hand, Eberhard's use of chronologically widely separated data for reconstructing an ancient myth (in contrast to his main endeavor, that of isolating a cluster of long-term cultural components) has its obvious dangers. No doubt Eberhard is correct in asserting that "a myth reported only in a later text, may very well represent a form reflecting quite an early stage of development." However, as he himself then goes on to say, "Of course, we have to prove this in every single case." Unfortunately, the proofs presented by followers of this methodology are by no means always convincing, nor are they sometimes even seriously attempted. In many cases, indeed, they can never be really convincing, simply because the data themselves make this impossible.

In what follows, therefore, we shall try to steer a middle course: that of limiting ourselves (save for the first myth, which is a special case) to those myths for which at least *some* factual basis can be found in the Chou literature. However, we shall not hesitate to add to this what the Han writers have to say, in every instance being careful to warn the reader accordingly.

III. THE MYTHS

The following are five examples of cosmogonic myth; as explained earlier, space does not permit us to discuss, more than incidentally, those having to do with cultural heroes, unless (as in the fifth myth) they also have cosmogonic significance.

1. The P'an-ku Creation Myth

In the *San-wu li-chi* (Record of Cycles in Threes and Fives), an obscure work of the third century A.D. now known only through quotations in later encyclopedias, there appears the following story (here paraphrased):

Heaven and Earth were once inextricably commingled (*hun-tun*) like a chicken's egg, within which was engendered P'an-ku (a name perhaps meaning "Coiled-up Antiquity"). After 18,000 years, this inchoate mass split apart, what was bright and light forming Heaven, and what was dark and heavy forming Earth. Thereafter, during another 18,000 years, Heaven daily increased ten feet in height, Earth daily increased ten feet in thickness, and P'an-ku, between the two, daily increased ten feet in size. This is how Heaven and Earth came to be separated by their present distance of 90,000 *li* (roughly 30,000 English miles).

Other texts, probably somewhat later in date, add the further information that after P'an-ku died, his breath became the wind and clouds, his voice the thunder, his left and right eyes the sun and moon respectively, his four limbs and five "bodies" (fingers?) the four quarters of the earth and five great mountains, his blood the rivers, his muscles and veins the strata of the earth, his flesh the soil, his hair and beard the constellations, his skin and body-hair the plants and trees, his teeth and bones the metals and stones, his marrow gold and precious stones, and his sweat the rain. The parasites on his body, impregnated by the wind, became human beings. In graphic portrayals of much later date, he is often shown as a horned demiurge who, with hammer and adze, chisels out the universe.

Here, in these works of the third century A.D. and later, we find China's *only* clearly recognizable creation myth. Most Chinese scholars believe it to be of non-Chinese origin and link it to the ancestral myth of the Miao and Yao tribal peoples of South China (also first recorded in the third century), in which these tribes trace their origin to a dog named P'an-hu. This dog, a pet of the Chinese legendary ruler Ti K'u (trad. ca. 2400 B.C.), succeeded in bringing to his imperial master the head of a certain troublesome barbarian general, and in accordance with a previously promised reward was given the emperor's own daughter as wife. The dog then carried her off to the mountain fastnesses of South China, where the progeny of the two became the ancestors of the present Miao and Yao tribes. Aside from the phonetic similarity between the names P'an-ku and P'an-hu, however, and the fact that both cults seem to have been centered in South China, where they were sometimes confused with one another, there is little apparent similarity between the myths.

Similarities to the P'an-ku story do appear, however, if we

look farther afield, for example at India and ancient Sumer. Thus the *Rig Veda* tells us that the cosmic waters were originally restrained within a shell, but that the fashioner god, Tvaṣṭṛ, created Heaven and Earth, who in turn engendered Indra. By drinking the soma, Indra became strong and forced Heaven and Earth apart, himself filling up the space between them and also slitting open the cover within which lay the cosmic waters, so that they could issue forth. Another later story in the *Rig Veda* also tells us that when Puruṣa was sacrificed by the gods, the parts of his cut-up body became the sun, sky, atmosphere, earth, four quarters, four social classes of mankind, and so forth.

In Sumer, similarly, it was believed that there first existed the primeval sea, which engendered the cosmic mountain, consisting of Heaven and Earth in undivided form. They in turn produced the air-god Enlil, who separated Heaven from Earth, carried off Earth for himself, and through union with his mother Earth set the stage for the organization of the universe.

Though in China itself the P'an-ku myth does not appear before the third century, Eberhard (in his *Lokalkulturen*, II, 467 ff.) would relate it conceptually to what he believes to be a much earlier Chinese idea: that of a primeval egg or sac, the splitting of which permits its undifferentiated contents to assume form as an organized universe. In its sophisticated version, this conception may well underlie the astronomical theory, current in Han times, according to which Heaven and Earth are shaped like an egg, Earth being enclosed by the sphere of Heaven just as the yolk of an egg is enclosed by its shell.

The first of our texts, it will be remembered, says that Heaven and Earth were once inextricably commingled (*hun-tun*) like a chicken's egg. In late Chou and Han philosophical texts, the same onomatopoeic term *hun-tun* is used to designate the state of undifferentiated chaos before an organized universe came into being. Curiously enough, the term appears again in modern Chinese parlance as the name for a small *sac*-like dumpling (a thin shell of dough enclosing chopped-up meat), used as the basic ingredient of the popular *hun-tun* soup served in Chinese restaurants.

In the *Shan-hai ching* or *Classic of Mountains and Seas* (bk. 2), of Han date, Hun-tun is personified as a being living southwest of the Mountain of Heaven (T'ien Shan), who has six feet and four wings, is the color of fire, lacks a face or eyes, and is *shaped like a sac*. Among Chou dynasty texts, the *Tso chuan* history (iv cent. B.C., with later additions), under the year 618 B.C., euhemerizes Hun-tun as the evil son of an early sage ruler. Describing his undesirable characteristics, it says, among other things, that he "screens [i.e., covers over or bottles up] righteousness." The best-known Chou reference to Hun-tun, however, is the charming allegory in the seventh chapter of the Taoist work *Chuang-tzu* (iii cent. B.C.). There we are told that Hun-tun or Chaos was the Ruler of the Center, and that he lacked the usual seven openings of other men (eyes, ears, nostrils, and mouth). Therefore his friends, Shu and Hu, having been well treated by him, decided to bore such openings in him. Each day they bored one hole, but on the seventh day Hun-tun died.

Such are the scattered data from which we must decide whether or not the cosmogonic *conception* underlying the P'an-ku myth (and not, of course, the myth as such) possibly goes back to early times. Marcel Granet, for his part (in his *Danses et légendes de la Chine ancienne*, 1926, p. 540 ff.), would link the *hun-tun* idea to another mythical theme in which, though the term *hun-tun* itself does not appear, a leather sack plays a central role. It concerns King Wu-yi (trad. reigned 1198–95 B.C.), one of the last evil rulers of the Shang dynasty, who made a human figure which he called the Spirit of Heaven (T'ien Shen), and played a game of counters with it, which he won. To show his contempt, he then hung up a leather sack filled with blood and shot at it with arrows, saying that he was shooting at Heaven. Soon afterward, while hunting, he was killed by lightning. The same theme recurs almost a millennium later in connection with the last king of Sung, a state which in Chou times was ruled by descendants of the Shang royal house. This king too hung up a leather blood-filled sack and shot at it, saying that he was shooting at Heaven. Shortly afterward, in 282 B.C., he was attacked by a coalition of other states, killed, and his state annihilated.

Possibly Granet is correct in believing that this theme is related to the *hun-tun* conception. On the other hand, a parallel has also been suggested between it and the theme of Archer Yi's shooting at the sun (see III, 4 below).

2. The Fashioning Deity Nü-kua

Nü-kua, the "Woman Kua," though fairly prominent in Han times, appears only twice in earlier literature. Despite her name, it is only in the first century A.D. that her sex is positively stated. At about the same time she also becomes identified as either the sister or consort of the much better known Fu-hsi (Subduer of Animals), a sage (trad. ca. 2800 B.C.) said to have taught men how to hunt and cook, to make nets, and so on. On the stone reliefs of the Wu Liang offering shrines (ca. A.D. 150), Fu-hsi and Nü-kua appear together; their upper bodies are human, but merge below into serpent tails that are intertwined with one another. Fu-hsi holds a carpenter's square in his hand and Nü-kua a compass, apparently as symbols of their constructive activities. The constructive work of Fu-hsi, however (other than as inventor and ruler), has not come down to us, and we may wonder whether the purported association between him and the fashioning deity Nü-kua really goes back before Han times.

The best account of the latter's activities occurs in the sixth chapter of the Han Taoist work, *Huai-nan-tzu* (ii cent. B.C., a work rich in mythological materials):

> In very ancient times, the four pillars [at the compass points] were broken down, the nine provinces [of the habitable world] were split apart, Heaven did not wholly cover [Earth], and Earth did not completely support [Heaven]. Fires flamed without being extin-

guished, waters inundated without being stopped, fierce
beasts ate the people, and birds of prey seized the old
and weak in their claws. Thereupon Nü-kua fused
together stones of the five colors with which she
patched together azure Heaven. She cut off the feet of
a turtle with which she set up the four pillars. She
slaughtered the Black Dragon in order to save the
province of Chi [the present Hopei and Shansi provinces in North China]. She collected the ashes of reeds
with which to check the wild waters.

The text goes on to say that thereafter there was universal
harmony: the seasons followed their due course, beasts
sheathed their claws and teeth and serpents hid their poison,
the people lived lives of undreaming sleep and uncalculating
wakefulness.

The "four pillars" mentioned in this myth belong, of course,
to the cosmological belief, found in many cultures, that
Heaven is supported on pillars or some other kind of foundation. In China (where the pillars were thought of as mountains), the earliest mention is that in the *T'ien wen* poem
(iv cent. B.C.), which, however, speaks not of four but of
eight pillars. The same poem, as well as the Kung-kung story
below (and other texts as well), further makes mention of
the *wei* or "cords" of Earth. As a technical term, *wei* designates the cords which, on a chariot, secure its canopy to the
frame or body. By analogy, therefore, the *wei* of Earth
(sometimes stated to be four in number) must likewise serve
to attach the canopy of Heaven to Earth below. (The comparison of Heaven to a chariot's canopy and Earth to its
body is a common one in the texts.) Just how the *wei* function in relation to the (four or eight) pillars of Heaven is,
however, unstated.

The story of Nü-kua is by several Han writers linked to
the cosmic struggle between Chuan-hsü (legendary ruler,
trad. xxv cent. B.C.) and Kung-kung (euhemerized in Chou
writings as a human "rebel," but in late Han times described
as a horned monster with serpent's body). Wang Ch'ung

(A.D. 27–ca. 100), for example, in his *Lun heng* or *Critical Essays* (chs. 31 and 46), says that anciently, when Kung-kung fought unsuccessfully with Chuan-hsü to become ruler, he blundered in his rage against Mount Pu-chou (in the northwest quarter), thereby causing the pillar of Heaven and the cord of Earth to break off at that point. It was then that Nü-kua patched up Heaven with melted stones and cut off a turtle's feet to hold it up. Nonetheless, Heaven and Earth have since that time sloped toward one another in the northwest, but have tilted away from one another in the opposite direction. This is why the astral bodies of Heaven continue to this day to move in a westerly direction, whereas the rivers (of China) on Earth flow toward the ocean (in the east). In the *T'ien wen* there is already mention of the gap in the southeast between Heaven and Earth, from which we may infer that at the time of this poem the story of Kung-kung was already current.

We may question, however, whether this story and the Nü-kua myth properly belong together. In the *Huai-nan-tzu* (ch. 3), for example, the Kung-kung story appears alone, without any mention of Nü-kua at all, and though the two are joined in the fifth chapter of *Lieh-tzu* (a Taoist work, trad. Chou but prob. Han), their order is there reversed (the story of Nü-kua given first, followed by that of Kung-kung). This, of course, destroys any logical connection between them.

In a passage (now known only through later quotation) from the *Feng-su t'ung-yi* (Comprehensive Meaning of Customs), by Ying Shao (ca. 140–ca. 206), Nü-kua is also portrayed as the creator of mankind:

> It is popularly said that when Heaven and Earth had opened forth, but before there were human beings, Nü-kua created men by patting yellow earth together. But the work tasked her strength and left her no free time, so that she then dragged a string through mud, thus heaping it up so as to make it into men. Therefore the rich and the noble are those men of yellow earth,

whereas the poor and the lowly—all ordinary people—
are those cord-made men.

Another passage from the same work (likewise now known
only in quotation) tells us further that Nü-kua is prayed to
as the goddess of marriage, because it is she who first instituted marriage. (In other words, having created men, she
taught them how to propagate.)

Finally, we are told in the *Shan-hai ching* (bk. 16) that
beyond the northwest sea there are ten spirits, called "Nü-
kua's intestines," because (after she died) they were transformed into spirits (from her intestines).

Whether or not Nü-kua as the creator of mankind represents simply a popular addition to the primary theme of
Nü-kua as the repairer and organizer of the world, it is evident that neither theme constitutes a true creation myth (in
the sense of the P'an-ku myth), since both take place in an
already existing universe. We might assume the entire Nü-
kua cult to be a Han creation, were it not for two bare references to her occurring in Chou literature. The more important of these is one of the riddles in *T'ien wen:* "Nü-kua had
a body. Who formed and fashioned it?" This certainly suggests that Nü-kua's fashioning activities were already known
in Chou times if, as seems reasonable, it should be interpreted as meaning: Nü-kua was a fashioner of other things.
Who then fashioned her?

3. The Separation of Heaven and Earth

We have already encountered the theme of the separation
of Heaven and Earth in the P'an-ku myth. It crops up again,
though in a very different context, in two texts of Chou
date. The first is one of the major classics, the *Shu ching* or
Classic of History (sect. *Lü hsing*, trad. x cent. B.C., but
prob. some cents. later). There we are told that the Miao
(a tribe or confraternity, notorious as troublemakers during
the reigns of Yao and Shun, trad. xxiv–xxiii cent. B.C.) created
oppressive punishments which threw the people into disorder. Shang Ti, the "Lord on High" (name of the most

prominent ancient divinity), surveyed the people and found them lacking in virtue. Out of pity for those who were innocent, the August Lord (surely another name for Shang Ti, though the euhemerizing commentators interpret him as either Yao or Shun) had the Miao exterminated. "Then he charged Ch'ung and Li to cut the communication between Heaven and Earth so that there would be no descending and ascending [of spirits and men between the two]." After this had been done, order was restored and the people returned to virtue.

The second much more detailed account—actually an early exegesis of the foregoing—is that in the *Kuo yü* or *Narratives of the States* (iv cent. B.C. with later additions; sect. *Ch'u yü*, II, 1). In it King Chao of Ch'u (515–489), puzzled by the *Shu ching*'s statement about the separating of Heaven from Earth, asks his minister: "If it had not been thus, would the people have been able to ascend to Heaven?" To which the minister, after making denial, supplies his own metaphorical explanation:

Anciently, men and spirits did not intermingle. At that time there were certain persons who were so perspicacious, single-minded, and reverential that their understanding enabled them to make meaningful collation of what lies above and below, and their insight to illumine what is distant and profound. Therefore the spirits would descend into them. The possessors of such powers were, if men, called *hsi* (shamans), and, if women, *wu* (shamannesses). It is they who supervised the positions of the spirits at the ceremonies, sacrificed to them, and otherwise handled religious matters. As a consequence, the spheres of the divine and the profane were kept distinct. The spirits sent down blessings on the people, and accepted from them their offerings. There were no natural calamities.

In the degenerate time of Shao-hao (trad. xxvi cent. B.C.), however, the Nine Li (a troublesome tribe like the Miao) threw virtue into disorder. Men and spirits became intermingled, with each household indiscriminately performing for itself the religious observances which had hitherto been conducted by the shamans. As a consequence, men lost their reverence for the spirits, the spirits violated the rules of men, and natural calamities arose. Hence the successor of Shao-hao, Chuan-hsü, charged Ch'ung, Governor of the South, to handle the affairs of Heaven in order to determine the proper places of the spirits, and Li, Governor of Fire, to handle the affairs of Earth in order to determine the proper places of men. "And such is what is meant by 'cutting the communication between Heaven and Earth.'"

Still later, however, the Miao, like the Nine Li before them, stirred up new disorders, obliging the ruler Yao to order the descendants of Ch'ung and Li to resume the tasks of their forebears. Since that time members of the same two families have continued to maintain the proper distinctions between Heaven and Earth. Under King Hsüan of Chou (827–782), one of them remarked of the two ancestors: "Ch'ung lifted Heaven up and Li pressed Earth down."

A detailed comparison of these two texts is unnecessary, other than to say that the first telescopes events which by the second are placed in two different periods (the troubles caused by the Nine Li during the reigns of Shao-hao and Chuan-hsü, and the similar troubles caused by the Miao during that of Yao); that both accounts are in part euhemerized; but that this is especially evident of the second, with its added "human" details and metaphorical explanation of what, in the first text, might be understood as a literal separating of Heaven from Earth. However, the second text also reveals the real state of affairs in its significant final quotation: "Ch'ung lifted Heaven up and Li pressed Earth down."

The idea that Heaven and Earth were once joined together, thereby permitting free communication between men and the divine powers, but later became separated, is extremely widespread among many cultures. It and related concepts have been brilliantly analyzed by Mircea Eliade in his two books, *The Myth of the Eternal Return* (1954; first published in French in 1949) and *Le chamanisme et les techniques archaïques de l'extase* (1951). In the former (p. 12 ff.) he discusses the concept of an *axis mundi*. This cosmic symbol, widely found among Asian peoples, may take the form of a mountain, a sacred temple, palace or city, or a tree or a vine; its distinguishing characteristic is that it is believed to occupy the center of the world and to connect Earth with Heaven. Concerning the ideas underlying this belief, Eliade writes further (p. 91):

> . . . the myths of many peoples allude to a very distant epoch when men knew neither death nor toil nor suffering and had a bountiful supply of food merely for the taking. *In illo tempore,* the gods descended to earth and mingled with men; for their part, men could easily mount to heaven. As the result of a ritual fault, communications between heaven and earth were interrupted and the gods withdrew to the highest heavens. Since then, men must work for their food and are no longer immortal.

In his *Le chamanisme,* Eliade has also discussed at length what it is that motivates the shaman when he enters his ecstatic trance. It is his desire to be able thereby to ascend to Heaven and thus momentarily restore, in his own person, that contact between Heaven and Earth which had more generally existed prior to the "fall."

It can hardly be doubted that our two Chinese texts are reflections of these widespread concepts. For in them, too, the cutting of communication between Heaven and Earth follows upon a "ritual fault," and the second text, in particular, describes in some detail the male and female shamans who enjoy contact with the spirits.

There is, however, also an important shift of emphasis: the fact that in the Chinese story it is the shamans only, and not the people as a whole, who originally enjoyed communication with the spirits, and that the usurpation of this prerogative by other persons then constituted the "ritual fault" leading to the cutting of communication between Heaven and Earth. Conceivably this shift in emphasis is not, after all, deeply significant, for it may be merely an attempt on the part of the author (or of the minister whose speech he is ostensibly recording) to enhance the prestige of the shamans by emphasizing their dominant role in earliest times. We cannot really know. (In his *Le chamanisme*, pp. 396–97, Eliade has also discussed this second text, basing himself, however, on an inexact translation which has led to certain misunderstandings on his part.)

The Miao, it will be remembered, are mentioned in both texts as one of the two groups responsible for the ritual disorder. Maspero ("Légendes mythologiques," pp. 97–98) has already pointed out that in the *Shan-hai ching* (bk. 17) these Miao are described as winged human beings living in the extreme northwestern corner of the world, while in a still later text they are said to have wings but to be unable to fly. Here, perhaps, is a symbolic expression of the "fall": the fact that the Miao had once been able to communicate with Heaven, but lost this power when, because of their ritual fault, the Lord on High exiled them to their distant region and ordered the (shamans) Ch'ung and Li to sever the communication between Heaven and Earth.

Are there other passages in Chinese literature expressive of a paradisal era followed by a "fall"? The Taoists often write about man's state of innocence before the rise of human institutions, but it is hard to know whether this is simply a Taoist philosophical abstraction, or may be inspired, at least in part, by popular traditions concerning a primordial paradise. The latter hypothesis, however, seems quite reasonable.

Among such passages, one of the most vivid is that in the eighth chapter of *Huai-nan-tzu*, describing the era of Great Purity, when men were genuine and simple, sparing of speech and spontaneous in conduct. "They were joined in body to Heaven and Earth, united in spirit to the *yin* and *yang* [the negative and positive cosmic forces or principles], and in harmonious oneness with the four seasons." At that time wind and rain brought no calamities, sun and moon equably distributed their light, the planets did not deviate from their courses. But then came the era of decline: men began to mine the mountains for minerals, to make fire with the fire drill, to fell trees for houses, to hunt and fish, and to do the many other things which destroyed their original purity.

A later passage in the same chapter is even more suggestive of an ancient Chinese Garden of Eden: In ancient times men entrusted their children to birds' nests and left the grain in the fields. Without fear of injury, they could freely grasp the tails of tigers and panthers and tread upon serpents. Then, however, came the inevitable decline. It is notable that nowhere here or elsewhere do the Taoists provide a mythological explanation for the "fall"; it is simply, for them, the inexorable concomitant of the rise of human civilization.

4. Sun Myths

Anciently there existed not one but ten suns, each of which would appear in succession on each day of the Chinese ten-day week. Once, however, at a time usually placed in the reign of Yao, all ten suns, through some confusion, appeared simultaneously, so that it seemed as if the world were about to burn up. At this climactic point the Chou texts (*Chuang-tzu*, ch. 2; *Lü-shih ch'un-ch'iu*, XXII, 5; etc.) leave off; for the denouement we must turn to the *Huai-nan-tzu* (ch. 8). There we are told that when the suns appeared, a certain Yi (or Hou Yi), famous as an archer, shot down all but one, thus rescuing the world and leaving the single sun which moves in the sky today. At Yao's bidding he also killed a number of destructive monsters (described in gory detail in works like *Shan-hai ching*). So overjoyed were the people by this happy ending that (somewhat inconsequentially, as we might think) they thereupon established Yao as their ruler.

There is an ambiguous line in the *T'ien wen* which, as usually translated, reads: "Why did Yi shoot down the suns? Why did the ravens shed their feathers?" Here we have the earliest reference to the belief that in the sun (or in each individual sun) there is a raven. (In *Huai-nan-tzu*, ch. 7, it is said to be three-legged.) From this line one might also conclude that the story of Archer Yi's shooting at the ten suns goes back at least to the fourth century B.C.

Karlgren, however, believes the story to have originated only in Han times, and therefore, as we have seen (II, 2 above), would translate the line in the singular: "Why did Yi shoot at the sun? Why did the raven shed its feathers?" His main reason for so doing is the chronological difficulty that, in other Chou texts, Yi appears as a great but arrogant hunter who lived in the early part of the Hsia dynasty (a century or more after Yao), and who, after usurping the throne, came to a bad end. Yi's shooting at a *single* sun (and not ten of them) is, therefore, as interpreted by Karlgren, simply "a sacrilegious act," expressive of Yi's hybris, but having nothing to do with the threatened burning up of the earth; he compares it with the act of the two kings (see III, 1 above) who shot at a leather sack filled with blood, calling it Heaven.

There are several arguments, however, which—at least to this writer—speak in favor of the more usual interpretation. In the first place, Yi's shooting at the ten suns provides a necessary conclusion to a myth which otherwise—quite literally—would leave the several suns dangling in mid-air. In the second place, is it really fair to look for strict chronological and thematic consistency in what, after all, is not history but myth? Yi seems to have been the focus of several cycles of story. There is no real reason to be surprised, therefore, if he appears as a hero in one cycle, but as a villain in another.

Thirdly, and perhaps most important, the theme of saving the world from multiple suns is by no means peculiarly Chinese. On the contrary, as shown by Eduard Erkes ("Chinesisch-amerikanische Mythenparallelen," 1926), it has many parallels on both sides of the Pacific. Among the Battaks of Sumatra and the Semangs of Malaya, for example, the sun is believed to be the parent of several children suns, but is tricked by the moon into devouring them when they threaten to burn up the world. Among the Shasta Indians of California it is the coyote who slays nine of ten brother-suns (a striking numerical agreement with the Chinese myth). And among the Golds of eastern Siberia there is even a national hero who, in the manner of the Chinese story, shoots down two of three suns when they make the world unbearably hot.

Returning to China, we find considerable lore concerning the daily course taken by the sun (or suns) across the sky. Perhaps the earliest source is the opening chapter of the *Shu ching* (Classic of History), which, as usual for this work, is considerably euhemerized:

> He [the sage Yao] then charged Hsi and Ho, in reverent accordance with august Heaven, to calculate and delineate the sun, moon, stars and constellations, and respectfully to give the people the seasons. He separately charged the younger Hsi to reside among the Yü barbarians, [at the place] called the Valley of Light (Yang-ku), there to receive the rising sun as a guest and regulate its activities in the east. . . . He further charged the youngest Hsi to reside in Southern Chiao, there to regulate its doings in the south. . . . He separately charged the younger Ho to reside in the west, [at the place] called the Valley of Darkness (Mei-ku), there respectfully to see off the setting sun and regulate the completion of its work in the west. . . . He further charged the youngest Ho to reside in the Northern Region (Shuo-fang), [at the place] called the City of Obscurity (Yu-tu), there to supervise its operations in the north.

Other Chou texts make it evident that the two sets of three brothers, here spoken of as supervising the movements of the sun and other heavenly bodies, are in actual fact mere multiplications of a single person, Hsi-ho. (The multiplication was no doubt motivated by the desire to provide enough brothers to take care of all celestial operations in all quarters of the sky.) As pointed out by Karlgren, Hsi-ho appears in the Chou texts simply as an ancient cult-master (sex unspecified) who observes the heavenly bodies, creates the calendar, prognosticates by means of the sun, and controls the sun in its movements.

In the *Shan-hai ching* (bk. 15), on the other hand, Hsi-ho for the first time becomes the mother of the sun or suns (for ten are specifically mentioned). She lives beyond the Southeast Sea, in the midst of the Sweet Waters (Kan-shui), where she bathes the suns one by one in the Sweet Gulf (Kan-yüan). The same work (bks. 9 and 14) tells us further that in the eastern Valley of Light (already mentioned in the *Shu ching*) there grows a tree known as the Fu-sang (Supporting Mulberry; other names for it appear in other texts). Its trunk reaches a height of 300 *li* (about 100 miles), yet its leaves are no bigger than mustard seeds. It is in the branches of this tree that the suns (personified, it will be remembered, as ravens) rest when they are not crossing the sky; as soon as one of them returns from its journey, another starts forth.

The daily itinerary of the sun (or suns) is best described in the third chapter of *Huai-nan-tzu* (though several of its place names also occur in other texts, both of Chou and Han time). At dawn, we are told, the sun first emerges from the Valley of Light and bathes in the Hsien Pool (presumably the same as the Sweet Gulf mentioned in *Shan-hai-ching*, and identified in some texts as a constellation). Maspero points out ("Légendes mythologiques," pp. 26–27) that at the Chou royal court there was a Hsien Pool Dance, the details of which are uncertain, but which is said to have been performed at the summer solstice on a square outdoor altar in the middle of a pond.

The *Huai-nan-tzu* goes on to say that after bathing, the sun ascends the Fu-sang tree and from there crosses the sky, passing en route a dozen or more places of which we know little more than the names. Finally it arrives at Yen-tzu, said to be a mountain in the extreme west of the world. There, at its setting place, grows another mythological tree known as the Jo tree, the flowers of which shine with a reddish glow. It has been suggested by modern scholars that these flowers symbolize either the glow of sunset or the twinkling of stars as they appear after sunset.

The *Ch'u tz'u* anthology contains a poem, probably of the

third century B.C., called *Tung chün* (Lord of the East), which, though it never mentions the sun by name, seems to be a hymn sung in its praise. From it we may infer that the sun uses a chariot when it traverses the sky, for the poem's opening lines read (as translated by David Hawkes, *Ch'u Tz'u, the Songs of the South*, Oxford, 1959, p. 41):

> With a faint flush I start to come out of the east,
> Shining down on my threshold, Fu-sang.
> As I urge my horses slowly forward,
> The night sky brightens, and day has come.

The last two lines of this hymn give us the one and only hint in all early Chinese literature as to how, after setting, the sun makes its way (perhaps under the earth?) back to its eastern starting point:

> Then holding my reins I plunge down to my setting,
> On my gloomy night journey back to the east.

5. Flood Myths

Of all the mythological themes of ancient China, the earliest and by far the most pervasive is that of flood. It appears in writings belonging to the beginning of the Chou dynasty (*Shih ching* or *Classic of Poetry* and *Shu ching*), and thereafter the references are too numerous to be listed here. Though it crops up in localized form in conjunction with several minor figures (including Kung-kung, whom we have already encountered in connection with Nü-kua in III, 2 above), its really universal version is that in which Yü, together with his father Kun, play the major roles. The former is renowned in history not only as conqueror of the flood, but also as founder of China's first hereditary dynasty, that of Hsia (trad. in 2205 B.C.). Though Yü and his father are portrayed in the orthodox accounts as human beings, the written graphs for their names betray their non-human origin: that for Kun contains the element meaning "fish," and that for Yü is written with an element often found in the names of reptiles, insects, and the like.

The euhemerized version of the Kun-Yü myth, notably as found in the early chapters of the *Shu ching,* may be summarized as follows:

"Everywhere the tremendous flood waters were wreaking destruction. Spreading afar, they embraced the mountains and rose above the hills. In a vast flow they swelled up to Heaven. The people below were groaning." In response to their appeals, a being who in the *Shu ching* is referred to simply as Ti, "Lord," rather reluctantly (because he had reservations about his ability) commanded Kun to deal with the flood. (By the commentators this "Lord" is equated with the sage ruler Yao; in all probability, however, he was none other than the supreme divinity, Shang Ti, the "Lord on High.")

For nine years Kun labored without success to dam up the waters. At the end of that time either Yao or his successor Shun (the texts differ) had Kun executed at the Feather Mountain (Yü-shan), and ordered Kun's son, Yü, to continue the task. The latter, instead of trying to dam up the waters in the manner of his father, adopted the new technique of channeling passages for them to drain off to the sea. In this way he eventually conquered the flood and made the land fit for habitation. As a reward, he was given the throne by Shun and became founder of the Hsia dynasty.

In contrast to this "historical" account, we can, by piecing together the fragments found both in Chou and Han literature, produce another version which is much more "mythological":

On being ordered to deal with the flood, Kun stole from the Lord the "swelling mold" (*hsi jang*)—a magical kind of soil which had the property of ever swelling in size. With this he tried to build dams which, through their swelling, would hold back the waters. When his efforts failed, the Lord, angered by his theft, had him executed at Feather Mountain, a sunless place in the extreme north. There his body remained for three years without decomposing, until somebody (unspecified) cut it open with a sword, whereupon Yü emerged from his father's belly. (One tradition says that

Yü was born from a stone, which would apparently signify that Kun's body had turned to stone.) Following Yü's birth, Kun became transformed into an animal—variously said to be a yellow bear, black fish, three-legged turtle, or yellow dragon—and plunged into the Feather Gulf (Yü-yüan). A cryptic line in the *T'ien wen* poem, however, suggests that he subsequently managed to get to the west, where he was restored to life by a shamanness.

Yü, we are told, "came down from on high" to continue his father's work. He was helped by a winged dragon which, going ahead of him, trailed its tail over the ground and thus marked the places where channels should be dug. For some eight or ten years Yü labored so intensely that, though several times passing the door of his home, he had no time to visit his family within. He wore the nails off his hands, the hair off his shanks, and developed a lameness giving him a peculiar gait which in later times came to be known as the "walk of Yü." Nonetheless, he eventually succeeded in draining the great rivers to the sea, expelling snakes and dragons from the marshlands, and making the terrain fit for cultivation. So great, indeed, were his achievements that the *Tso chuan* history, under the year 541 B.C., reports a noble as exclaiming: "Were it not for Yü, we would indeed be fish!"

There are many other stories about Yü, for example, that he used the same "swelling mold" which had brought disaster to his father to build China's great mountains. Or again, we read that he ordered two of his officials (presumably after he became ruler) to pace off the dimensions of the world from east to west and north to south. In this way they determined it to be a perfect square, measuring exactly 233,500 *li* (roughly 77,833 miles) and 75 paces in each direction. Yü himself also traveled extensively. His itinerary included mythological places like that of the Fu-sang tree (where, as we have seen, the sun comes up), as well as the lands of the Black-teeth People, the Winged People, the Naked People, and many more; among the latter he even stripped himself naked so as to accord with local custom. Furthermore, Yü was a mighty warrior who conquered notorious rebels and gained the allegiance of ten thousand states. On one occasion he held a great assembly on a mountain consisting, in its euhemerized version, of dependent nobles, but elsewhere described as an assembly of spirits.

One curious episode concerns Yü's wife, the Girl of T'u, whom he met and married in the course of his flood labors. Later, while digging a passage through a certain mountain, he was changed (for unexplained reasons) into a bear. His wife, seeing him, ran away and herself became changed to stone. She was pregnant at the time, and so when Yü pursued her and called out, "Give me my son!" the stone split open on its north side and a son, Ch'i, came forth. It should be added that the name of this son (who succeeded Yü as second ruler of the Hsia dynasty) means "to open."

Of the foregoing episodes, most are already attested by the Chou texts. Some, however—notably Kun's theft of the "swelling mold," Yü's use of it to build the great mountains, and the measuring of the world by his two officials—are known only from Han works (primarily *Huai-nan-tzu* and *Shan-hai-ching*). Of still later date, moreover, is the story of Ch'i's birth, which first appears only in a seventh-century A.D. commentary, where it is claimed, quite erroneously, to come from the *Huai-nan-tzu*. At first sight the story appears to be nothing more than the clumsy repetition of two already attested themes, since in it Ch'i (like his father Yü) is born from a stone, and Yü (like his father Kun) is changed into a bear. Yet it would be unwise to dismiss it simply as a late and deliberate literary invention, for already in 111 B.C., according to the sixth chapter of *Han shu* (History of the Han Dynasty), Emperor Wu of that dynasty issued an edict in which he said: "We have seen the mother-stone of the Hsia sovereign Ch'i." This can only mean that at that time the belief that Ch'i was born from a stone was already current.

The story of Kun's transformation into an animal also raises a problem: the fact that in its Chou version (see *Tso chuan* under the year 535 B.C.) the animal in question is a bear, whereas in other much later versions it is variously described as a fish, turtle, or dragon. Kun's close associations with water make any one of these latter interpretations much more plausible. Nevertheless, the earlier bear version cannot be rejected out of hand, since its context is a story in which a noble, having dreamed that he was visited by a bear, is told that this is none other than Kun's spirit.

The fact that the bear is associated both with Kun and Yü (if the story of the latter's change into a bear can be accepted as more than literary invention) has been adduced as evidence for an ancient (and possibly totemistic) bear cult in China. Certainly it accords very poorly with the otherwise overwhelmingly aquatic associations of Kun and Yü alike. This contradiction, together with other thematic disparities, suggests that the Kun-Yü myth (aside from its central theme of flood) is by no means a homogeneous entity, but rather an amalgam of several cultural components which, originally, may have been geographically and perhaps ethnically quite distinct from one another. Just how these diverse cultural components should be interpreted and localized, however, is by no means an easy question. To cite only two of several hypotheses: both Maspero ("Légendes mythologiques," pp. 70–73) and Eberhard (*Lokalkulturen*, I, 365; II, 380–81, etc.) believe that the Kun-Yü myth originally had two major centers of development. Maspero, however, would locate these in North China (along the upper and lower reaches of the Yellow River), whereas by Eberhard they would be placed much farther south (very roughly along a west-east axis extending from eastern Szechuan to coastal China).

In closing, let us repeat (in slightly expanded form) two conclusions already suggested by Maspero: (1) The flood motif is by no means uniquely Chinese, for it is widely found among other peoples of East and Southeast Asia. Hence it could not have been inspired by the localized memory of any particular flood, whether along the Yellow River or elsewhere. (2) Between the Chinese and the Biblical or other Near Eastern flood stories there is this basic difference: in the Chinese version the flood is not inflicted as divine retribution for human sin, but simply epitomizes the condition of the world before there yet existed an organized human society. What is emphasized, therefore, is not the flood as such. Rather it is the task of draining the land and rendering it fit for settled human life. In essence, therefore, the Chinese myth is one about the origins of civilization, in which a divine being, Yü, descends from on high, creates a habitable world for mankind, and founds the first civilized state, the perpetuation of which he ensures by marrying a human mortal.

IV. CONCLUSIONS

1. The fragmentary and episodic nature of China's ancient myths suggests that they are not homogeneous creations, but rather the amalgams—still incomplete at the time of their recording—of regionally and perhaps ethnically diversified materials.

2. The intense historical-mindedness of the Chinese—displayed already in very early times—together with their tendency to reject supernatural explanations for the universe —caused them to "humanize" or "euhemerize" much of what had originally been myth into what came to be accepted as authentic history. No doubt this trend was encouraged by the eagerness of the noble houses of feudal China to find convincing genealogies for themselves among the shadowy figures of ancient tradition. So early did the process begin, in relationship to the development of written literature, that it largely prevented the myths from being recorded in this literature in their pristine mythological form. This situation is perhaps well-nigh unique among the major civilizations of antiquity.

3. Chinese scholars of the past few decades—notably the historian Ku Chieh-kang—have devoted much energy to the problem of the chronological stratification of early Chinese myth. In so doing they have demonstrated a widespread

phenomenon: the fact that the "historical age" of a myth (the period of history to which it purports to belong) usually stands in inverse ratio to its "literary age" (the period when it is first actually recorded in the literature). In other words, the earlier the purported age of a myth, the later is its actual appearance in the literature.

This phenomenon quite possibly reflects the gradual geographical expansion of Chinese civilization, in the course of which it absorbed the cultural traditions—including myths—of peoples originally lying outside the Chinese orbit. As these myths were thus successively acquired, the historically minded Chinese tried to fit them into a chronological sequence, in which each new acquisition had to be dated earlier than its predecessor, since the lower chronological levels had already been pre-empted. Confirmation of this phenomenon is in general supplied by the five myths we have studied (aside from the fourth, that of the ten suns), as shown by the following table (in which, of course, the dates under the middle column are traditional only):

Myth	Historical Age	Literary Age
P'an-ku	Beginning of creation	iii cent. A.D.
Nü-kua	Fu-hsi (2852–2738)	Only two pre-Han references (one of iv cent. B.C.)
Separation of Heaven and Earth	Chuan-hsü (2513–2436)	First half of Chou
Ten suns	Yao (2357–2256)	Second half of Chou
Flood	Yü (2205–2198)	Early years of Chou

Of these five examples, the flood myth of Yü, indubitably the oldest in literary age, also has by far the greatest hold on the Chinese consciousness. That of P'an-ku, on the other hand, is both the youngest and the most obviously alien (unless, which is far from certain, it can be *conceptually* linked with the possibly Chou-time notion of the primordial universe as an egg or a sac).

4. It is rather striking that, aside from this one myth, China—perhaps alone among the major civilizations of antiquity—has no real story of creation. This situation is paralleled by what we find in Chinese philosophy, where, from the very start, there is a keen interest in the relationship of man to man and in the adjustment of man to the physical universe, but relatively little interest in cosmic origins.

5. Violence and drama, boisterous humor or morbid macabreness, a frank concern with sex or the other bodily functions: all these are traits often found in other mythologies, but softened or absent in the myths we have examined. No doubt the selectivity of these myths—the fact that they are cosmogonic rather than intimately "human" in their subject matter—is partly responsible for this situation. Yet there also seems to be a reflection here of a broader phenomenon: the didactic tone and concern for moral sensibility found in much early Chinese literature. It is striking, nonetheless, that when it comes to actual human history, the writers of ancient China could, if need be, record quite unflinchingly the raw facts of life.

6. That the themes of ancient Chinese myth are by no means peculiar to China is demonstrated by the outside parallels noted by us for four out of our five examples (all save that of Nü-kua).

7. Virtually the only texts recovered in original form from pre-Han China are the short and restricted inscriptions on Chou bronze vessels or the even shorter and more restricted inscriptions on Shang divination bones. Almost none of the more extensive literature written on bamboo slips has come down to us physically, owing to the North China climate. This fact, coupled with the rarity of anthropomorphic portrayal in pre-Han art, makes it unlikely—though prophesy is admittedly dangerous—that future archaeology will add very greatly to what we already know about the myths of ancient China from traditional literary sources.

SELECTED BIBLIOGRAPHY

Only modern studies, and not original sources, are
here included.

Eberhard, Wolfram. *Lokalkulturen im alten China*, I (Leiden,
1942); II (Peking, 1942).

————. Review of Karlgren, "Legends and Cults in Ancient
China," in *Artibus Asiae*, IX (1946), 355–64.

————. *Typen chinesischer Volksmärchen* (Helsinki: FF
Communications No. 120, 1937).

All of Eberhard's writings display stimulating originality, admirable organization, and encyclopedic knowledge. They have sometimes been criticized, however,
for an occasional tendency toward overly sweeping conclusions and carelessness as to details.

Eliade, Mircea. *Le chamanisme et les techniques archaïques
de l'extase* (Paris, 1951).

————. *The Myth of the Eternal Return*, translated from the
1949 French original by Willard R. Trask (New York:
Bollingen Series XLVI, 1954).

Salient ideas from these two stimulating works (discussed in III, 3 of our essay) are conveniently summarized in Eliade, "The Yearning for Paradise in
Primitive Tradition," *Daedalus* (Spring 1959), pp.
255–67.

Erkes, Eduard. "Chinesisch-amerikanische Mythenparallelen,"
T'oung Pao, n.s. XXIV (1926), 32–54.

A useful comparative study of the Chinese ten-sun
myth and its circum-Pacific parallels.

Ferguson, John C. "Chinese Mythology," in J. A. MacCulloch, ed., *The Mythology of All Races*, VIII (Boston, 1928), 1–203.

This and the compendia by Maspero (on "Modern China") and Werner have little relevance for *ancient* Chinese mythology.

Granet, Marcel. *Danses et légendes de la Chine ancienne* (2 Vols.; Paris, 1926).

A notable pioneer work, the results of which, however, are often questioned today, and which should be used only with extreme caution.

Hentze, Carl. *Mythes et symboles lunaires (Chine ancienne . . .)* [Antwerp, 1932].

Listed primarily as an example of the highly questionable theorizing that should be avoided.

Karlgren, Bernhard. "Legends and Cults in Ancient China," *Bulletin of the Museum of Far Eastern Antiquities,* No. 18 (1946), 199–365.

For the controversy between Karlgren and Eberhard, see II, 3 of our essay. Regardless of the validity of Karlgren's theories (presented with uncompromising finality), this monograph is invaluable for its incredibly complete coverage of a huge mass of data.

Ku Chieh-kang. Numerous articles in *Ku shih pien* (which see) and elsewhere.

Ku is one of the greatest of present Chinese historians. See our "Conclusions" for his theory of the stratification of Chinese myth. Though the writings of him and other Chinese scholars here listed are not explicitly cited in our essay, they have been indispensable in its preparation.

Ku Chieh-kang and Yang Hsiang-kuei. *San-huang k'ao* (The History of the "Three Emperors" in Ancient China) [Peiping: Yenching Journal of Chinese Studies, Monograph Series No. 8, 1936].

A notable product of modern Chinese scholarship.

Ku shih pien (Symposium on Ancient Chinese History) [Vols. 1–5, Peiping, 1926–35; Vols. 6–7, Shanghai, 1938–41].

    A huge repertory of studies by China's best-known scholars.

Maspero, Henri. "Légendes mythologiques dans le *Chou king*," *Journal Asiatique*, CCIV (1924), 1–100.

    Like all of Maspero's writings, a fine piece of work, even though open to criticism on particular points.

————. "Mythology of Modern China," in P. L. Couchoud, ed., *Asiatic Mythology* (London, 1932), pp. 252–384.

    See comment under Ferguson.

Thompson, Stith. "Myths and Folktales," in *Myth: A Symposium* (Bibliographical and Special Series of the American Folklore Society, Vol. 5, 1955), pp. 104–10.

Werner, Edward T. C. *Dictionary of Chinese Mythology* (Shanghai, 1932).

————. *Myths and Legends of China* (London, 1922).

    See comment under Ferguson.

Yang K'uan. *Chung-kuo shang-ku shih tao-lun* (Introduction to Ancient Chinese History), in *Ku shih pien*, Vol. 7, Pt. 1 (Shanghai, 1938), pp. 65–421.

    An attempt to prove that some forty personages of ancient Chinese "history" were actually gods or animal divinities. Though not always convincing, the work presents a wealth of valuable material.

Yüan K'o. *Chung-kuo ku-tai shen-hua* (Ancient Chinese Myths) [Shanghai, 1950].

    A popular retelling of the myths, untrustworthy as to theory, but convenient for its careful citation of the original texts.

Japanese Mythology

BY E. DALE SAUNDERS

The Japanese islands were populated perhaps some 5000 years ago[1] by peoples[2] coming probably in great part from the Asiatic mainland. Two ethnic currents are discernable in the make-up of the Japanese: a northern current shows undeniable parentage with Ural-Altaic (Mongols, Huns, Tungusic tribes) peoples—to use a philological term—while a southern element is doubtless to be placed in relationship with the culture of the South Seas. Just where or when the fusion of the several elements that have gone into the composition of the Japanese "race" took place is not certain, nor is it within the scope of these few pages to go more deeply into this question, except to point out the more striking similarities that exist between the Japanese and the "foreign" myths belonging to these two principal streams. In fact, these similarities should incline students of mythology toward some reserve in using such a term as "native myths," that certain scholars have applied to the earliest recorded legends of the Japanese, for it is hard to avoid the conclusion that the Japanese, like their myths, are of a composite nature.

Japan stretches like a great bow aimed toward the Pacific and lying not far to the east of the Asiatic coast. The climate is diversified, ranging from the northern temperate type in the far north to a semi-tropical south. Largely mountainous, the islands are endowed with an abundance and diversity of natural beauty to which the Japanese have ever been susceptible. The early growth of poetry, inspired by nature and emphasizing the harmony of human life with its natural environment, bears witness to this association. Sentiments toward nature, moreover, are expressed in terms of human emotion. Yet the degree of personification in Japanese mythology never attains that which is apparent in, say, the highly anthropomorphized Greek myths. Never, in Japanese myths, does personification obscure the sources in the actual, physical world of which the Japanese remain pre-eminently aware.

Interestingly enough, too, in a country in which natural calamities such as typhoons, earthquakes, and floods are a frequent occurrence, the Japanese view of nature has always been a singularly benign one, stressing the qualities of tranquillity and beauty, rather than those of turbulence or menace. Nowhere in Japanese mythology is to be found the idea of a great catastrophe, of eternally threatening natural divinities. Folklore provides examples of irksome, meddlesome, and mischievous spirits, but no overpowering, ominous divinity. In fact, the Japanese have generally eschewed the personalization of catastrophes and menace. Invariably, the conflicts which do occur in their mythological accounts are de-emphasized, and, unlike the Greeks with their appreciation of sublime tragedy, the outcome of dissension in the Japanese myths is regularly presided over by a spirit of compromise. Such an attitude is not incompatible with the Japanese emphasis on a harmonious existence with the environment in which they live.

This all-important harmony with nature, fundamental in the Japanese outlook, led to an animistic view of the world. The things of nature, like human beings, were considered animated by, or imbued with, a vital spirit; they had a kind of personal vitality. This vitality in things which depart from the ordinary through shape or color, or in any other way, was felt to be "superior." It was hence characterized by the word *kami*, the fundamental meaning of which is "above," "upper part," "superior." Anything with unusual power or beauty or form was an object for reverence, or more precisely, was entitled *kami*, and the list of *kami* is infinite: an awe-inspiring mountain, an oddly shaped rock, a torrential mountain stream, a secular tree. . . .

The above concepts may well be borne in mind, for they will enable one better to relate the course of Japanese mythology to the natural background from which it sprang and from which it was never to dissociate entirely. They bear directly on the following pages in which an attempt will be made, first, to set forth the sources of Japanese mythology, those earliest records which tell most about the ancient myths; and secondly, to trace in some detail the so-called "central mythological current" contained in the Yamato cycle. The third section of this essay will deal with the branch currents represented by the Izumo group of regional myths, parallel rather than secondary to the Yamato set. And lastly, a final section drawn up in the light of what has been presented will close the discussion.

SOURCES

Japanese myths present a somewhat disorganized pattern, episodic rather than epic in nature. They form a miscellaneous body of superstition rather than a co-ordinated system of legends. So confused are these myths that aside from the difficulty of assigning them in all cases to specific groups, it is often hard to distinguish later accretions from the earlier legends. However, the student of Japanese mythology is in something of a better position than certain of his continental counterparts, for the bulk of early Japanese legends were gathered together at the beginning of the VIII century A.D. in two important collections: the *Kojiki*, or "Records of Ancient Matters," and the *Nihongi*, or "Chronicles of Japan." These two works to some considerable extent represent legends of a period anterior to the VIII century.

Both the *Kojiki*, which appeared in 712, and the *Nihongi*, which appeared in 720, were the products of a milieu chiefly interested in the Chinese culture which dominated VIII cen-

tury Japan. Both volumes were written in Chinese, although
sometimes, particularly in the case of the *Kojiki*, the characters were used phonetically to stand for Japanese sounds.
Both volumes set out to prove a point of a politico-cultural
nature, namely, that the people who termed themselves
Yamato (i.e., those who settled in the present-day Kyōto-
Ōsaka region) had attained a superiority over other political
and cultural centers. Hence, the aim of both books was to
form a kind of official dynastic history based on Chinese
models, and the compilers viewed their historical narrative
with a prejudicial and rational eye. They also tended to view
the history of their own preceding ages with an unabashedly
Sinicized attitude characteristic of the VIII century. They
attributed to them in many instances a sophistication that
could hardly have been obtained long before the influences of
Buddhism and Chinese culture in general were felt. In spite
of the political motives and the cultural prejudice that characterize these two volumes, they do, with the exercise of
appropriate caution, provide a wealth of material on early
Japan and are to be considered the chief sources of Japanese
mythology.

The *Kojiki*[3] (Records of Ancient Matters), or *Furu koto
bumi* as the title is sometimes read, although commanded in
the latter part of the VII century, appeared only in A.D. 712.
It is the oldest extant Japanese book. Its compilation was
begun under the emperor Temmu (673–86), who in 681
decided to assemble the records of former ages lest they be
irreplaceably lost. A certain Hieda no Are, reputed to have
a prodigious memory and doubtless a member of the *katari-
be*, or guild of reciters, was commissioned to transmit the
legends orally to a scribe, Ō no Yasumaro (d. 723), who wrote
them down. Since the aim of the compilers was to glorify the
reign and to establish dynastic claims, the tales and myths
as recorded in the *Kojiki* were subjected to considerable
change and elaboration for the ends of national unification.
Moreover, the preface reflects the current Chinese ideas that
animated the writers, for to them history was seen as a basis
of action in, and as a standard for, the present. The *Kojiki*

then is a "selection" of myths thought to be worthy of transmission, for among these records of ancient matters are to be discerned prescriptions applicable to the present.

The *Nihongi*,[4] or "Chronicles of Japan," appeared a scant eight years after the *Kojiki*, in 720. While the *Kojiki* purported to cover the period from oldest times until A.D. 628, the *Nihongi* spanned much the same space of time, except that it brought history up to the date 700. Flagrant instances of Chinese influence are more frequent in the *Nihongi*, from the introduction of the creation myth explained by the interaction of *yin* and *yang*, to passages lifted bodily out of the Chinese dynastic histories.[5] While covering essentially the same material as the *Kojiki*, the *Nihongi* presents two features absent in the earlier work: a system of chronology and variant versions of recorded legends. The system of dating in the *Nihongi* is arbitrary and reflects the desire of the authors to provide the flow of Japanese history with a chronology in the Chinese style. In the earlier reigns it must be radically modified so as to correspond with reality, and it is not until the beginning of the VI century that the dating becomes to any great degree trustworthy. Characteristic of the *Nihongi* is the listing after each mythological episode of variant accounts that the authors have been at pains to mention. These supplementary narrations differ usually in minor details, but they expand considerably the basic accounts as they are presented in the *Kojiki*.

In addition to the chief sources mentioned above, a number of contemporaneous works constitute valuable, although less concentrated, sources for Japanese mythology. Chief among these are the *Kogoshūi*, or "Gleanings from Ancient Stories," the *norito*, or ritual prayers, the *fudoki*, or provincial gazetteers, and the *Manyōshū*, the great VIII century collection of poetry.[6]

The *Kogoshūi*, compiled in 807 by Imbe no Hironari, was written chiefly as a protest against a rival family, the Nakatomi, who had, to the detriment of the Imbe, assumed considerable power in ritual matters. Containing much the same material as the *Kojiki* it is not, however, a systematic pre-

sentation of myths but rather a collection of traditions omitted
in some cases from the earlier books and preserved in the
Imbe family.

The *norito*, or official liturgies, perhaps dating as far back
as the VII century, are contained in a later work, completed
in 927, and called *Engi-shiki*, a collection of "Ceremonies of
the Engi Period" (901–23). Some scholars maintain that
these prayers represent formulas of great antiquity, and it is
certain at least that they antedate by several centuries their
commitment to writing. It is difficult to know just how much
change the *norito* were subjected to at the hands of the compilers of the *Engi-shiki*, but in all probability they contain
some ancient elements.

Perhaps most important of these "secondary" sources are
the *fudoki*, or gazetteers. Commanded in 713, provincial
records were to contain for the edification of the central government detailed descriptions of the provinces—ethnography,
flora and fauna, legends, etymologies of place names, in brief,
a rather exhaustive miscellanea of regional lore. Of the many
fudoki that must have existed, the only ones extant are those
of Harima, Hitachi, Hizen, Bungo, and Izumo, this last being
the only complete one. It was finished in A.D. 733. Of the lost
fudoki, a number of fragments quoted in later works still
survive, and as a whole this body of literature provides a rich
source for provincial mythology and folklore.

Finally, a number of mythological elements are to be found
in the great VIII century collection of poetry called the *Manyōshū*. This collection, brought together sometime after A.D.
760, contains some few poems composed as early as the IV
century, although the great majority were made between
the last half of the VII and the first half of the VIII centuries.

Such are the principal sources of Japanese mythology. It
is to be observed that the composition of all of them (especially the *Kojiki* and the *Nihongi*), or rather their commitment to writing, takes places some considerable time after
the myths they recount were formulated. In some cases the
written texts, for political, family, or religious reasons, are
plainly tendentious. In all instances, from the earliest written

texts on, Chinese influence on writing and on ideas is apparent, and it would be wrong to think of any of these volumes as representing a "purely Japanese" viewpoint. Yet, it is none the less evident that underneath the Chinese flourishes lies a fundamentally Japanese core, and it is principally on this that the following exposition of Japanese mythology is based.

THE CENTRAL MYTH

In the beginning was chaos, like an ocean of oil or like an egg, ill-defined but containing germs.[7] From this confusion sprang a "thing" likened to a reed shoot but conceived of as a divinity and given a name.[8] Almost at once other divinities came into being, varying according to different accounts, but all of minor importance, and disappearing immediately. In all there were seven generations, or pairs, of these secondary deities; they seem to personify germinating powers such as mud, vapors, seeds . . . and they appear in brother-and-sister couples. It is only the eighth, and last, pair of this group, who are to assume a considerable, but passing, importance in the subsequent account. They are in the order of their appearance Izanagi, the Male-who-invites, and his sister Izanami, the Female-who-invites.

At the command of the so-called "celestial divinities," who had been produced before them, Izanagi and Izanami stood together on the Floating Bridge of Heaven (*ama no uki-hashi*) and plunged a heavenly jeweled spear into the chaotic brine beneath them. They stirred until the liquid curdled and thickened. Thereupon they drew up the spear, and the drops of brine falling back into the ocean formed the island of Onogoro, that is, Self-curdling [island].[9]

Izanagi and Izanami descended onto this new island and made it the "Central Pillar"[10] of the land. Then, Izanagi questioned his sister, saying: "In what manner is your body made?" To which Izanami answered: "My body grows in all parts except one," and Izanagi continued, "My body grows in all parts, especially in one. Would it not be well to unite my part which is in excess to your part which is in deficit, and so produce many [regions]?"[11] And the younger sister replied, "It would [indeed] be well." Then the two deities, at the suggestion of the August Male, decide to circumambulate the island-column, Izanagi proceeding to the left, Izanami to the right. When they meet, the younger sister cries out at the beauty of her brother, "Oh, what a handsome man!" and Izanagi exclaims, "Oh, what a beautiful woman!" But later Izanagi rebukes her for such unrestrained enthusiasm, saying: "I am a man, and by right should have spoken first. How is it that on the contrary you a woman should have been the first to speak? This was unlucky. Let us go round again."[12] So they repeat the ritual and this time the male deity speaks first and so rectifies the ceremonial error. According to another version of the legend, the two deities were desirous of uniting, but they were ignorant of the art of sexual intercourse. They noticed a wagtail characteristically moving its head and tail violently, and by imitating the bird the two gods were able to copulate. From the union of the two originated a number of islands and a number of deities, one of whom was a deformed child, who even at the age of three could not stand erect, and who was consequently styled the "leech child."[13] This offspring in view of its imperfection was abandoned in a reed boat[14] and left to float away.

It is interesting to note that in the Japanese myth the birth of the leech child is not associated with a sense of guilt over the brother-and-sister marriage. Although incestuous unions are not infrequent in other mythologies, a simple mistake in ceremonial is not usually considered an adequate apology. The Amis of Formosa, for example, tell of a brother and sister who, having escaped a great flood in a mortar, unite and give birth to a snake and a frog. The first they throw in the bushes and the second they abandon next to the house. The disintegration of the bodies and the resultant odor cause the sun goddess to begin inquiries. Frightened at the punishment that will be meted out to them for their censurable act, they flee, and although they are later pardoned, emphasis rests on the knowledge of their wrongdoing.[15]

Izanami continued producing a variety of divinities: the sea, the waves, the mountains, and so on, until finally she brought forth the god of Fire. The private parts of the August Female were so burned in giving birth to this last divinity, that she mortally sickened, and various other divinities came into existence from her vomit (mountains), her offal (mud), and her urine. At last she dies. Izanagi is sick with rage and despair, and as he creeps around her pillow, lamenting, still other divinities spring into existence from his tears. Then he seizes his sword, ten handbreadths long, and cuts off his son's (the Fire god) head; from the blood are born still more deities.

At this point begins one of the most striking sequences in the story. Izanagi, unable to contain his desire to see his dead sister-wife, decides to visit her in the Land of Darkness. There she has built a castle. Izanagi tries to entice her back to the upper world where their creative work is still unfinished. But she hesitates, saying it is too late, for she has eaten the food of the Land of Darkness. She bids her brother not to look upon her and retires into her palace. But Izanagi is impatient. He breaks off the left end-tooth of his comb, ignites it, and enters to discover why she tarries so long. He finds her in a shocking condition of disintegration, covered with maggots, putrescent, and rotting. Frightened at the sight, he turns and flees. But his sister, angry at being discovered in such a shameful state, launches the hags (shikome) of the Land of Darkness in his pursuit. As he flees Izanagi takes his headdress and throws it behind him; it immediately turns into grapes, which the hags stop to devour. But the pursuit resumes, and Izanagi snatches from his hair the right comb, which he casts behind him; it immediately turns into bamboo sprouts, which the hags also tear up and eat.[16] Izanami then sends an army of fifteen hundred warriors on her brother's traces. However, the August Male keeps them at a distance by brandishing his ten-grasp sword.

Finally, at the Even Pass between the world of light and the Land of Darkness, he finds three peaches with which he pelts his pursuers so that they are obliged to retreat. Without further ado he blocks the Even Pass with a great rock, from either side of which he and his sister address each other menacingly. She threatens to kill a thousand beings a day in the land of light, to which Izanagi replies that in such a case he will set up fifteen hundred parturition houses, that is, he will cause fifteen hundred births each day, thereby establishing a just proportion between births and deaths.[17] He further severs connection with his sister by pronouncing the formula of divorce.[18]

This legend, which establishes the contrasting cycles of light and dark, birth and death, presents obvious analogies with the Greek Orpheus and Eurydice, or, more precisely, with the Persephone myth. Like Persephone, Izanami has tasted of the food of the Land of Darkness, and because of this act she is prevented from returning to the land of light. However, unlike the Greeks, the Japanese do not develop the tragic possibilities inherent in the situation, which in the Japanese myth is resolved by a kind of compromise. Similar conciliatory denouements may be observed at other points in the course of the Japanese mythological account and must doubtless be laid to some fundamental difference of outlook from that of the Greeks.

From his contact with death and the defiled nether land, Izanagi proceeds to purify himself. This he does in a small river in Tsukushi (i.e., Kyūshū). As he throws his clothing on the ground some twelve deities[19] are born of the individual garments and jewelry. Avoiding the water of the upper river as being too fast and that of the lower river as being too sluggish, he bathes himself in the middle course, and from the maculations on his body are born other divinities—some fourteen in all. At last, from his left eye is born the sun goddess, Amaterasu, the "Heaven Shining," and from his right eye, the moon god. From his nose is born Susanowo, the "Impetuous Male."[20] Of these three divinities, Amaterasu and

Susanowo are to occupy henceforth the central place in the legend; the moon god fades rapidly from the account.

Amaterasu is resplendent and shining; Izanagi places under her domination the Plain of High Heaven and bestows upon her a necklace of jewels. Susanowo is impetuous and dark, and to him is given the rule of the Sea Plain.[21] But the Impetuous Male is disconsolate; he weeps and laments loudly without ceasing until the mountains wither and the seas dry up. All the gods are baffled and distracted. At last, Izanagi questions him on his clamorous despair, to which, indeed, he seems more devoted than to his duties as ruler of the Sea Plain. Susanowo answers that he is lamenting because he wishes to visit his mother (Izanami) in the Land of Darkness, and that such is the cause of his distress. Izanagi is furious at such impertinence and as punishment banishes him from the land.

Susanowo resolves then to take leave of his sister the sun goddess and sets off for her realm in the heavens. But so boisterous is his approach that the sun goddess is frightened lest his arrival mean a coming encroachment on her own domains. So she prepares herself for meeting him. She slings a thousand-arrow quiver on her back, and another holding five hundred, and, grasping her bow, she takes her stance with such vigor that her legs sink to the thighs in the ground, and her appearance is that of a mighty warrior. Face to face with this formidable amazon, Susanowo assures her he has come only to take his leave, that he arrives with "no strange intentions." In order that she may know the sincerity of his motives, he suggests they take an oath together and produce children, which they do. She accepts the ten-grasp sword he gives her and, breaking it into three pieces, puts them in her mouth and chews them. He does the same with the jewels she has presented to him. And as they spew out the bits, numerous divinities come into being.[22]

In spite of all his assurances, the Impetuous Male does not give up his rude ways. In fact, in certain respects his behavior worsens. He breaks down the divisions in the rice fields, which had been laid out by Amaterasu, fills the irrigation ditches,[23] defiles her dwelling place with excrement.

Curiously enough, she at first excuses him, blaming his actions on drunkenness. But when he flays a piebald colt with a backward flaying and flings it into the weaving hall where she is working with her attendants so that they are fatally wounded in their private parts by the flying shuttles, she is profoundly annoyed. To underline her displeasure, she retires into a rock cave and makes the entrance fast.

With the retirement of the sun goddess, light leaves the world, and the alternation of day and night ceases. The myriads of divinities are deeply perturbed at this turn of events and gather in the river bed of heaven to consult among themselves as how best to entice the goddess from her hiding place. They place long-singing night birds (i.e., roosters?) near the entrance of the cave and cause them to crow; they suspend from a tree a string of curved jewels, a mirror, and offerings of white cloth,[24] and they all recite official liturgies (*norito*). But what is to prove finally efficacious is a lascivious, madcap dance performed by the goddess Ama no uzume, who, stamping loudly on the ground, pulling the nipples of her breasts, and lowering her skirt, so delights the assembled gods that they break out in raucous and appreciative laughter.[25] Piqued with understandable curiosity, the sun goddess peers out of the cave, whereupon the mirror is pushed to the door and the goddess, intrigued with her own image, gradually steps out. A rope is passed in back of her, beyond which she is forbidden[26] to return. With the appearance of the sun, light returns once again to the world, and the alternation of night and day recommences.

The reappearance of the sun goddess constitutes the climax of the cosmological myth. It is difficult to ascertain just what this occurrence signifies in mythological symbolism. Is it the return of the sun after some prolonged natural disturbance in the form of a great storm or even of a solar eclipse? From the cultural point of view, it doubtless stands for the understandable exaltation, on the part of the compilers, of an imperial ancestor; the victory over barbarians through the peace, instituted by a more or less centralized government, over lesser clans. In any case, with this climax the legend seems to lose a good part of the continuity it had up to this point and largely breaks down into a series of episodes and incidents among which it is often difficult to establish a fully satisfying sequence.

THE PROVINCIAL CURRENTS

Susanowo is censured in the high council of the gods for the whole episode of the sun [goddess]'s retirement, and, accordingly, a heavy fine of "1000 tables" is levied on him, his finger- and toenails are extracted, and he is banished from heaven.

Here follows an interesting myth of origin that deserves some detailed notice. Susanowo, or according to another version, the moon god,[27] Tsuki-yomi, is commanded by Amaterasu to descend and wait upon the Food goddess, Ukemochi. Upon his arrival at her palace, the goddess welcomes him by turning her head toward the land, and from her mouth spews forth boiled rice; facing the sea there pour out all kinds of fishes; confronting the mountain she discharges the various species of game. All these products are presented to the moon god as a great banquet. But the divine messenger, flushed with anger at being offered the filth of the goddess' vomit, draws his sword and kills her. Returning to heaven, he recounts these circumstances to the sun goddess, who in turn is exceedingly irritated with her messenger's intemperate action. And, in the case of the moon god, she marks her disapproval by refusing henceforth to meet face to face with him. As a result, the sun and moon dwell apart and are separated by one day and one night. But the story does not end here. Another messenger is dispatched to the dead Food goddess, who discovers that a number of things have been produced from her lifeless body (compare with Izanami above): from her head, the ox and horse; from her forehead, millet; from her eyebrows, silkworms; in her eyes, panic grass; in her belly, rice; in her genitals, wheat and beans.[28] These commodities are taken up by the messenger and shown to the sun goddess. Thereupon Amaterasu makes seeds of the grain and appoints a divinity to sow them for the future sustenance of mankind. Moreover, placing the silk worms in her mouth, she reels thread from them and thus founds the art of silkworm culture.

But to return to the adventures of Susanowo. The Impetuous Male, having been banished, descended into the land of Izumo in western Japan across from Korea, at the headwaters of the principal river, the Hii. Noticing a pair of chopsticks (sic) floating down the stream, he surmised that people must be dwelling in the upper reaches and so proceeded upstream. He soon came on an old man, his wife, and daughter, all three weeping bitterly. In answer to Susanowo's questions, the old man revealed their sorry plight. An eight-headed, eight-tailed serpent had for the last eight years been terrorizing the country and had devoured eight daughters of the old couple. Now the time had come again for the serpent to claim still another. It is a terrifying monster; its eyes are red, and it has eight heads and eight tails, moss grows on its back and cryptomerias, and its belly is bloody and inflamed.[29] Susanowo, on condition that he receive their daughter in marriage, offers to help the old couple. He has them prepare a refined liquor (*sake*), which they place in eight vats, on eight platforms surrounded with a fence having eight apertures. The serpent approaches of course, and, putting a head into each of the eight vats, drains them dry. Soddenly drunk, he falls into a deep sleep, whereupon the Impetuous Male draws his sword and cuts him to pieces. The river Hii flows red with blood. As he strikes the middle tail something dents the edge of his blade. He cuts open the flesh and finds buried in the meaty tissue the famous Herb-Quelling (*kusanagi*) sword, about which more later.

Before continuing with the career of the Impetuous Male, it will be worth-while to record here the famous *kunibiki*,[30] or land-drawing, myth. This legend accounts for the origin of Izumo, the area of Susanowo's subsequent activities. The god Yatsuka-mizu-omi-tsunu, noting the narrowness of Izumo, looked over toward Korea (Shiragi: Silla) to see whether there was not an excess of land there that he could borrow. There was indeed, and with a spade he dug away a parcel "like the space between a maiden's breasts," and broke it off with blows as one strikes the gills of a great fish. He made a triple-strand hawser fast to it and drew it toward him like a slow barge, speaking the words: "Come, Land! Come, Land!" and made it fast on the coast of Izumo. He performed this land-drawing act four times, attaching the new land to different parts of the Japan coast.[31]

Susanowo builds a great palace at Suga, in Izumo, and, espousing the princess whose life he had saved from the eight-headed dragon, he lives therein and together with his wife produces a number of generations of gods. Their most renowned offspring is Ōkuninushi, Master of the Great Land (i.e., Izumo).[32] From this point on, it is largely Ōkuninushi's career that the legend pursues, and it is apparent that here begins a new cycle, the Izumo myths, which, although not in opposition to the preceding Yamato group, are nevertheless distinct from it. The tales concerning Susanowo's descent into Izumo[33] may best be thought of as a kind of transition between the two cycles.

Ōkuninushi had numerous brother gods. These divinities conceive the desire to marry the princess Yakami, who dwells in Inaba, a province not far from Izumo, and they take Ōkuninushi along as their attendant, piling him high with their baggage. On the way to Inaba, they encounter a hare stripped of its fur, lying on the ground. The mischievous deities advise him to bathe in salt water and then to lie on the mountainside exposing himself to the winds. The hare follows their directions, but when the sea water dries, the skin of the unfortunate beast splits open and he lies writhing in acute pain. Ōkuninushi arrives with some delay at the spot where the suffering hare is lying and asks him the cause of his present predicament. The hare tells the following story: "Being on the island of Oki, off the Izumo-Inaba coast, I wished to cross over to the mainland but could find no way. I therefore gathered together the crocodiles of the sea and proposed a competition to see which [one] of our two species was more numerous. I suggested they lie end to end, while I, treading on their backs, would count their numbers. This they did, and I ran across them toward land. Just as I reached the last crocodile, who realized my deception, he reached up and stripped me of my fur." And he continues telling how he himself had been deceived by the mischievous deities and has so come to his present sorry plight. Ōkuninushi out of compassion advises the hare to bathe in fresh water and to dust his body with sedge pollen. This the hare does, and he is restored to his original health. Now, the hare was in reality the Hare Deity of Inaba, and for the favor he had received he promised that not the mischievous deities, but Ōkuninushi himself should obtain the princess Yakami in marriage.[34]

Angered at their failure to obtain the princess' hand, the deities plan to do away with the Master of the Great Land. Thus, when they arrive at the foot of Mt. Tema, they propose a boar hunt, in which Ōkuninushi is to catch the beast, which they will drive down the mountain. He accedes to their wishes, but instead of a boar the mischievous deities heat a great stone and send it crashing down the mountainside. In catching the boulder Ōkuninushi is fatally burned. But heaven intercedes by sending a cockleshell and a clam, two deities; the former triturates her carapace and the latter carries water, and, anointing him, they bring the lifeless god back to life in the form of a beautiful young man. But his ordeals are not over yet. The mischievous deities cut down a large tree, in the trunk of which they insert a wedge. Ōkuninushi is placed in the slot and the wedge removed, with the result that he is squeezed to death. However, he is again revived, this time by his parent, who, disabused of the motives of the other deities, counsels flight. So Ōkuninushi takes to his heels and escapes the arrows of the pursuing deities, dips under the fork of a tree, and disappears.

Ōkuninushi then set out for the nether land to seek the advice of Susanowo, who was dwelling there. As he drew near the palace, the Impetuous Male's daughter, Forward Princess, came out and saw him. The two exchanged glances and so were married. The princess announces the coming of a beautiful young deity, whom the Impetuous Male with paternal captiousness at once names Ugly Male of the Reed Plains. He sends him to sleep in a snake house. But Ōkuninushi's wife provides her husband with a snake scarf, which protects him during the night. On the following evening he is made to sleep in a centipede and wasp house, and again he is given a protective scarf, which sees him through the ordeal. Then, Susanowo lets fly an arrow into the middle of a meadow and bids the harassed god fetch it. No sooner has Ōkuninushi departed into the field than the Impetuous Male sets the grass afire. Just as the luckless deity is to be consumed by the flames, a mouse appears and indicates a narrow hollow where he can hide. Thanks to the protection of this cache he is preserved from the fire as it burns past. Then the mouse presents him with the arrow, which he has kept safe from the flames. Exasperated at Ōkuninushi's success, Susanowo takes him into the palace and demands that he delouse himself. The Master of the Great Land chews some *muku* berries his wife has given him, along with a quantity of red earth, with which he makes a fine, vermilion spittle. Susanowo, thinking the expectorations are masticated centipedes, is amused and contentedly falls asleep. Ōkuninushi quickly grasps the Impetuous Male's hair, ties it fast to the rafters, and, taking the great god's sword, bow and arrows, and lute, he flees with Forward Princess on his back. But as he departs the lute brushes against a tree and Susanowo is awakened. He leaps up; the rafters of the house spring from their sockets and the palace tumbles down about his ears. Despite the delay, he sets out in pursuit of the Master of the Great Land and follows him up to the Even Pass between the land of light and that of darkness. There, giving up the chase, he calls out to Ōkuninushi with belated indulgence to use the sword and bow against the mischievous deities and to take the Forward Princess as his consort, all of which the Master of the Great Land does.

Ōkuninushi now proceeds to the construction of the non-celestial world. In this he is aided by a curious divinity called Sukuna-bikona, a dwarf who comes riding over the crest of the waves to the coasts of Izumo, where Ōkuninushi is dwelling. Clad in goose skins,[35] he is borne on a tiny boat made of bark. Even his attendants do not know his name. Ōkuninushi places him in the palm of his hand to inspect him, and as he is looking the little deity leaps up and bites him on the cheek. Perplexed, Ōkuninushi reports this to the heavenly divinity,[36] who recognizes the tiny god as one of his own children, an evil one, who had slipped between his fingers and fallen to earth. He none the less recommends that the small god be well treated. Together Sukuna-bikona and Ōkuninushi construct the world, and on behalf of mankind they formulate the "method of healing diseases" (i.e., the medical arts) and "in order to do away with the calamities of birds, beasts, and creeping things, establish(ed) means for their prevention and control."[37] Sukuna-bikona is lost from the account when, on climbing to the top of a millet stalk, he is projected by the rebounding stem into the Everlasting Land.[38]

Ōkuninushi continues for a time as the ruler of Izumo, that is, until the sun goddess determines to send her grandson, Ninigi, to take possession of the Central Land of Reed-Plains (i.e., Japan) and there to assume sovereignty. Asked if he will deliver up the land to the heavenly chosen ruler, Ōkuninushi consults with his son and at last accedes. However, in recognition of the Master of the Great Land's power and position, it is a kind of divided rule according to which the divine grandchild (Yamato) assumes sway over public, that is, political matters, while Ōkuninushi (Izumo) retains control over secret (religious) affairs. As a sign of his charge, Amaterasu gives Ninigi three treasures: a curved jewel, a mirror, and the famous Herb-Quelling sword, taken by Susanowo from the eight-headed dragon. These three articles to the present day constitute the three imperial symbols of sovereignty. With Ninigi begins divine rule on earth.[39]

Among the children of the divine grandchild are the princes Fireshine and Fireshade, and the story of their exchange of luck is famous.[40] Fireshine, the elder brother, gained his livelihood from the sea catching things broad of fin and things narrow of fin. Fireshade lived from the land, catching things rough of hair and things soft of hair. One day Fireshade proposed an exchange of luck, the sea-luck going to him who frequented the land, and the land-luck, to him who lived by the sea. Reluctantly, Fireshine accepted, and the two set out to try their new fortunes. But the luck of the sea is for the sea, and the luck of the mountain is for the mountain; Fireshade could catch not a single fish with the hook[41] his elder brother had given him. What was worse, while fishing he lost his brother's hook in the sea, and although he offered five hundred hooks in return, the elder brother persistently demanded the return of the original one. As Fireshade stood lamenting by the shore, a sea divinity approached and, learning the young man's plight, made a boat and set the prince afloat. Drifting into the seaways, Fireshade soon arrived at the fish-scale palace of the Sea god and took his place in a cassia tree beside a well near it. When the handmaidens of the princess who dwelt within came to draw water, they saw Fireshade and offered him some. He accepted, and as he drank he removed a jewel he was wearing and, putting it in his mouth, spat it into the bowl which the maidens had offered him. The jewel adhered firmly to the side of the container with the result that the maidens were obliged to present both jewel and bowl to the princess. Thinking this event most curious, the princess and her father went out to greet Fireshade, whom they recognized as the divinity he was. They received him with a great show of splendor. The two were married and Fireshade dwelt in the sea-land for three years. With the passage of time, he began to think more and more of his former life, until one day he heaved a great sigh. He was at once questioned as to its cause, and he revealed then the story of his coming to the Sea castle and of the losing of the fishhook his brother had given him. Thereupon the Sea god interrogated all fishes to see if by chance the hook might be caught in one of their throats. Sure enough, it was found in the sea bream's (*tai*) gullet and returned to Fireshade. The Sea god instructed the young prince to restore the hook to his brother, and he gave him two water-ruling jewels and taught him their use. "Give this hook to your brother," he said, "and say to him: 'This fishhook is a big hook, an eager hook, a poor hook, a silly hook.' And then, if your brother cultivates fields in the uplands, you must cultivate fields in the lowlands. By so doing, your brother will be impoverished in three years. If at any time you are attacked, use the jewels to protect yourself." Then Fireshade was escorted back to land on a crocodile's back. After the return of the hook, the elder brother became poorer and poorer until finally in desperation he made an attempt on Fireshade's life. Thereupon Fireshade, following the advice of the Sea god, used the jewel which causes the tides to flow. The water rose and Fireshine was almost drowned. When Fireshine, fearing death, repented, Fireshade used the jewel which causes the tides to recede and thus saved his brother's life. Moved by this compassion, the elder brother vowed eternal submission.

In the meantime, back at the Sea palace, the Sea princess had found herself to be with child. As her time for delivery approached she came to join her husband Fireshade on land, thinking it would be wrong to bear a god's child in the ocean. On the shore she built a parturition house thatched with cormorant feathers and took her place within. She warned Fireshade not to look upon her during delivery, for at that time, she, like all foreigners, must take her primary shape. Of course, Fireshade is unable to curb his curiosity, and, peeping into the parturition house he sees that she has turned, at the moment of childbirth, into an immense crocodile. Deeply ashamed at having been discovered, she flees to the sea and disappears. Yet, the two cannot completely suppress their deep attachment for each other. Although they will never meet again, the princess offers her eternal love, and Fireshade answers by a song in which he grieves: "To the end of life, I shall never forget my younger sister with whom

I slept on the island where the wild duck light, and the birds of the offing."

The legend of Fireshine and Fireshade will doubtless recall to many the folk tale of Urashima of Mizunoe.[42] Urashima had gone fishing for three days and three nights, and yet he had caught nothing. At length he snared a turtle who, when captured, changed into a beautiful maiden. The girl bade Urashima close his eyes, whereupon she led him to a wondrous island in the middle of the sea where the ground was set with pearls and jewels hung from the trees. They entered the palace of the maiden's father and there were sumptuously entertained until the day darkened. The two were left alone. They made love, and Urashima, enamored of the princess, completely forgot his former life. Yet, at the end of three years, he began to sigh for his homeland, and the princess, taking pity on his disconsolateness, agreed to his departure. She gave him a comb box set with jewels, but admonished him never to open it, lest they be eternally parted. Urashima closed his eyes, and when he opened them again he found himself in his homeland. There he looked in vain for friends and family but could find no one he knew. When he questioned he was told that in the village there existed an ancient legend about a certain Urashima, who some 300 years ago had gone down to the sea and disappeared. Disconsolate, he opened the box from which a white mist arose and dissipated in the breeze. Seeing this, Urashima realized he would never again meet the sea princess. He turned toward the island in the sea and spoke his love, while on the breezes the maiden's voice came softly to him urging him never to forget.[43] In one version,[44] the unfortunate Urashima runs about wildly and stamps his feet in his grief. And finally he dies, his beautiful white skin creased with wrinkles, his lustrous black hair spotted with white.

In something of the same category of legends as Urashima is that of the folk hero Yamato-dake, the Brave of Yamato. This worthy early gained a reputation for decisive action when his father requested him to discipline his elder brother for his absence at meals. Yamato-dake did so by accosting the mannerless sibling during his morning visit to the privy. There he crushed the life from him, wrapped his dismembered limbs in matting, and threw them away. Yamato-dake was no less efficient in dealing with the Kumaso braves, two braggardly and uncouth brothers. Dressing in woman's clothes, he quite intrigued the two men with his feminine seductions. At a banquet, where he was a guest much made over by the two hosts, he drank with them until they were quite intoxicated. He then drew the sword that he had smuggled in under his garments, stabbed the one and, plunging his sword into the buttocks of the other, ripped him up like a ripe melon.[45] Subsequently, in Izumo he did not hesitate to have recourse to questionable subterfuge in order to gain his ends. Entering into friendship with the Izumo warrior whom he planned to defeat, he fashioned a sword of wood. After bathing together in a river with the brave, he proposed an exchange of weapons. The transfer completed, he at once challenged the defenseless man to battle, with the result that the latter was promptly dispatched. Yamato-dake then set out to the east and during his travels met the princess Miyazu to whom he became engaged and whom he later married. He was given a sword by his aunt, and a bag, and he then continued on to Sagami. There he was subjected by the ruler to an ordeal by fire similar to the one in which Susanowo entrapped Ōkuninushi in a burning field. On the point of being consumed by the flames, Yamato-dake opened the bag and found therein a fire-striker with which he started a counter blaze and so saved himself. He was accompanied on a part of his journeyings by his mistress, Ototachibana. At one melodramatic point in a sea crossing, threatened by monstrous waves, the princess offered herself as a sacrifice to the sea, and her act saved the life of her lord. Yamato-dake's career came to an end on the plain of Tagi ("rudder") where, despite his light heart, his legs became like rudders and he could no longer walk. To commemorate his death, a great mausoleum was built for him at Ise and there occurred great lamenting over the loss of so great a hero. Yamato-dake changed into a white plover and soared away into the heavens, where he disappeared. His tomb was hence called the Mausoleum of the White Plover.

CONCLUSION

The preceding account of Japanese mythology cannot pretend to be exhaustive. This would be difficult in the space allotted. An attempt has been made rather to provide a simple, working description of the principal Japanese myths. It will be worth-while, in conclusion, to emphasize certain characteristic elements of the Japanese tales as they have appeared in the foregoing account.

The legends of Japan are fundamentally theogonic myths. In them, manifestations of nature are deified, but not highly anthropomorphized. As a consequence, an important part of the legend aims at establishing a relationship between the birth of gods and corresponding objects and categories. Moreover, creation is not the result of some exterior force, some *prima causa*, but occurs through a kind of spontaneous generative process, the exact workings of which the legend does not make clear.

From the very beginning, it is apparent that Japanese myths are of a composite nature. Resemblance to Polynesian legends is most striking, but tales like Izanagi's descent into the world of darkness, the creation of Amaterasu from Izanagi's eye, along with the tales of Fireshade and Urashima are of a universal type to be found in other mythologies.

What has been termed here the central legend, that is, the story of Amaterasu and Susanowo, is largely solar in nature, and although, as in frequent other instances, the divinities are conceived of as a male-female pair, emphasis is largely on the inherent polarity of their natures, the extremes of light and dark, purity and impurity, of tranquillity and impetuosity. Although Amaterasu, the sun goddess, is assigned the central role, her character is vague and symbolic, while Susanowo, of all the divinities, is most sharply defined. Although the solar, or Yamato, cycle is made arbitrarily to dominate the mythological account, this is largely the result of the political tendencies of the compilers. Actually, the provincial tales of Ōkuninushi and his career in Izumo must be considered parallel rather than secondary. And the mythical division of power, temporal to Yamato and religious to Izumo, would seem to reflect the existence of not one, but at least two, chief cultural centers from which these myths arose. A third center was doubtless situated in Tsukushi (Kyūshū). And yet, contrary to what one might expect, Japanese mythology did not develop into a distinct dualism. Rather, a compromise was arranged in the form of a separation of spheres of interest between the deities concerned and their descendants.

In general, then, Japanese myths are at once sensitive and earthy, jestful and sometimes melancholy; at no time do they show a strong tragic sense. The dominating tendency is rather toward compromise, and despite the boisterous exploits, such as the deeds of Susanowo and the Brave of Yamato, one is nowhere struck with the overbearing sense of catastrophe that characterizes certain other mythologies. Perhaps this is due to the strong feeling of harmony with their natural surroundings, which the Japanese have always nurtured. It should not, then, be surprising that in animating the aspects of nature that struck their imagination, they have stressed not only an earthy functionalism but also such qualities as productivity, purity, and beauty.

NOTES

1. Sansom, p. 12.
2. For an authoritative treatment of the origins of the Japanese, see Haguenauer, *Origines de la civilisation japonaise.*
3. The *Kojiki* has been translated into English by B. H. Chamberlain (see Bibliography). Subsequent references are to this translation, which will be abbreviated to *Kojiki.*
4. The *Nihongi* has been translated by W. G. Aston (see Bibliography). Subsequent references are to this translation, which will be abbreviated to *Nihongi.*
5. *Nihongi*, pp. 371–72, under Yūryaku (457–79).
6. References to these four sources in the following pages will be: for the *Kogoshūi*, Katō, *Gleanings from Ancient Stories;* for the *norito*, Satow, "Ancient Japanese Rituals"; for the *fudoki*, Florenz *Japanische Mythologie;* for the *Manyōshū*, Pierson, *The Manyôsû.*
7. The *Nihongi* (pp. 1–2) uses the expression "egg." The *Kojiki* is silent on this but compares the young earth to floating oil and its movement to the jellyfish (p. 15).
8. Kunitokotachi in the *Nihongi* (p. 3) and Ame no tokotachi in the *Kojiki* (p. 15), i.e., Eternally Land [Heaven] Standing.
9. Identified with one of the small islands off the coast of Awaji, not far from present-day Kōbe. The implica-

tion is that this island produced itself, while all other islands were created by the deities. Compare the primeval couple of the Ainu legend, who work together to make the island of Ezo (Hokkaidō). While the husband works assiduously in the west, the wife, in the east, spends her time chattering with other goddesses, with the result that, when she is at last joined by her husband, she is obliged to finish her part in great haste. The coasts of western Hokkaidō are accordingly rough and ill-wrought, while those in the east are smooth and finished. For similarities with the Ryūkyū creation myth, see Matsumoto, p. 114; with Tai myths, see idem, pp. 116–17.

10. The *Kojiki* (p. 20) says that they erected a pillar, as well as a palace. And there is a tradition that they made the jewel spear the center pillar of it (*Nihongi*, p. 12, n. 2).

11. *Kojiki*, p. 20.

12. After the *Nihongi*, p. 13; also *Kojiki*, p. 21. The following version concerning the art of sexual intercourse is from the *Nihongi*, p. 17.

13. The *Kojiki* (p. 21) and the *Nihongi* (pp. 13–19) accounts differ slightly.

14. The *Nihongi* (p. 19) says "rock-camphor-wood boat of Heaven."

15. Matsumoto, pp. 122–23. For an Annamite legend concerning brother-and-sister marriage, see idem, p. 124.

16. At this point a *Nihongi* (p. 25) version tells that Izanagi making water against a tree forms a great river, the crossing of which delays the hags.

17. Cf. the *Nihongi* account, pp. 24–25. This "Orpheus motive" is present among the Manchous, Polynesians, and North American Indians.

18. *Nihongi*, p. 25; not in the *Kojiki*.

19. For the enumeration of these deities, see *Kojiki*, pp. 44–45, and *Nihongi*, pp. 25–26.

20. According to the P'an-ku legend in China, the sun and moon come from the left and right eyes (cf. Mackenzie, pp. 260–61), while in the *Rig Veda* (X. 90) the moon is Brahmā's mind and the sun his eye (cf. the Bṛhadāraṇyaka Up., i, 1). For a Buddhist parallel, see Katō, p. 92; for Egyptian parallels, see Mackenzie, p. 264.

21. The moon god becomes ruler of the night (*Kojiki*, p. 50). The *Nihongi* (p. 28) assigns the rule of the ocean to the moon god and the rule of the world to Susanowo.

22. The male divinities from Amaterasu and the females from Susanowo (*Kojiki*, pp. 58, 61). *Nihongi* (p. 40) reports all male children from Susanowo. Concerning other mythological accounts of brother-and-sister marriage to produce mankind, see Matsumoto, pp. 118–24.

23. Acts particularly abhorrent to an agricultural society. He also drives "piebald colts" into the rice fields (*Nihongi*, p. 40).

24. White cloth made from paper mulberry and, the *Nihongi* (p. 44) adds, blue cloth made from hemp.

25. For an Ainu parallel to this dance, see Matsumoto, pp. 130–31.

26. *Kojiki* (p. 65). *Nihongi* (p. 45) says, "begged."

27. Susanowo in the *Kojiki* (p. 70); moon god in the *Nihongi* (pp. 32–33). The two accounts differ somewhat; the account given here is according to the *Nihongi*, more likely the original form of the story according to Aston.

28. The parts of the body and the articles produced form kinds of word plays, but in Korean, and point doubtless to a Korean origin for this legend. For the word plays, see Anesaki, p. 379. *Kojiki* (p. 70): head—silkworms; eyes—rice seeds; ears—millet; nose—small beans; rectum—large beans; genitals—barley.

29. The description is from the *Kojiki* (p. 72).

30. From the Izumo *fudoki* (Florenz, pp. 282–85).

31. For the lands involved, see Florenz, pp. 284–85. Also, cf. Anesaki, p. 248. For a parallel Polynesian legend in

which land is drawn from the sea by deities fishing with human ears as bait, see Matsumoto, p. 117.

32. *Kojiki* (pp. 78–79); the *Nihongi* (p. 54) makes Ōkuninushi the son of Susanowo.

33. According to one account, Susanowo descends into Korea (*Nihongi*, p. 57).

34. *Kojiki*, pp. 81–82. This legend does not appear in the *Nihongi*. For a parallel Ainu myth concerning a fox, otter, and monkey, see Chamberlain, p. 25 ff.

35. *Nihongi* (p. 62) says "the feathers of a wren."

36. That is, Takami-musubi. On this divinity, see *Nihongi*, p. 5, n. 3.

37. *Nihongi*, p. 59.

38. Hitachi? (see *Nihongi*, p. 60, n. 2).

39. Curiously enough, however, when Ninigi descends from heaven he arrives not in Izumo but on the peak of Takachiho, in Hyūga (Kyūshū); see *Nihongi*, p. 70.

40. The story here is according to the *Kojiki* (pp. 145–56). The five versions of the *Nihongi* (pp. 92–108) differ somewhat.

41. A number of Polynesian legends present closely parallel stories, which involve hooks and which are resolved in much the same way as the Japanese tale: see Matsumoto, pp. 110–12, 117.

42. Urashima is absent from the *Kojiki* and given but passing mention in the *Nihongi* (p. 368; also see n. 2). The full story is contained in the Tango *fudoki* (Florenz, pp. 293–99), which is the basis of the tale given here, and in the *Manyōshū* (IX), pp. 85–93.

43. See Mackenzie (pp. 97–98) for a parallel Indian legend; Egyptian (pp. 98–99); Babylonian (pp. 99–100); Ainu (p. 328).

44. *Manyōshū*, p. 89.

45. *Kojiki* (pp. 256–57). The *Nihongi* (p. 201) version differs slightly.

BIBLIOGRAPHY

Anesaki Masaharu. *Japanese Mythology*, in *The Mythology of All Races*, Vol. VIII, ed. by C. J. A. MacCulloch. Boston: Archaeological Institute of America, 1928.

Aston, W. G. *Nihongi; Chronicles of Japan from the Earliest Times to A.D. 697*. London: Allen and Unwin, 1956.

Chamberlain, Basil Hall (tr.). *Ko-ji-ki; "Records of Ancient Matters."* Supplement to Vol. X of *Transactions of the Asiatic Society of Japan*, Tokyo: Asiatic Society of Japan, 1906.

————. *The Language, Mythology and Geographical Nomenclature of Japan Viewed in the Light of Aino Studies*. Tokyo: Imperial University, 1887.

Florenz, Karl. *Japanische Mythologie*. Tokyo: Hobunsha, 1901.

Haguenauer, Charles M. *Origines de la civilisation japonaise; introduction à l'étude de la préhistoire du Japon*. Part I. Paris: Imprimerie Nationale, 1956.

Katō Genchi and Hoshino Hikoshirō (trs.). *Kogoshūi: Gleanings from Ancient Stories*. 2nd edn., rev'd. Tokyo: Meiji Japan Society, 1925.

Mackenzie, Donald A. *Myths of China and Japan*. London: Gresham, 1923.

Matsumoto Nobuhiro. *Essai sur la mythologie japonaise*. *Austro-Asiatica*, Vol. II. Paris: Geuthner, 1928.

Pierson, J. L. *The Manyôsû.* Vol. I—latest Vol. X. Leiden: Brill, 1929–58.

Sansom, George. *A History of Japan to 1334.* Stanford: Stanford University Press, 1958.

Satow, Ernest. "Ancient Japanese Rituals," *Transactions of the Asiatic Society of Japan* (Tokyo), Vol. II (1927 reprint), 5–164.

IMPORTANT NAMES IN JAPANESE MYTHOLOGY

(Note on pronunciation: Pronunciation of Japanese is very simple. Vowels are pronounced as in Italian, consonants as in English. There are no silent syllables: e.g., Ukemochi = u-ke-mo-chi)

Ama no uzume	goddess who dances outside the cave of heaven
Amaterasu	sun goddess
fudoki	provincial gazetteers
Inaba	province in western Japan, to the north of Izumo, opposite Korea
Izanagi	Male-who-invites; August Male
Izanami	Female-who-invites; August Female
Izumo	province in western Japan across from Korea
kataribe	guild of reciters
Kogoshūi	"Gleanings from Ancient Stories"
Kojiki	"Records of Ancient Matters"
kunibiki	"land-drawing"
kusanagi	Herb Quelling [sword]
Manyōshū	VIII century collection of poetry

Miyazu	princess, wife of Yamato-dake
Nihongi	"Chronicles of Japan"
Ninigi	grandson of Amaterasu
norito	ritual liturgies
Ōkuninushi	Master of the Great Land
Ototachibana	mistress of Yamato-dake
shikome	hags of the nether world
Sukuna-bikona	helpmate of Ōkuninushi
Susanowo	the Impetuous Male, brother of the sun goddess
Tsukiyomi	moon god
Ukemochi	food goddess
Urashima	visitor to the Sea god's palace
Yakami	wife of Ōkuninushi
Yamato	province in central Japan near the Inland Sea
Yamato-dake	Brave of Yamato
Yatsuka-mizu-omi-tsunu	the "land-drawing" god

Mythology of Ancient Mexico

BY MIGUEL LEÓN-PORTILLA

An ancient myth smoothed the way for the entry of the conquistadores into the Aztec world in 1519. The appearance of Hernán Cortés and his men was held by the Aztecs to be the return of the benevolent *Quetzalcóatl* of Toltec times—the white, bearded god and inventor of the arts—an event foretold by pictures in Pre-Columbian codices which said that one day he would return from the east, from the direction of the Gulf Coast. On this subject the Spanish chronicles and the accounts of the native wise men are eloquent and their descriptions of the initial convergence of the two distinct civilizations and modes of thought are themselves stamped with the full impress of the myth.

The quickening into life of this myth by the presence of the Spaniards revived some of the ancient rites. The Aztecs offered the conquistadores the vestments of *Quetzalcóatl* and other gods and even went so far as to consider sacrificing slaves and captives to them, since "the gods might, perhaps, be utterly fatigued after so long a journey."

However, the hypnotic effects of the myth endured but a short time. The supposed *Quetzalcóatl* did not play the part of the benevolent hero and creator of the arts, nor did his gods conduct themselves in a godlike manner. "Those bearded men," as the Indians said, "were not *Quetzalcóatl* and his

This chapter was translated into English by Thelma Sullivan.

gods. They were strange and mighty *popolocas* [barbarians] who had come to destroy the ancient civilization and religion."

The minds of those mighty conquistadores contained myths also. For one, they thought that the Indians were descendants of the lost tribes of Israel, and many years were to pass before they left off believing this. This notion salved their consciences more than once in their efforts to obliterate the religion of the conquered and their concept of the universe, and if they did not achieve full success, as is evident by the vast treasure of documents and archaeological remains that still exist, it was not for lack of zeal. Only the patient and untiring work of some of the surviving native wise men and a handful of humanistic missionaries, such as Fray Bernardino de Sahagún, often fraught with obstacles and persecutions, rescued for all time those native texts so essential for the study of the civilization of ancient Mexico. This rich documentation makes possible the study of the various Pre-Hispanic institutions, in general and, in this case, its mythology.

The Sources

The Indians of Mexico's central plateau left us a triple documentary legacy. The first consists of about ten codices, or books of pictures, dating back to Pre-Hispanic times, which are still preserved in American and European libraries. In addition to these there are about thirty other codices which are copies made during the sixteenth century of Pre-Hispanic codices that had disappeared. Many of these books of pictures, written principally in ideographs but also in the partially phonetic representation of Náhuatl (the language of the Aztecs and Toltecs) are indispensable documents in the study of this mythology.

The second source consists of the hundreds of folios written by some of the natives in the Náhuatl language, using the Latin alphabet they had learned, by which means they preserved the poems, songs, chronicles, and traditions they had been made to learn by rote in their schools, during the era prior to the conquest. Some of these documents were also compiled by humanistic friars, such as Sahagún, who asked the Indians acting as his informants to write from memory what they knew about their ancient civilization. It is no exaggeration to say that these hundreds of folios constitute the richest record we have, one which still has been barely tapped as a source for study.

Archaeological findings, with their inscriptions and their representations of the gods, which become richer day by day, make up the third source for penetrating the mysterious world of the myths. And to all these sources can be added the various histories and chronicles written during the sixteenth century by missionaries and authorities of the Crown, also based upon information supplied by the Indians, which, if they often interpret Náhuatl thinking in terms of their own, nevertheless allow us a glimpse into the first reaction of the Europeans to the multiple evidences of the superior civilization of the Aztecs and the other Náhuatl-speaking peoples.

1. THE MYTHS OF ORIGIN

Before continuing, it is essential to caution the reader, who might be unfamiliar with the nature of the Pre-Hispanic Mexican cultures, against the often mistaken notion that the Aztecs are singularly representative of this region of America. In reality, the Aztecs with all their military and political greatness constituted only one branch of the great tree of Náhuatl peoples. Since the Aztecs arrived in the valley of Mexico at about the middle of the thirteenth century, the important role they played was confined to the last century prior to the conquest. Around 1428 they embarked upon an extraordinary social and religious reform, and, in accordance with their notion of being the Sun's chosen people, they adapted several of the cultural institutions of more ancient peoples to their warlike ends.

Archaeology places the origin of civilization in ancient Mexico between the second and third millenniums before Christ, in the light of which, the duration of Aztec power coming at the end, is brief indeed. In the second millennium B.C. agriculture and ceramic making appear to have begun. Dating back to the first millennium, the innumerable small clay heads and the figures of such gods as *Huehuetéotl*, "the old god," the god of fire, serve to give us some notion as to the religious ideas of those ancient inhabitants of Mexico, whose ethnic filiations have not, as yet, been precisely defined.

In this study of ancient Mexican mythology we will take as our point of departure what is called the *classical* period, which began more or less at the start of the Christian era. In the central plateau at that time, there arose the imposing religious center of Teotihuacán, "the city of the gods," which is mentioned in the earliest written documents. Almost simultaneously, to the south the Mayans also erected such great cities as Tikal, Uaxactún, Palenque, and others. The oldest traditions which relate the sacred sites to various myths concerning the cosmic and human origins, appear to go back to this time. Limiting ourselves to the religion and mythology of central Mexico we mention only that many of the early Náhuatl myths are not a little similar to those of the Mayans to the south, permitting us to discern in them some common cultural origin.

In agreement with ancient Náhuatl lore, there appears to have occurred a definite fusion of peoples in the central plateau, where, prior to the Christian era, the already established agriculturists and worshipers of the "old god" *Huehuetéotl* came into contact with peoples migrating from the northeast, namely, from the direction of the Pánuco River on the Gulf Coast. These migrants are described as a people with a high degree of culture, possessing books of pictures, music and song, and as followers of a supreme god whom they designated as "Master of the Everywhere, who is like the night and the wind" (*Tloque, Nahuaque, Yohualli, Ehécatl*).

It appears that one group of migrants went on toward the

Maya region of Guatemala, while others came to settle on Mexico's central plateau. There, according to myth, the latter founded a city called *Tamoanchan,* which means "we are seeking our home," doubtless a mythical place and, as yet, undiscovered by archaeology. Continuing their march, they arrived at Teotihuacán, "the city of the gods," which is some twenty-eight miles northeast of the present city of Mexico. There, as one text states, "they established themselves and the wise men became the rulers." After the decline of Teotihuacán, the Toltecs took up these beliefs. They were descendants, at least in part, of Náhuatl-speaking peoples who had come down from the northern plains and created Tula, around the ninth century A.D. (Tula is approximately forty miles north of Mexico City). Their ideas probably constitute the most ancient roots of a mythology which was to spread, later, throughout the entire central plateau of ancient Mexico.

The Supreme Dual God

Influenced by the mysterious wise men from the northeast, the religion of the ancient agriculturists appears to have been joined with the doctrine of the supreme god, "Master of the Everywhere, who is like the night and the wind." The supreme god, evolving, perhaps, from the ancient worship of the sun and earth, regarded both as the source of fecundity and as the universal mother, was considered a dual being. Never losing his oneness, for the ancient hymns always evoke him in the singular, he is held to be the *dual god* (*Ometéotl*), Master and Mistress of our flesh (*Tonacatecuhtli, Tonacacíhuatl*) who, in a mysterious cosmic coupling and conception, has given origin to all that exists.

He is, as is frequently repeated, "Mother of the gods, Father of the gods, the Supreme God." In the first burgeoning of his own reality he caused the birth of his four sons, the *Tezcatlipocas—The Smoking Mirrors—*white, black, red, and blue. These gods make up the primordial forces which were to generate the history of the world. With one of them *Quetzalcóatl,* symbol of divine wisdom, is often identified.

Their colors, sometimes symbolic of the natural elements, other times of the four quarters of the universe, and still others of epochs in time under their influence, allow the supreme god to continue his multiple activity. It is through the sons of the supreme dual deity that space and time, as dynamic factors which give life and abundance to all, make their presence felt in the world.

The Cosmic Ages

In the beginning the sons of the *dual god* worked peacefully together laying down the foundations of the earth, of the heavens, and of the region of the dead. In this way, the first of the worlds which existed in ancient times made its appearance. Soon, however, one of the *Tezcatlipocas*, eager to dominate over his brothers, transformed himself into the Sun and for his own use brought about the advent on earth of the first humans, who were made of ashes and had no food other than acorns. The other gods were angered by the audacity of their brother who had attempted to place himself above them, and *Quetzalcóatl* stepped in to destroy this first sun and earth and so "all disappeared, all was swept away by the water, the people became fish." With this cataclysm ended the first age, or "Sun," as the Indians called it.

Three more ages existed before the present one, according to the ancient Mexicans, and all were the results of the attempts of each of the sons of the *dual god* to rise above his brothers. The second age, or "Sun," brought with it the giants, those strange beings who, on greeting each other said: "Fall not, for he who falls, falls forever." This second Sun perished because the crumbling of the heavens and the earth monsters destroyed everything. The third and fourth ages also ended tragically. In the third, one of the *Tezcatlipocas* caused a rain of fire which consumed everything. Finally, the fourth age was devastated by the wind which destroyed all that had been on the earth. In that epoch lived the beings which the native text calls "ape-men" (*tlacaozomatin*).

The Restoration of the Earth, the Sun, and the Moon

After the universe had been destroyed four consecutive times because of conflicts among the *Tezcatlipocas*, these gods concerned themselves with putting an end to this disgrace. They met in Teotihuacán to reconcile their jealousies and to create a new age, the fifth of the series, in which present-day man was to be born. The fifth age was given the name "The Sun of Motion" and was to be the result of the direct intervention and voluntary sacrifice of all of the sons of the *dual god*.

Their first task was to re-establish the earth. For this purpose they brought in the goddess of the earth, a species of monster entirely made up of eyes and mouths. Two of the *Tezcatlipocas* transformed themselves into serpents and encircled this goddess, squeezing her with such force that they split her in two. From one of the halves they made the surface of the earth, from the other, the firmament. After this was done, the gods arranged that all things should be born of her, in order to compensate for the harm they had done her. Out of her hair sprouted the trees, the flowers, and the herbs. In her skin the small plants put out their shoots. Out of her myriad eyes were created the springs and small caverns and out of her mouth the rivers and great caves. The mountains and valleys came from her nose and her shoulders. In this way, all that exists arose from the living reality of the goddess.

With the earth restored, the gods again met in Teotihuacán to concern themselves with the remaking of the sun and moon, as well as human beings and their sustenance.

"As yet it was night. There was still neither light nor warmth." With these words the myth of the creation of the Sun in Teotihuacán begins. For four days the gods remained around the "divine hearth," trying to determine who would be the god to cast himself into the fire and thus become transformed into the heavenly body which would illuminate the day. There were two candidates: the arrogant *Tecuciztécatl, Lord of the Snails,* and the modest *Nanahuatzin, The Pimply*

One. The former, seeking pomp and glory, made offerings of golden thorns and quetzal plumes. *Nanahuatzin*, on the other hand, modestly did his ritual penance, the ritual which was to be adopted, later, by the ancient Mexican priests.

Finally, the moment arrived for the ordeal. *Tecuciztécatl*, in the sight of all the gods, prepared to throw himself into the fire. He made four attempts and a few more, but was fearful of the lighted coals, and so the gods decided that now the humble *Nanahuatzin* could make his attempt. *Nanahuatzin* heard the invitation of the gods, and, closing his eyes, he cast himself into the fire which consumed him in an instant. Seeing this, *Tecuciztécatl* also cast himself into the fire, but was too late. The humble god, *The Pimply One*, who was the first to be consumed by the flames, finally appeared transformed into the sun and *Tecuciztécatl*, fearful and too late, only achieved transformation into the moon. The sun and moon now appeared in the firmament. But to the great surprise of the gods, they did not move. It was then necessary for all the gods who were meeting in Teotihuacán to sacrifice their lives in order to set the sun and moon in motion, the one to move during the day, the other at night.

In this act was contained the seed which, much later, flowered into ritual of the Aztec religious cults. If by the sacrifice of the gods the life and the motion of the sun was made possible, then only by the sacrifice of men who, on earth, play the role of gods could the life and motion of the sun be preserved, thus preventing the cataclysms which had put an end to the sun and to the human beings who had lived during the previous ages.

The Re-establishment of Man on Earth

As they did for the creation of the sun and moon, the gods met to ponder the re-establishment of man on earth. On this occasion it was *Quetzalcóatl*, the symbol of divine wisdom, who agreed to go to the "Region of the Dead" to search for the precious bones of the human beings from other ages. Accompanied only by his *nahual*, a kind of alter ego, he descended to the world of the dead where he had to face a series of trials and ordeals imposed by *Mictlantecuhtli, Lord of the Region of the Dead.* Finally, *Quetzalcóatl* collected the bones of a man and a woman and carried them to the mythical place of *Tamoanchan.* Once again the gods gathered together, and after they ground the bones in a beautiful earthen tub, *Quetzalcóatl* caused the blood he drew from his penis to drip over them to give them life. Once more a blood sacrifice becomes the origin of motion and life. Man, as the myth recounts, was given the name *macehual,* which originally means "the achieved one," because in this fifth age his existence was made possible by the sacrifice of *Quetzalcóatl.*

The Finding of the Corn

A final myth belonging to the cycle which we call "the origins" concerns the provision of the proper food for man. Again, it is *Quetzalcóatl* who is charged with the task of finding the corn, the grain which is an epithet for America. He goes in search of the red ant who lives beside the "Mountain of our sustenance," where it has the grain hidden. *Quetzalcóatl* transforms himself into a black ant and after a long conversation between the two, he receives permission from the red ant to take out the grains of corn. Several other gods now make their appearance in the myth. These are the *Tlaloques,* the gods of the rain, who come in from the four corners of the universe to consummate the theft of the corn, making possible its germination in the earth. Once again, *Quetzalcóatl* goes to *Tamoanchan* and there delivers the precious seeds to the gods. The gods take a little of the corn and masticate it, after which they place it in the mouths of the first human beings, named *Cipactónal* and *Oxomoco,* so that they might live and be strong.

These, in brief, are the ancient myths concerning the origins of the world, the sun, the moon, man and corn, which the ancient Mexicans told, linking them with *Tamoanchan* and the great religious center of *Teotihuacán.* From these old myths they were to derive several of their principal rites, aimed at repeating, in some way, the divine act which made possible life and motion in this fifth age of the world.

2. THE TOLTEC CYCLE OF QUETZALCOATL

As the myths concerning the cosmic and human origins appear linked with *Tamoanchan* and *Teotihuacán,* what might be called ancient Mexico's "golden age" is closely related in the texts with the Toltec splendor owed to the human *Quetzalcóatl,* the great priest and cultural hero of the Pre-Columbian world, who seems to have lived during the ninth century. Probably taking his name from the god who, as has been indicated, symbolized the wisdom of the supreme *dual god,* Quetzalcóatl, the priest, appears to have created a new religious concept of a higher spirituality. Whoever studies his life and his thought in the rich documentation available in the Náhuatl language will easily understand why many investigators of the nineteenth century tried to see him as a Christian missionary, or perhaps a Buddhist, who accidentally arrived in the New World. Without formulating any hypothesis at this point, we will deal directly with the figure of Quetzalcóatl, the originator of religious doctrines and himself the subject of an extraordinary myth.

Culturally, the people of Quetzalcóatl, the Toltecs, appear as a result of new fusions of distinct ethnic groups. On the one hand, there is found in them the spirit of the ancient Teotihuacán world. On the other, there are also indications that remind us of the ancient nomads who came from the northern plains. From this point of view, the city of Tula, probably founded in the ninth century A.D., takes on the character of the civilizing center of the nomadic hordes who came from a mythical place to the north, *Chicomóztoc,* "the place of the seven caves," from which the Aztecs will later also claim to have come.

The delineation of Quetzalcóatl's rule is the description of a life of abundance and riches of all kinds. The Toltecs received from Quetzalcóatl his wisdom and the entire roster of the arts. Among them were extraordinary sculptors and painters, artisans who worked the precious feathers and metals, and ceramists who put their deified hearts into the works they executed. The Toltecs were so rich that their foodstuffs were not priced. In their homes nothing was lacking, and no one was ever sorrowful or poor: "They said that the ears of corn were as long and as thick as the pestle of a grinding stone. They affirmed that their cotton germinated in diverse colors: red, yellow, pink, white, purple, and green. It had these colors of itself. Thus it sprouted from the earth. No person colored it."

The palaces in which Quetzalcóatl lived were of various colors and oriented toward the four points of the universe. There he lived a life which approached divinity, a life of abstinence and chastity. He practiced several types of penance, some quite similar to those which had been introduced by the ancient gods. Above all, however, he devoted himself to meditation and to the search for new forms in which to conceive the supreme god and all that exists.

Quetzalcóatl's New Concept of the Supreme God

It is asserted that Quetzalcóatl, in his meditation *mo-teotia,* "searched for a god for himself," endeavoring, for his own sake, to get close to the supreme mystery of divinity. In this way, he went on discovering new attributes of the ancient *dual god,* the master of two distinct faces. Among many others, he invoked him with the following pairs of designations: "She of the star-speckled skirt, He who illuminates all things; Mistress of our flesh, Lord of our flesh; She who sustains the earth, He who covers it with cotton; the supreme *dual god,* who dwells beyond the nine heavenly beams."

That Quetzalcóatl the priest took his name from *Quetzal-cóatl* the god, symbol of the wisdom of the supreme dual principal, is made plain in an ancient Toltec hymn:

> *Only one god did they have,*
> *and they held him as the only god,*
> *they invoked him,*
> *they supplicated him;*
> *his name was Quetzalcóatl.*
> *The supreme guardian of their god,*
> *his priest,*
> *his name was also Quetzalcóatl . . .*
> *He told them, he preached to them:*
> *"This one god,*
> *his name is Quetzalcóatl.*
> *Nothing does he exact*
> *but serpents, but butterflies*
> *that thou shouldst offer him,*
> *that thou shouldst sacrifice to him."*

The Toltec Concept of the World

The god, *Quetzalcóatl*, symbol of the wisdom of the ancient dual deity, had given origin and form to the world in which we live. This world, drenched in symbols, in which man attempts to draw closer to the deity through sacrifice and meditation, takes on a definite shape in the Toltec mind. The surface of the earth is a great disc situated in the center of the universe which extends horizontally and vertically. Around the earth is the vast water which causes the world to be "entirely encircled by the water" (*cemanáhuac*). The earth and its vast ring of water are divided into four great quadrants or sectors which, opening out from the center of the world, extend to where the water joins the heavens and receives the name "the heavenly waters." The four great parts of the world swarm with symbols. The east, where the sun rises, is the region of light and fertility symbolized by the color white; the north is the region of death, the black sector of the universe; the west is the dwelling place of the sun, the region of the color red; and, lastly, to the left of the sun's course is the south, the place of thorns and of the color blue.

Vertically above and below this water-encircled earth are nine celestial tiers and nine regions associated with the world of the dead. The heavens, together with the water which completely encircles the earth, form a kind of vault furrowed with courses separated from each other by the great celestial beams. In the first five tiers are the courses of the moon, the stars, the sun, the evening star, and the comets. Above them are the heavens of the different colors and, finally, the region of the gods. Over all is the *Omeyocan* (the place of the duality) where the *dual god,* the Giver of Life and Guardian of the Universe, exists.

Because he is in all places, the supreme god is designated as the "Master of the Everywhere" (*Tloque-Nahuaque*). From beyond the clouds he rules the movement of the moon and the stars which are "the skirt which covers his feminine aspect," and by giving the sun the power to illuminate the day he reveals his masculine characteristic of creator, endowed with a marvelous life-giving power. The other gods, popularly considered as the sons of the *dual god,* form the multiple extensions which make possible his omnipresence. First they were the four forces, the four *Tezcatlipocas,* each being equivalent to one of the four elements—earth, air, fire, and water (an interesting parallelism with classic Greek and Hindustani philosophy). They took action from the four sections of the universe in each of the four prior ages, introducing into the world conflict, the cataclysms, and the evolution of all things.

The Flight of Quetzalcóatl

But the figure of the human Quetzalcóatl, the cultural hero, the inventor of the arts and the calendar, itself engendered a new myth which is doubtless based upon certain historical facts dealing with the destruction of the Toltec world and the flight of the wise priest toward the east, from which, it was believed, he would return one day.

The ancient hymns recount that one day, during the time of Toltec grandeur, three sorcerers—workers of magic—turned up in Tula. They had gone there for the purpose of persuading Quetzalcóatl to introduce the rite of human sacrifice. But the priest and cultural hero firmly refused because "he loved the Toltecs, who were his people, very much." As a result, the sorcerers decided to derange his heart and thus provoke his flight.

They spoke with Quetzalcóatl, who was now old and infirm, and gave him a mirror with which to contemplate himself. In a long conversation they tried to persuade him to drink an intoxicating brew which, they said, they had brought to cure him. After resisting for quite a time, Quetzalcóatl finally tasted the brew, then drank it all until he became inebriated. The great priest, who had lived a chaste and abstemious life, then had the princess *Quetzalpétatl* brought to him. He continued drinking and finally retired with her, giving way to the pleasure he had for so long denied himself.

Meanwhile, the sorcerers devoted themselves to casting their evil spells over Tula. Their charms caused the death of innumerable Toltecs. When Quetzalcóatl finally realized what had happened, his pain became increasingly great. He determined not to stay in Tula any longer. He decided to go eastward toward the region of light.

To this end, he abandoned the splendor he had created during his lifetime—his palaces, his temples, his works of art and, above all, his subjects, the Toltecs. The ancient hymns relate, in some detail, the course of Quetzalcóatl's journey until he finally reached the edge of the sea, on the Gulf Coast. He then disappeared forever. According to one version, he set off on a magic raft made of serpents. According to another, he cast himself into an enormous, blazing fire, emerging from it in the form of a heavenly body. In search of the unknown place of wisdom, the cultural hero had, in any event, to withdraw from the earth. Despite his mysterious disappearance, there forever remained among the Nahuas the belief in the return of Quetzalcóatl, the priest. The following brief Náhuatl text, in translation, expresses the deep-rootedness of this longing:

> *Thus spoke*
> *the old ones in ancient times:*
> *"Verily, the same Quetzalcóatl lives yet,*
> *as yet, he is not dead;*
> *he will come to rule."*

The god and the priest, so often undifferentiated in the thinking of the Nahuas, continued to be symbols for them of spiritual loftiness in the subsequent periods prior to the conquest. When the Nahuas finally believed that they had received news regarding the eagerly awaited return of Quetzalcóatl, the supreme tragedy consisted in the fact that those who came to their shores were to put an end to their ancient civilization.

However, several centuries were still to pass between his flight from Tula and the arrival of the Spanish conquistadores. Probably in the middle of either the eleventh or twelfth centuries A.D. the ruin and abandonment of Tula took place. The scattering of the Toltecs and the arrival of other Náhuatl-speaking groups coming down from the northern plains created the formation of many city-states in the valley of Mexico on the lake shores, and in the valley of Puebla beyond the volcanoes. In the middle of the thirteenth century appeared the last nomadic group—the Aztecs or Mexicans—who spoke the same language as the other peoples who dwelled in the valley, and who possessed one of the greatest of all treasures, an indomitable will. The establishment of the Aztecs in Mexico's central plateau and their influence, especially during the fifteenth century, which was the period of their military and economic hegemony, molded the final phase of Pre-Hispanic mythology and religion into the shape of their particular aims.

3. AZTEC MYTHS AND RITES

According to their lore, the Aztecs, who were the last of the Náhuatl-speaking peoples, came to the valley of Mexico from the same mythical "place of the seven caves" (*Chicomóztoc*). There, in ancient times, their tutelary numen, *Huitzilopochtli*, had spoken to them, ordering them to move on in search of a kind of "promised land." The place in which they finally were to settle was to be marked by the presence of an eagle sitting on some cactus and devouring a serpent.

The prolonged wandering of the Aztecs was fraught with difficulties, and the vicissitudes which they suffered are described in several of their ancient codices. Their presence in the valley awakened suspicion and provoked persecution on the part of those ancient peoples who were the heirs of the Toltec culture. Barely a century after having made their appearance in the valley of Mexico did they arrive at the site designated by their god, and in 1325, the will of the gods made manifest, they finally became established on the little island where they found an eagle devouring a serpent.

However, another hundred years were to pass before the Aztecs would initiate the period of their real greatness, which, in 1428, was given its impetus by their victory over their neighbors, the Tecpaneca rulers of Azcapotzalco who, up until that time, had been masters of the island on which was erected the city of Mexico-Tenochtitlan. The result of their victory was a rapid change in all phases of Aztec life. An extraordinary Aztec figure by the name of Tlacaélel, supreme counselor to three successive rulers, who also had been instrumental in the conquest of Azcapotzalco, was to be responsible for the cultural and ideological transformation of his nation.

The Remodeling of Náhuatl History by Tlacaélel

Determined to augment the grandeur of the Aztecs, not merely by titles and lands, Tlacaélel resolved to furnish his people with a new rendering of their history, for he felt that the ancient hieroglyphic books did not give either the Aztecs or their god Huitzilopochtli sufficient importance. Hence, he set out to burn the old codices "because they preserved many falsehoods and, in them, many have been falsely held as gods . . ." As is evident, this new perspective on Aztec history resulted from the desire to exalt a hitherto persecuted people, and his action provided a firm foundation for the subsequent grandeur of the Aztecs. There is no doubt that the Aztec myths and rites, as we know them today, originated from the reform undertaken by the royal counselor, Tlacaélel.

In spite of the Aztec determination to change ancient history, it survived among certain Náhuatl nations which were not completely subjugated by the Aztecs. Ideologically, however, Aztec influence became increasingly great and, as a consequence, was responsible for the many myths and doctrines concerning the ancient tutelary numen, Huitzilopochtli. Elevated to the level of those gods who had been the creators of the various ages or "Suns," that is, the *Tezcatlipocas* and *Quetzalcóatl*, Huitzilopochtli came to be identified with the sun itself, the result being that the Aztecs assumed the role of a chosen people whose mission was the subjection of all the nations of the earth.

In this new rendering of Náhuatl history, implemented and imposed by Tlacaélel, the myth of Huitzilopochtli singularly reveals his predominating characteristics. The Aztecs said that in the remote past there had lived on "Serpent Mountain" the goddess *Coatlicue*, "Serpent-Skirt." She was the mother of four hundred gods, called "The Huitznahua"— The Gods of the South—and of the goddess known as "The-One-Whose-Face-Was-Tattooed-with-Rattlesnakes" (*Coyolxauhqui*). One day while the goddess *Coatlicue* was sweeping in her temple, a ball of fine feathers dropped down upon her. She gathered them up and placed them within her bosom close to her abdomen. After she had finished sweeping, she wanted to take out the ball of feathers but it was gone. She immediately became aware that she was with child.

When *Coatlicue's* children saw that their mother was with child, they became suspicious and attempted to kill her. The little *Huitzilopochtli*, still in his mother's womb, spoke to her in order to calm her fears. One day, when the time for the childbed was close at hand, the four hundred *Huitznahua* and their sister *Coyolxauhqui* decided to carry out their resolve to kill *Coatlicue*. The minutiae of the myth, which are both interesting and abundant, will have to be sacrificed in favor of the denouement which is more pertinent to this discussion. At the very moment that *Coatlicue* was attacked by all of her children, *Huitzilopochtli* was born. He arrayed himself at once in the gear of a warrior and successfully defended his mother from the attacking *Huitznahua*. Believers in the astral interpretation of the myths saw in this act of *Huitzilopochtli*, afterward identified by the Aztecs with the Sun, the triumph of the celestial body which illuminates the day over the multitudinous stars, symbolized by the four hundred *Huitznahua*, and over the moon, represented by their sister, the goddess *Coyolxauhqui*. However, the myth may possibly have a more profound meaning. When *Huitzilopochtli* beheads his sister, *Coyolxauhqui*, and kills most of the *Huitznahua*, his action also embodies the prophetic statement of the Aztecs' primary mission as designated by *Huitzilopochtli*, namely, the conquest of the multitudinous peoples to the south and the extension of the Aztec empire to the most remote regions of Central America.

Mystico-Martial Concepts of Tlacaélel

In addition to the shaping of this myth, Tlacaélel and the Aztec priests shaped new religious doctrines. The ancient Toltecs had believed that there had been several ages or "Suns" prior to the fifth age in which they were living, which had always ended in cataclysms. With these ancient myths as a basis, the Aztecs formulated a mystico-martial concept of the universe for the purpose of preventing the disintegration or death of this fifth "Sun," called "The Age of Motion."

From the myth of the sacrifice of the gods who, by means of their death and their blood gave life to the sun, the Aztecs concluded that the sun and the universe required a certain vital energy in order to exist which, as the gods had established, was the blood—the miraculous substance which kept human beings alive, also. Therefore, the offering of human victims to the sun was vital because their blood would provide the sustenance that would prevent its death. "The Florid Wars," ritual wars, were organized for capturing prisoners to be offered up to the sun *Huitzilopochtli*. Combining the idea of war and the conquest of peoples with their prime mission of preserving the life of the sun and of this fifth age, the Aztecs aptly fused their drive for martial superiority with the supreme—almost mystic—religious image of themselves as the chosen people and cosmic collaborators of the deity.

Closely related to their mystico-martial philosophy was the Aztec belief that all those who fell in "The Florid Wars" became the attendants of the sun. Transformed into exquisite birds, the warriors became part of the entourage which accompanied the sun as it moved across the sky illuminating the day. Similarly, women who died in childbirth, with a prisoner in the womb, also became the attendants of the sun.

The Aztec Concept of the Hereafter

In the hereafter were three other places dsignated for distinct types of deceased. *Tlalocan*, the abode of *Tláloc*, god of the rains, was the place of pleasure and of happiness. To *Tlalocan* went all those selected by the god of rain for a specific death—by drowning, by being struck by lightning, from dropsy and from gout. Unlike the other Náhuatl dead, these were not cremated but were interred. Close to *Tlalocan* was situated another region called *Chichihuacuauhco*, "The Place of the Wet Nurse Tree," for children who died without having attained the use of reason. There the babies received nourishment from an immense tree whose branches dripped milk. This particular fate, assigned to the children, brought to the minds of many of the Spanish missionaries the image of the Christian limbo.

Finally, the place where the majority of deceased humans went was simply called "The Region of the Dead" (*Mictlan*). It was known also by other names which in themselves reveal a great deal about the Náhuatl concept of death: "Our Common Abode, The Region Where We Lose Ourselves, The Place Where One Somehow Lives, or The Region of the Unfleshed Ones," etc. According to some texts, those who went to *Mictlan* had to suffer a series of ordeals before they could end their journey into the beyond. These ordeals lasted for years, after which the dead definitely ceased to live.

These Náhuatl concepts of the hereafter seem to indicate a certain superposition of beliefs. It is undeniable, however, that the concept of the paradise of the sun reserved for those who died in combat was a belief indigenous to the Aztecs.

Aztec Sacrificial Rites

As a suitable background for the sacrifices of those captured in combat, the Aztecs erected a sumptuous and richly ornamented temple in honor of *Huitzilopochtli*. Now dedicated to war, this once unknown people reorganized its armies and persevered in its conquests until its empire extended from one ocean to the other and reached as far south as what today is Guatemala. The ancient calendar which they inherited from the Toltecs set the cycle of the sacrifices to the gods which they held during the year. In this way was established what might be called "a perpetual drama" in which the human victims before being sacrificed were actors playing the roles of the gods, and, hence, reliving in these rites the ancient prodigy of the gods who also died that their blood make possible the life of the Sun and consequently of all that exists.

The celebrations and sacrifices which the Aztecs held in honor of their gods throughout the year and which were rooted in their mystico-martial ideals kept alive their own interpretation of the ancient myths. The priests of the innumerable temples which had been erected in all of central Mexico had in their charge the cult of the various deities who, in great part, were nothing more than the divers names and representations of the supreme *dual god* and of his first children *Quetzalcóatl* and the *Tezcatlipocas*. Thus the faith of the People of the Sun was kept vital and vigorous.

However, the native texts which speak of the mystico-martial splendor of the Aztecs also give testimony of other modes of thought current during the same period, which, in a certain way, were diametrically opposed to the martial ideal. These were developed by several princes and rulers of various Náhuatl cities.

The Doubts of the Wise Men and the Revival of Toltec Concepts

Familiarity with the glorious traditions of the Toltec period of the supreme *dual god*, Master of the Everywhere and Giver of Life, as well as of such ancient precepts as the repudiation of human sacrifices and war, which emphasized the superior morality of the Toltecs, provided a fertile soil for seeds of doubt in regard to the mystico-martial concept of the Aztecs.

There are several illustrious names counted among those wise men who adopted this new Náhuatl intellectual position. Among them were the great kings Nezahualcóyotl and Nezahualpilli of Texcoco, Tecayehuatzin of Huexotzinco; Ayocuan of Tecamachalco. Even more noteworthy were the Aztec priests and wise men who attempted, albeit with some timidity, to direct their thinking into channels which were different from the official doctrines. The operational presence of all these thinkers who questioned the Aztec concepts of man, the world, and deity in its most profound sense provide additional material for the study of the ancient Mexico civilization.

The first inquiries that these wise men embarked upon concerned the concept of God. They were aware of the ancient Toltec concept of a *dual god*, invisible as the night and impalpable as the wind. However, through their own experience they were also aware that this doctrine had fallen into oblivion when the ancient cults were replaced by the bloody and bellicose veneration of the tutelary numen of the Aztecs, *Huitzilopochtli*. Texts have been preserved which contain such reflections as these on the part of the wise men:

You are in the innermost region of the heavens, giving origin
    to your word . . .
You, who are God.
What is it that you determine there?
For us here on earth have you, perchance, been overcome
    by sloth?
Must you hide from us your glory and splendor?
What is it that you are to determine
Here upon this earth?

In a certain way, these questions give us a glimpse into the doubts of the wise men regarding the presence and the action on earth of the ancient *dual god*. Further on in the same document can be found other questions concerning the place where one should look for the *dual god, Ometéotl*:

Where am I to go?
Where am I to go?
Which is the road toward Ometéotl, *god of duality?*
Perchance your abode is in the place of the unfleshed ones?
In the innermost region of the heavens?
Or is it the earth alone, that is the place of the unfleshed ones?

Little by little the problematic, as we call it, of these thinkers, who had separated themselves from the official doctrine, was becoming more extensive. Thus, for example, in a dialogue, the form which symbolically represents the dual Giver of Life, the question is framed concerning the possibility of speaking words that are true on this earth:

Perchance, Giver of Life, we speak some truth here?
We merely dream, we merely arise from our dreams.
All is like a dream . . .
Here no one speaks truth. . . .

Another text even more abstract, poses philosophy's paramount anthropological problem:

> *Man is real, perchance?*
> *If not, then our song is no longer real.*
> *What is to happen?*
> *What is it that comes out well?*

Starting with these problems, the Náhuatl wise men arrived at the construction of a new concept of the world, closely related to what today is known as Toltec philosophy. These modes of Náhuatl thought, side by side with the mystico-martial doctrine of the Aztecs, undeniably pose numerous problems for the modern investigator. Is it possible to ask oneself such questions as: To what extent did there exist an inner ideological conflict in the Pre-Hispanic Náhuatl civilization? Was there some possibility that the wise men, revitalizers of the ancient Toltec philosophy, might go so far as to exert authoritative influence on the priesthood and on the Aztec people?

Undoubtedly, something of the sort was taking place. Proof of this is to be found in innumerable discourses declaimed on solemn occasions in both family and public life, in which allusions are constantly made to the *dual god,* Master of the Everywhere, who is as the night and the wind. The Spanish conquest abruptly halted the inevitable and spontaneous evolution of these expressions of a more elevated intellectual development in the Pre-Hispanic world. There survived afterward during colonial times only the vestiges, largely incoherent, of what had been the popular religious practices of ancient Mexico. Some traces of their rituals and beliefs still exist in remote Mexican communities in a mixture confused with Christian ideas and practices.

CONCLUSION

Only the central themes in the evolution of the myth and religious thinking in ancient Mexico have been discussed here. There can be found in the abundance of available native documents the legends and traditions of many other gods not here mentioned. Innumerable divine couples are spoken of who, basically, symbolize the presence of the ancient *dual god* in all corners of the universe and in all the elements of nature.

Investigators of Asian and European mythologies will probably find several extraordinary parallelisms with the thinking of the ancient Mexicans. The belief in a supreme dual principle, mother and father of the gods and of man, as well as a concept of the world with the four corners of the universe, their characteristic colors, the four elements, the heavenly tiers and the nether world of the dead are undoubtedly analogous to some concepts in the civilizations of India, China, and Tibet. Are these simply parallelisms, or did there exist in ancient times some kind of cultural dissemination?

As yet, we believe that a definitive answer cannot be formulated. Those who are inclined toward the idea of cultural dissemination should remember the inexplicable absence of such cultural elements as the practical use of the wheel, the concept of weight and the development of balance scales, among other things, in the Pre-Columbian world. Besides, it cannot be ignored that many parallelisms in material or intellectual culture can also be explained as the independent result of the innate capacities of all human beings which make them apply relatively similar solutions to similar problems which crop up in distinct latitudes and times. It seems unquestionable that the peoples of ancient Mexico reached the climax of their culture in an isolated and independent way. From this point of view, they offer a unique opportunity for the study of man as the creator of civilization.

No testimony is as eloquent, regarding the esteem in which the ancient Mexicans held their religious doctrines, as the answer which several Náhuatl wise men gave to the first Spanish missionaries in the celebrated interview held among them in 1524:

> You say
> that we know not
> the Master of the Everywhere
> Creator of the heavens and of the earth.
> You say
> that ours are not the true gods.
> These are strange words
> which you speak.
> We are perturbed by them,
> we are annoyed by them.
> Because our forefathers,
> those who have been here,
> those who have lived upon this earth,
> did not speak thus.
> They gave us
> their precepts of life,
> they held as true,
> they paid homage to,
> they worshiped the gods.
> They inculcated us with
> all their forms of veneration,
> all their ways of worshiping (the gods) . . .
> But, if as you tell us,
> our gods are now dead,
> let us die now
> let us now perish,
> for now our gods are dead. . . .

BIBLIOGRAPHICAL REFERENCES

As already mentioned in this study, there are preserved in American and European libraries some Pre-Hispanic codices or "Books of Pictures" dealing with the mythology of ancient Mexico. There are also other manuscripts written in Náhuatl containing old Indian chronicles, hymns and songs concerned with their myths. Among them are to be mentioned: the *Colección de Cantares Mexicanos,* preserved at the National Library of Mexico; the *Codices Matritenses* of the Royal Palace and of the Spanish Royal Academy of History; the various collections of *Huehuetlatolli* or "Discourses of the Elders"; the *Vatican Codex A;* a Collection of Pre-Columbian Songs entitled *Romances de los Señores de Nueva España,* at the Latin American Collection of the University of Texas, etc.

The following are some bibliographical references concerning works of particular interest to the North American reader. Those wishing to consult a larger bibliography on this field are referred to the "Bibliography on Náhuatl Culture, 1950–1958," included in *Estudios de Cultura Náhuatl,* Institute of History, National University of Mexico Press, 1959, pp. 125–66.

CASO, Alfonso. *The People of the Sun,* Norman: University of Oklahoma Press, 1958.

FERNANDEZ, Justino. Coatlicue, *Estética del Arte Indígena Antiguo,* Prólogo de Samuel Ramos. México: Centro de

Estudios Filosóficos, 1954. México: 2nd revised edition, Instituto de Investigaciones Estéticas, 1959.

GARIBAY K., Angel Ma. *Epica Náhuatl* (Náhuatl Epics), Biblioteca del Estudiante Universitario, National University of Mexico Press, 1945.

———. *Historia de la Literatura Náhuatl* (A History of Náhuatl Literature), México: Editorial Porrúa, 2 vols., 1953–54. (A fundamental work on the literary creations of the various Náhuatl speaking groups of ancient Mexico.)

———. *Veinte Himnos Sacros de los Nahuas* (Twenty Sacred Hymns of the Nahuas). Fuentes Indígenas de la Cultura Náhuatl. Informantes Indígenas de Sahagún, 2. Introducción, paleografía, versión y comentarios de . . . México: Seminario de Cultura Náhuatl, Instituto de Historia, National University of Mexico Press, 1958.

GILMOR, Frances. *Flute of the Smoking Mirror* (a portrait of Nezahualcoyotl Poet-King of the Aztecs), New Mexico: The University of New Mexico Press, 1949.

LEHMANN, Walter. "Die Geschichte der Königreiche von Colhuacan und México" (The Annals of Cuauhtitlán), *Quellenwerke zur alten Geschichte Amerikas*, Bd. I, Text mit Uebersetzung von Walter Lehmann. Stuttgart, 1938.

LEON-PORTILLA, Miguel. *La Filosofía Náhuatl, estudiada en sus fuentes* (Náhuatl Philosophy, studied at its sources). Prólogo de Angel Ma. Garibay K., México: Ediciones Especiales del Instituto Indigenista Interamericano, 1956 (to be published in English, 1961, by The University of Oklahoma Press).

———. *Ritos, sacerdotes y atavíos de los dioses* (Rituals, Priests and Vestments of the Gods), Fuentes Indígenas de la Cultura Náhuatl. Informantes Indígenas de Sahagún, 1. Introducción, paleografía, versión y notas de . . . México: Seminario de Cultura Náhuatl, Instituto de Historia, National University of Mexico Press, 1958.

————. "A Náhuatl Conception of Art," *Evergreen Review,* Vol. 2, 7 (Spring Issue, 1959), New York, Grove Press, pp. 157–64.

ROBERTSON, Donald. *Mexican Manuscript Painting of the Early Colonial Period,* Yale Historical Publications, History of Art, New Haven: The Yale University Press, 1959.

SAHAGUN, fray Bernardino de. *Florentine Codex.* General History of the Things of New Spain, Books I, II, III, IV, V, VII, VIII, IX, and XII, translated from Aztec into English by Arthur J. O. Anderson and Charles E. Dibble. Santa Fe, New Mexico: School of American Research and the University of Utah, 1950–59.

SEJOURNE, Laurette. *Burning Water. Thought and Religion in Ancient Mexico.* London-New York: Thames and Hudson, 1956.

SELER, Eduard. *Gesammelte Abhandlungen zur Amerikanischen Sprach und Altertumskunde,* 5 vols., Berlin: Ascher und Co. (and) Behrend und Co., 1902–23.

SPENCE, Lewis. *The Gods of Mexico,* London, 1923.

VAILLANT, George C. *The Aztecs of Mexico, Origin, Rise and Fall of the Aztec Nation,* London: Penguin Books, 1953.

INDEX